A-Z EAST S

CW00410435

CONTENTS

REFERENCE

A Road	A22	Fire Station	■
Under Construction		Hospital	Ⓗ
B Road	B2247	House Numbers (A & B Roads only)	13 8
Dual Carriageway		Information Centre	🛈
One Way Street	→	National Grid Reference	560
Traffic flow on A Roads is also indicated by a heavy line on the driver's left.	→	Park & Ride	Withdean P+
Restricted Access		Police Station	▲
Pedestrianized Road		Post Office	★
Track / Footpath		Toilet:	
Residential Walkway		without facilities for the Disabled	▽
Cycleway	🚲	with facilities for the Disabled	▽
Railway	Station / Heritage Station / Level Crossing / Tunnel	for exclusive use by the disabled	▽
		Viewpoint	☀
Built Up Area	PARK RD	Educational Establishment	◨
Local Authority Boundary	— ∙ — ∙ —	Hospital, Hospice & Health Centre	◨
Posttown Boundary	———	Industrial Building	◨
Postcode Boundary	———	Leisure or Recreational Facility	◨
Map Continuation	80 Large Scale Centres 160	Place of Interest	◨
		Public Building	◨
Car Park (Selected)	Ⓟ	Shopping Centre or Market	◨
Church or Chapel	†	Other Selected Buildings	◱

SCALE

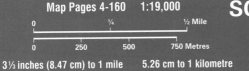

Map Pages 4-160   1:19,000

0 — ¼ — ½ Mile

0 — 250 — 500 — 750 Metres

3⅓ inches (8.47 cm) to 1 mile   5.26 cm to 1 kilometre

Map Pages 161-162   1:9,500

0 — ⅛ — ¼ Mile

0 — 100 — 200 — 300 — 400 Metres

6⅔ inches (16.94 cm) to 1 mile   10.52 cm to 1 kilometre

Copyright of Geographers' A-Z Map Company Ltd.

Head Office:
Fairfield Road, Borough Green, Sevenoaks, Kent TN15 8PP
Telephone: 01732 781000 (Enquiries & Trade Sales)
          01732 783422 (Retail Sales)
www.a-zmaps.co.uk

Copyright © Geographers' A-Z Map Co. Ltd.

Ordnance Survey® This product includes mapping data licensed from Ordnance Survey® with the permission of the Controller of Her Majesty's Stationery Office.

© Crown Copyright 2004. Licence number 100017302

Edition 1   2004   Edition 1A 2005 (Part Revision)

Every possible care has been taken to ensure that, to the best of our knowledge, the information contained in this atlas is accurate at the date of publication. However, we cannot warrant that our work is entirely error free and whilst we would be grateful to learn of any inaccuracies, we do not accept any responsibility for loss or damage resulting from reliance on information contained within this publication.

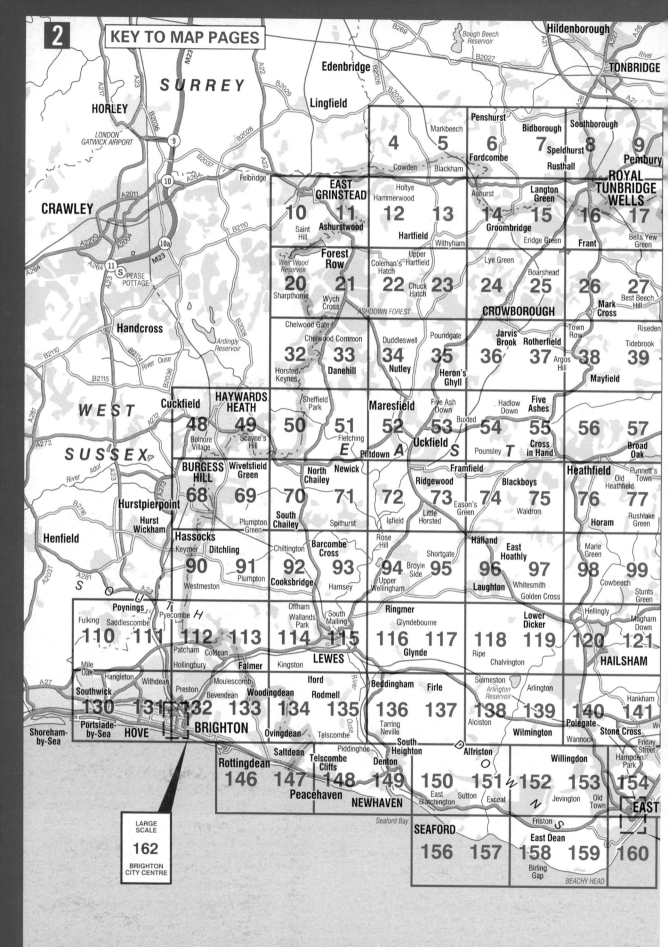

2

KEY TO MAP PAGES

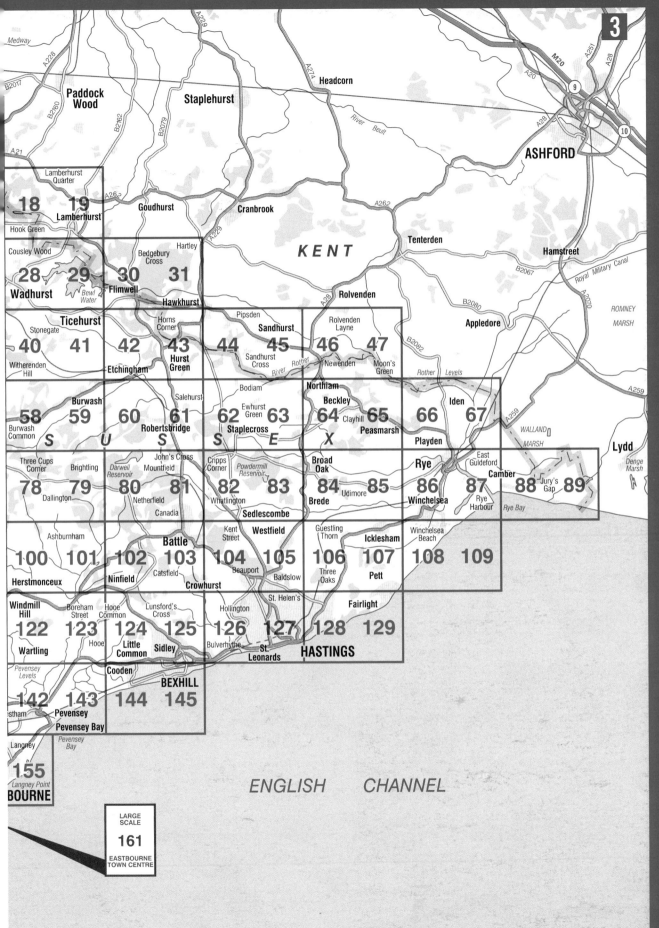

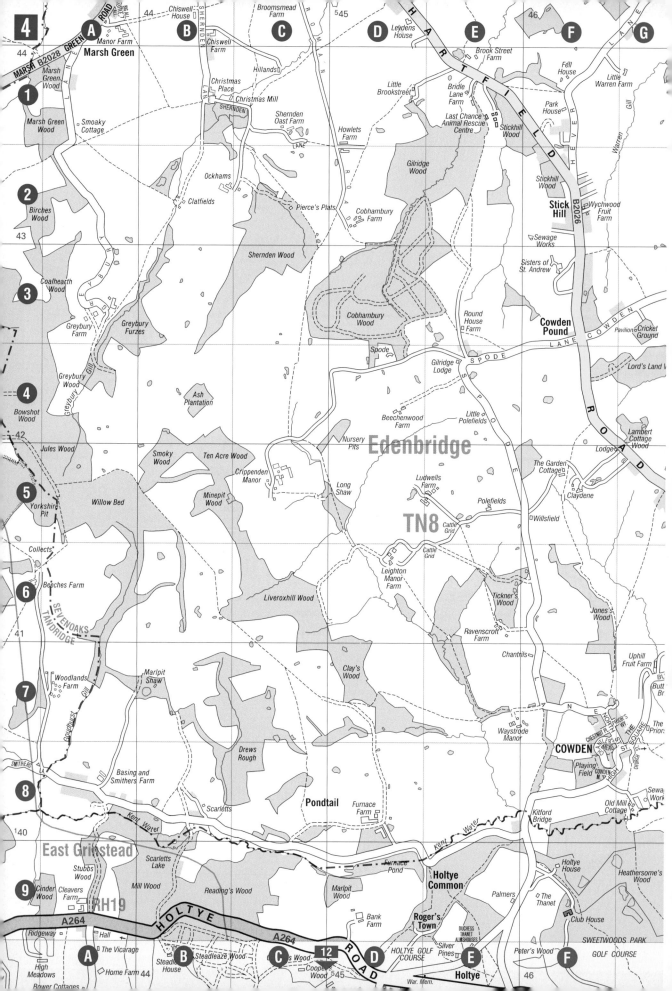

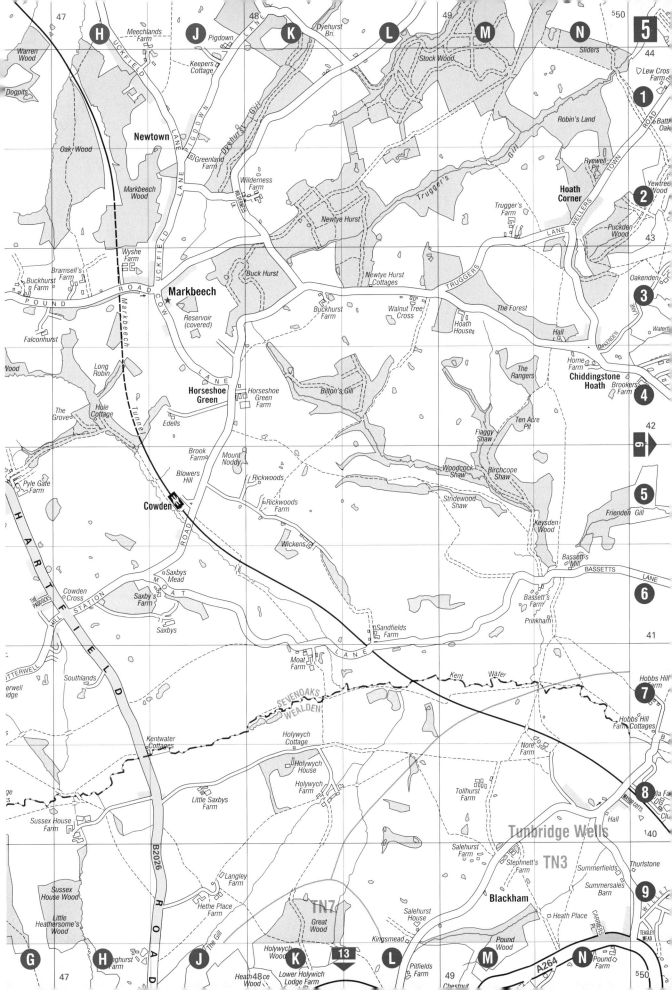

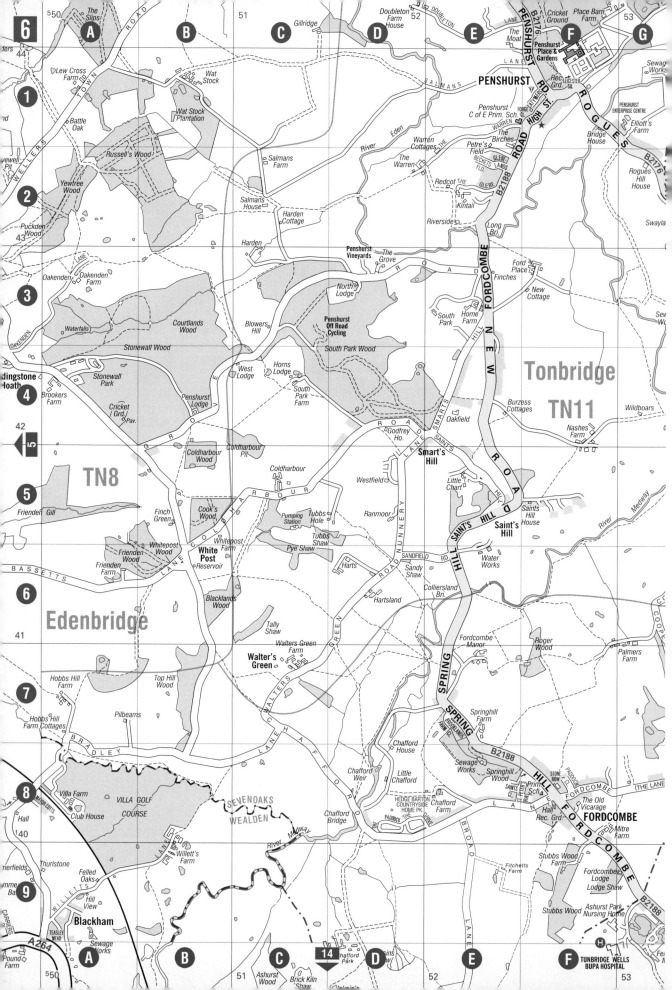

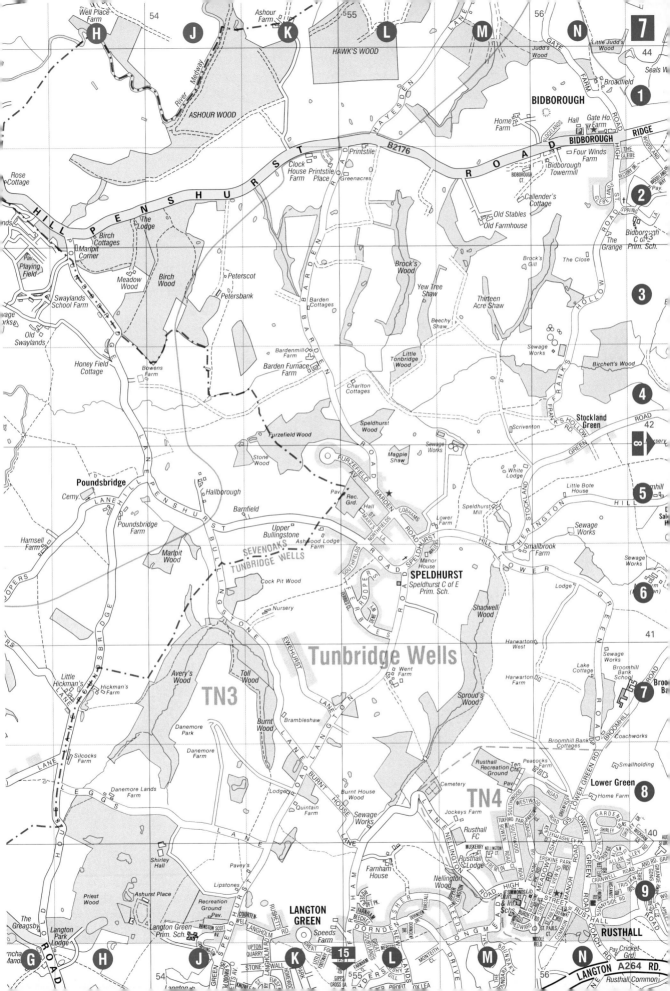

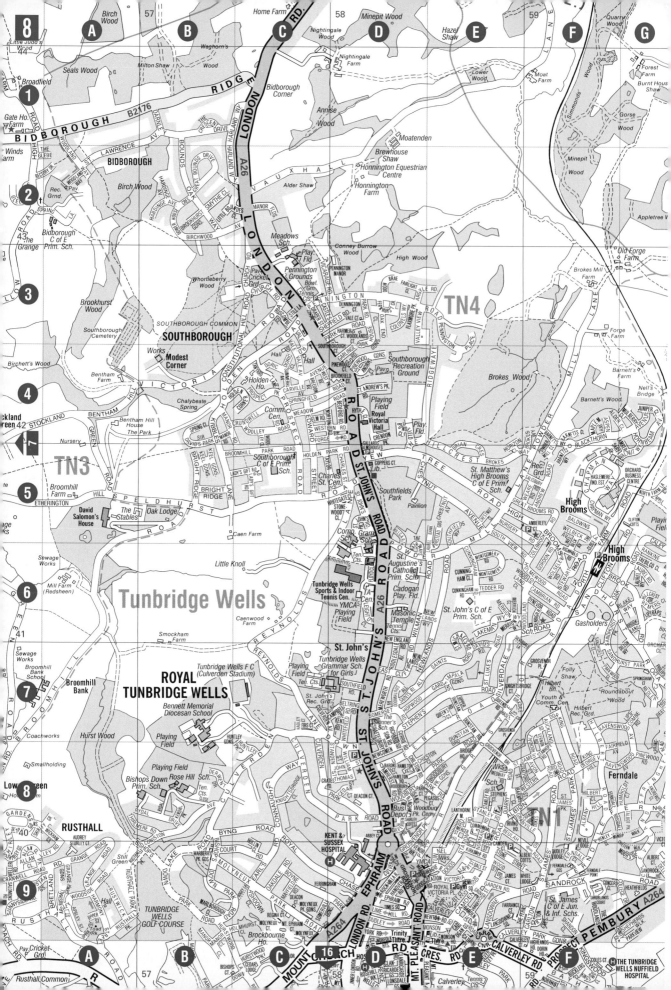

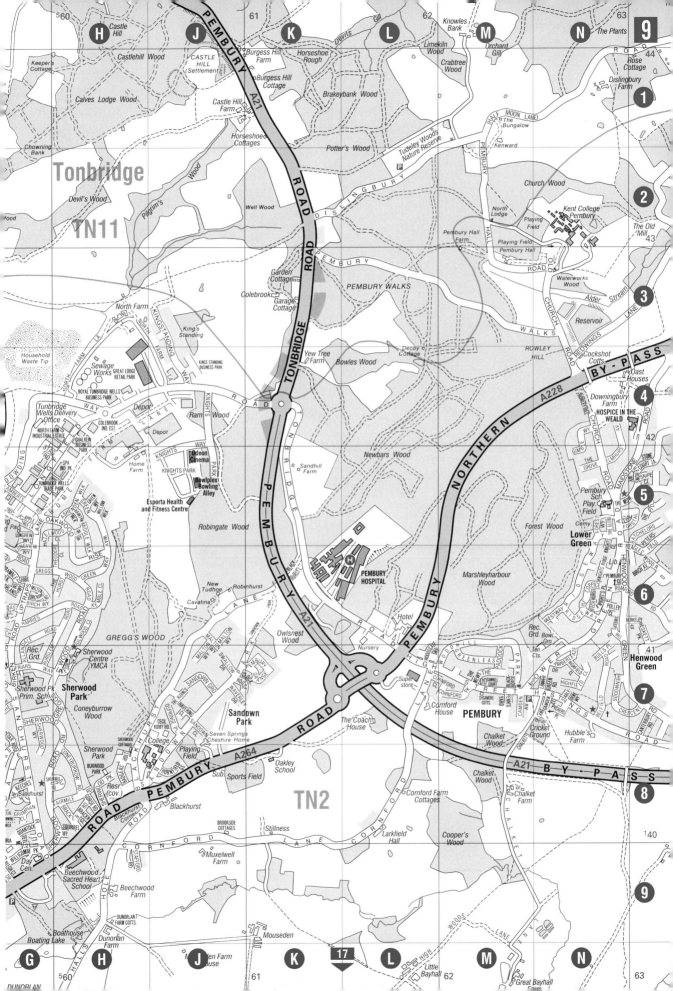

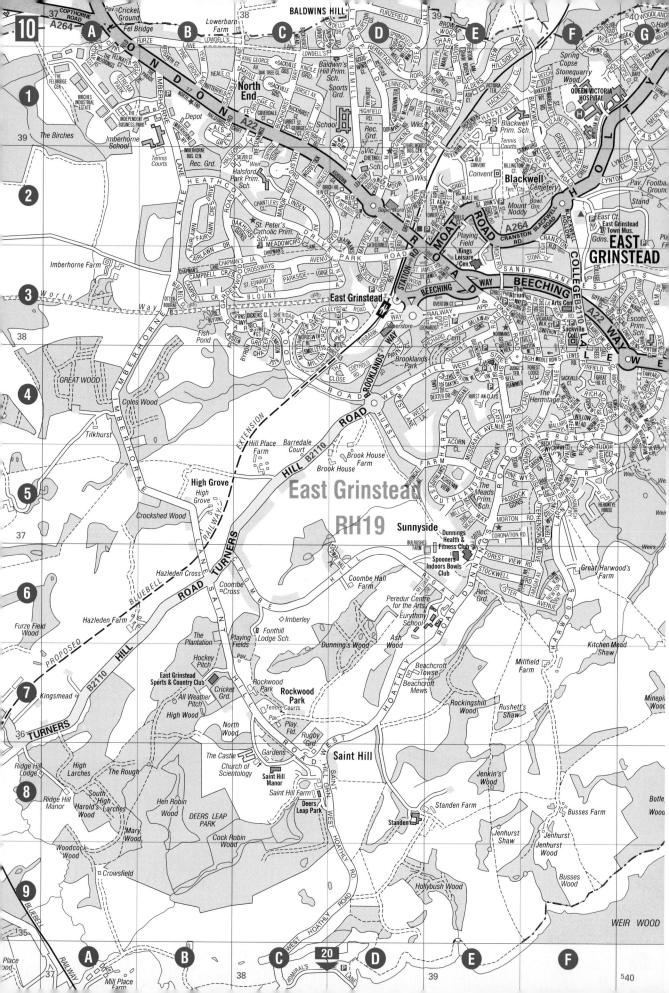

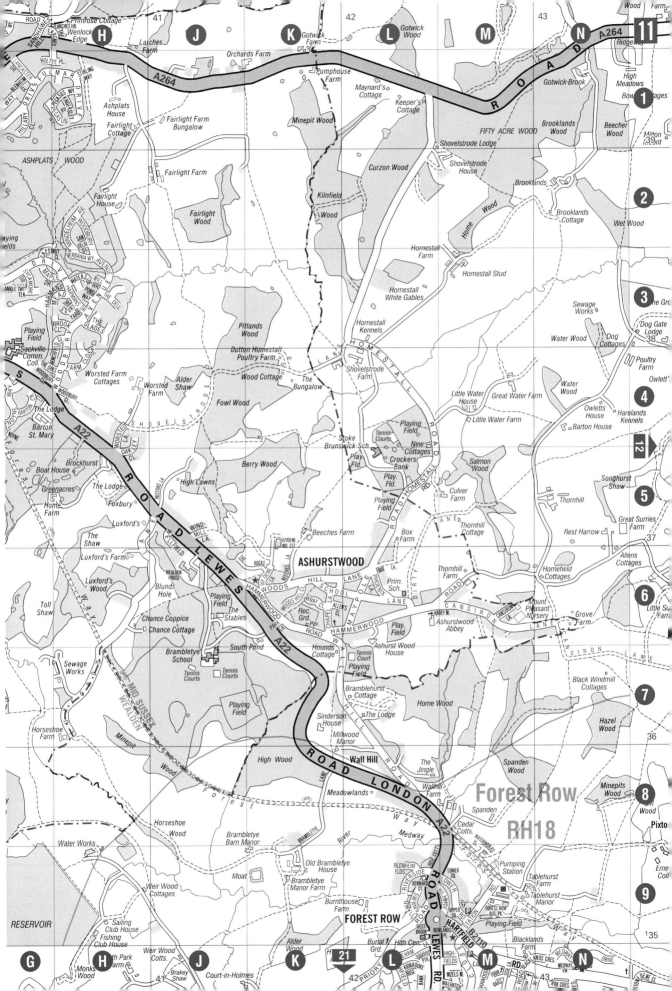

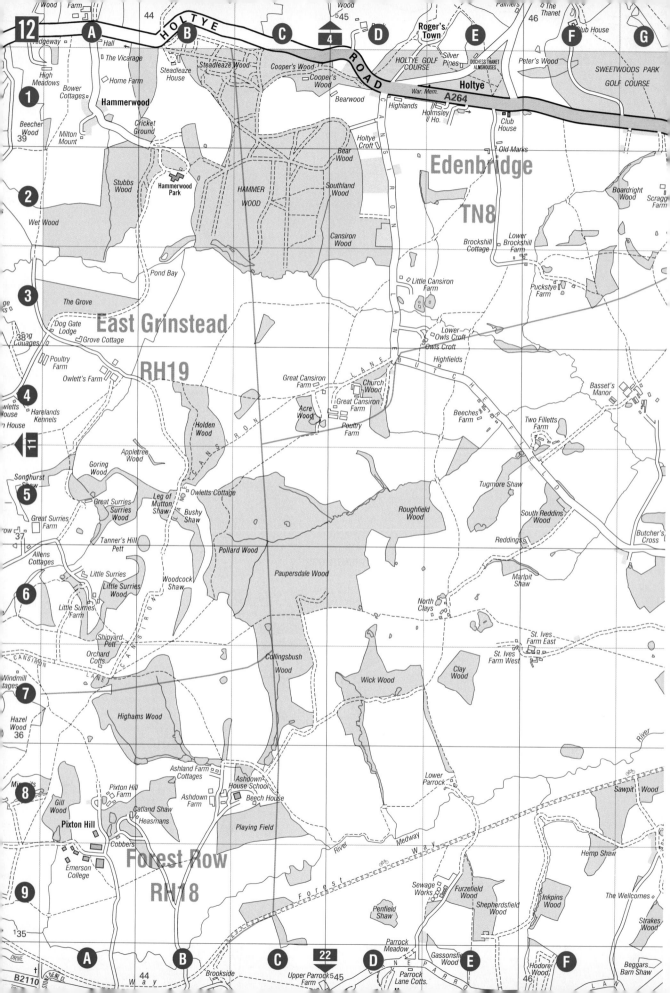

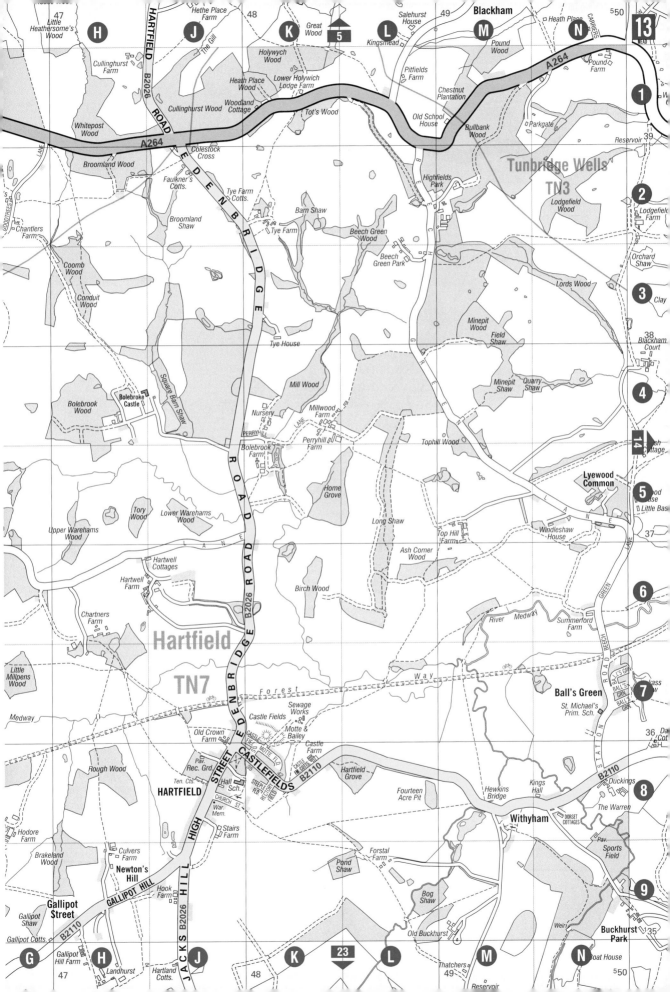

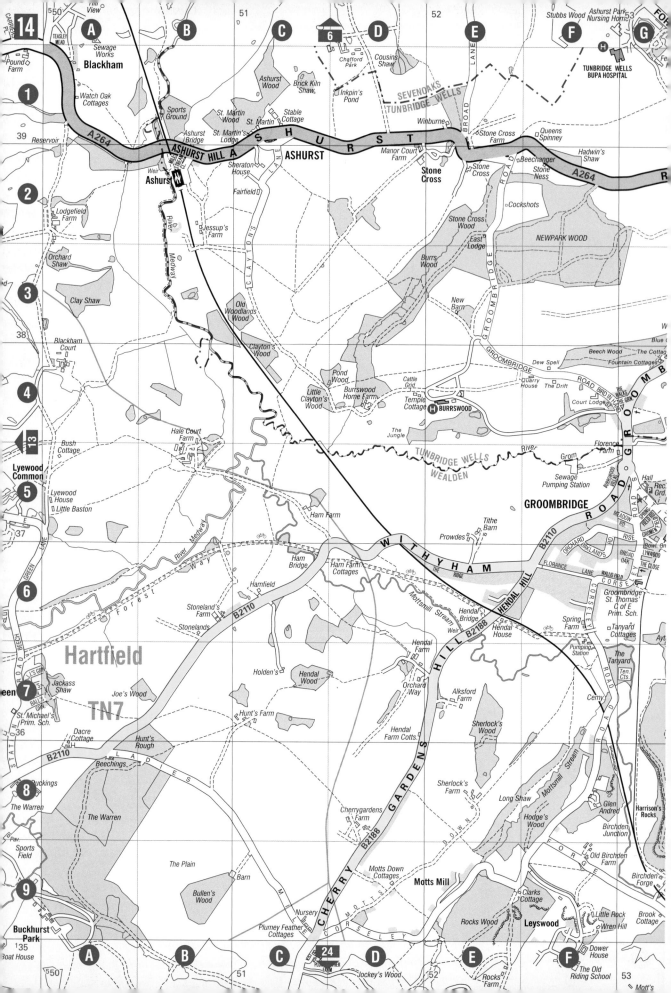

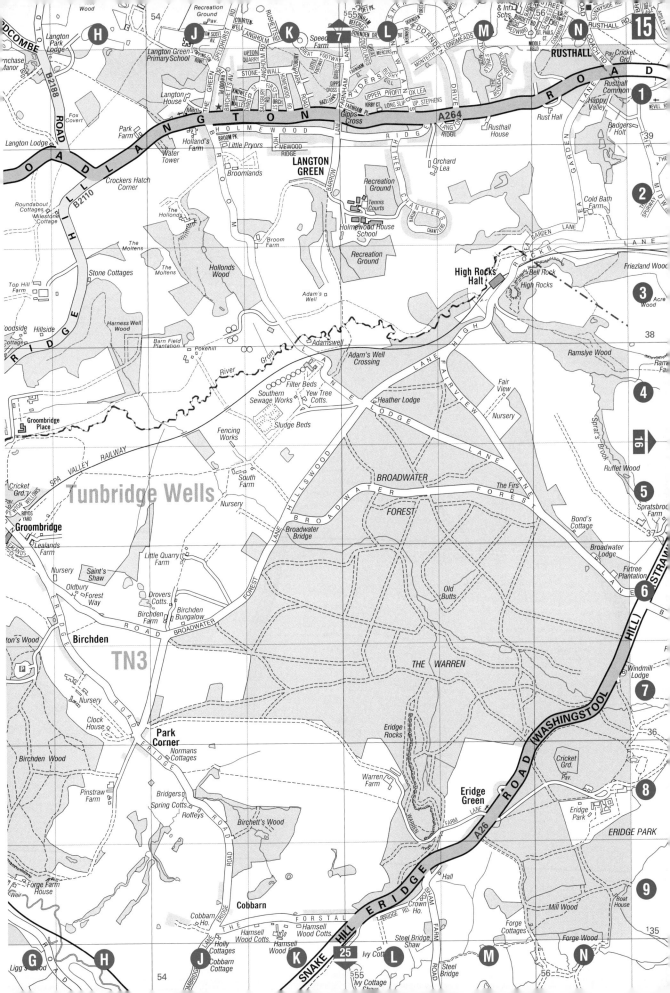

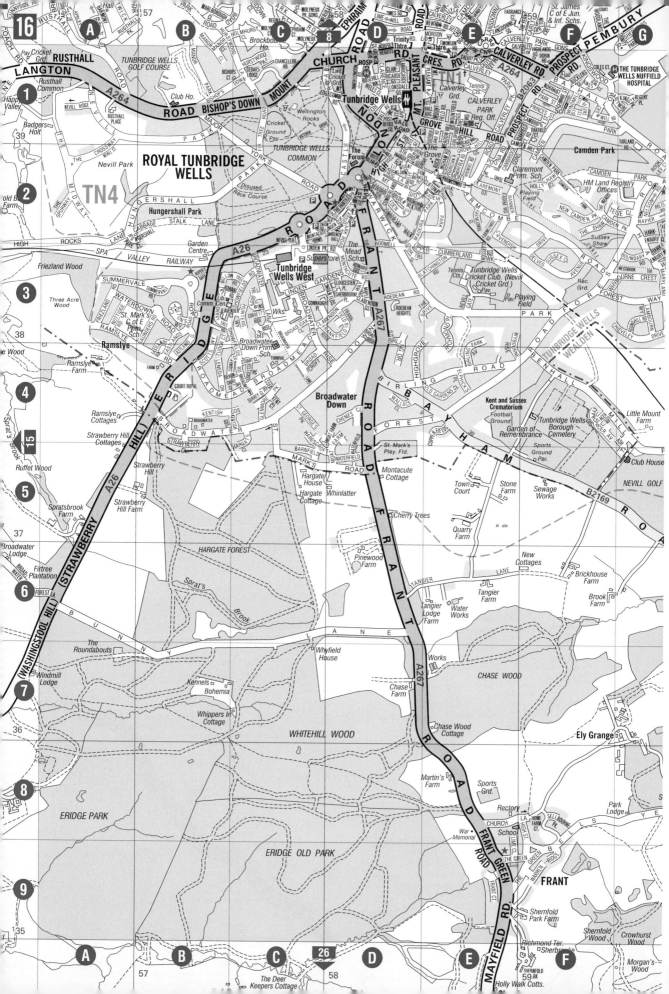

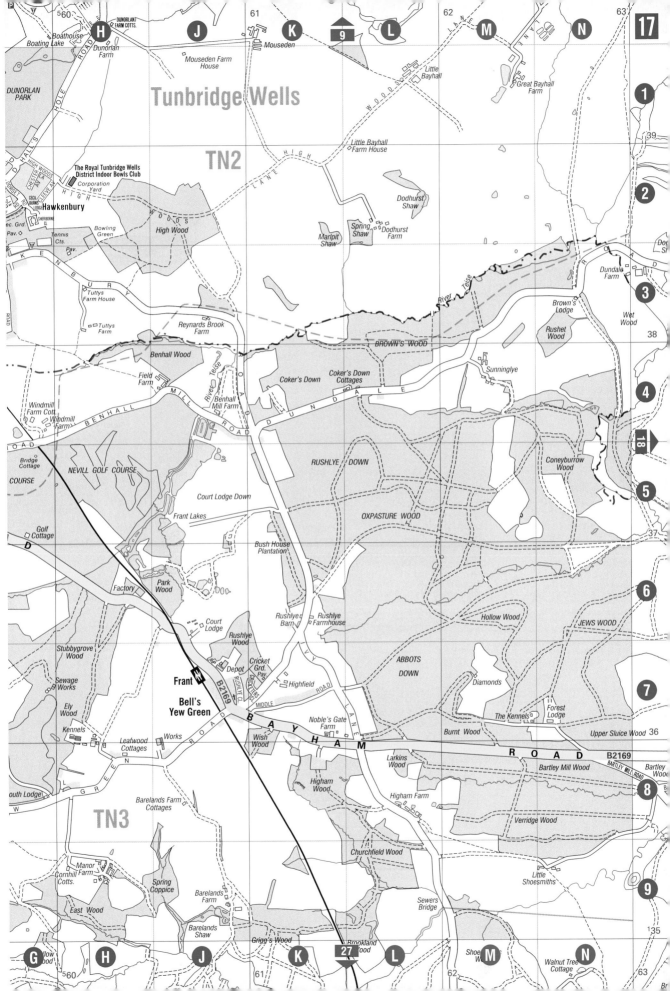

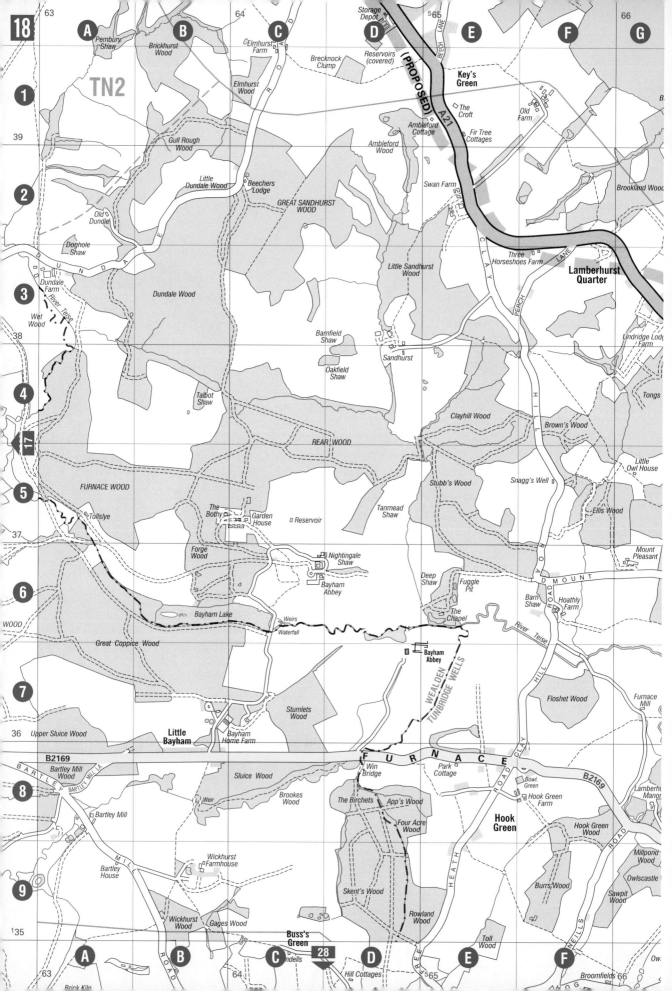

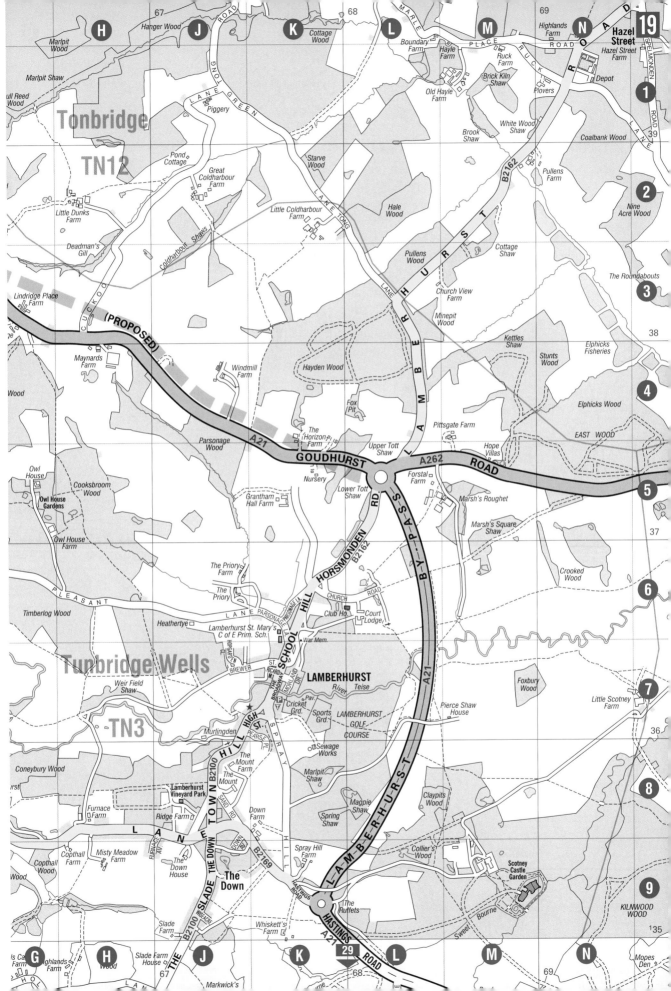

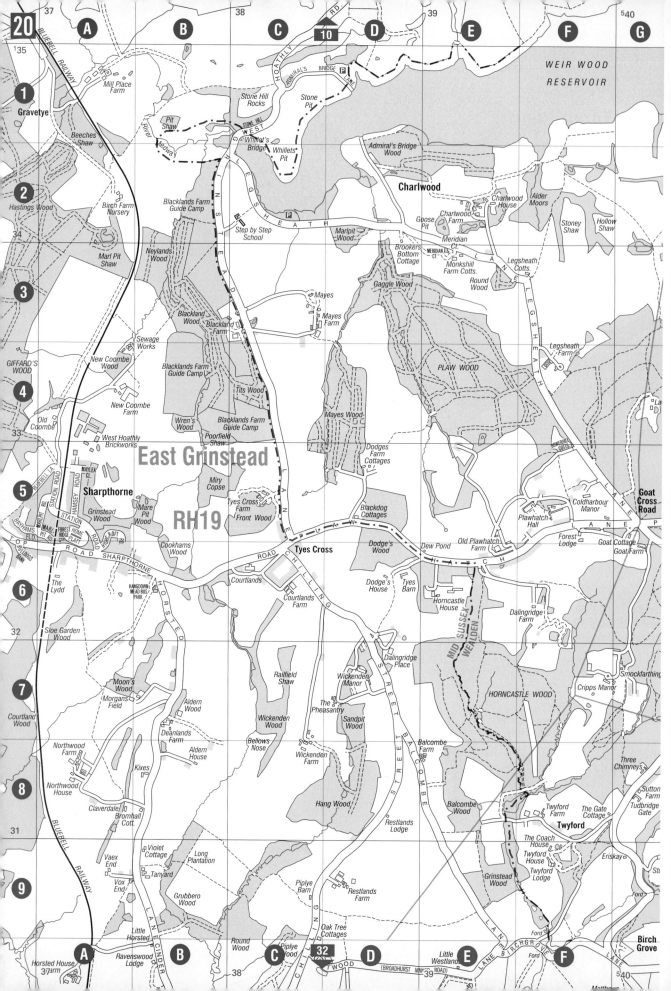

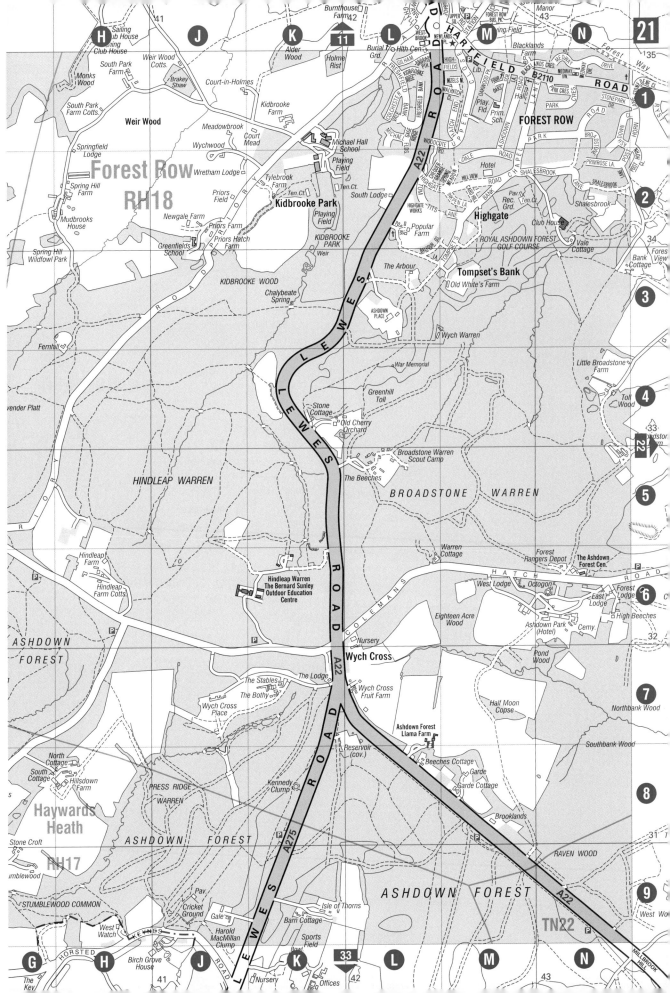

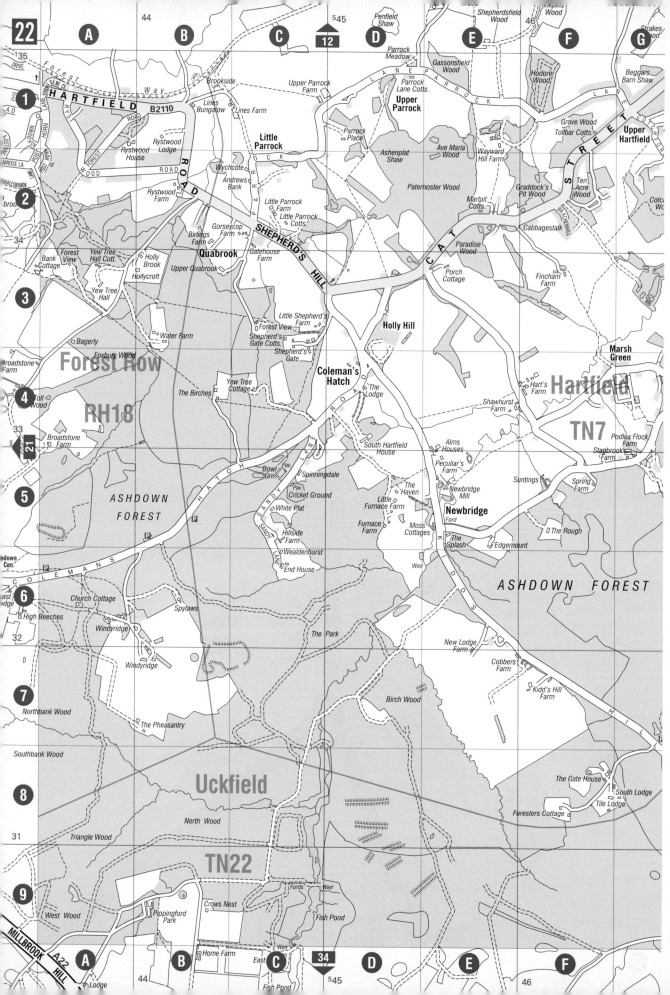

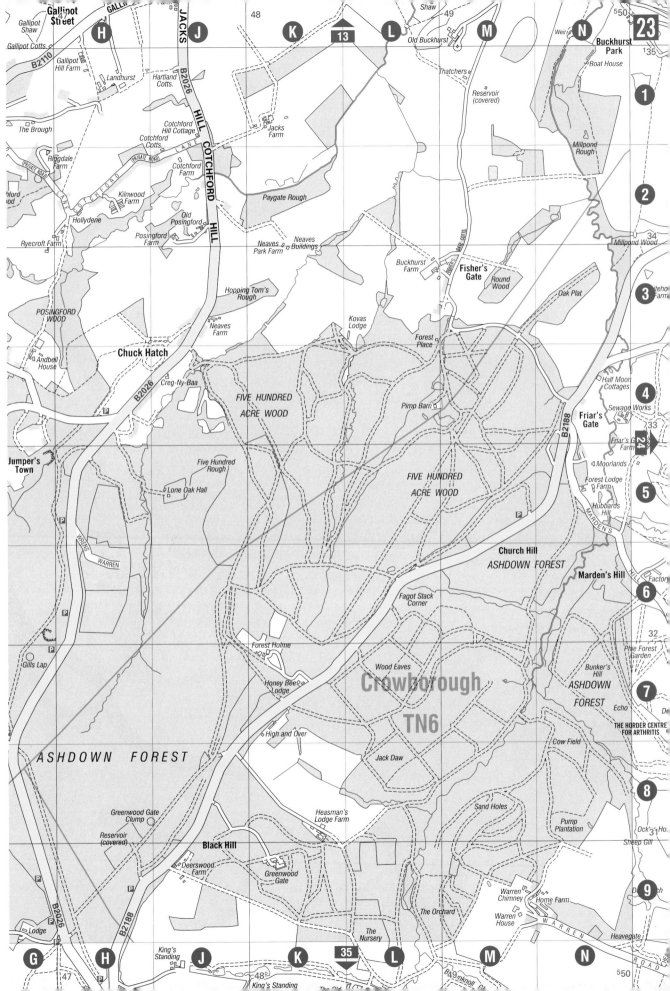

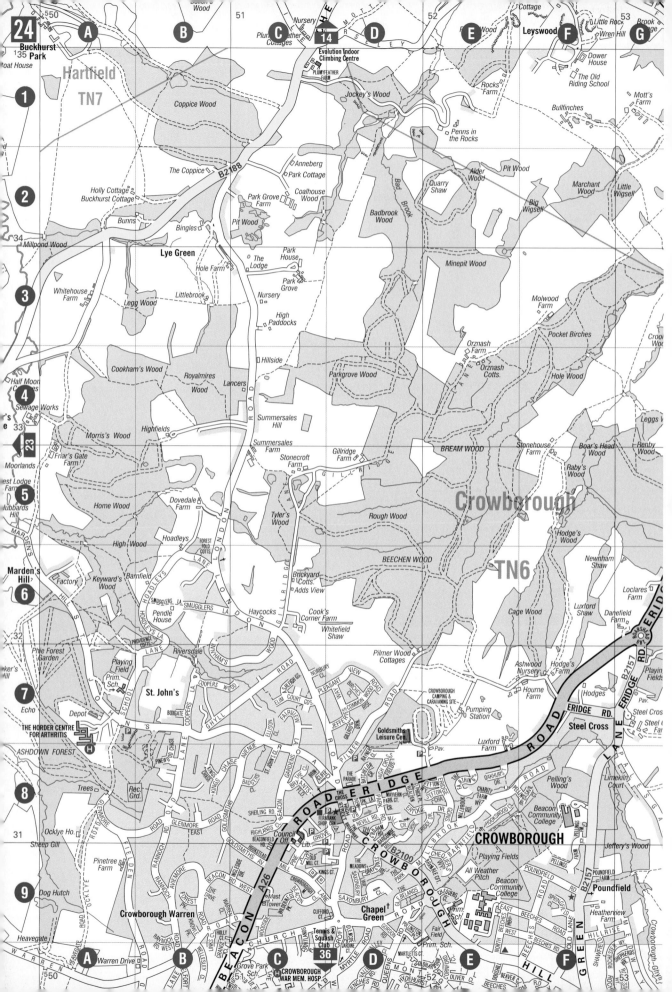

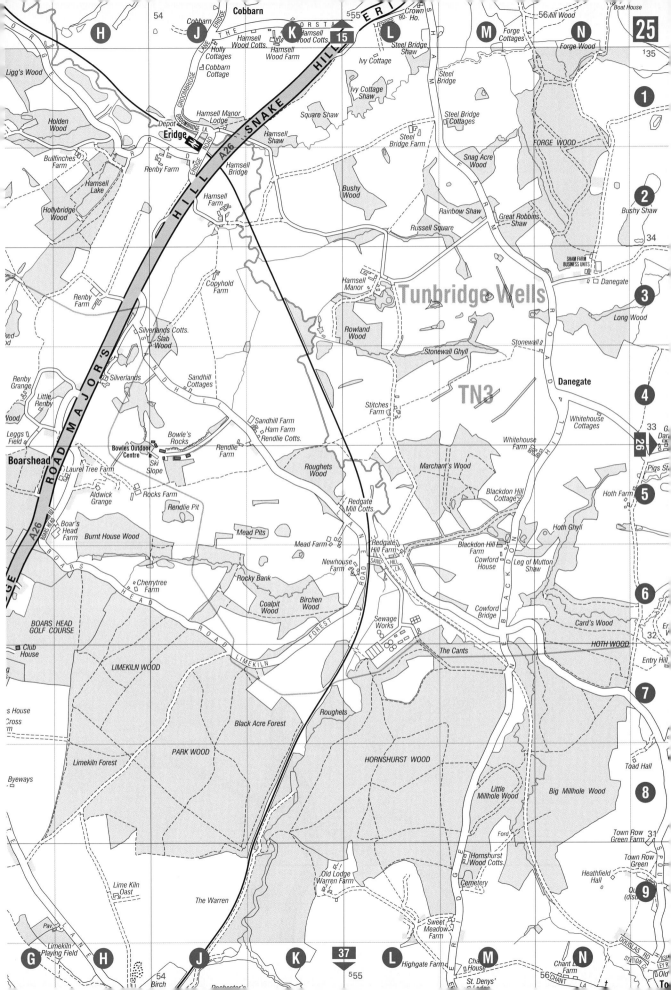

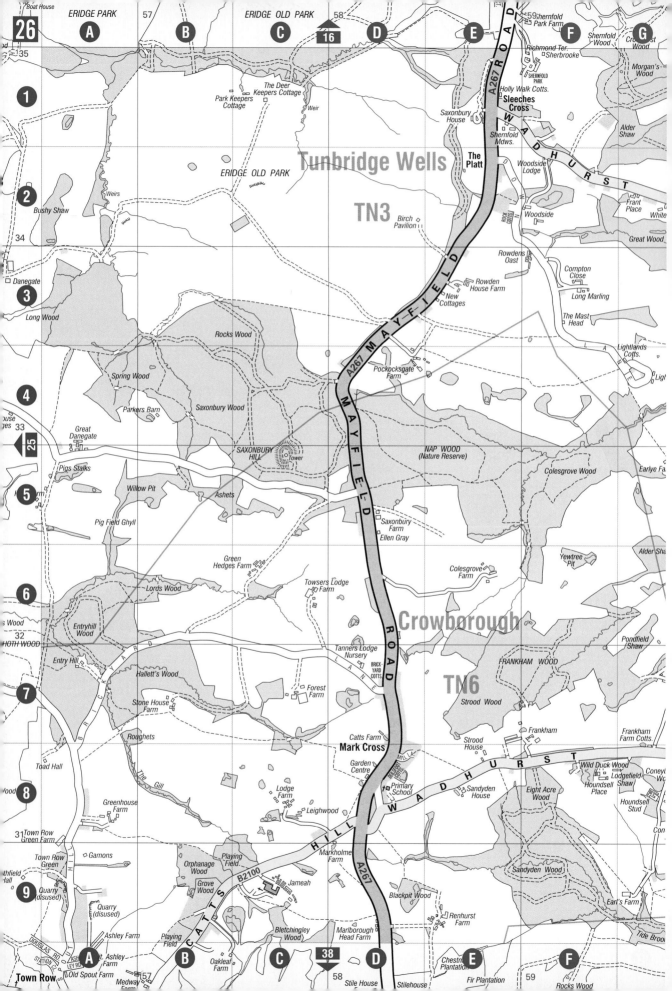

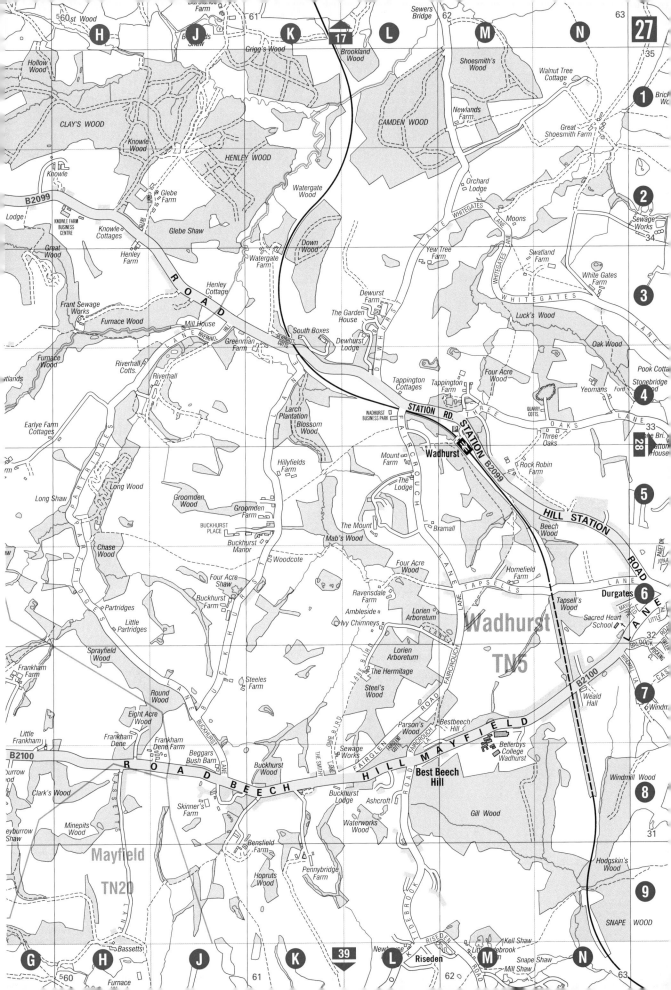

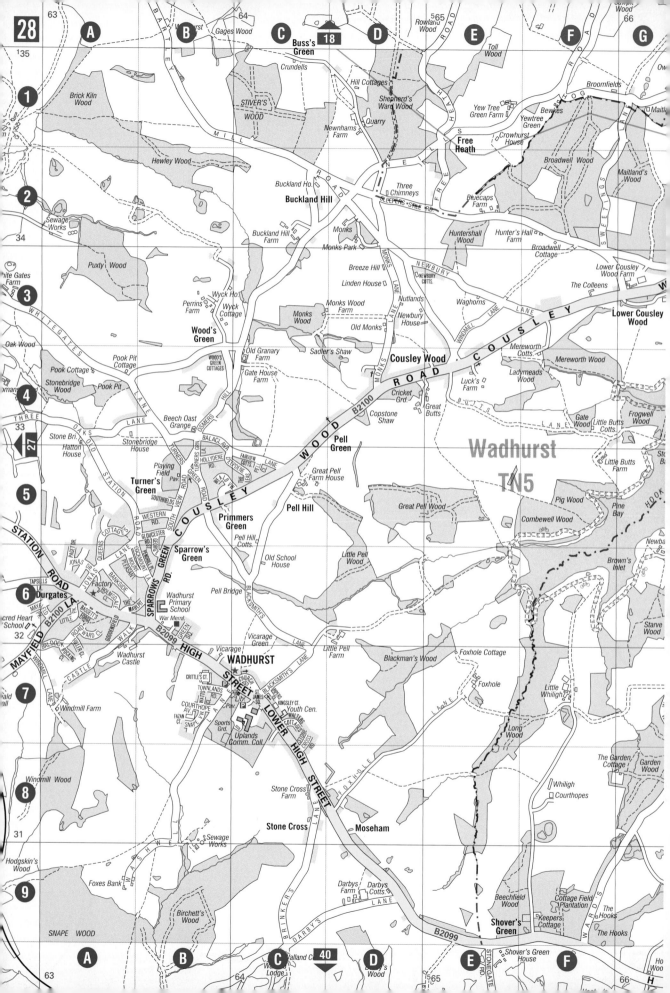

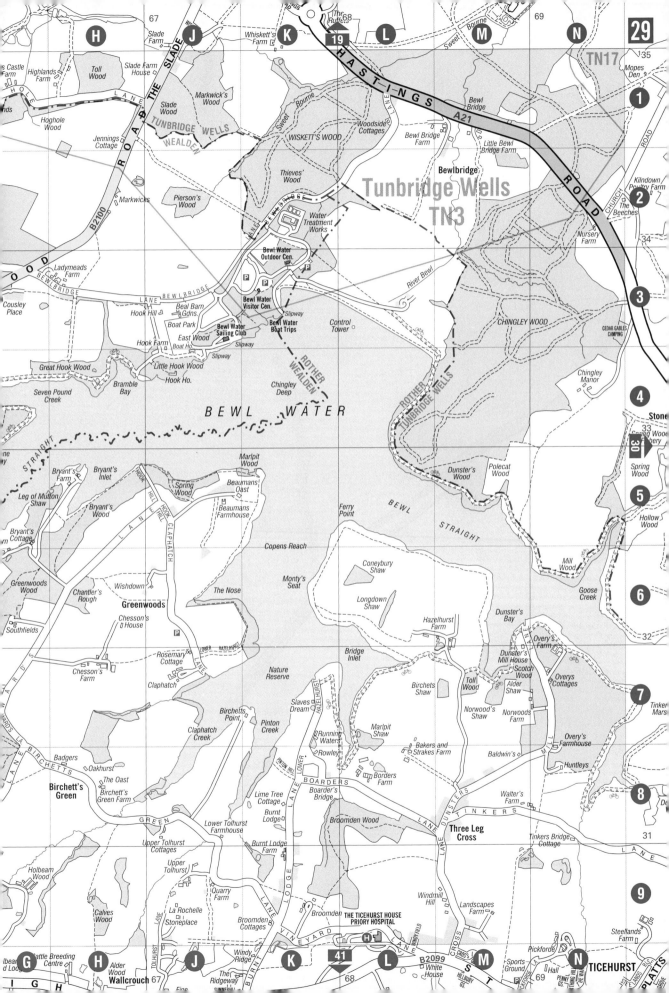

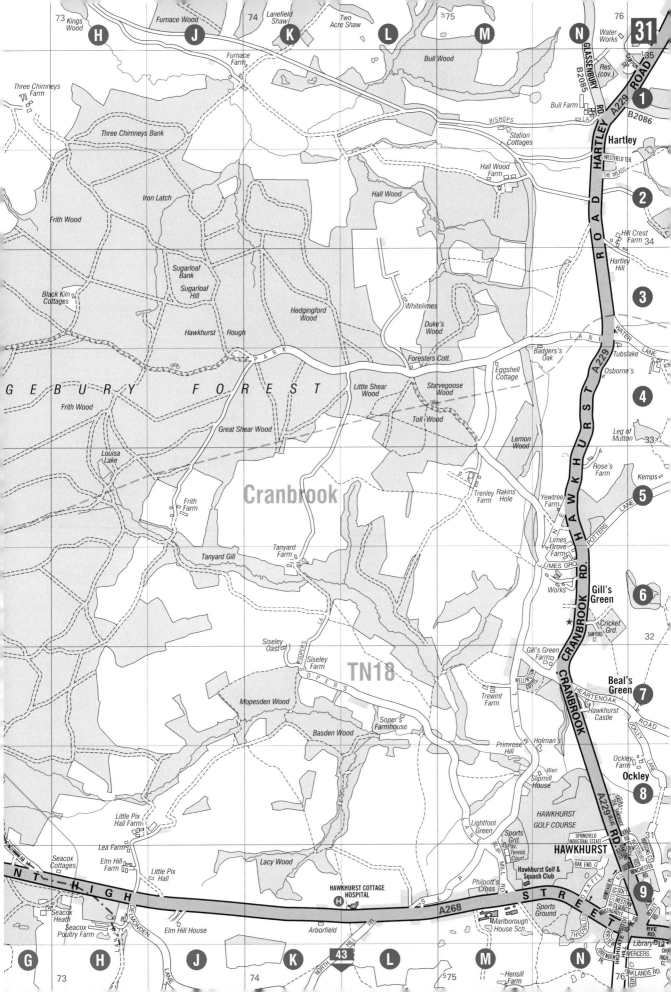

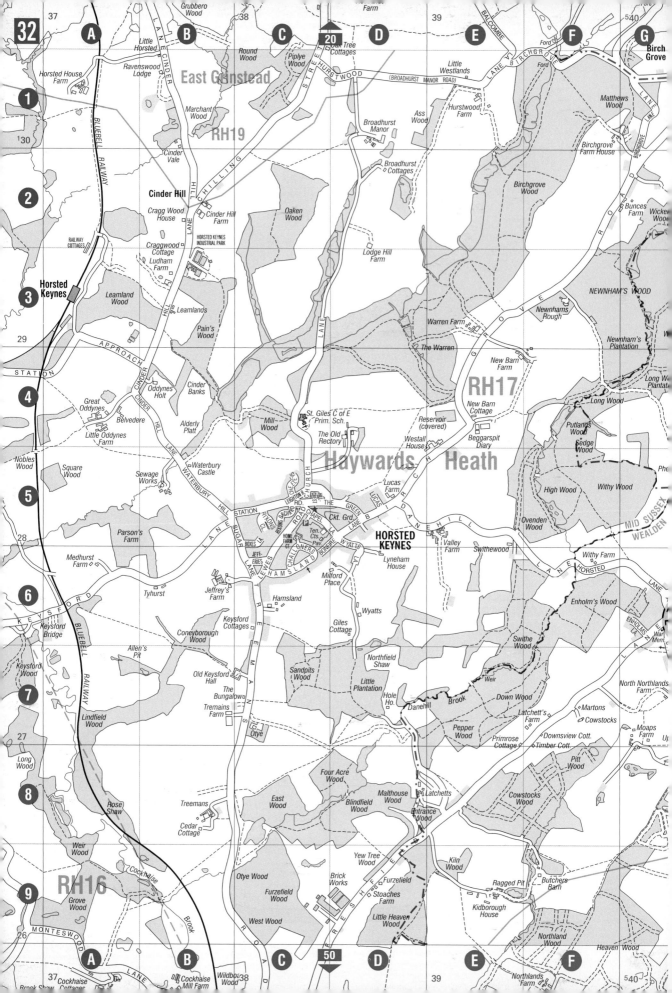

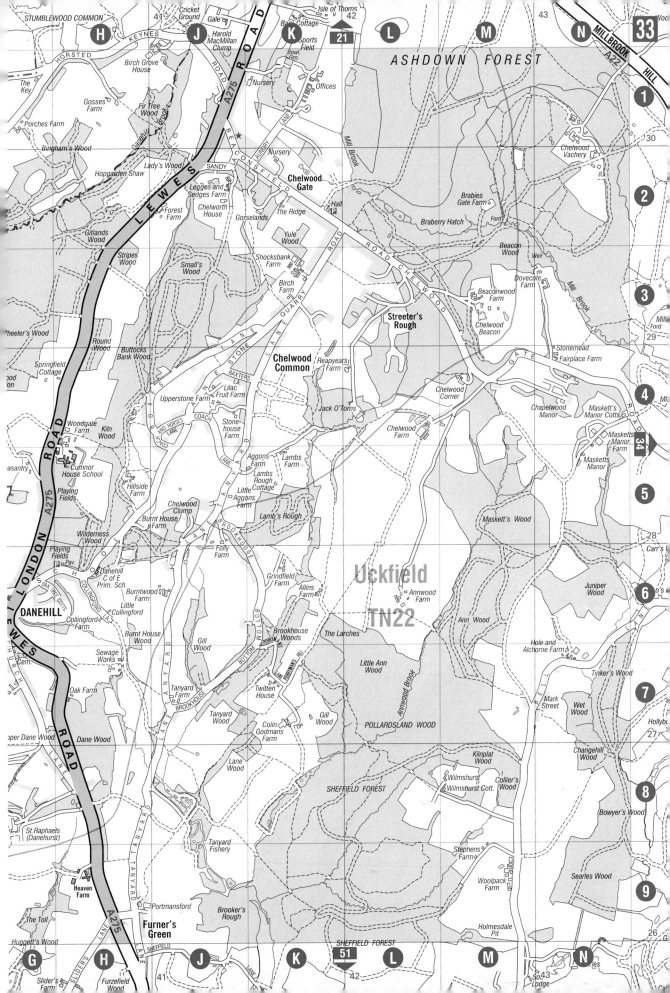

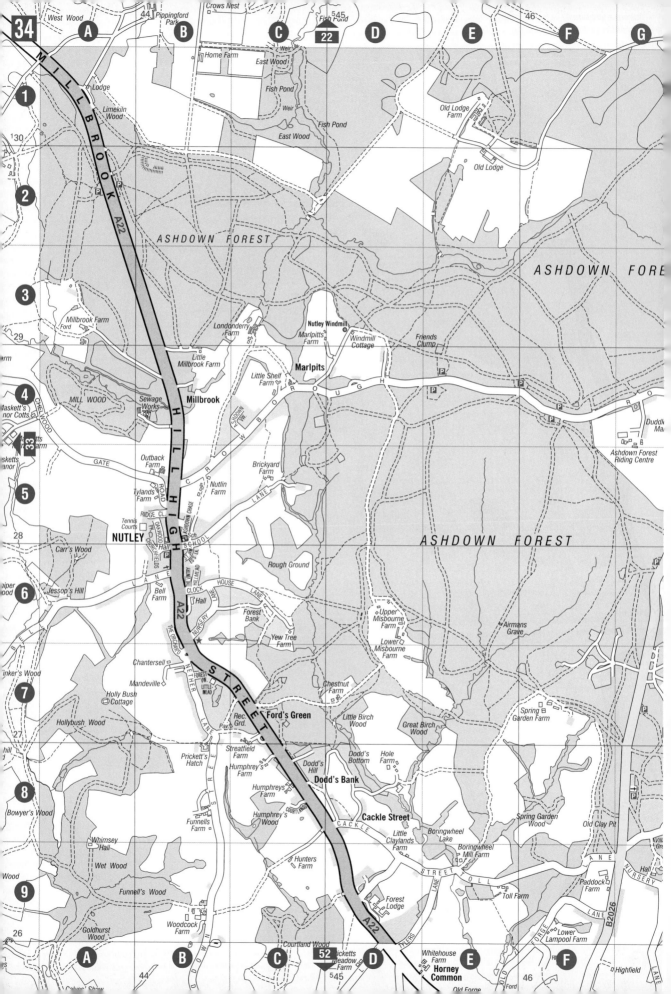

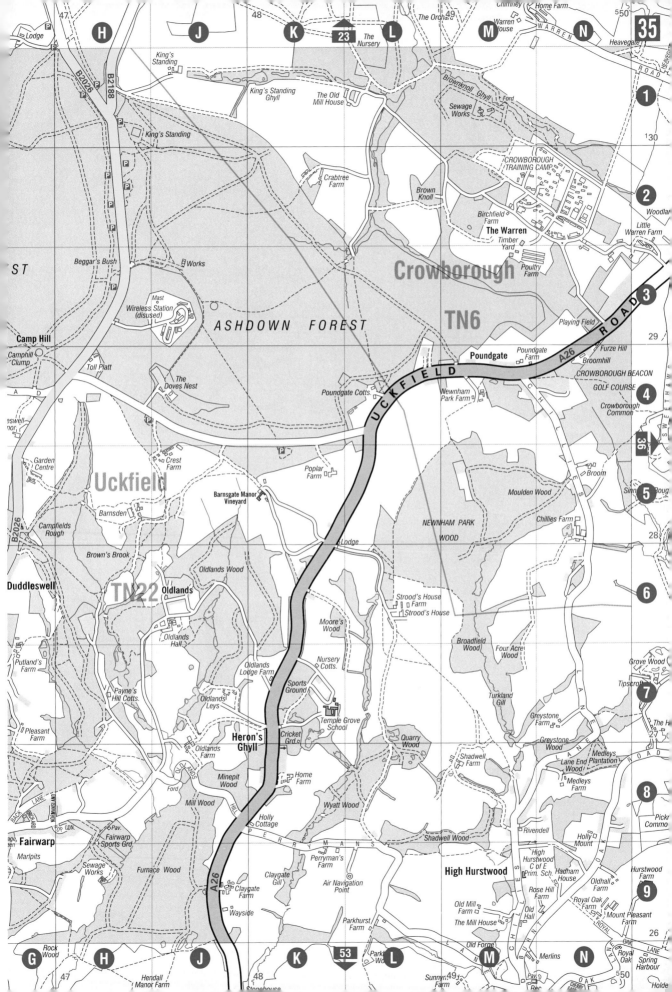

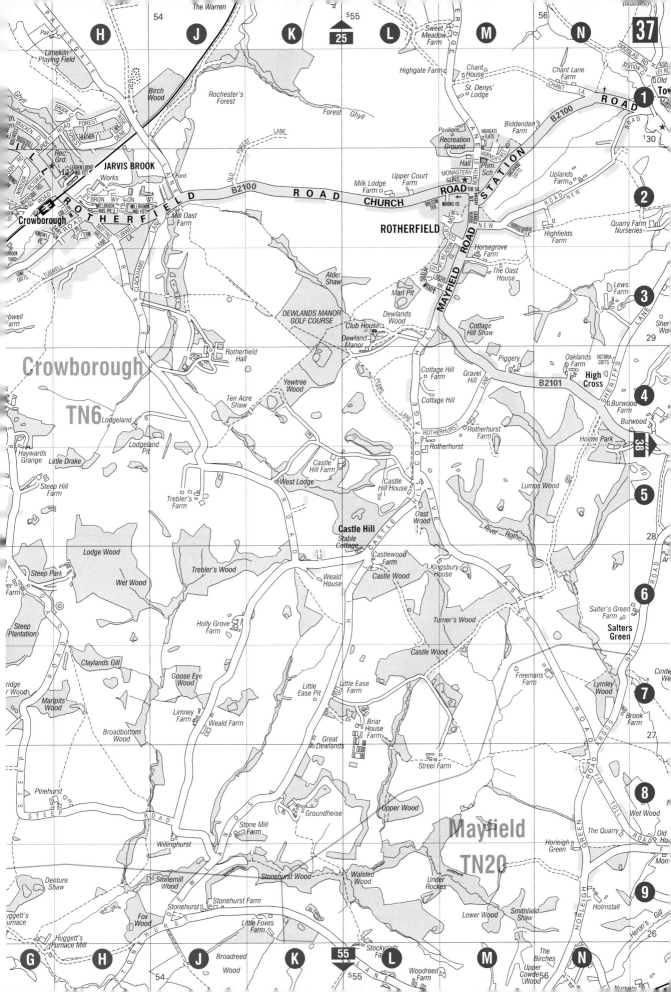

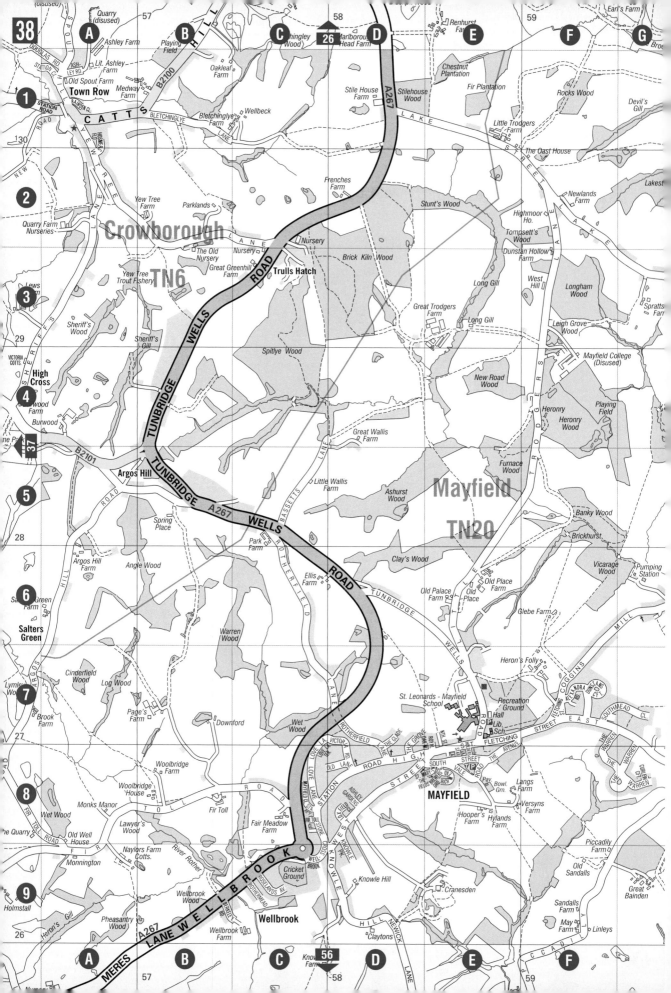

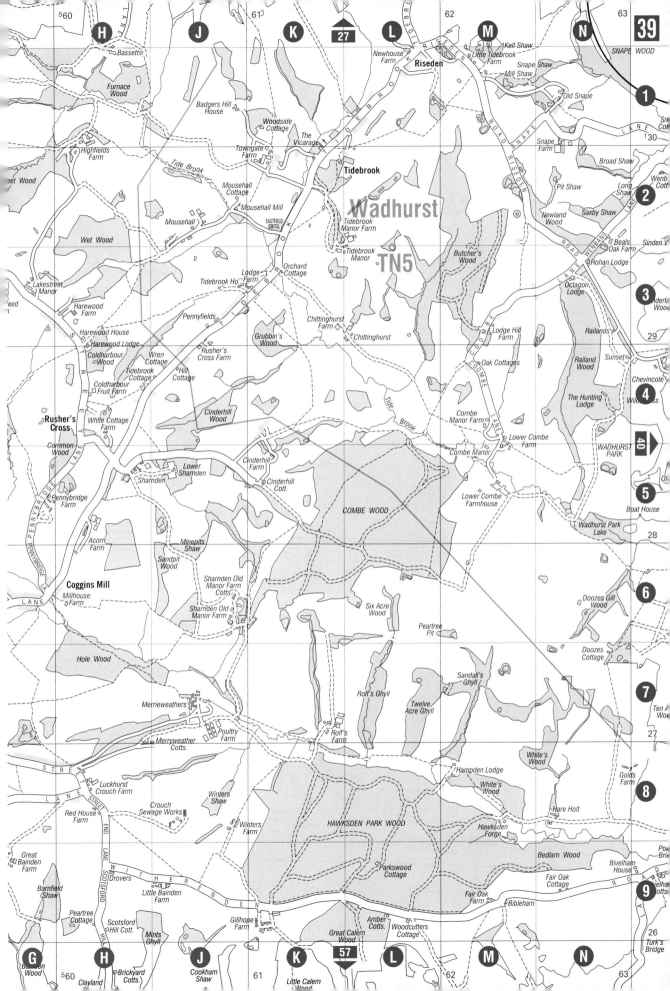

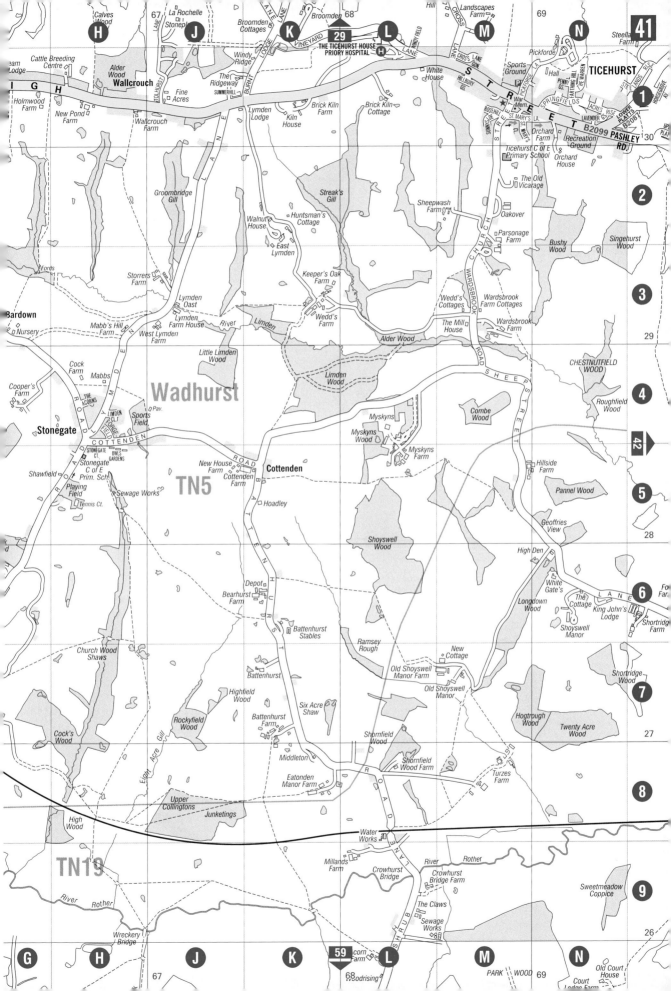

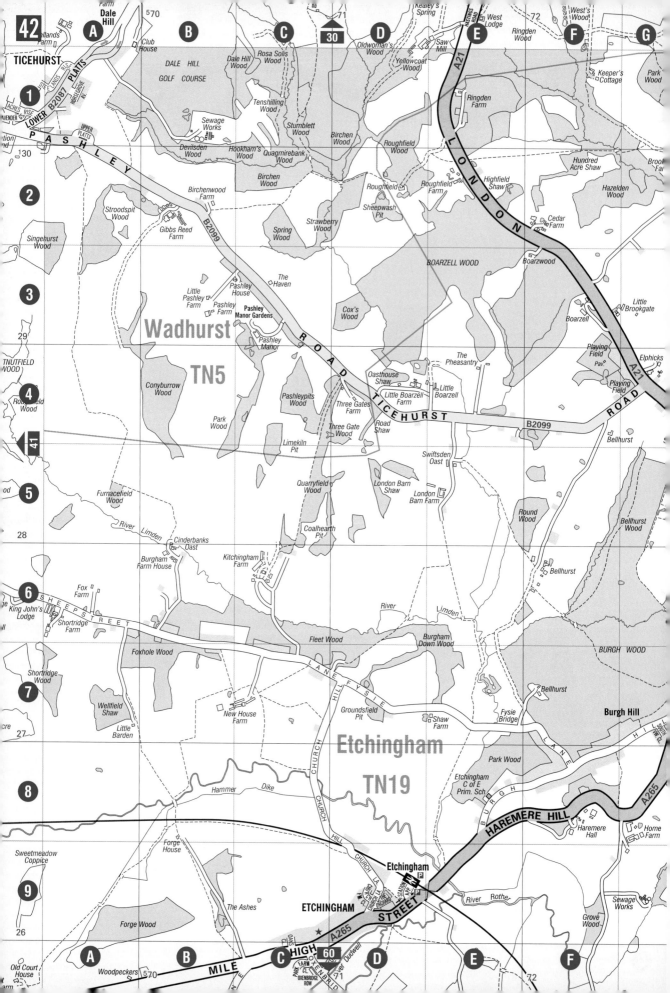

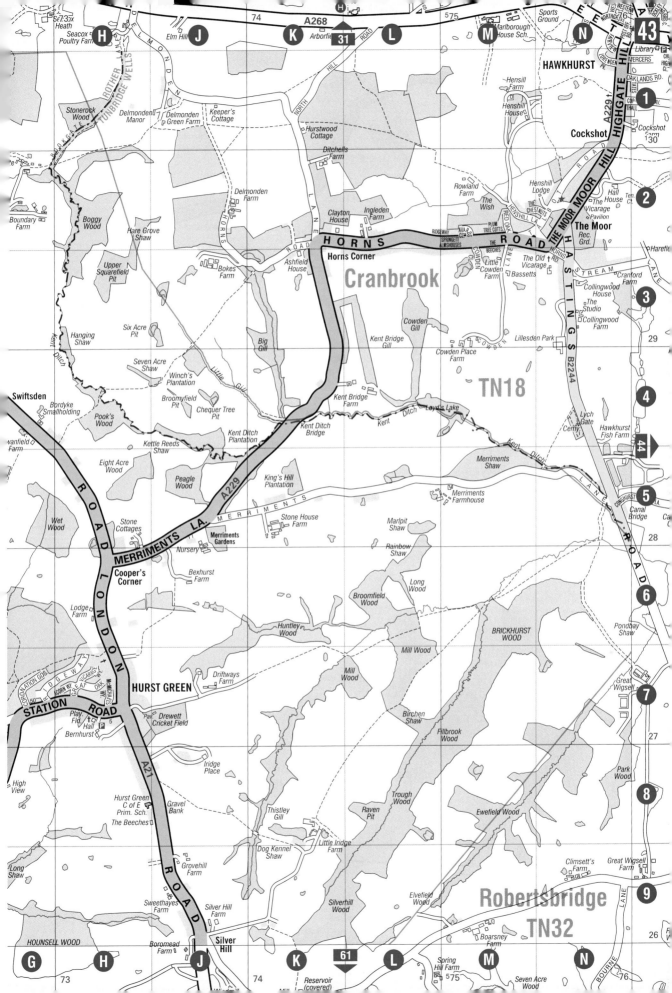

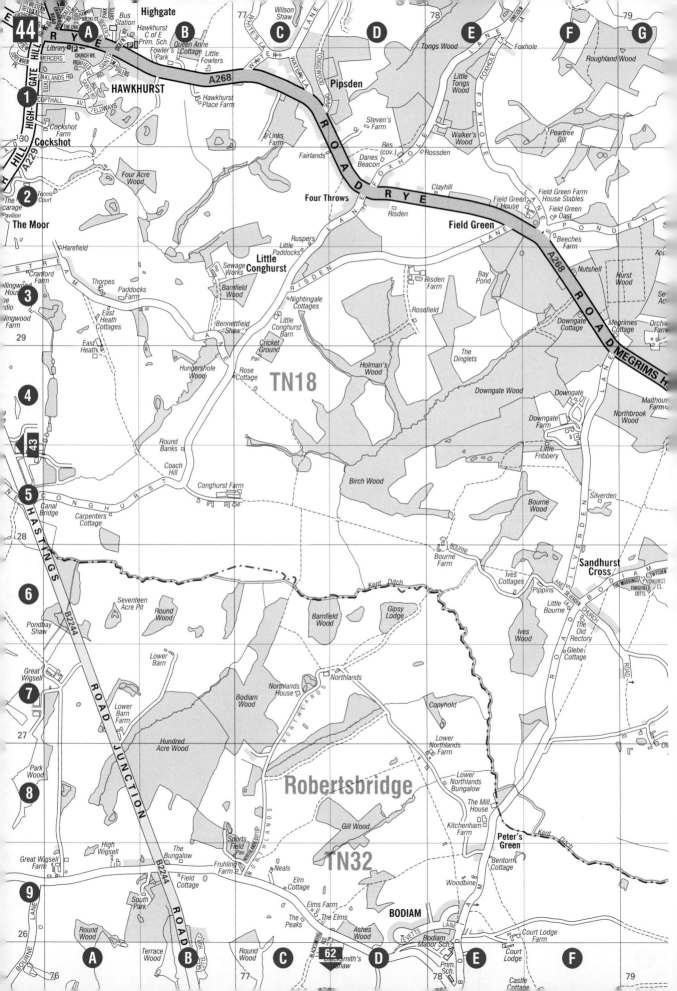

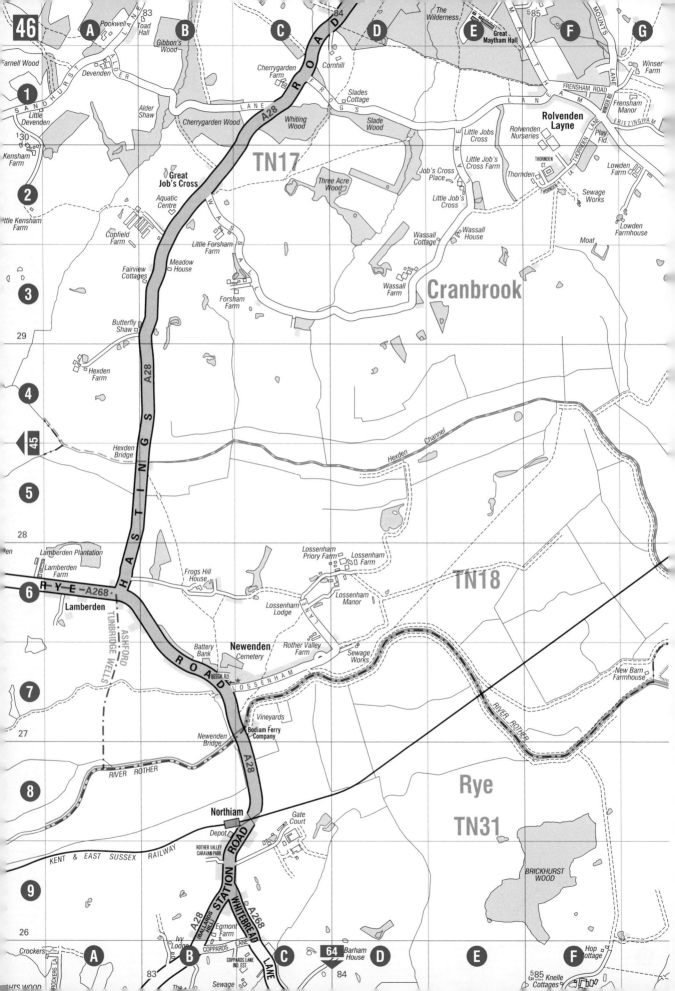

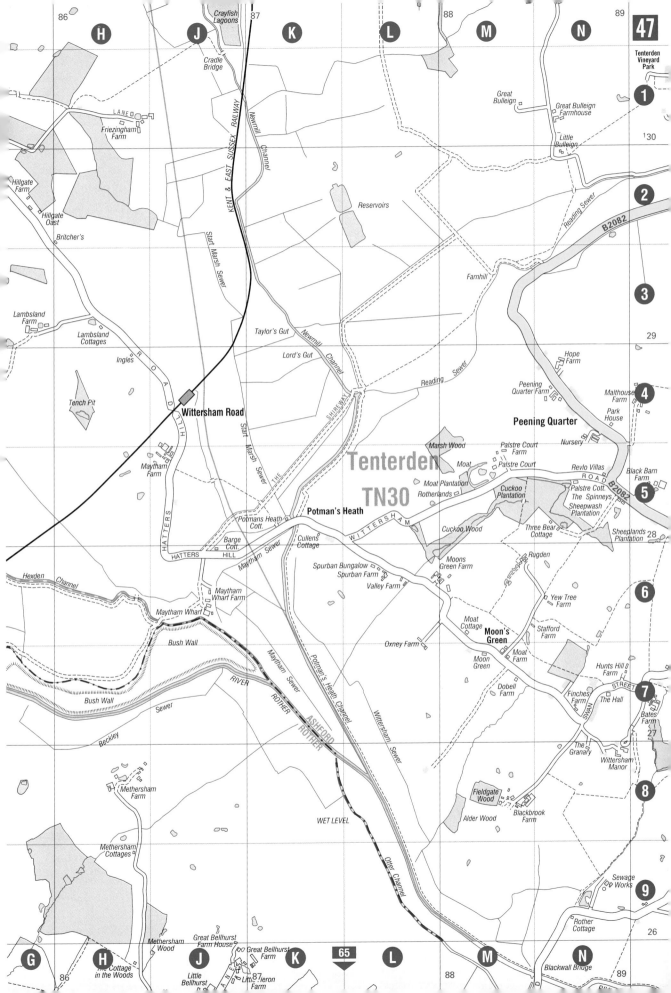

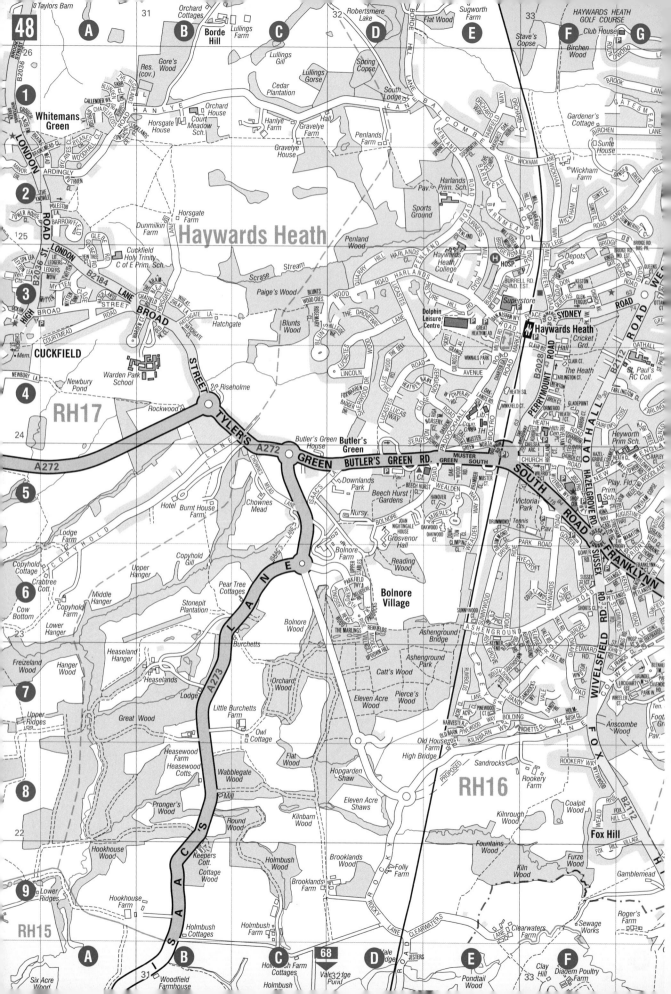

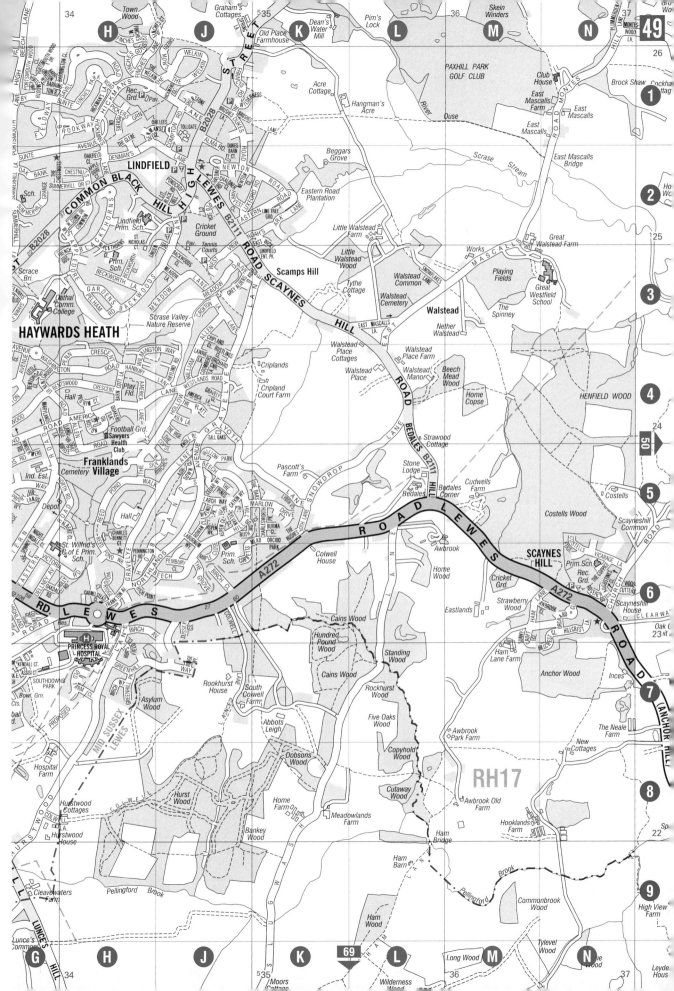

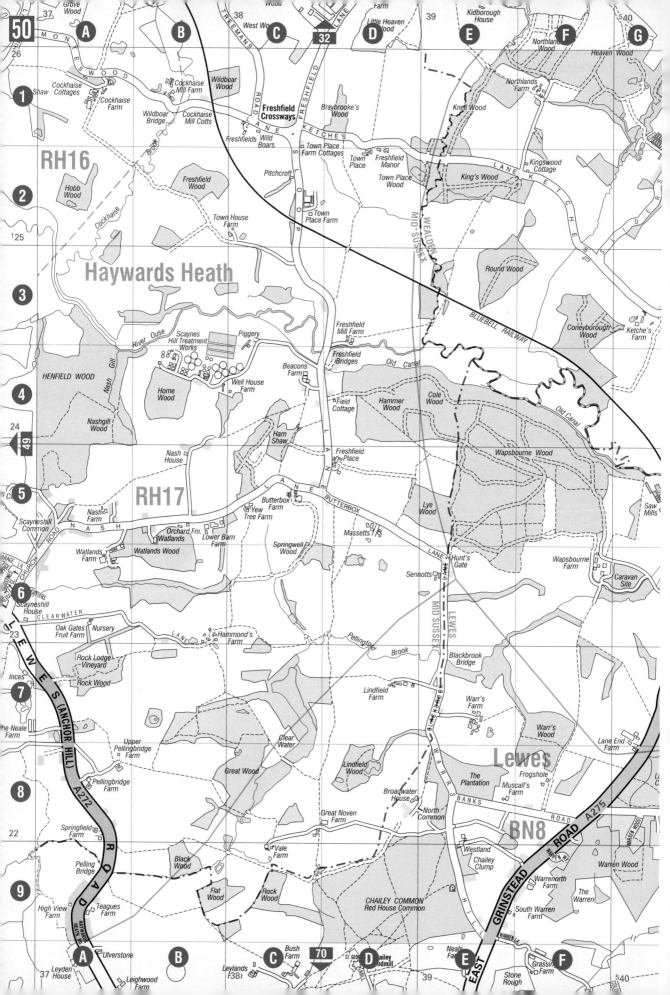

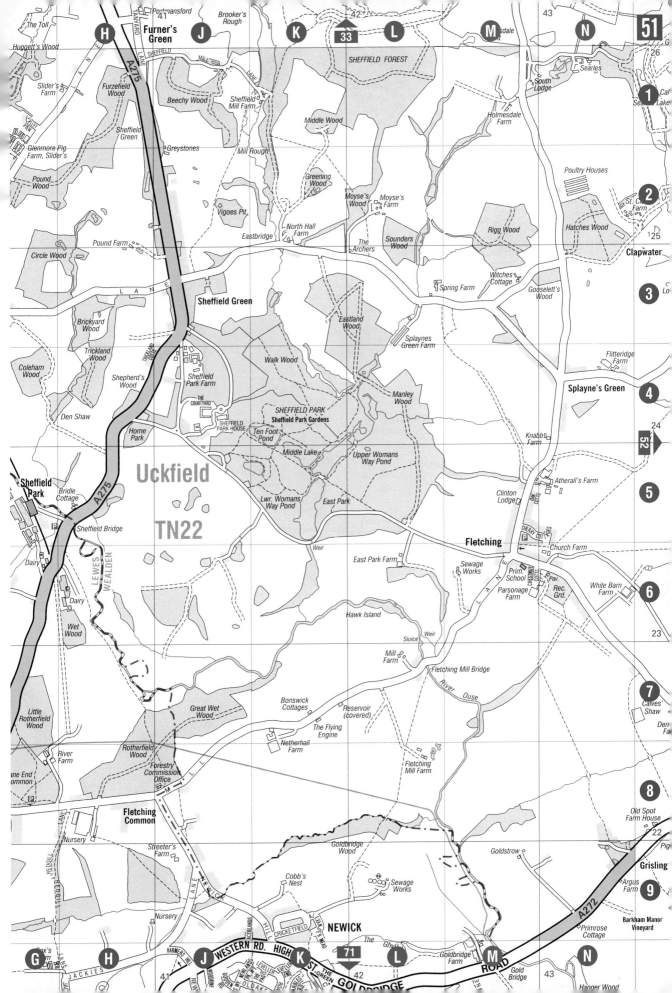

Portmansford
The Toll
Huggett's Wood
Furner's Green
Brooker's Rough

H J K 33 L M N

Slider's Farm
Furzefield Wood
Beechy Wood
Sheffield Mill Farm
Middle Wood
SHEFFIELD FOREST
South Lodge
Searles
Cal
Seale Lake

Glenmore Pig Farm, Slider's
Sheffield Green
Greystones
Mill Rough
Greening Wood
Moyse's Wood
Poultry Houses

Pound Wood
Vigoes Pit
Eastbridge
North Hall Farm
Moyse's Farm
Sounders Wood
Rigg Wood
Hatches Wood
St. Ch Farm

Circle Wood
Pound Farm
The Archers
Witches Cottage
Spring Farm
Gooselett's Wood
Clapwater
Lo

Sheffield Green
Brickyard Wood
Eastland Wood
Splaynes Green Farm
Flitteridge Farm

Coleham Wood
Trickland Wood
Shepherd's Wood
Walk Wood
Manley Wood
Knabb Farm
Splayne's Green

Den Shaw
SHEFFIELD PARK
Sheffield Park Gardens
Sheffield Park Farm
THE COURTYARD
SHEFFIELD PARK HOUSE
Home Park
Ten Foot Pond
Middle Lake
Upper Womans Way Pond
Knabb Farm

Uckfield

Sheffield Park
Bridle Cottage
Sheffield Bridge
Clinton Lodge
Atherall's Farm

TN22
Lwr. Womans Way Pond
East Park
Fletching
Church Farm

Dairy
Weir
East Park Farm
Sewage Works
Prim. School
Parsonage Farm
White Barn Farm

Dairy
Wet Wood
Hawk Island
Sluice
Weir
Mill Farm
Fletching Mill Bridge
River Ouse
Calves' Shaw
Den Fa

Little Rotherfield Wood
Great Wet Wood
Bonswick Cottages
Reservoir (covered)
The Flying Engine
Netherhall Farm
Fletching Mill Farm
Old Spot Farm House

River Farm
Rotherfield Wood
Forestry Commission Office
Fletching Common
Goldbridge Wood
Goldstrow
Grisling

Lane End Common
Nursery
Streeter's Farm
Cobb's Nest
Sewage Works
Argus Farm
Primrose Cottage
Barkham Manor Vineyard

Nursery
NEWICK
The Ghyll
Goldbridge Farm
Gold Bridge
Hanger Wood

Box's m
G H J 71 K L M N
Cricketfield
WESTERN RD. **HIGH ST** **GREEN** **GOLDBRIDGE** **ROAD**
A272

LEWES WEALDEN
A275
TANYARD LANE
SHEFFIELD
MILL LANE

Numbers: 41, 42, 43, 26, 1, 2, 125, 3, 4, 24, 52, 5, 6, 23, 7, 8, 22, 9

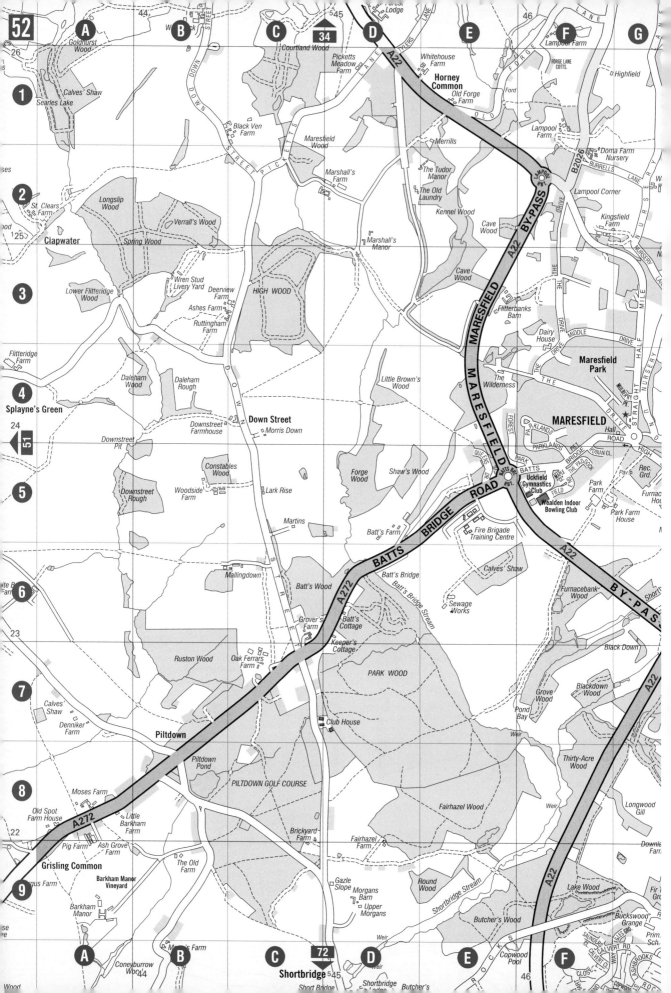

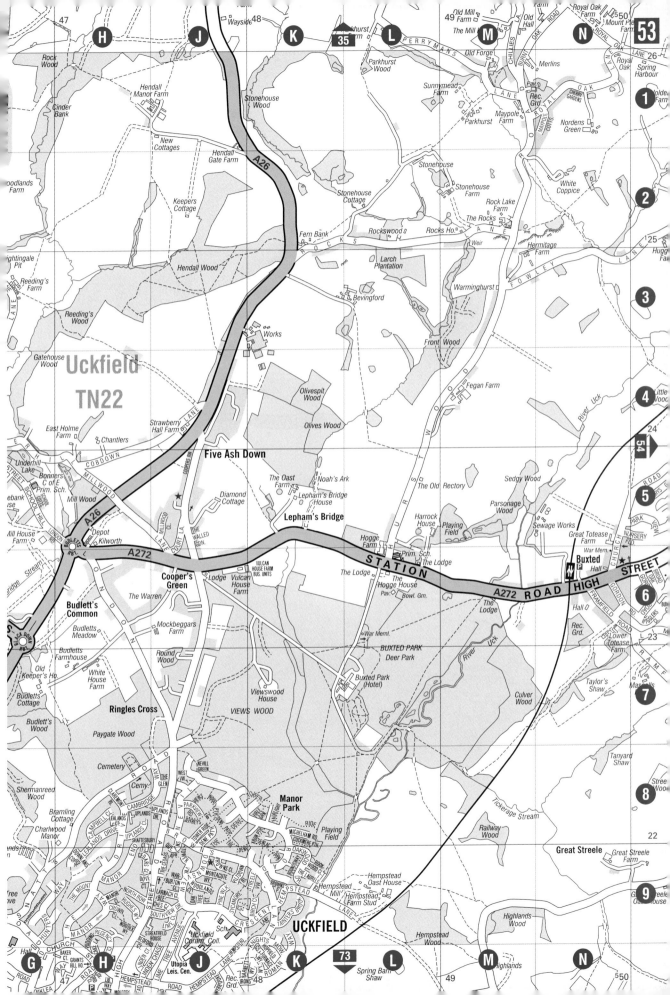

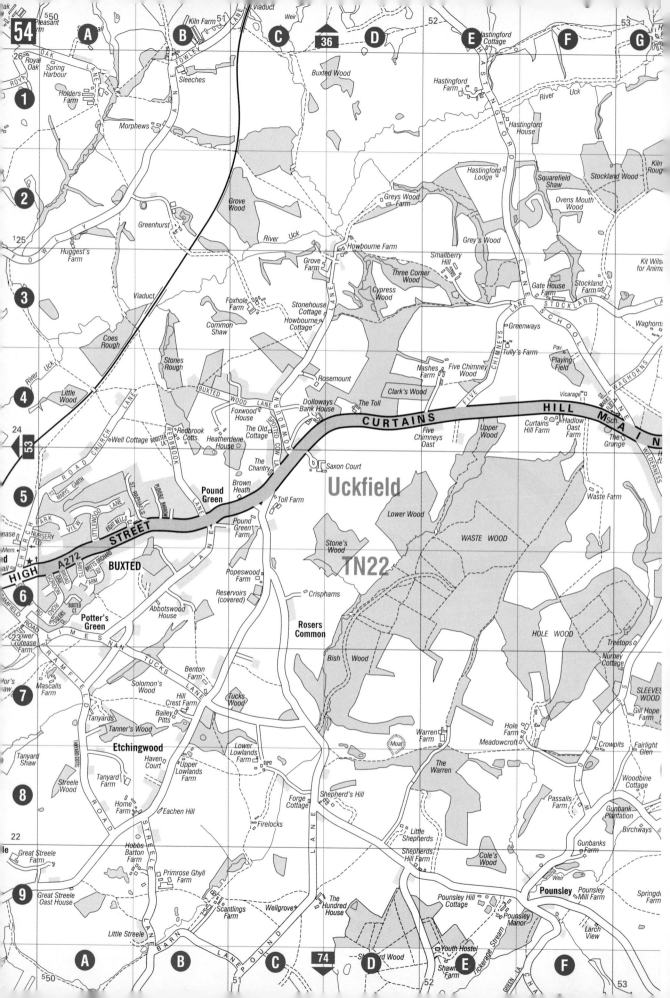

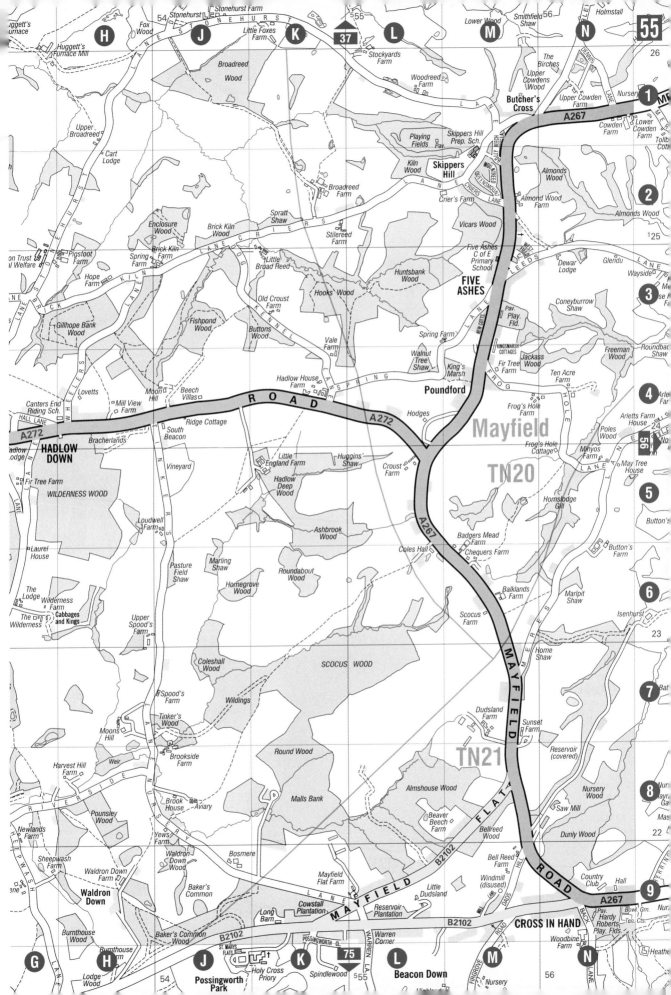

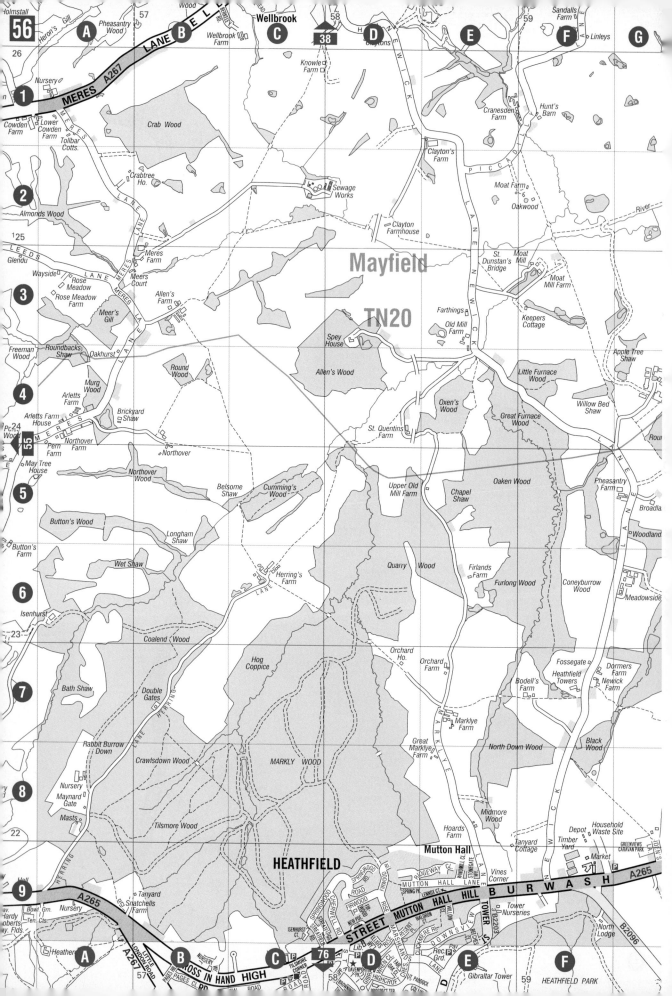

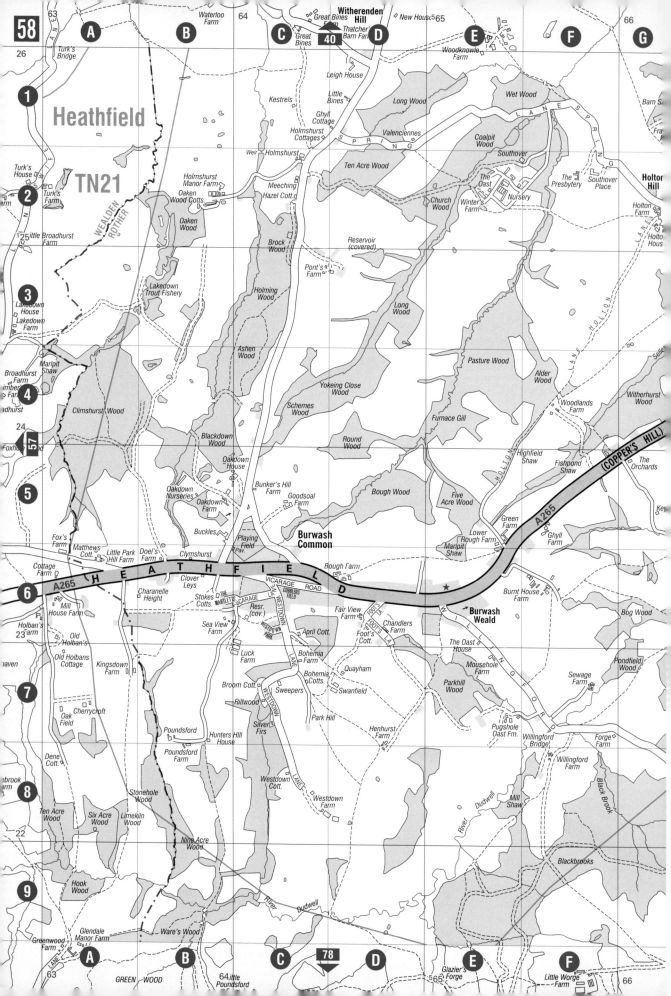

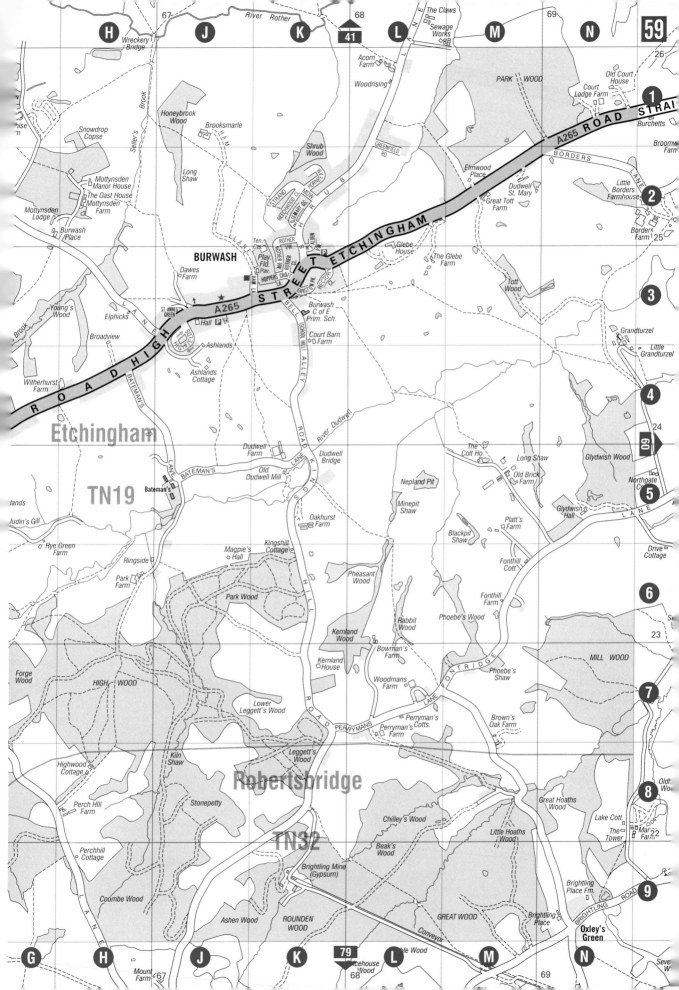

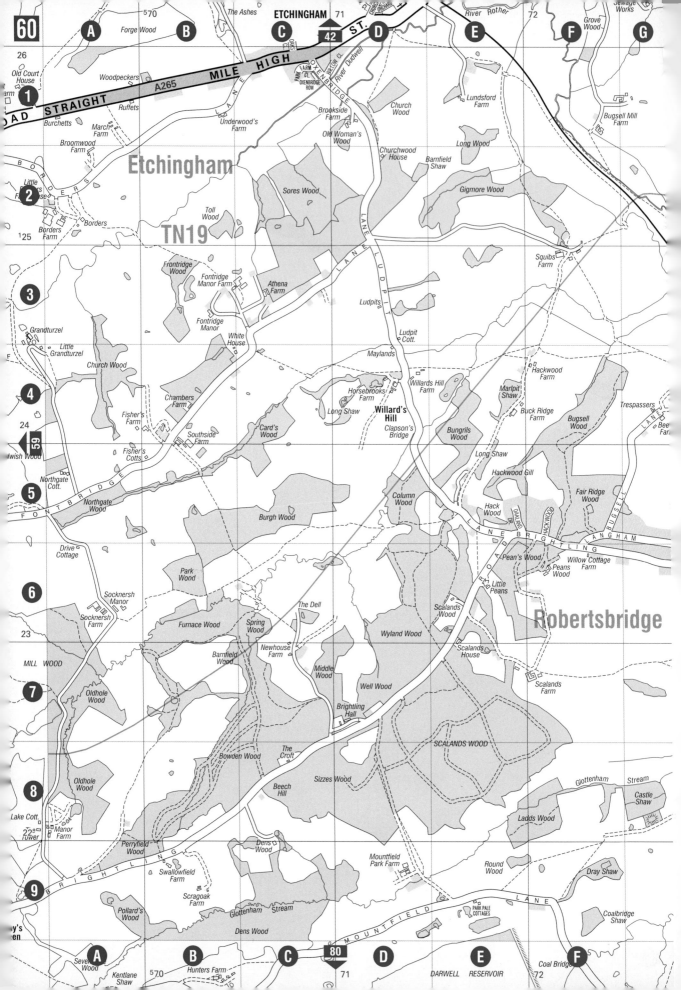

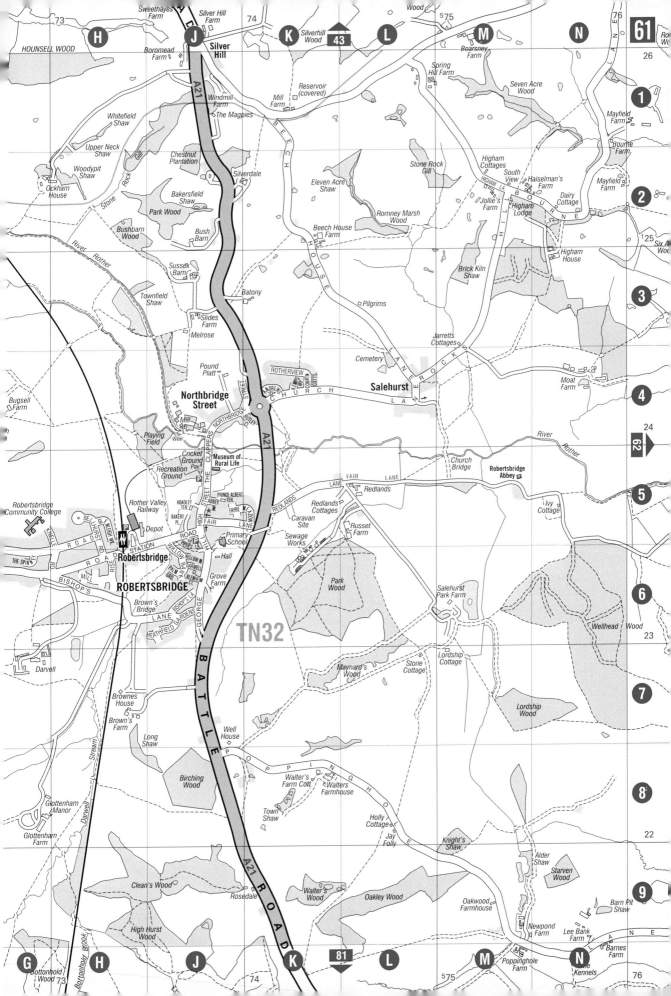

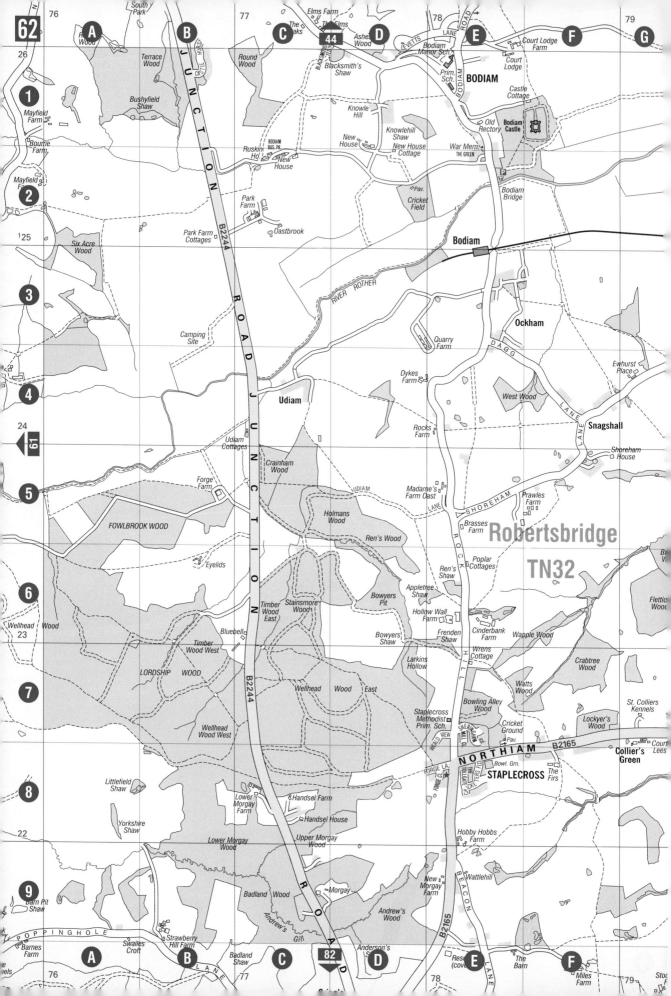

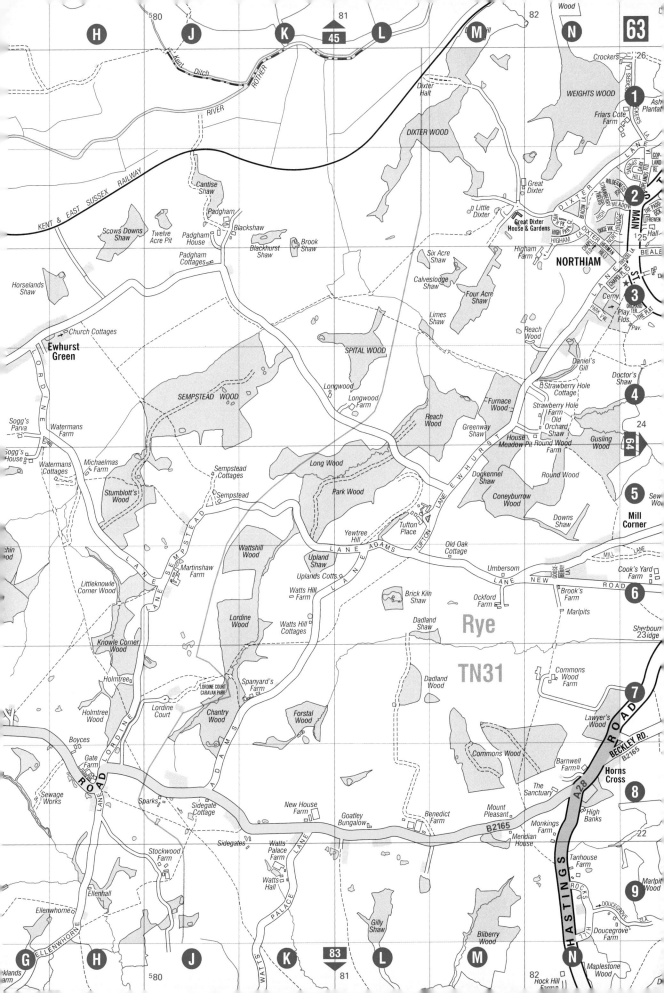

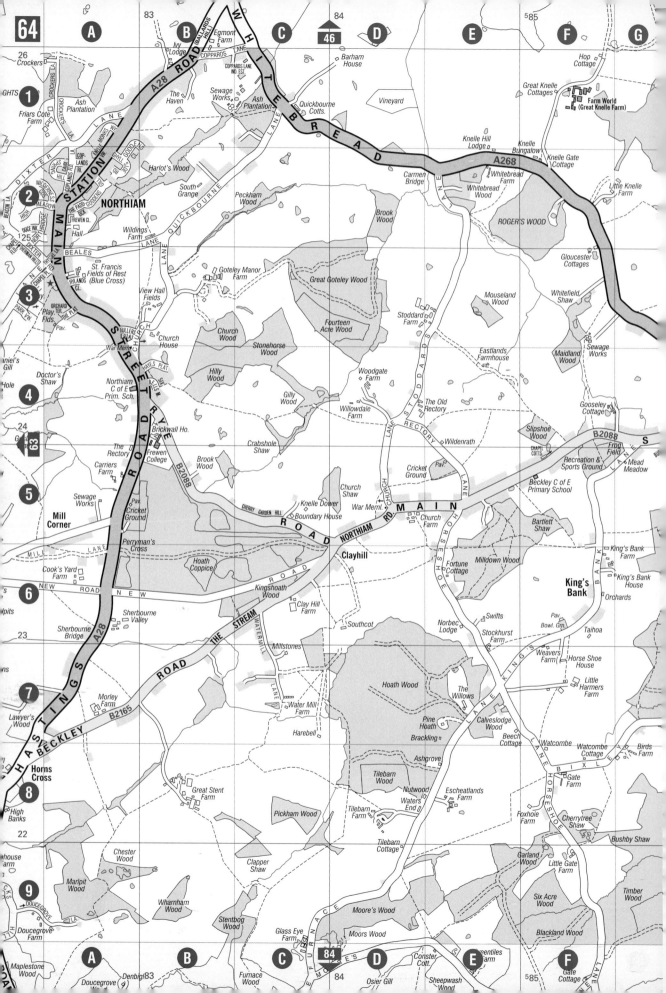

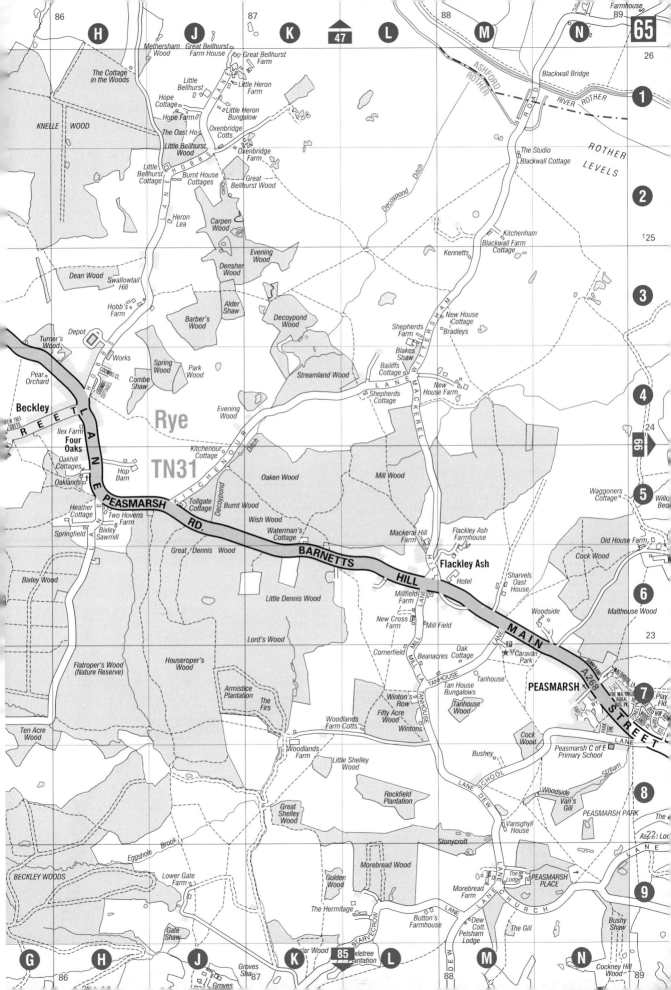

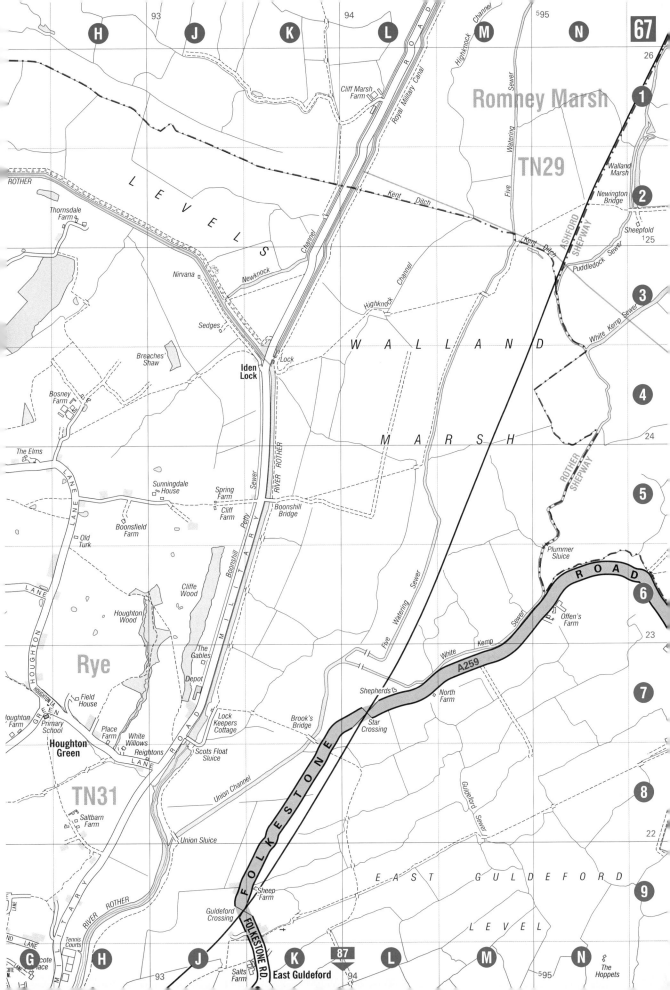

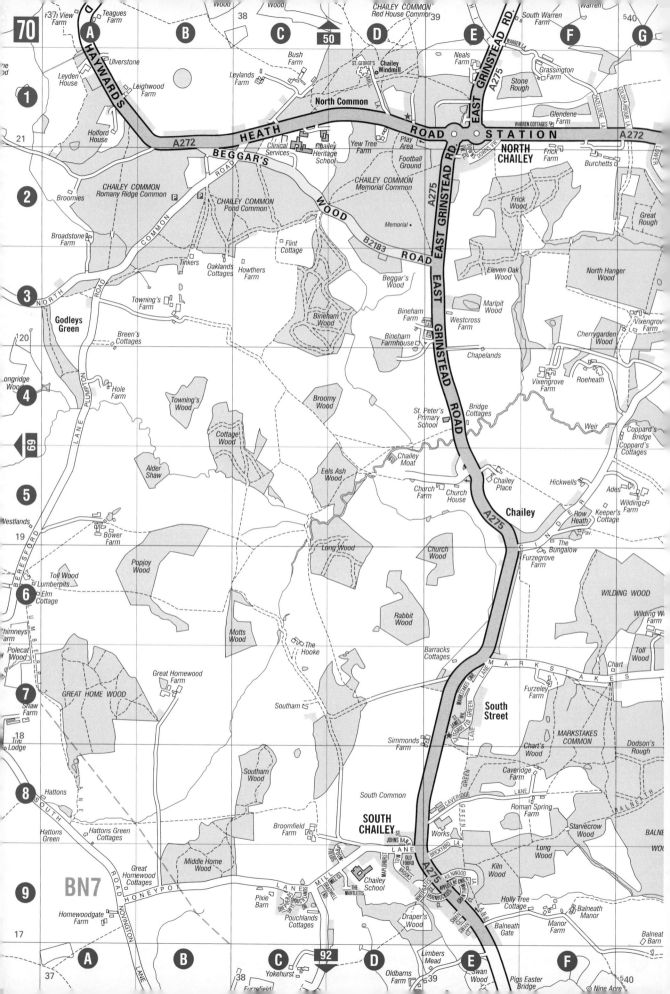

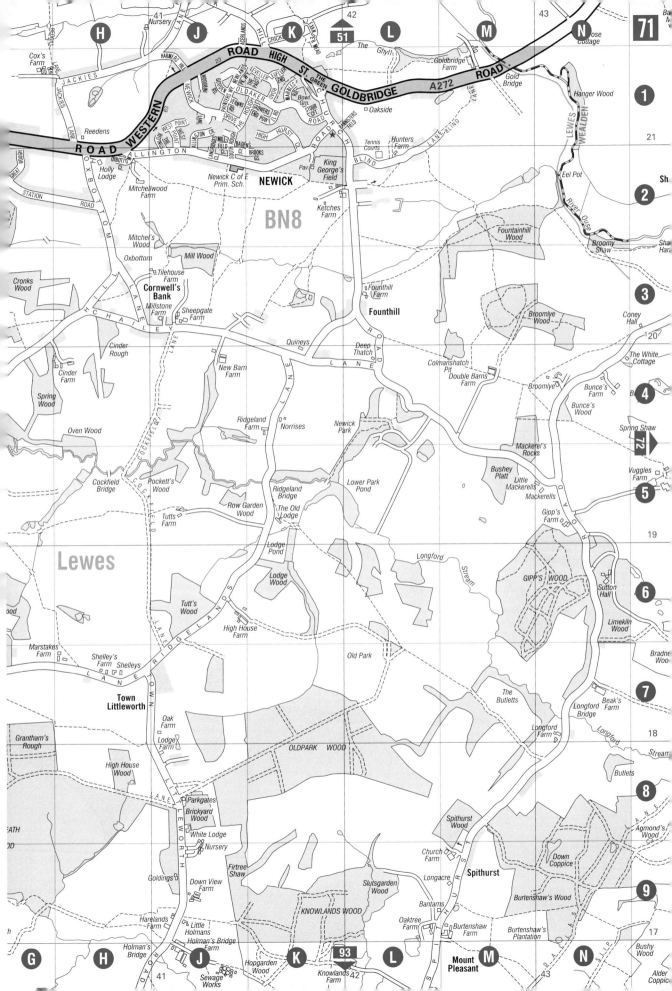

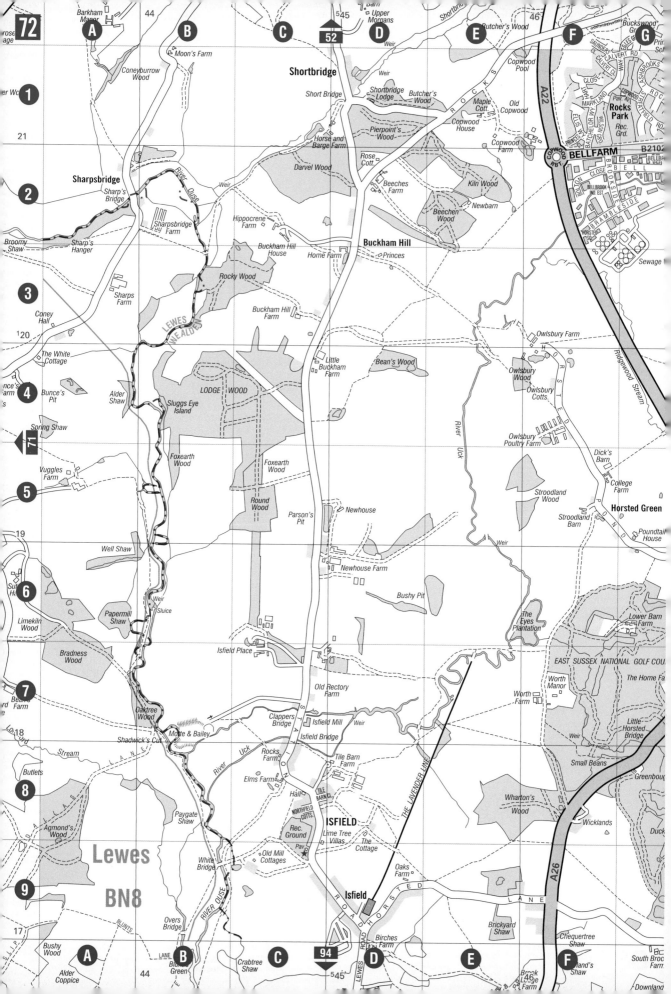

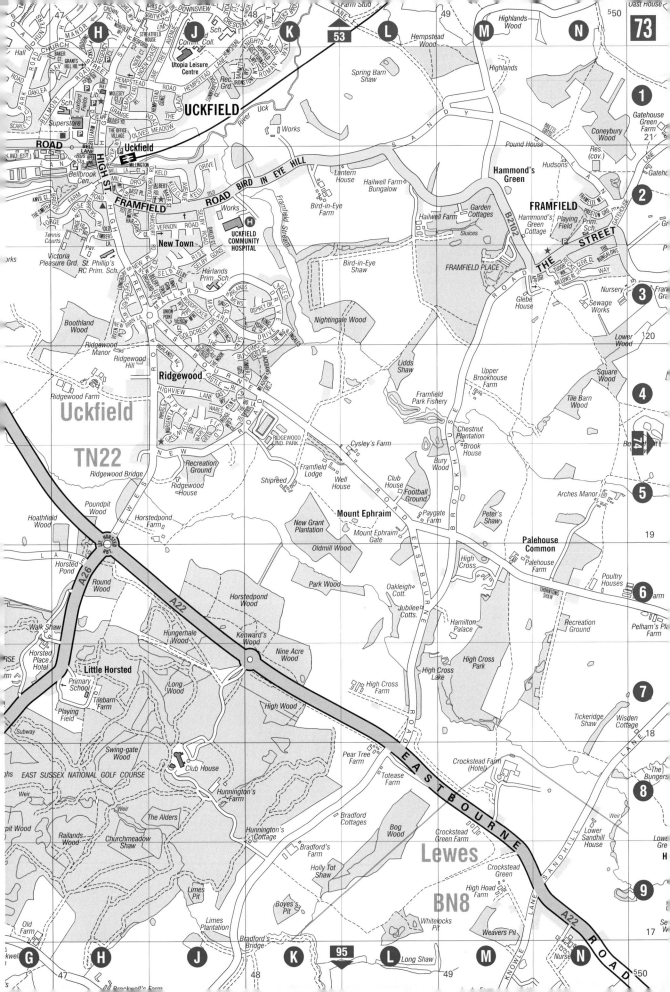

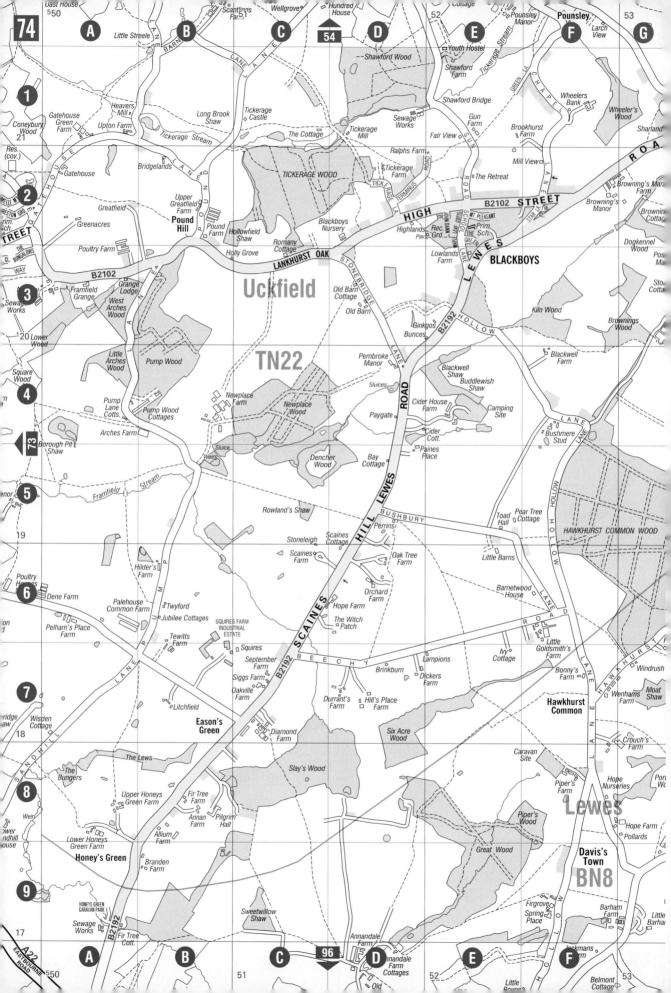

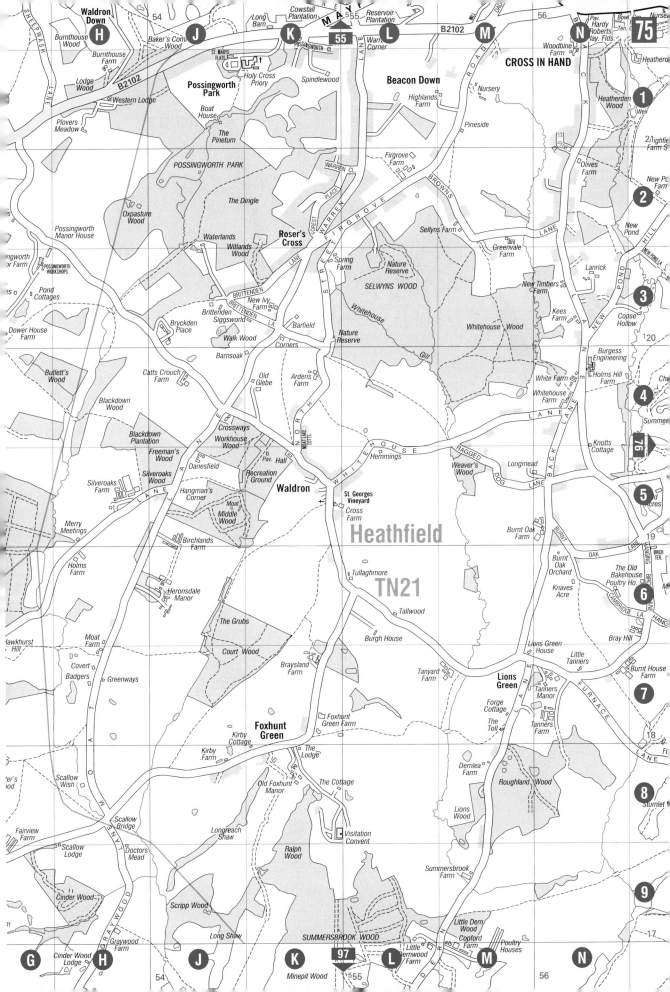

Waldron Down **H**
J
54
K
Long Barn
Cowstall Plantation
MAY
555
Reservoir Plantation
B2102
L
56
M
Pav.
Hardy Roberts
Play. Flds.
N
Bowl Ten.
Nurse
75

Burnthouse Wood
Baker's Comm. Wood
ST. MARYS FLATS
Holy Cross Priory
Possingworth Cl.
Warre Corner
Woodbine Farm
Heather

Burnthouse Farm
Possingworth Park
Spindlewood
Beacon Down
Highlands Farm
Nursery
CROSS IN HAND
Heatherden Wood
1
Weir

Lodge Wood
B2102
Western Lodge
Boat House
Pineside
Nightfie Farm 5
21

Plovers Meadow
The Pinetum
Firgrove Farm
BROWNS
Olives Farm
New P Farm
2
New Pond

Possingworth Manor House
POSSINGWORTH PARK
The Dingle
WARREN CL.
Sellyns Farm
Greenvale Farm
Lanrick
New Timbers Farm
NEW POND
3
Copse Hollow

gworth r Farm
POSSINGWORTH WORKSHOPS
Waterlands
Witlands Wood
Roser's Cross
Spring Farm
Nature Reserve
SELWYNS WOOD
Kees Farm
Burgess Engineering
120

Pond Cottages
BRITTENDEN
New Ivy Farm
Whitehouse
Whitehouse Wood
White Farm
Holms Hill Farm
4
Ch

Dower House Farm
Bryckden Place
Brittenden Siggsworld
Barfield
Nature Reserve
Gill
Whitehouse Farm

Butlett's Wood
Catts Crouch Farm
Walk Wood
Barnsoak
Corners
Old Glebe
Ardens Farm
Whitehouse Farm
Summe

Blackdown Wood
Crossways
Workhouse Wood
LANE
NORTH
WHITEHOUSE
Hemmings
RAGGED
Weaver's Wood
Longmead
BACK LANE
Knotts Cottage
76

Blackdown Plantation
Freeman's Wood
Danesfield
Pav. Hall
Recreation Ground
Waldron
5
d cres

Silveroaks Farm
Silveroaks Wood
Hangman's Corner
Moat
Middle Wood
St. Georges Vineyard
Cross Farm
DOG LANE
BURNT
Burnt Oak Farm
19

Merry Meetings
Birchlands Farm
Heathfield
Burnt Oak Orchard
Knaves Acre
The Old Bakehouse Poultry Ho.
BIRCH TER.
6

Holms Farm
Heronsdale Manor
Tullaghmore
TN21
Tallwood
Bray Hill
CAMBRIDGE LA.

Moat Farm
Hawkhurst Hill
The Grubs
Court Wood
Braysland Farm
Burgh House
Tanyard Farm
Lions Green House
Little Tanners
Burnt House Farm
7

Covert Badgers
Greenways
Foxhunt Green
Foxhunt Green Farm
Lions Green
Forge Cottage
The Toll
Tanners Manor
Tanners Farm
FURNACE
18

GRAYWOOD LANE
Kirby Cottage
Kirby Farm
The Lodge
The Cottage
Dernlea Farm
Roughland Wood
Sturmlet
8

r's od
Scallow Wish
Scallow Bridge
Old Foxhunt Manor
Lions Wood
Summersbrook Farm

Fairview Farm
Scallow Lodge
Doctors Mead
Longreach Shaw
Ralph Wood
Visitation Convent
9

Cinder Wood
Scripp Wood
SUMMERSBROOK WOOD
Little Dern Wood Copford Farm
Poultry Houses
-1.7

G
Cinder Wood Lodge
H
Graywood Farm
54
Long Shaw
J
K
97
555
Little Dernwood Farm
L
Minepit Wood
M
N
56

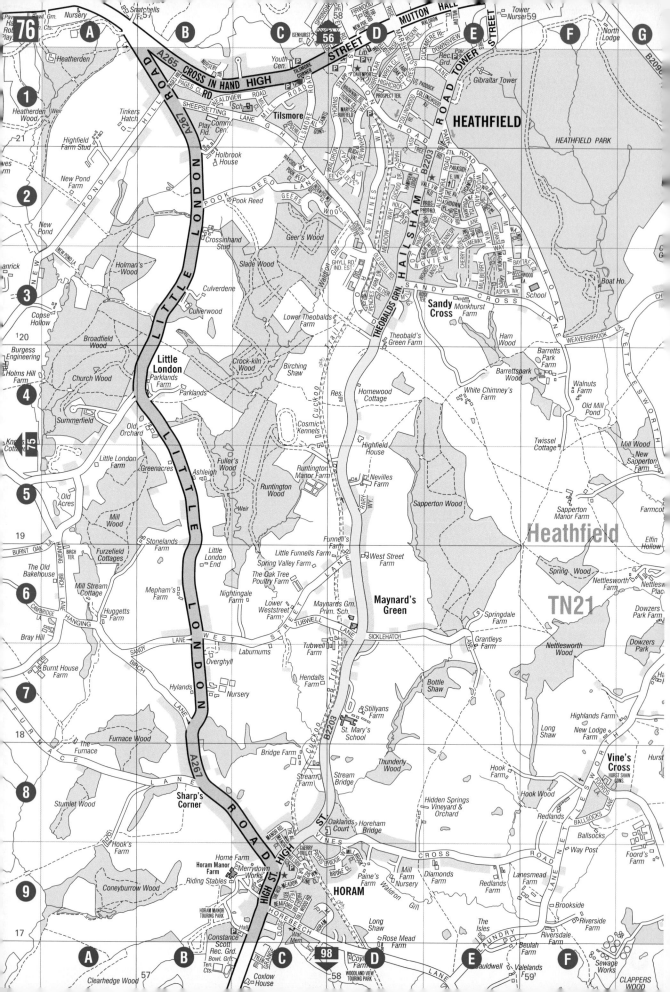

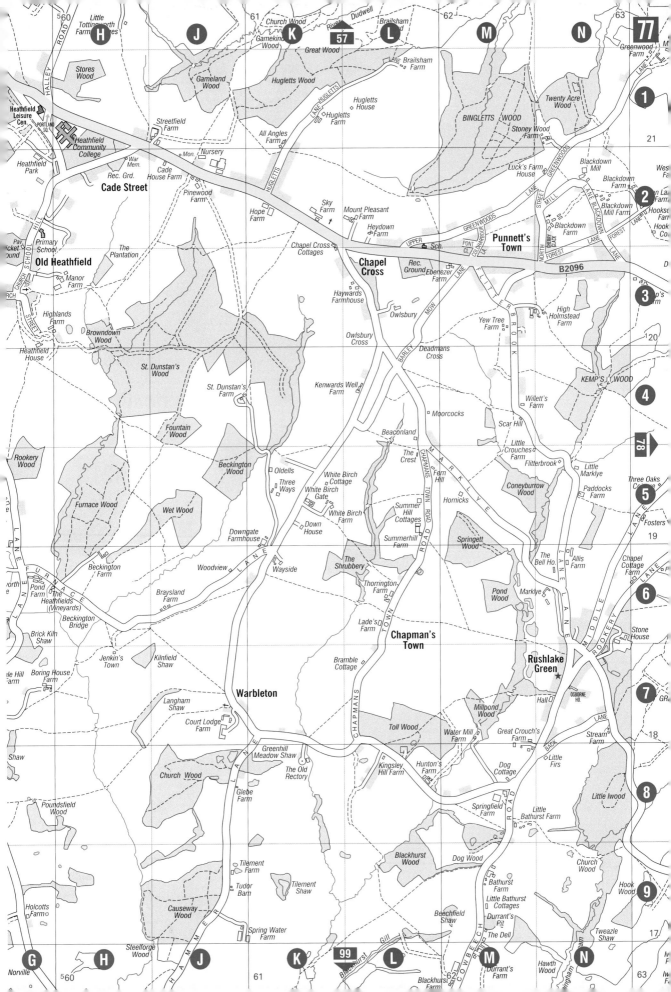

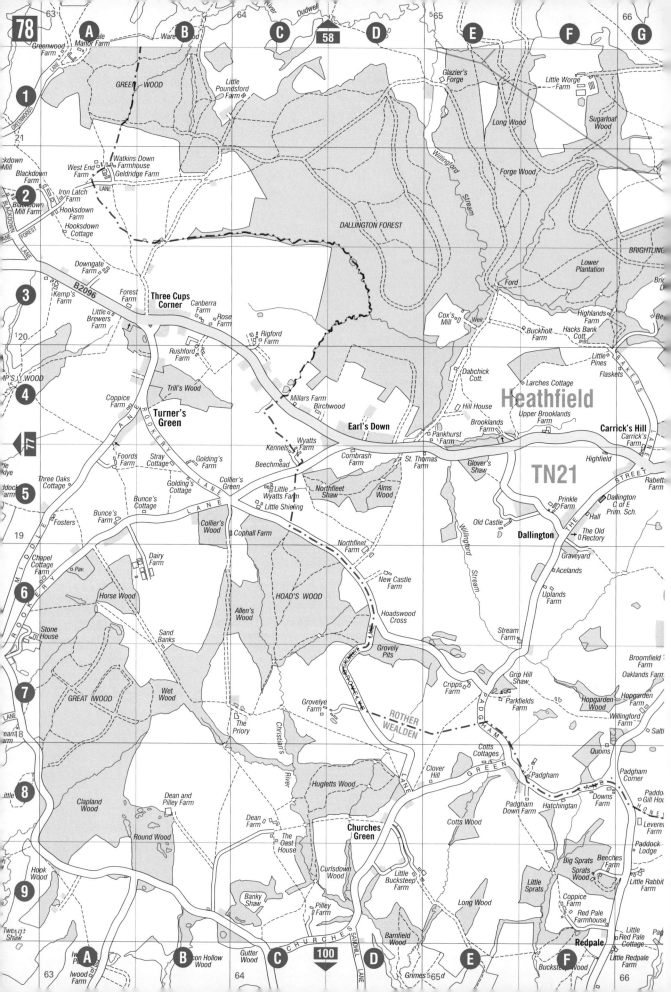

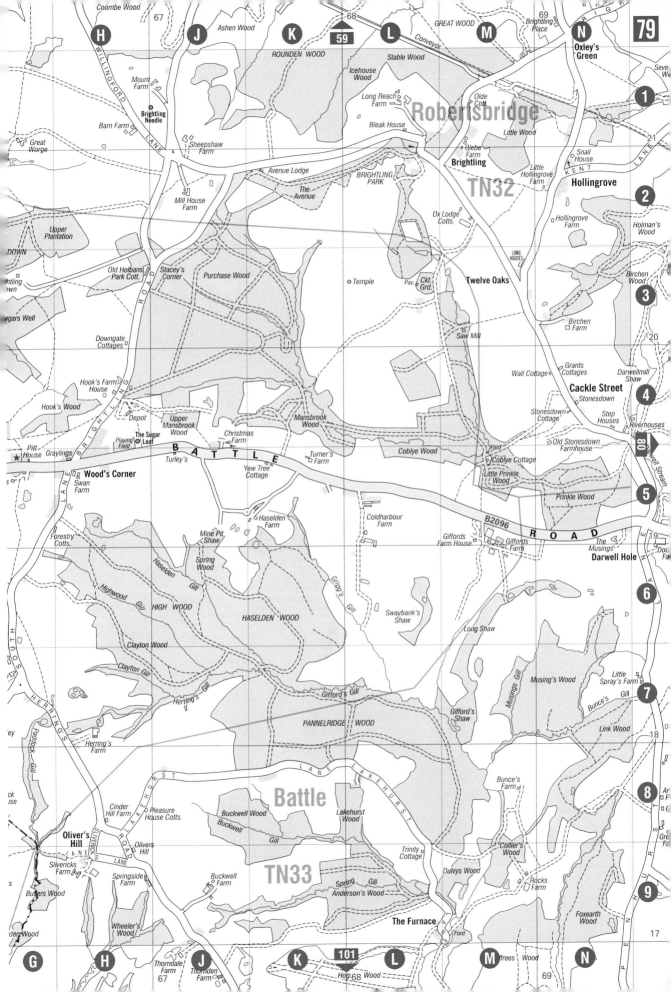

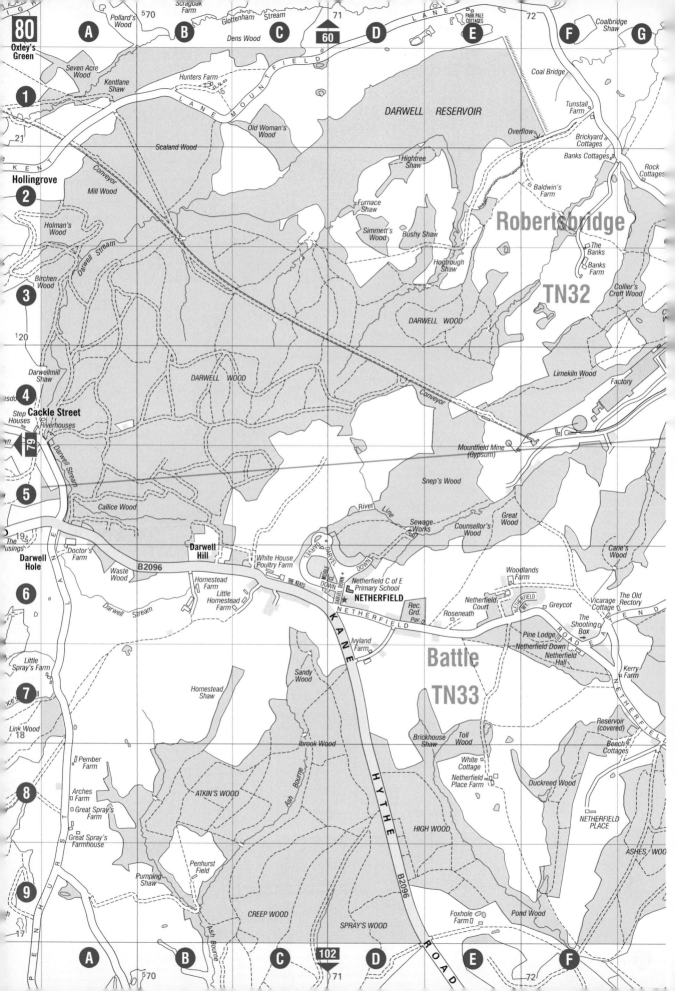

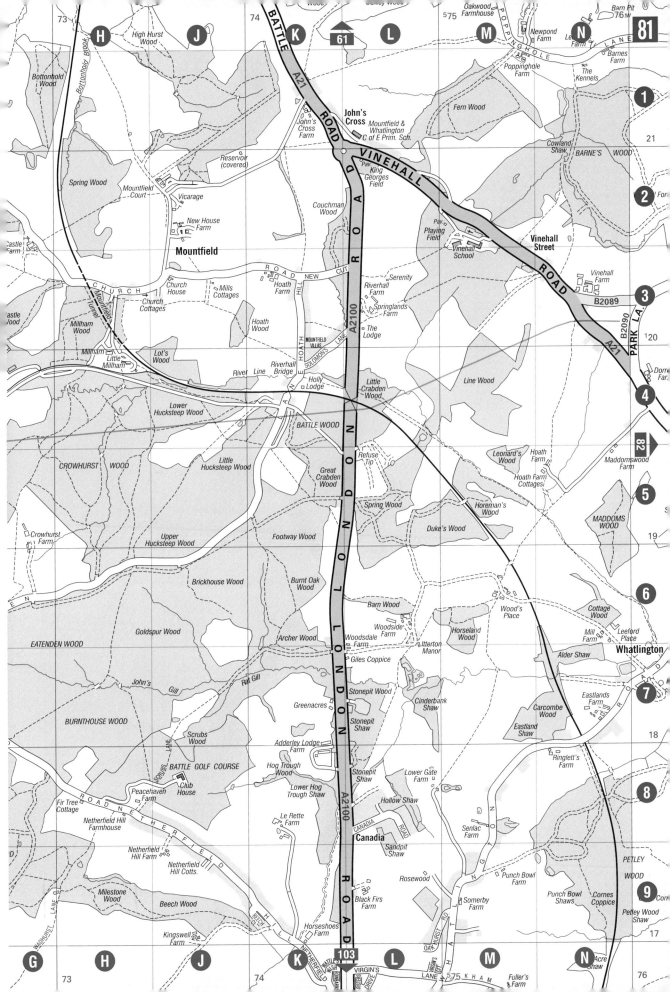

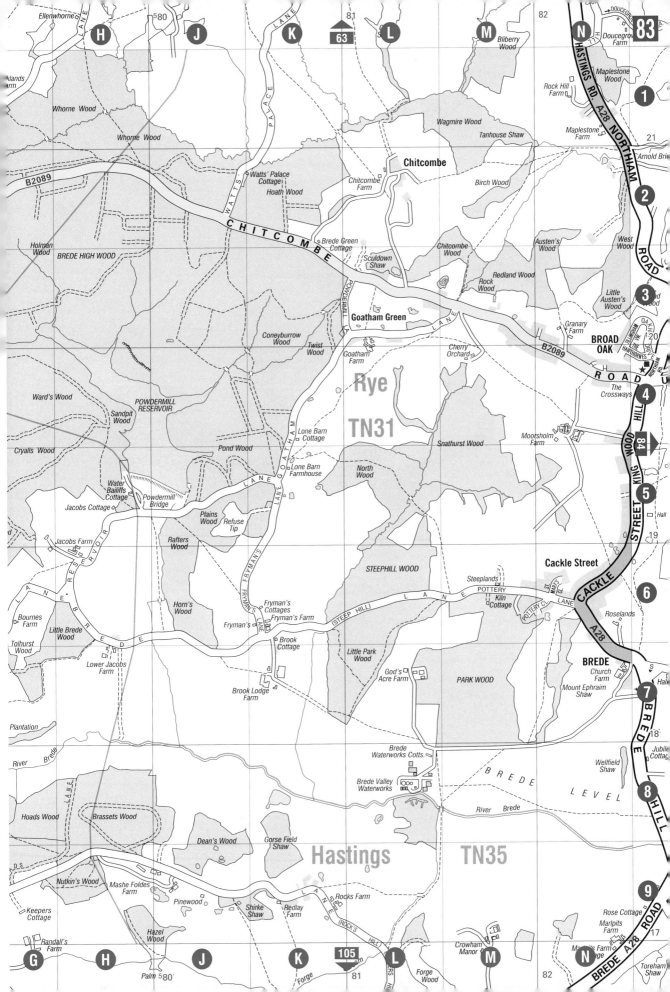

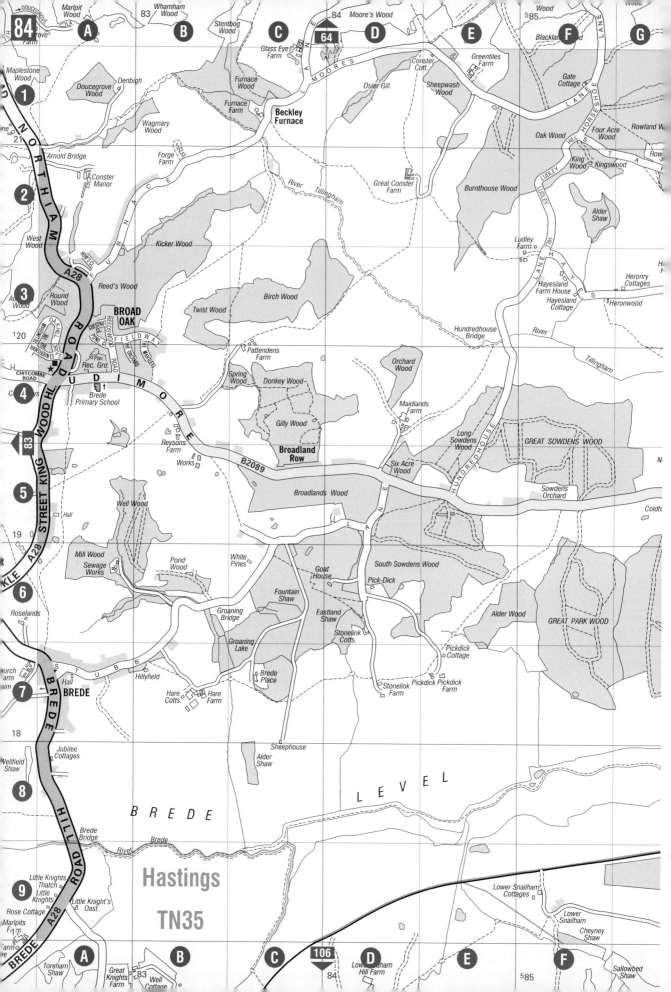

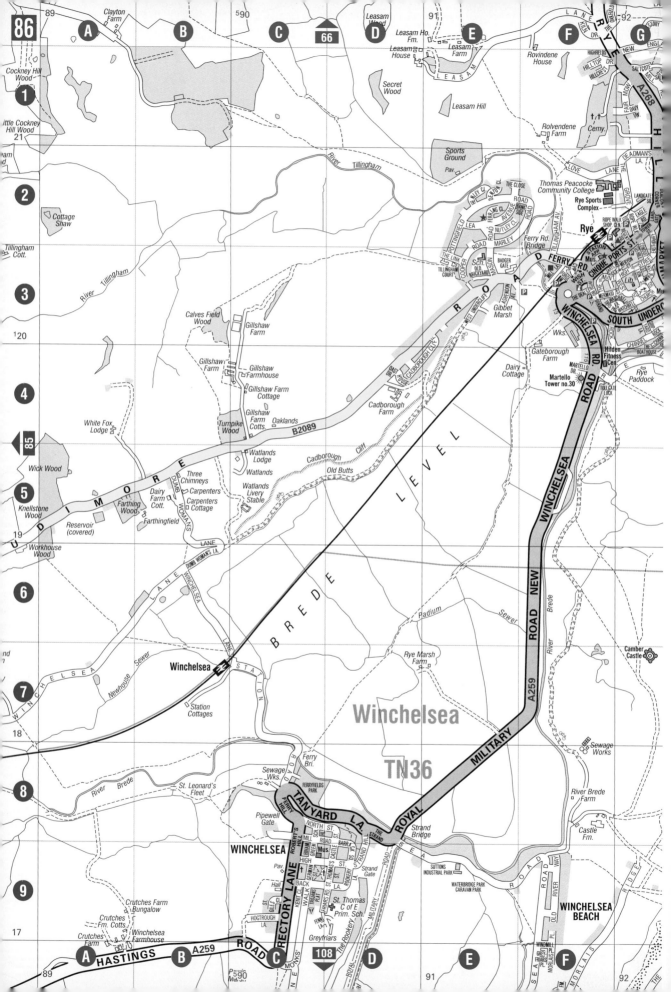

Playden

H **J** Guldeford Crossing **K** **67** **L** **M** **N**

Saltcote Place

Tennis Courts

Salts Farm

East Guldeford

Hoppets Farm

EAST   GULDEFORD

The Hoppets

1

Moneypenny Farm

LEVEL

21

Rye

A259

ROAD GULDEFORD

FOLKESTONE RD

ROAD

CAMBER

Black Ho. Farm

Guldeford

2

TN31

KING'S AVENUE

Sports Grd.

Playing Field

Freda Gardham Prim. Sch.

Walmway Wall

3

Monk Bretton Bridge

Bowl. Grn.
Putting Grn.

RYE

Town Salts

Northpoint   Sewer

120

River Brede

Northpoint Beach

Northpoint   Sewer

4

Hall

Northpoint Sluice

Sewage Works

ROAD

Northpoint Beach

CAMBER

88

RYE INDUSTRIAL PARK

Works
Wks.
Wks.
Depot

Oil Refinery

Depot

Works

Northpoint Beach

RIVER

ROTHER

Gorse Cott.

Northpoint Beach

Point Farm

Pound Field House

5

Depot

Club House

Poun Fiel Far

Works
Depot

Depot

Davis Land

Rye Harbour Nature Reserve

COASTGUARD SQUARE

Depot

Play. Fld.

Lifeboat Sta.

Harbour Masters Office
Harbour Cottages

Rye Harbour Sailing Club

Coastguard Office

19

RYE GOLF LINKS

Chief Coastguards Admiralty Cottages

6

Rye Harbour

Martello Tower no.28

FRENCHMANS BEACH HOLIDAY VILLAGE

Lime Kiln Cottage

Rye Harbour Sewer

Nook Drain

Rye Harbour Nature Reserve

CAMBER SANDS

East Pier

7

18

Nook Beach

The Nook

RYE   BAY

8

Watch Cotts.

Nook Drain

Ridge

9

17

Rye Harbour Nature Reserve

93

94

595

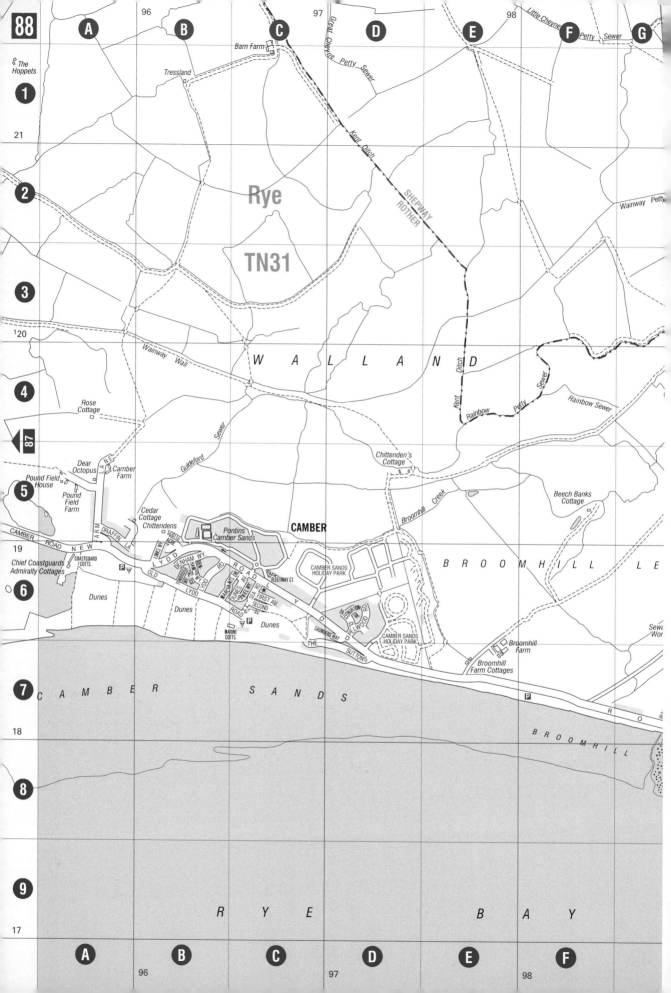

A   B   C   D   E   F   G

68

HASSOCKS

Keymer

Hassocks

DITCHLING

East End

Hassocks

BN6

New Barn Farm

Cricket Grd.

Woodside Grange

Ockley Wood

Ockley House

White Lodge

Acres

Broadhill Farm Ho.

Broadhill Farm

The Tole

The Millers

Oaks

Poultry Farm

Nursery

Townmead Garden Centre

Elphick's Farm

Little Shepherds

COTTAGE HOMES

Burntinholmes

Stocks Farm

Newtons

Ockley Manor Farm

Ockley Manor

Hill View

Oldland Mill House

Court Gardens Farm

Hampers Croft

MID SUSSEX LEWES

Lodge Hill

North End

Stoneywish Country Park

Sewage Farm

Playing Field

Inf. Sch.

Adastra Park

War Mem.

CHURCH

Lib.

Downlands Sch.

Windmills Jun. Sch.

ROAD

B2116

Keymer Ter.

BEACON H.

HURST

Cricket Grd.

Dumbrells Ct.

DUMBRELLS COURT

Mus.

Prim. Sch.

Cordons Farm

Grave Yard

Rec. Grd.

Larches Charter

Hooks Acre

Beards Place Farm

The Nye

Claycroft Farm

Butcher's Wood

Woodbine Cottage

Lag Wood

Southdown Farm

Park Av.

NEW ROAD B2112

ROAD CLAYTON RD.

B2112

Gospels Farm

Nevill Bungalows

Nevill Cottages

Millbrook

Lodge Cottage

Lodge Farm

Bungalow Farm

Molehilly Shaw

The Wilderness

Ditchling Nurseries

Claycroft House

Wellcroft Shaw

Blackdo Hill

Halfway

Weavers

Foxhole Farm

SPRING

Shaw

Whitelands

UNDERHILL

Park Barn Farm

Crossgoats Shaw

Beacon Nurseries

Southmead Cottage

Pond Farm

Westmest Place

Reservoir (covered)

Clayton Holt

Holt Valley Farm

Coombe Bottom

BOSTALL

DITCHLING

Wick Place

Wick Farm

LANE

Westmeston

Clayton Windmills

Jill

Jack

Reservoir (covered)

De Lilt Hill

BOSTALL

Ditchling Beacon

BOSTALL ROAD

Home Brow

New Barn Farm

Keymer Post

Home Bottom

MIDI

SOUTH DO

PYECOMBE GOLF COURSE

Rag Bottom

Dencher Bottom

112

trough ottom

Big Bottom

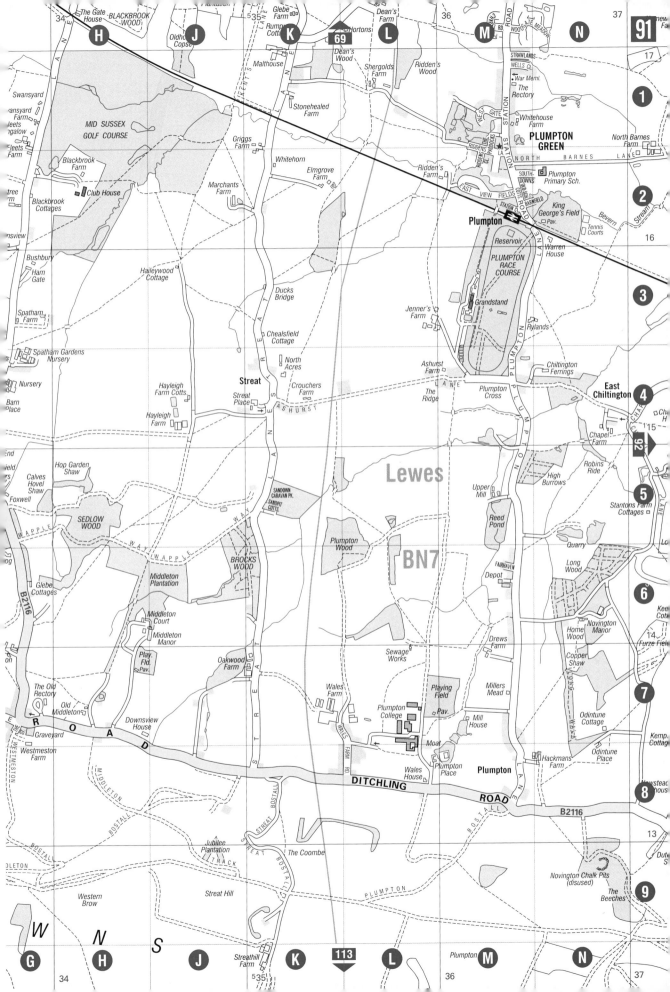

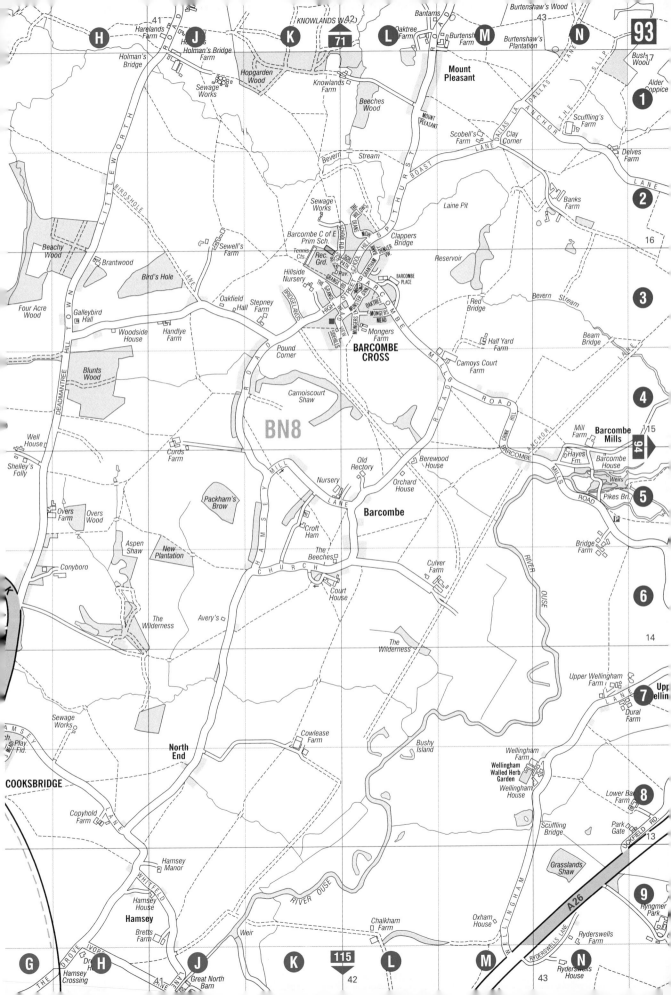

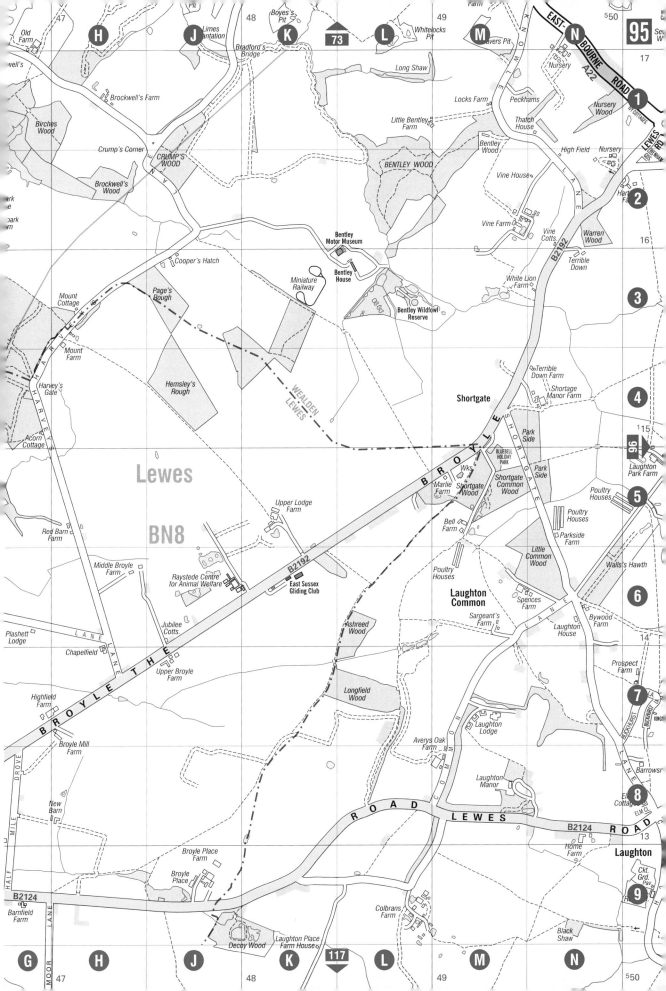

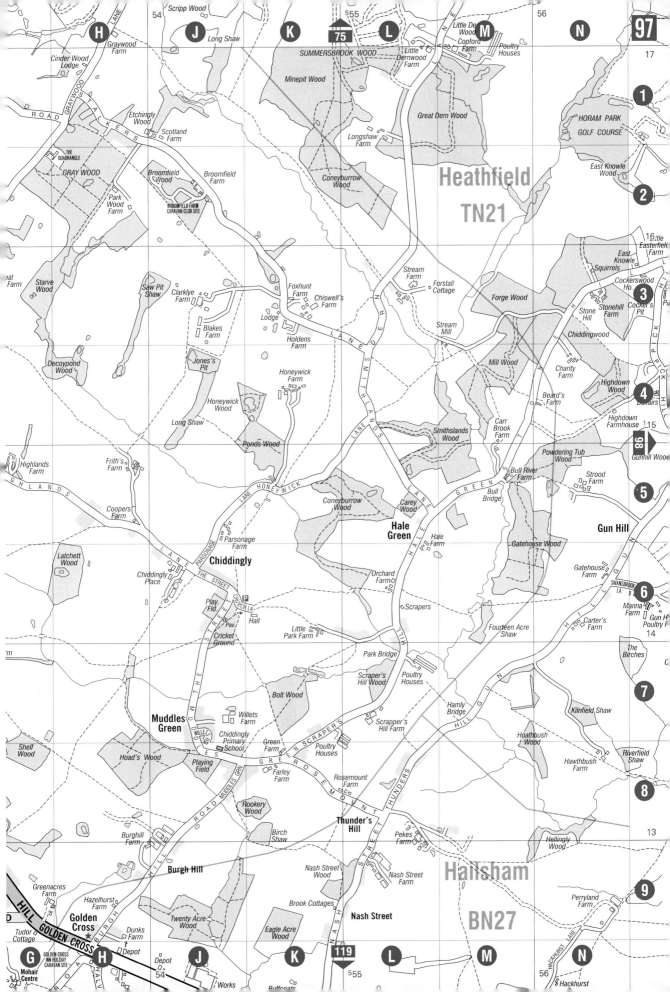

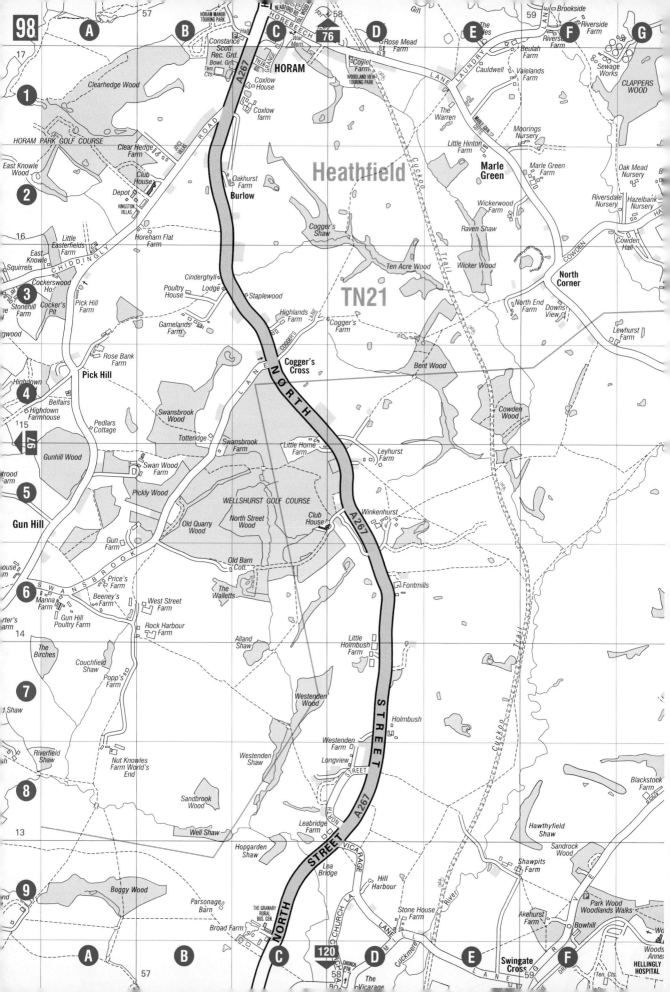

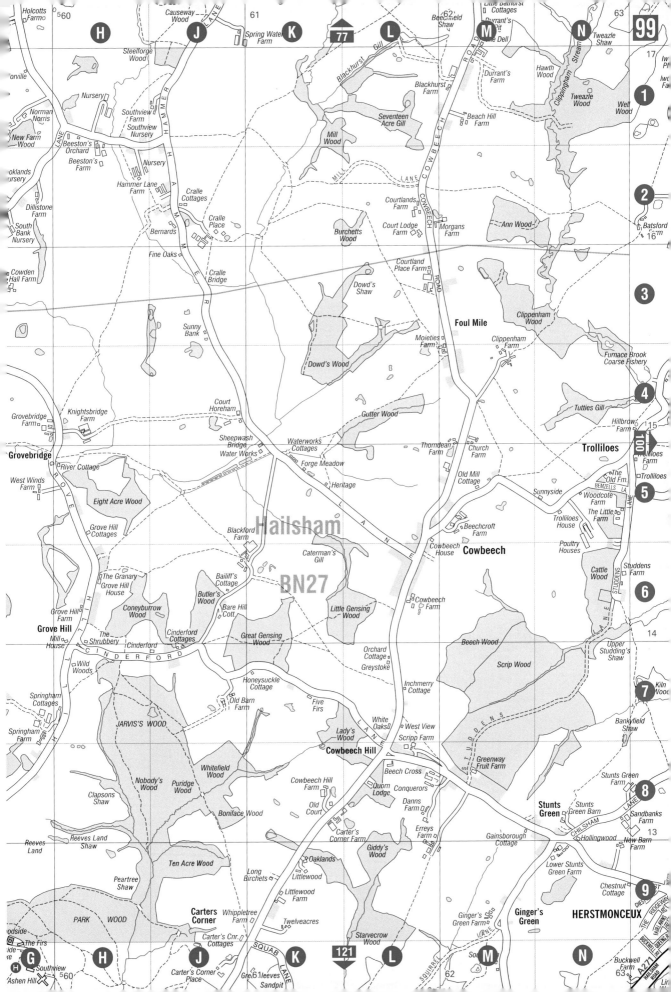

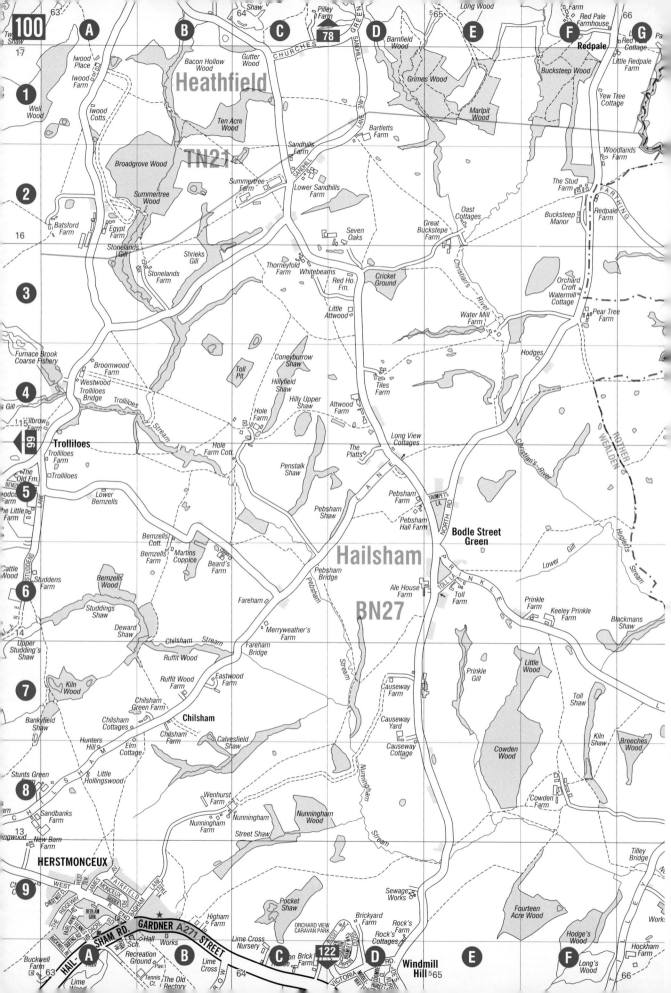

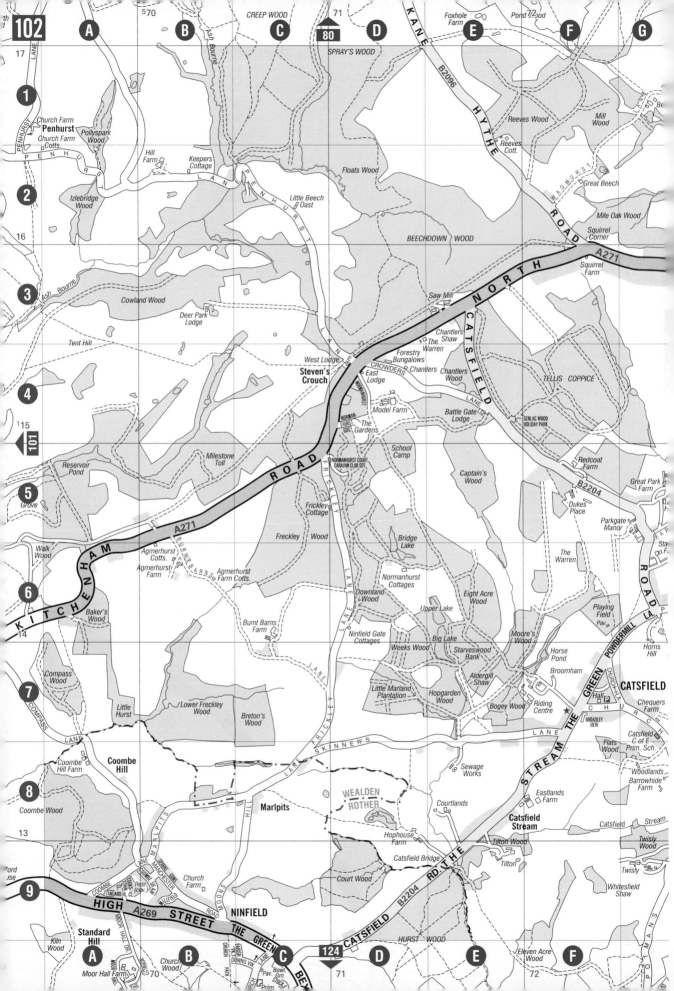

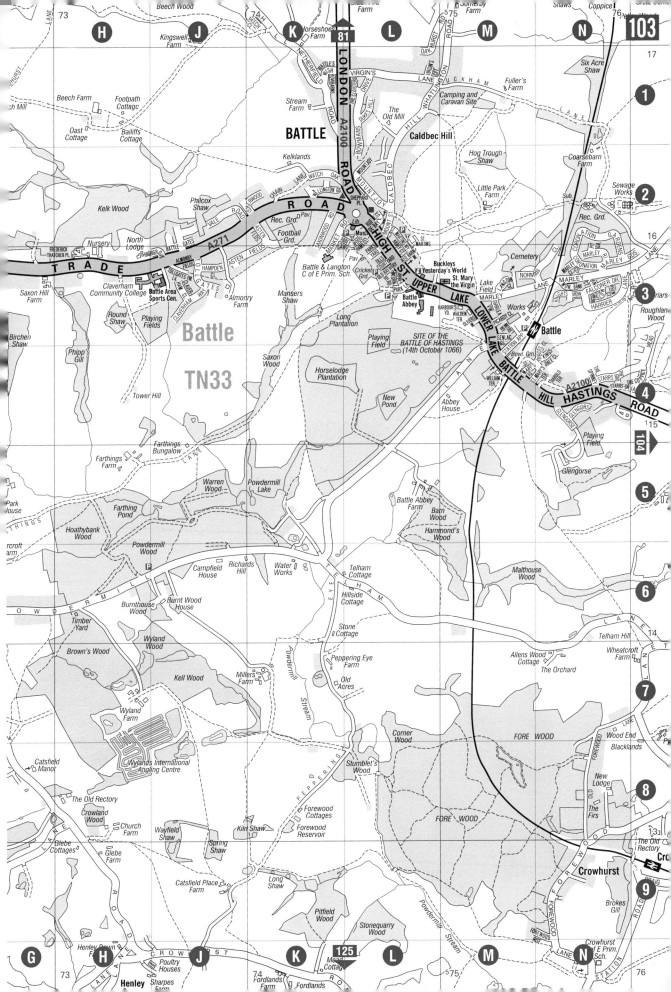

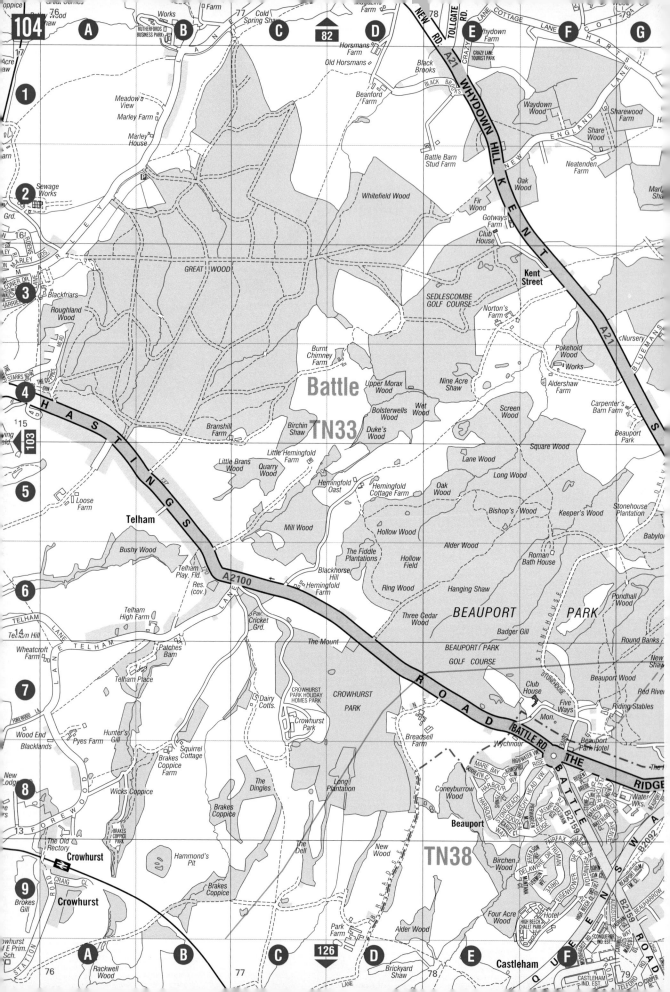

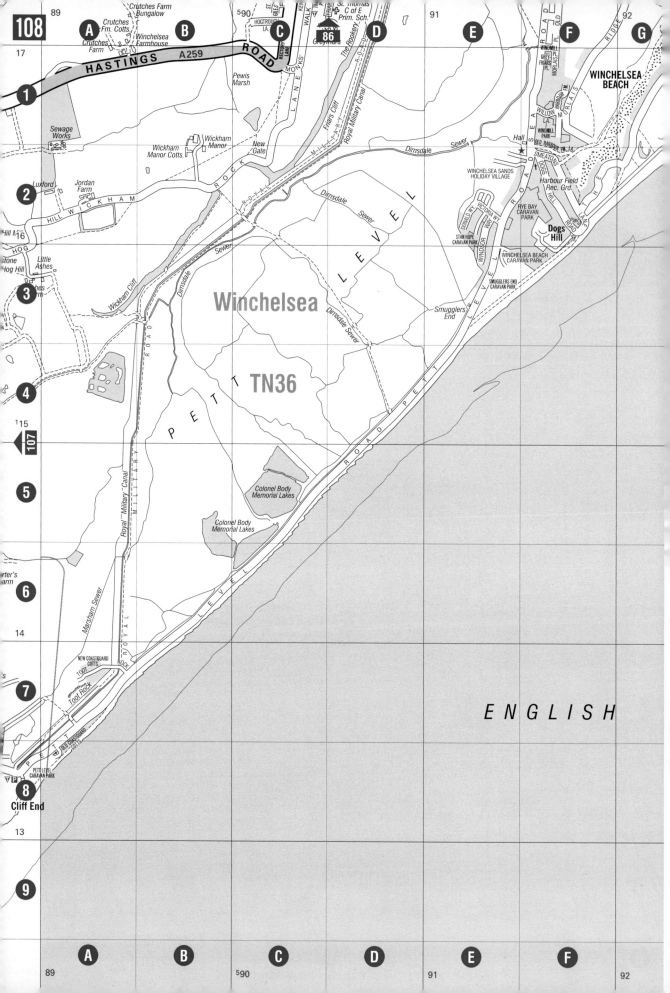

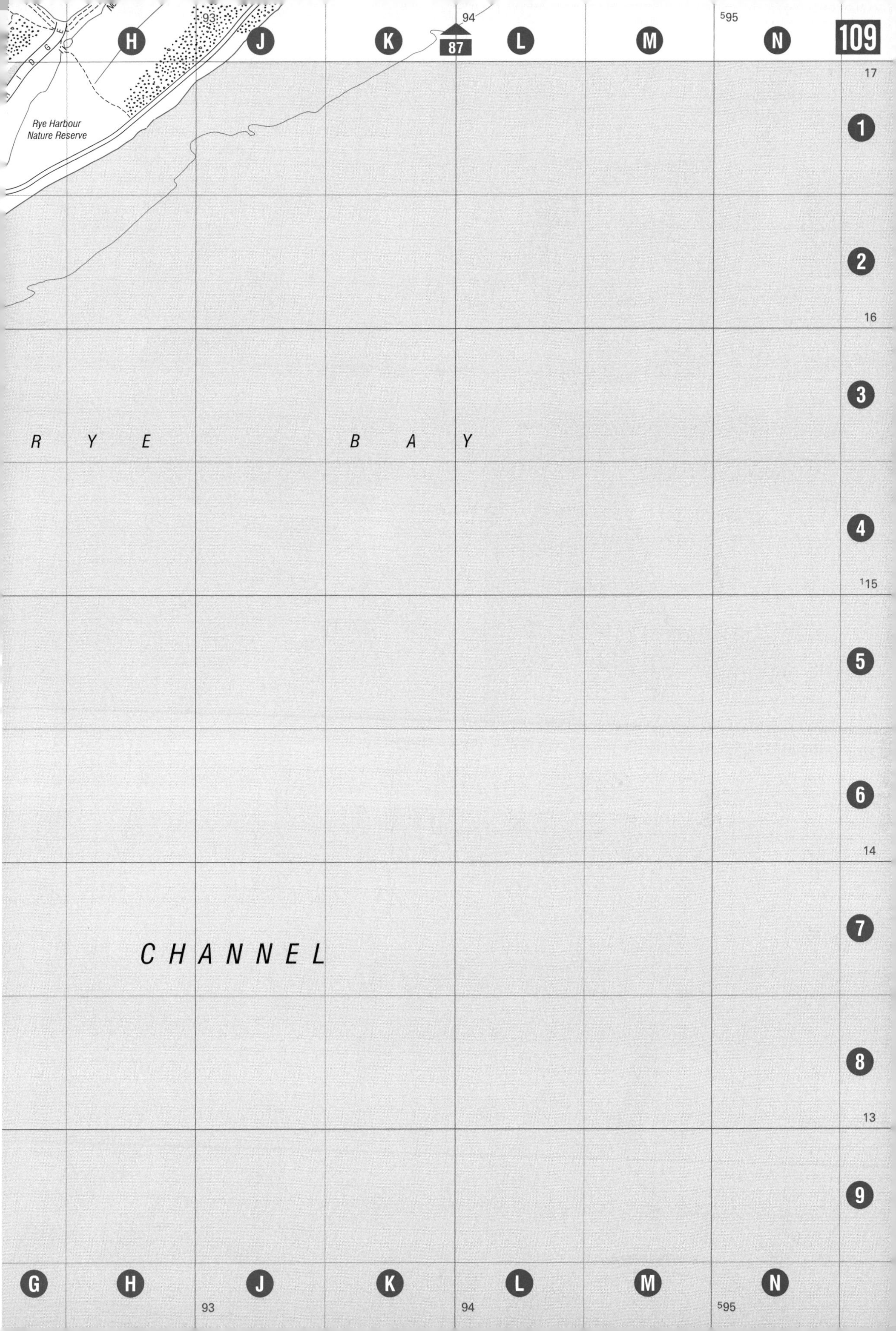

87

595

17

1

2

16

Rye Harbour
Nature Reserve

3

R   Y   E   B   A   Y

4

¹15

5

6

14

7

C H A N N E L

8

13

9

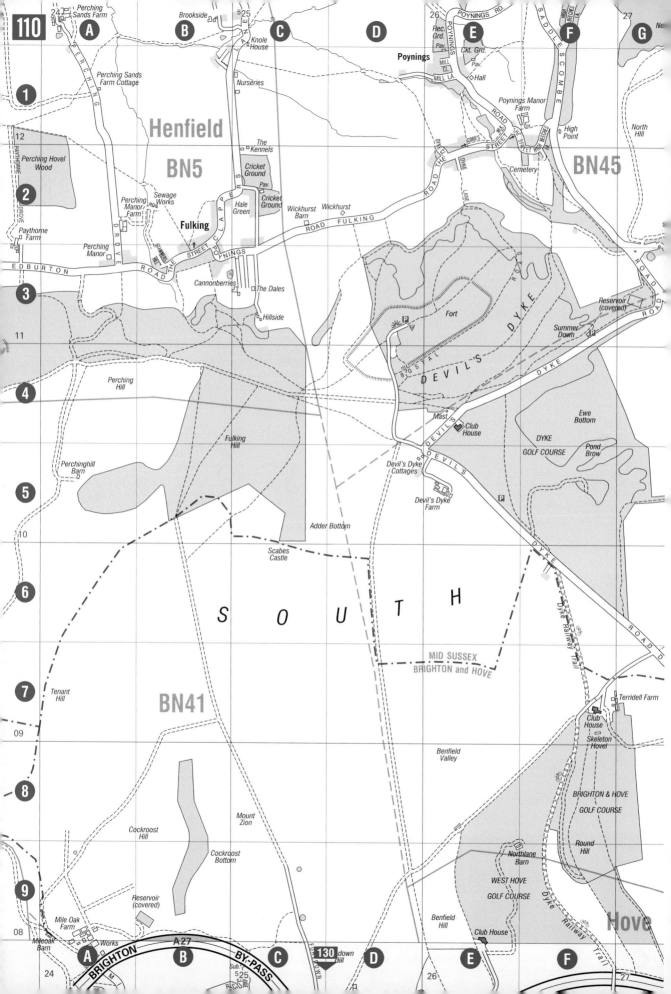

110

A · B · C · D · E · F · G

24
Perching
Sands Farm

Brookside

Knole
House

525

26
POYNINGS RD.
Rec.
Grd.
Pav.

Poynings

Ckt. Grd.
Pav.
Hall

MILL LA

27
Ne

1
Perching Sands
Farm Cottage

Nurseries

Poynings

Poynings Manor
Farm

North
HILL

12
Perching Hovel
Wood

The
Kennels

GORD'S

High
Point

Henfield

BN5

Cricket
Ground
Pav.

BN45

2
Perching
Manor
Farm

Sewage
Works

Cricket
Ground

Wickhurst
Barn

Wickhurst

Cemetery

Paythorne
Farm

Hale
Green

Fulking

3
Perching
Manor

ROAD FULKING

EDBURTON   ROAD

Cannonberries

The Dales

Fort

Reservoir
(covered)

Summer
Down

11

Hillside

DEVIL'S   DYKE

4
Perching
Hill

Mast

Club
House

Ewe
Bottom

Fulking
Hill

Devil's Dyke
Cottages

DYKE
GOLF COURSE

Pond
Brow

5
Perchinghill
Barn

Devil's Dyke
Farm

Adder Bottom

10

Scabes
Castle

6
S   O   U   T   H

MID SUSSEX
BRIGHTON and HOVE

Dyke Railway Trail

7
Tenant
Hill

BN41

Terridell Farm

Club
House

09

Benfield
Valley

Skeleton
Hovel

8
Cockroost
Hill

Mount
Zion

BRIGHTON & HOVE

GOLF COURSE

Cockroost
Bottom

Northlane
Barn

Round
Hill

9
Reservoir
(covered)

WEST HOVE

GOLF COURSE

08
Mile Oak
Farm

Benfield
Hill

Hove

Mileoak
Barn

Works

BRIGHTON

A27

BY-PASS

130
down
hill

Club House

Dyke Railway Trail

24

525

26

27

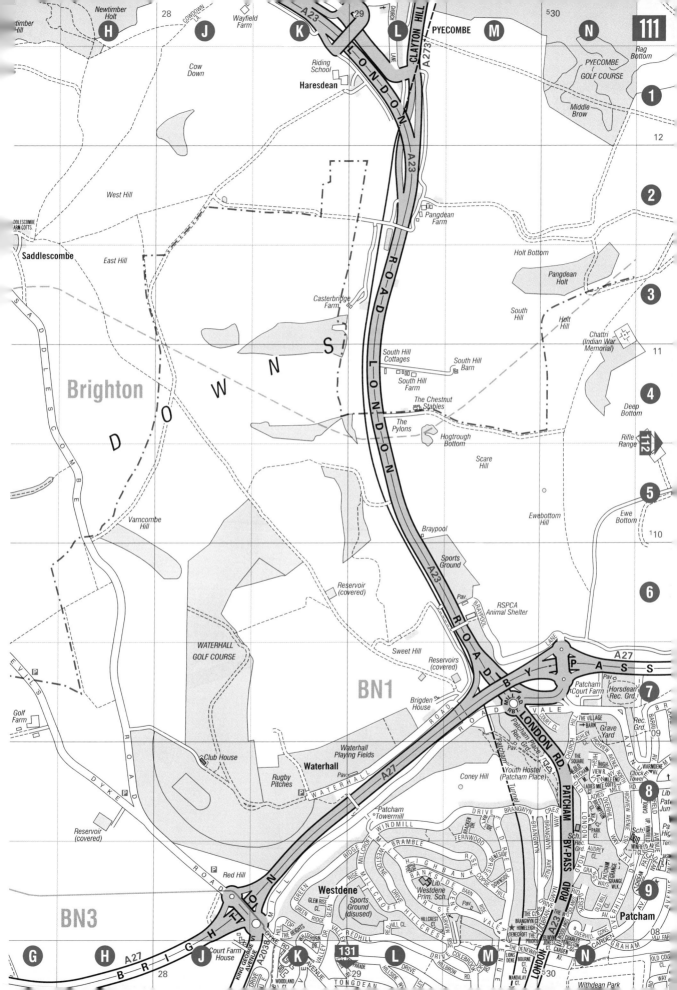

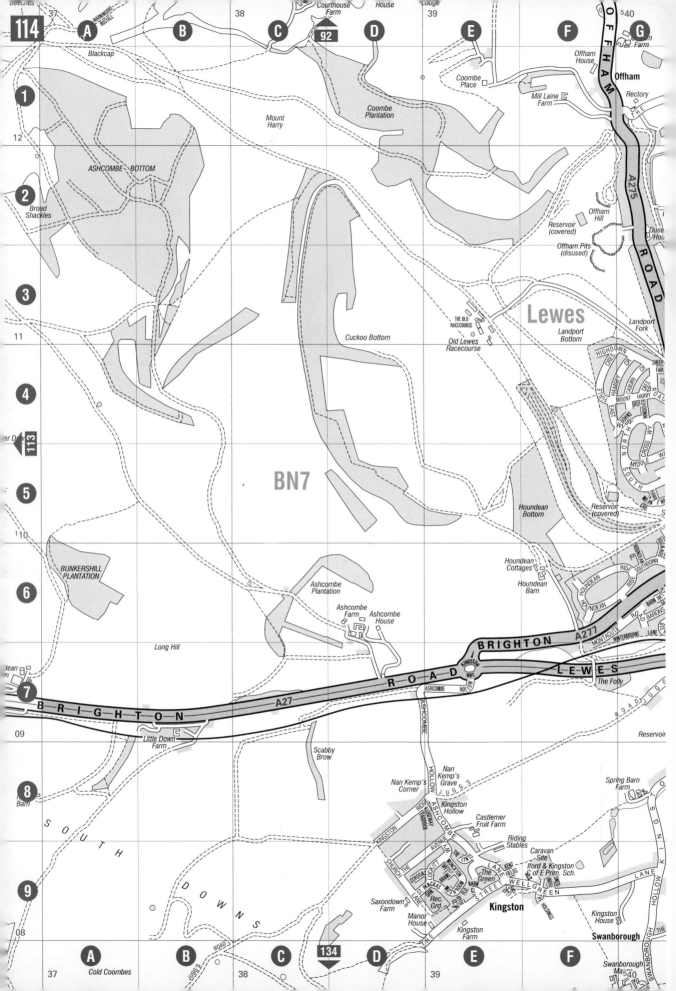

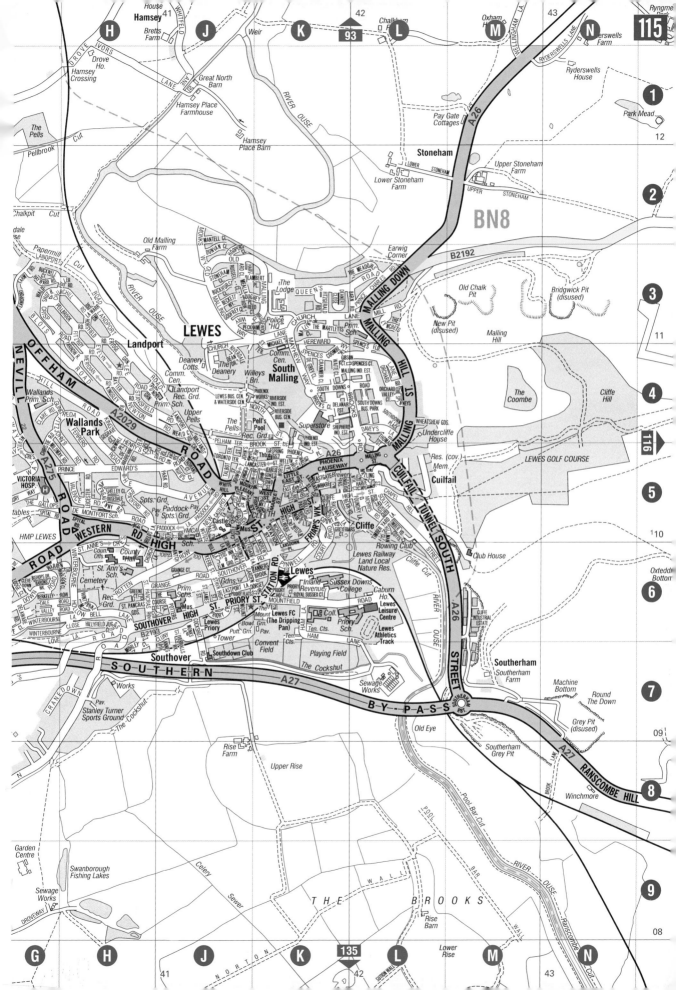

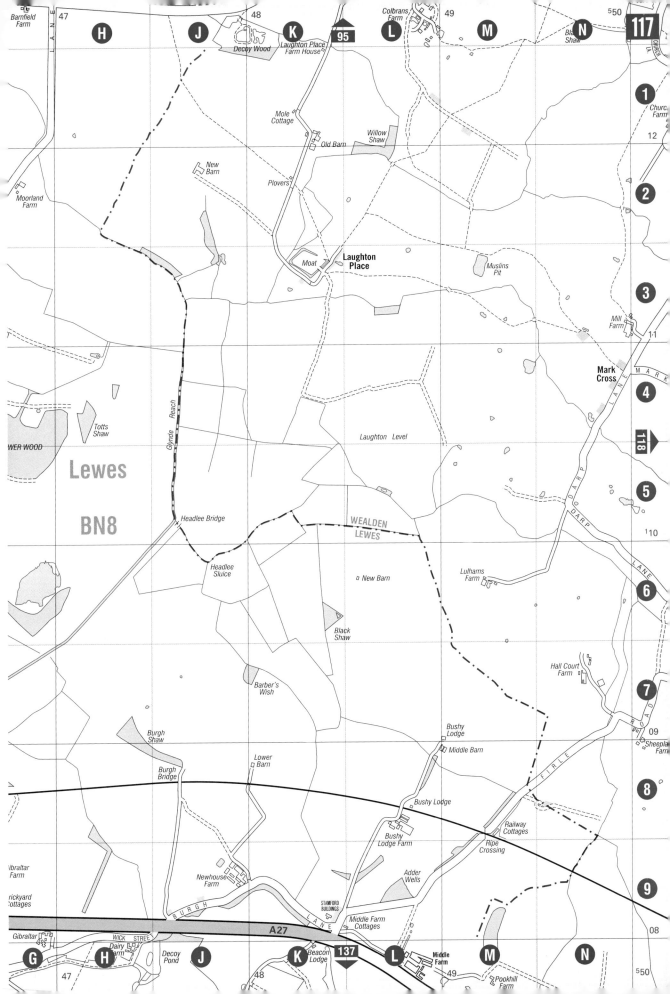

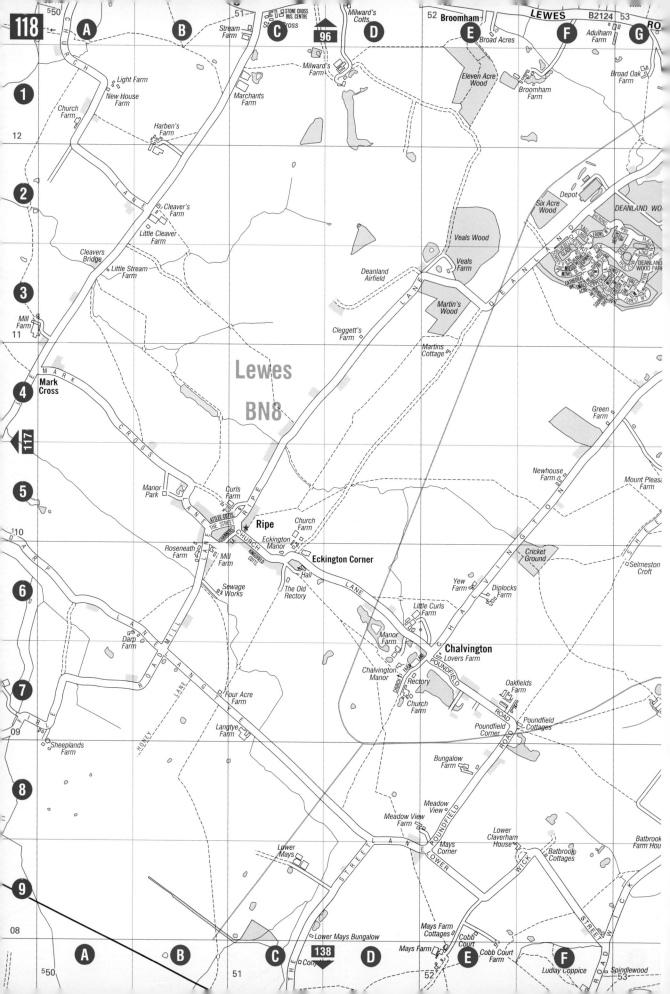

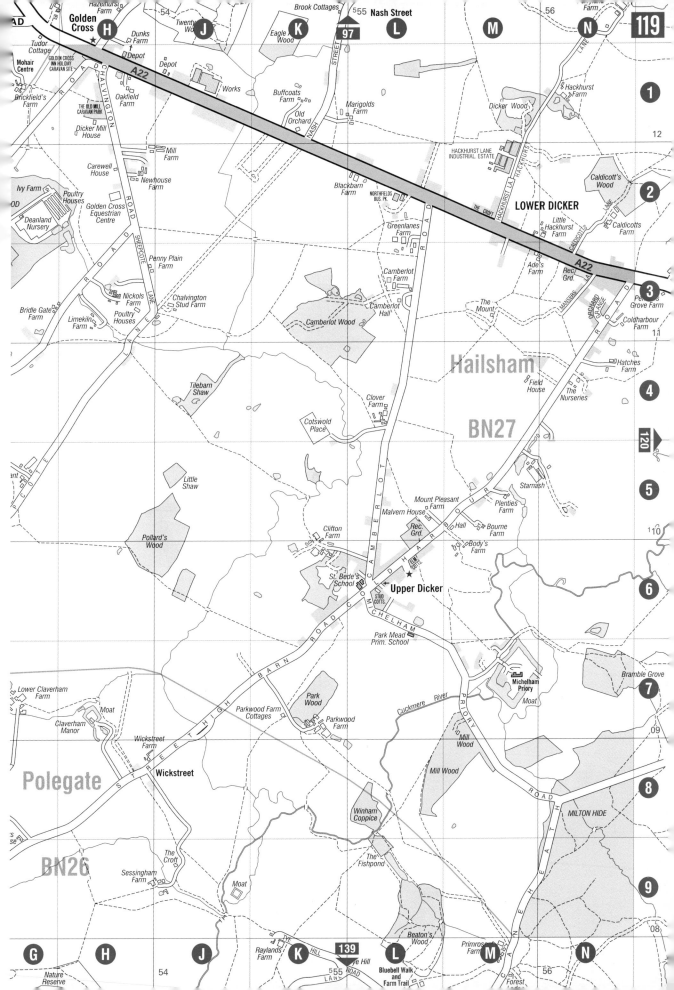

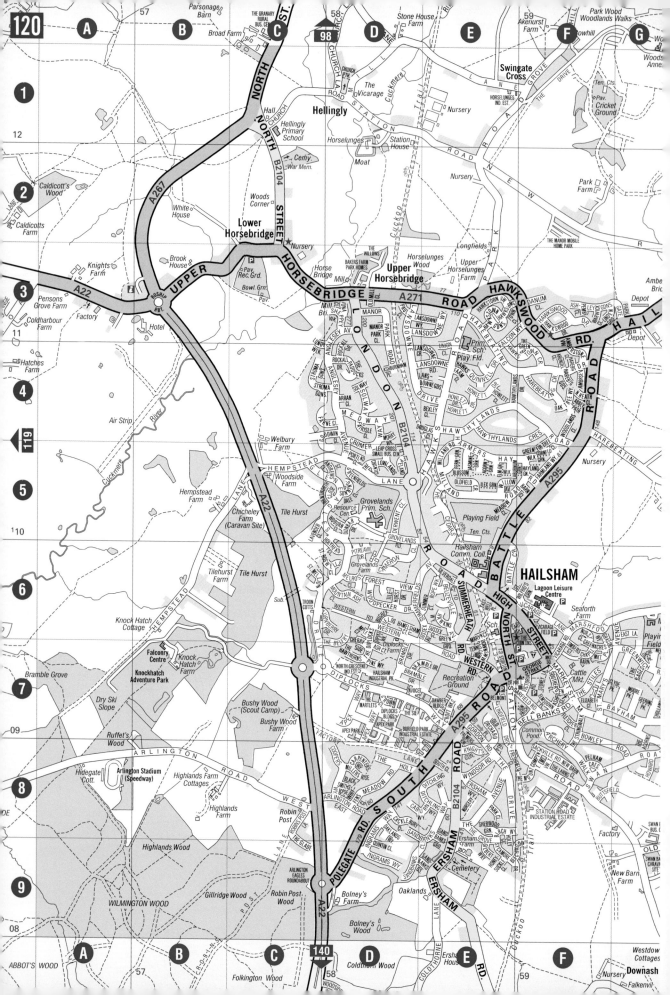

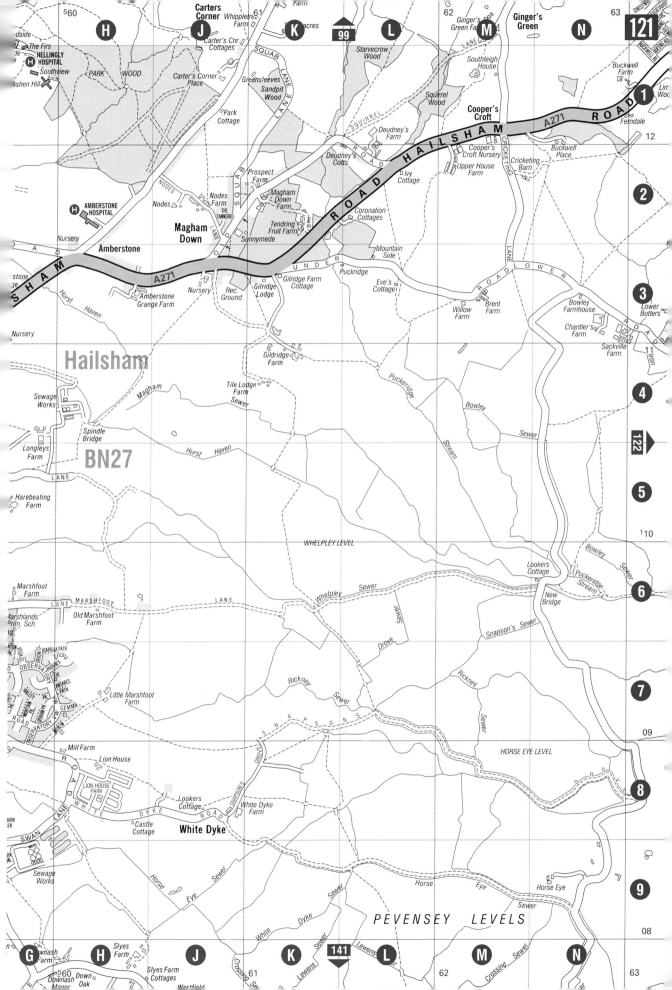

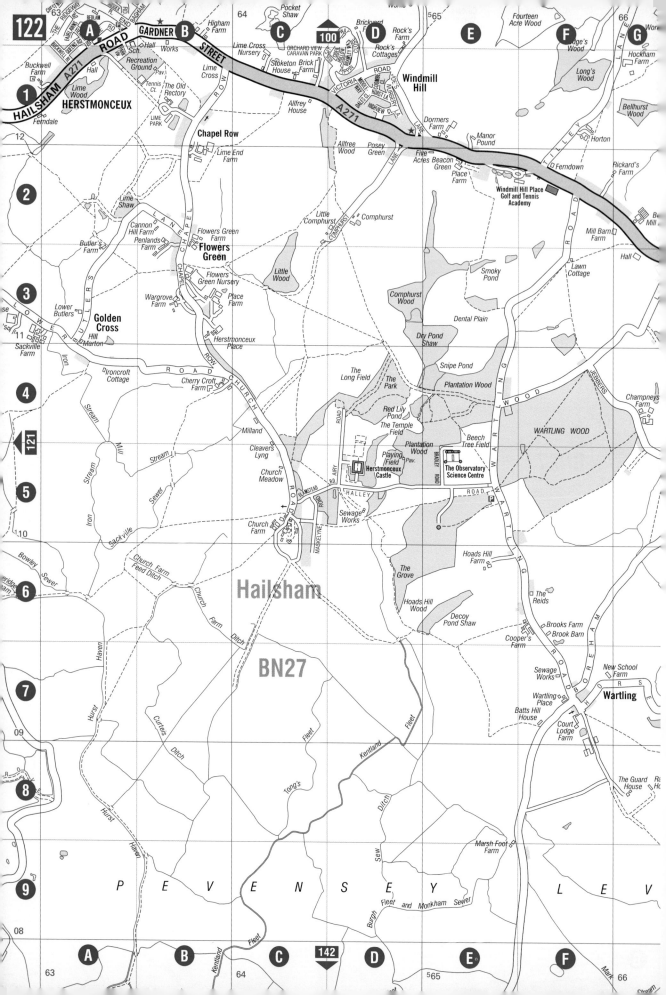

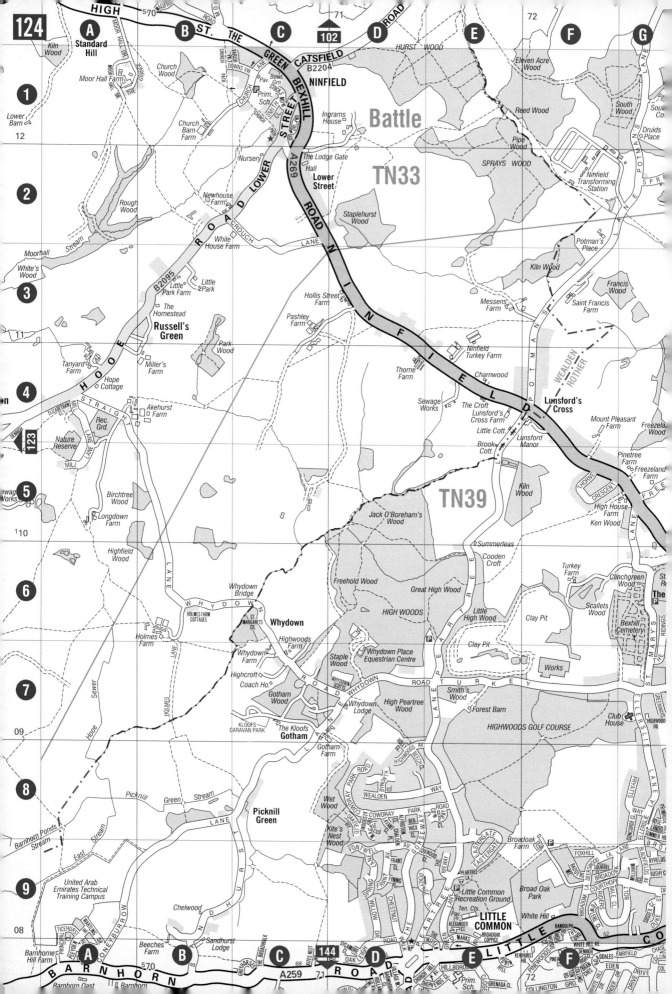

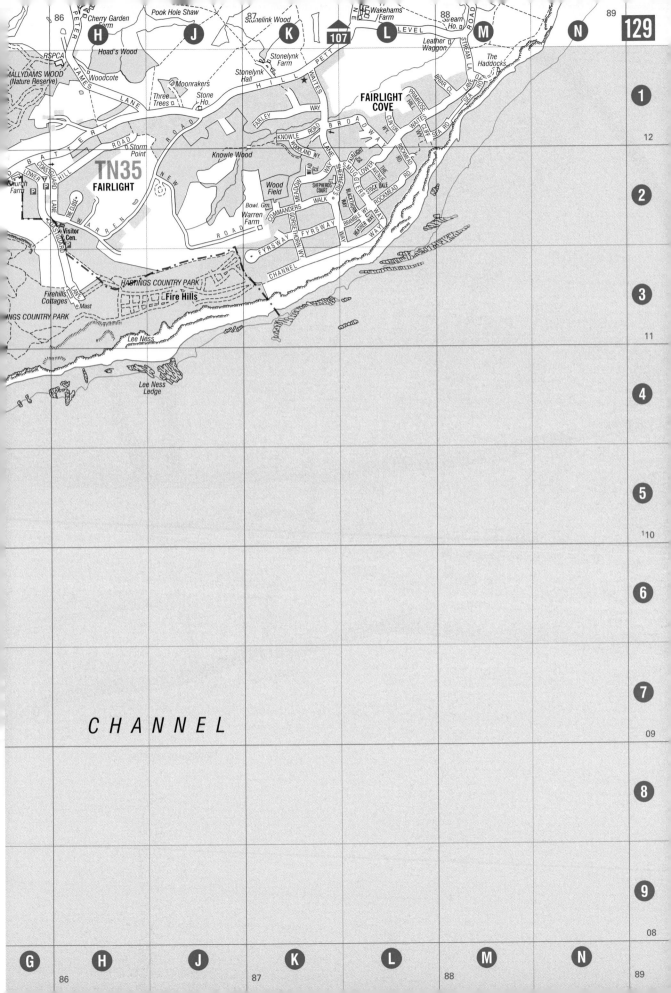

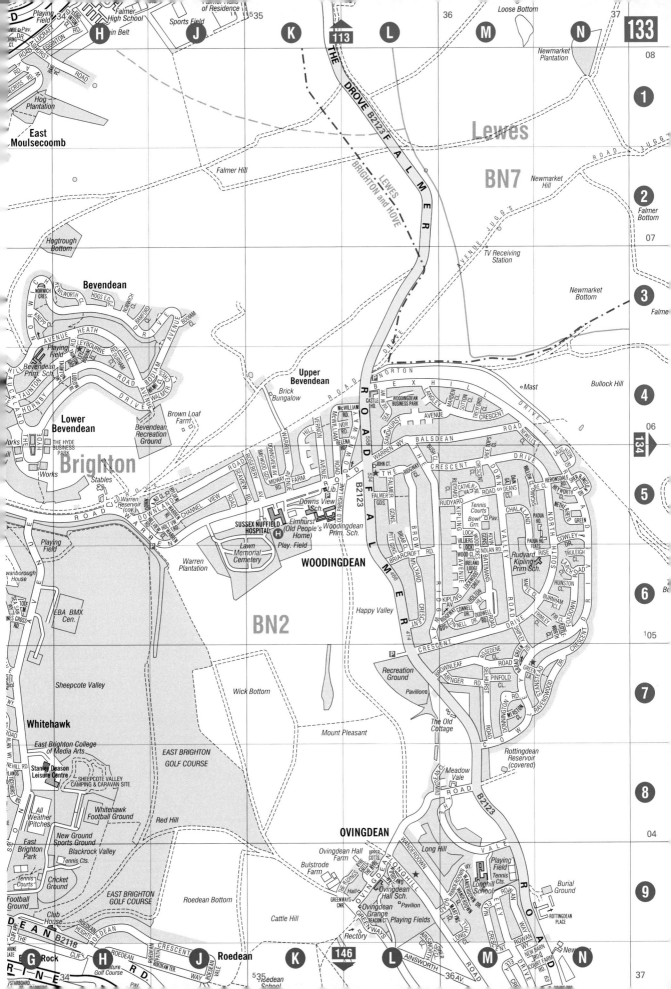

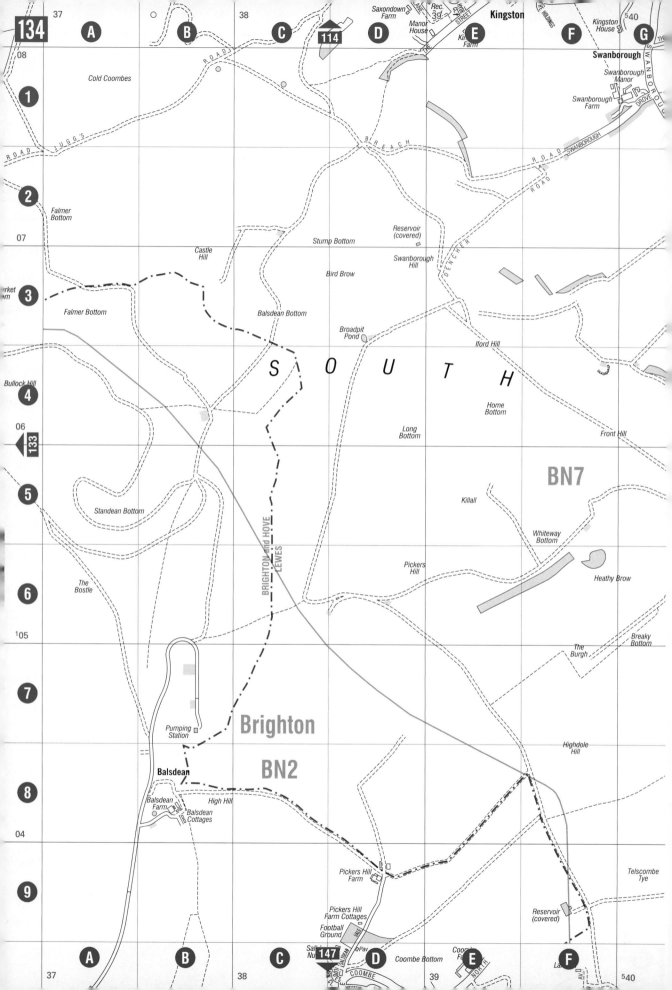

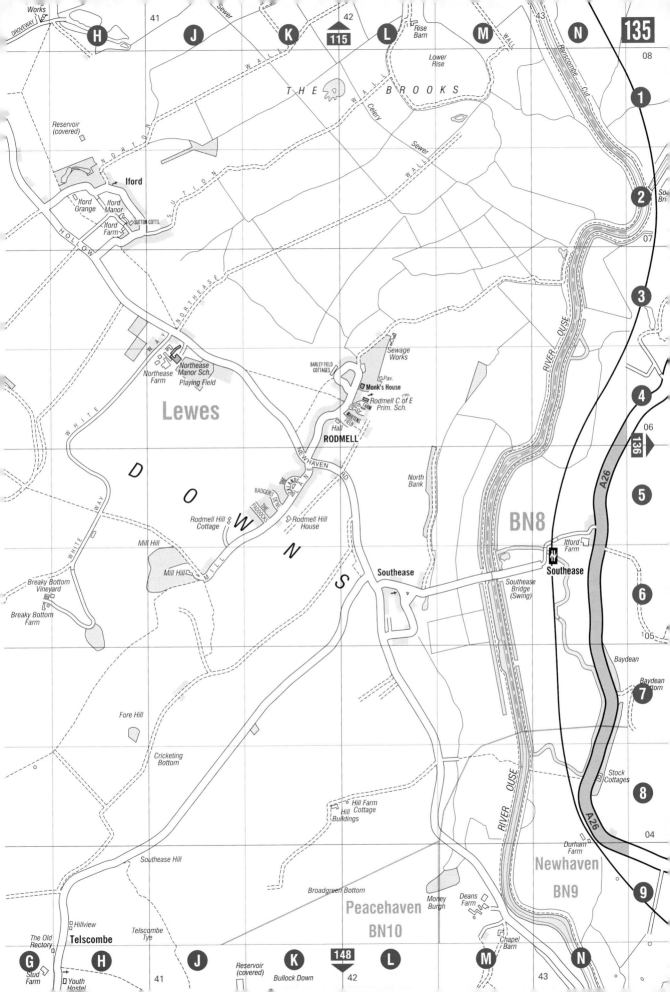

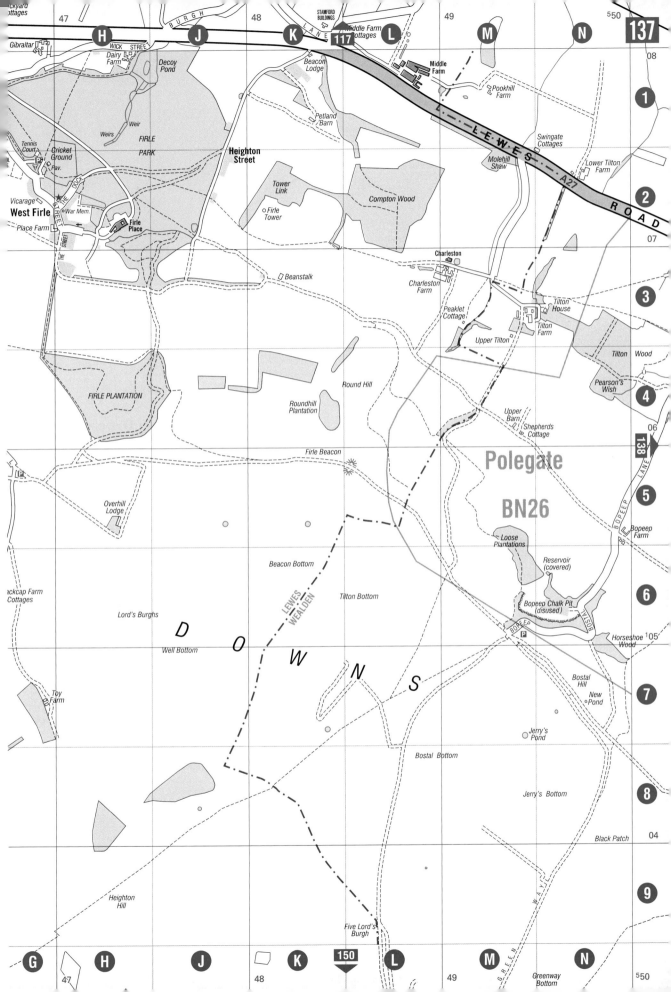

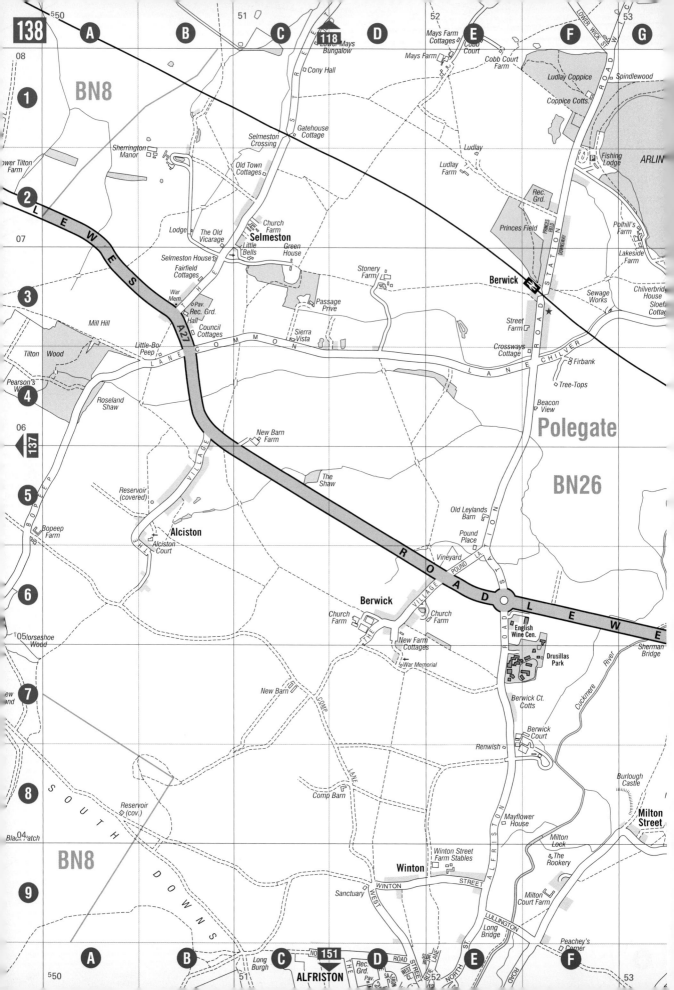

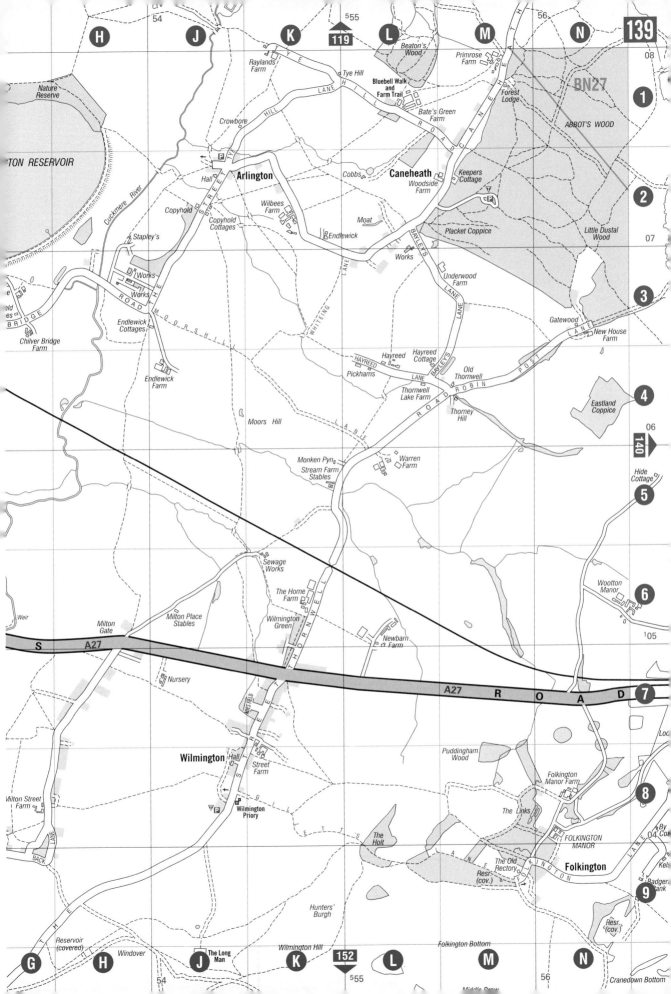

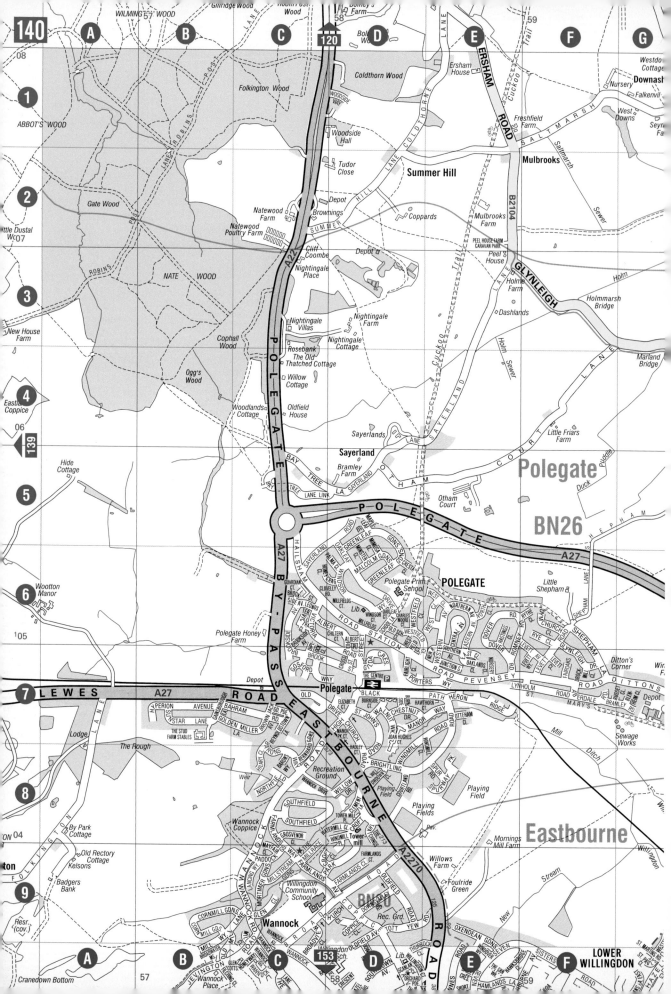

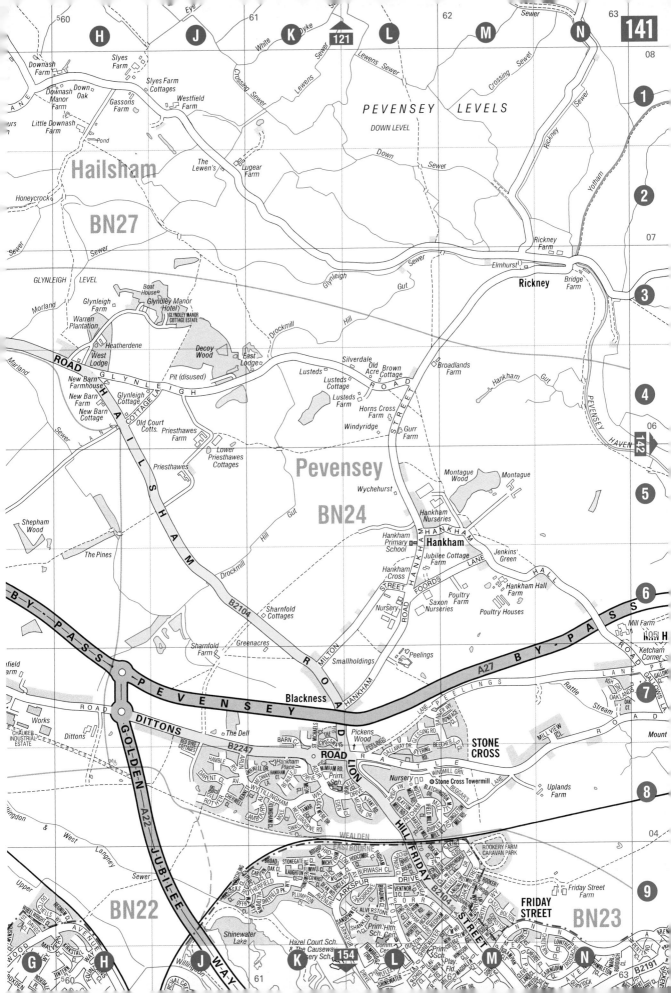

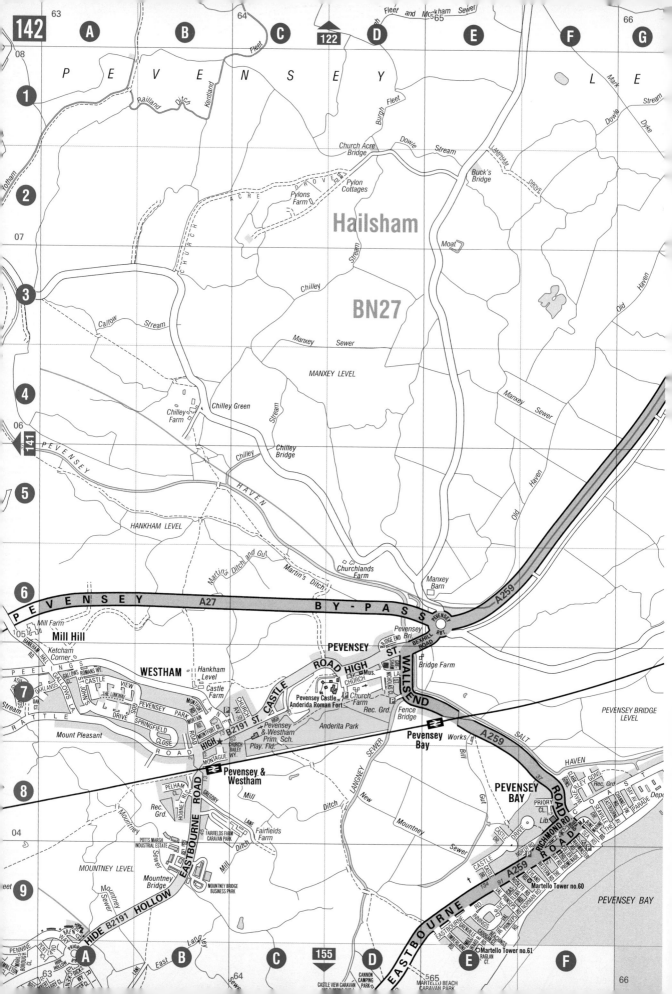

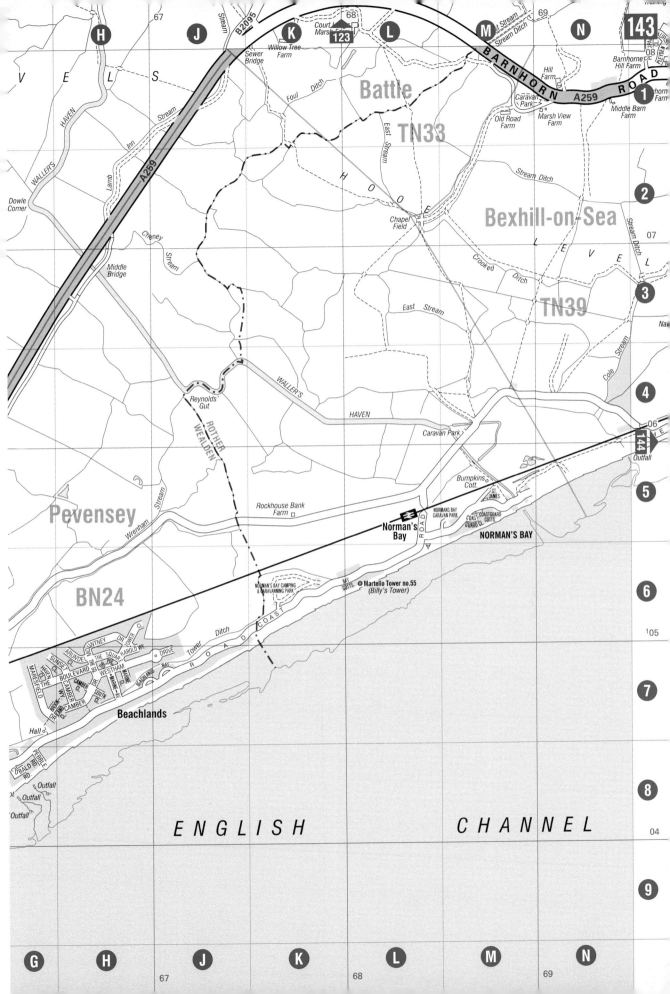

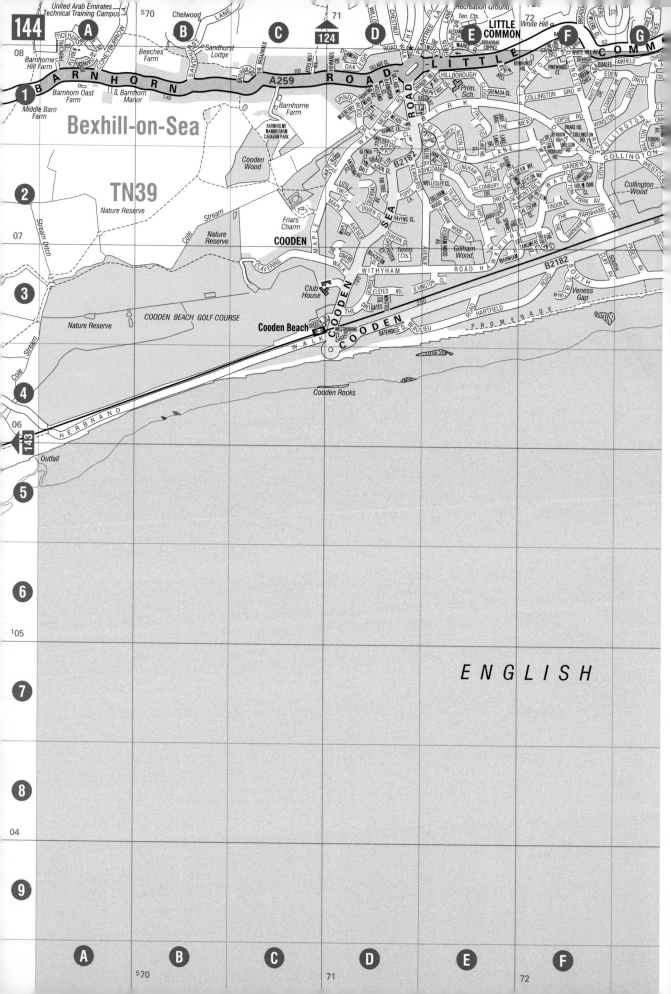

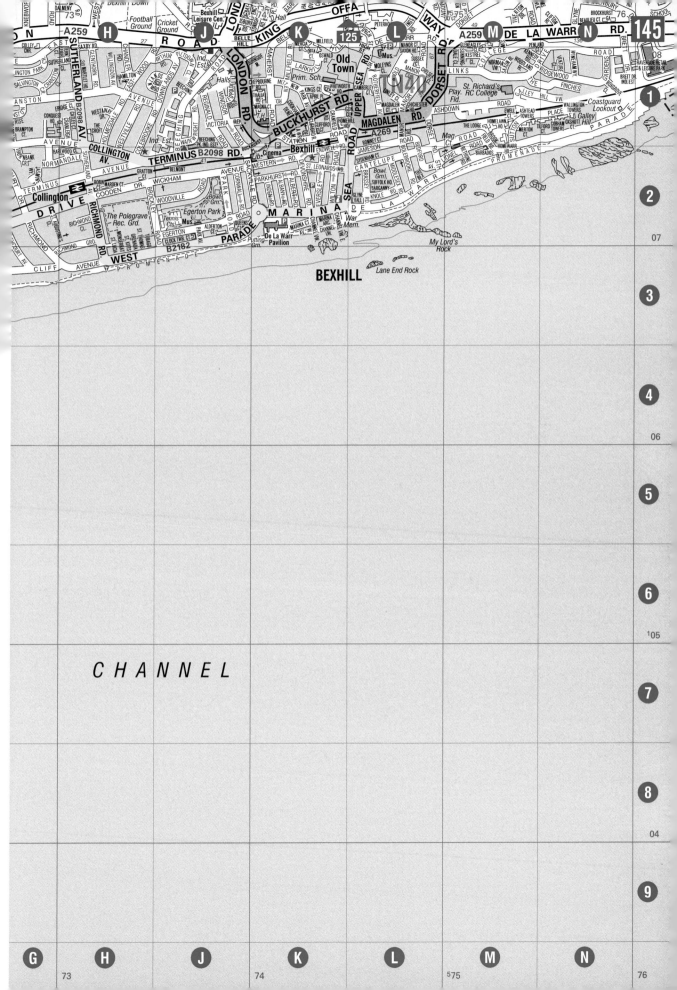

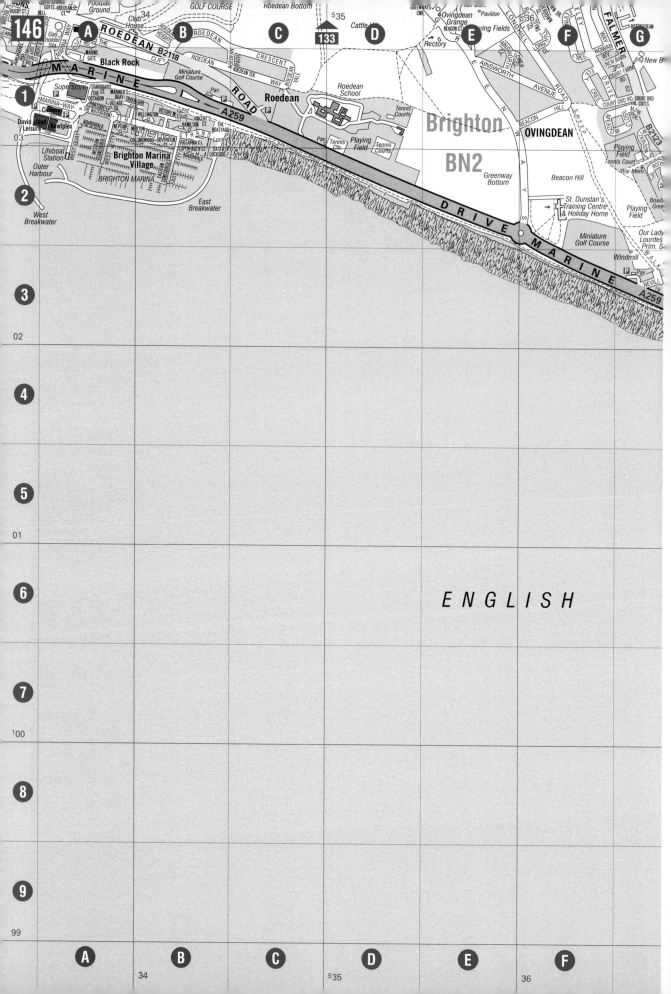

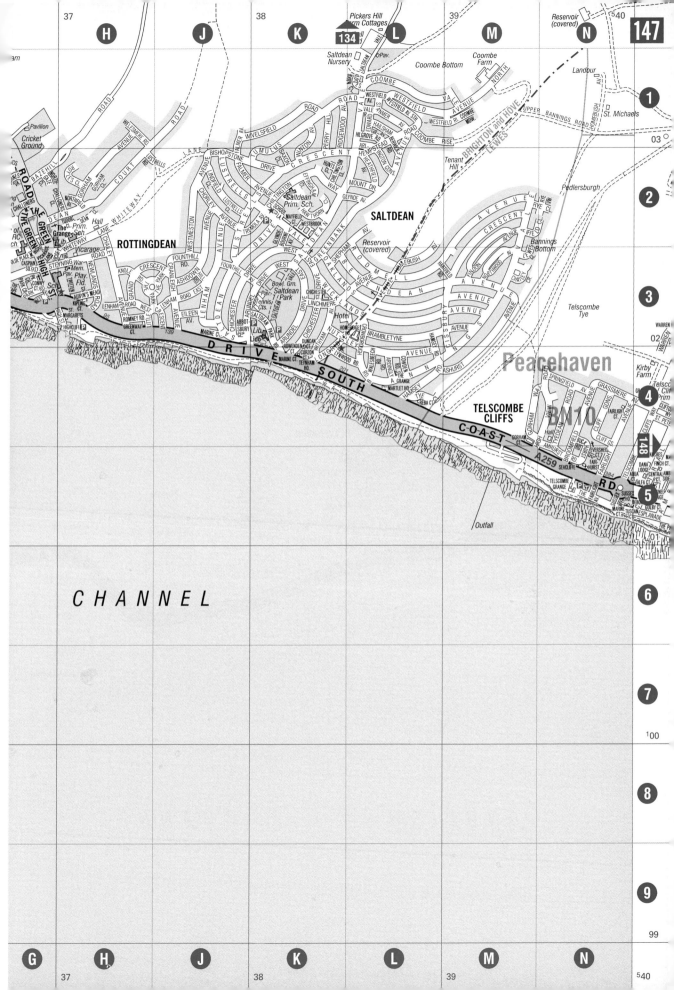

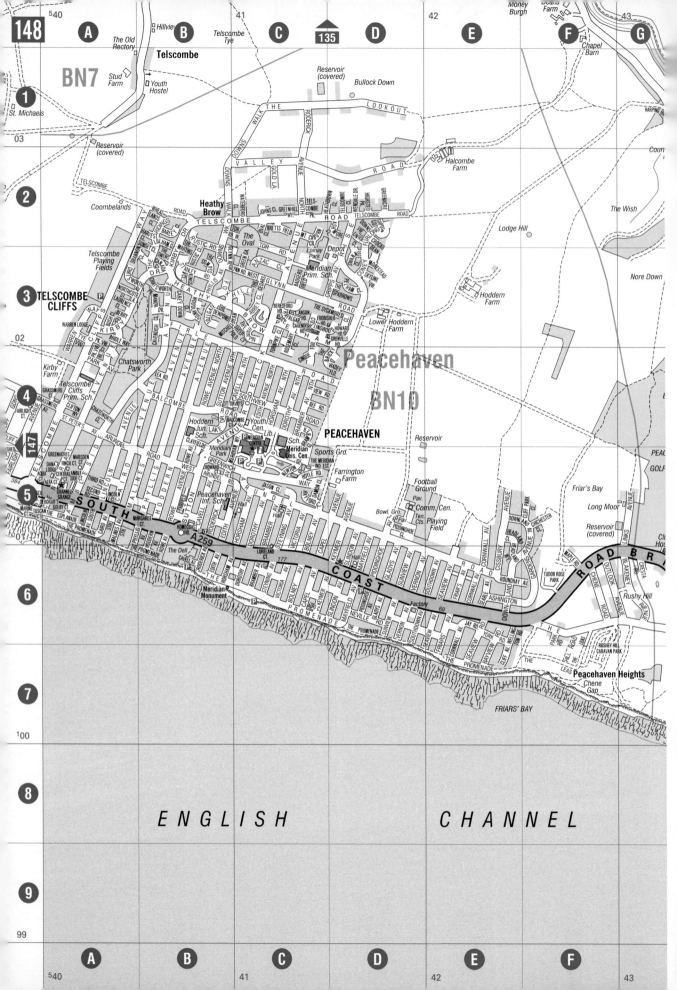

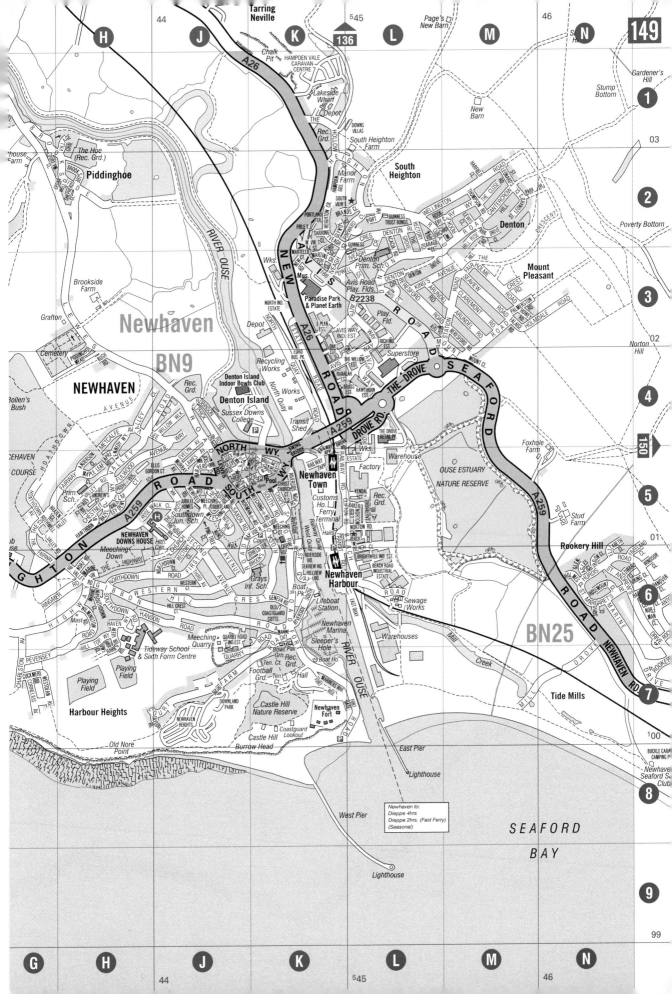

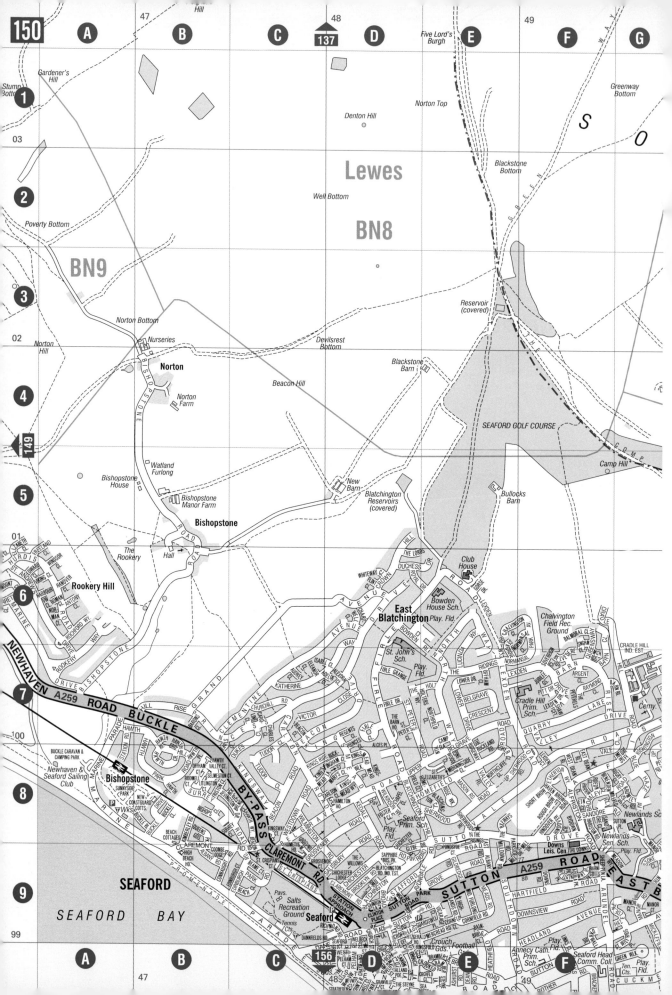

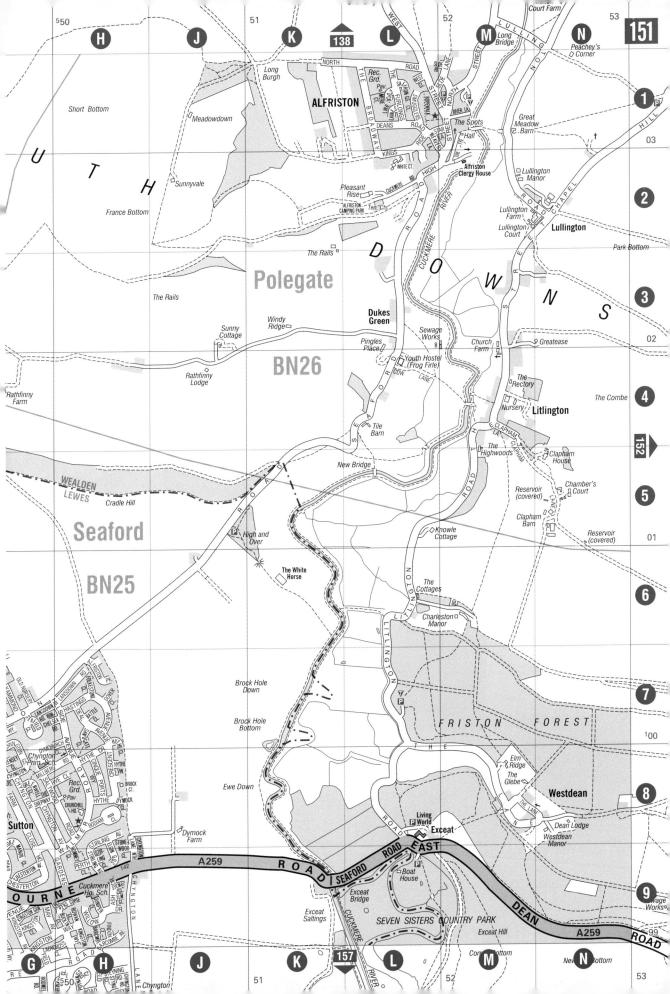

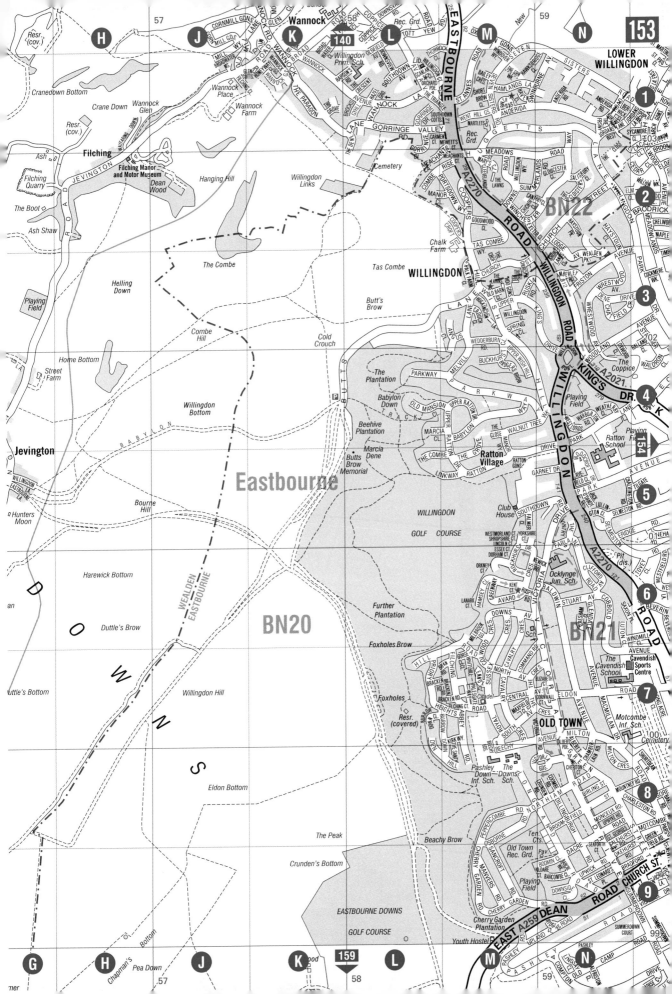

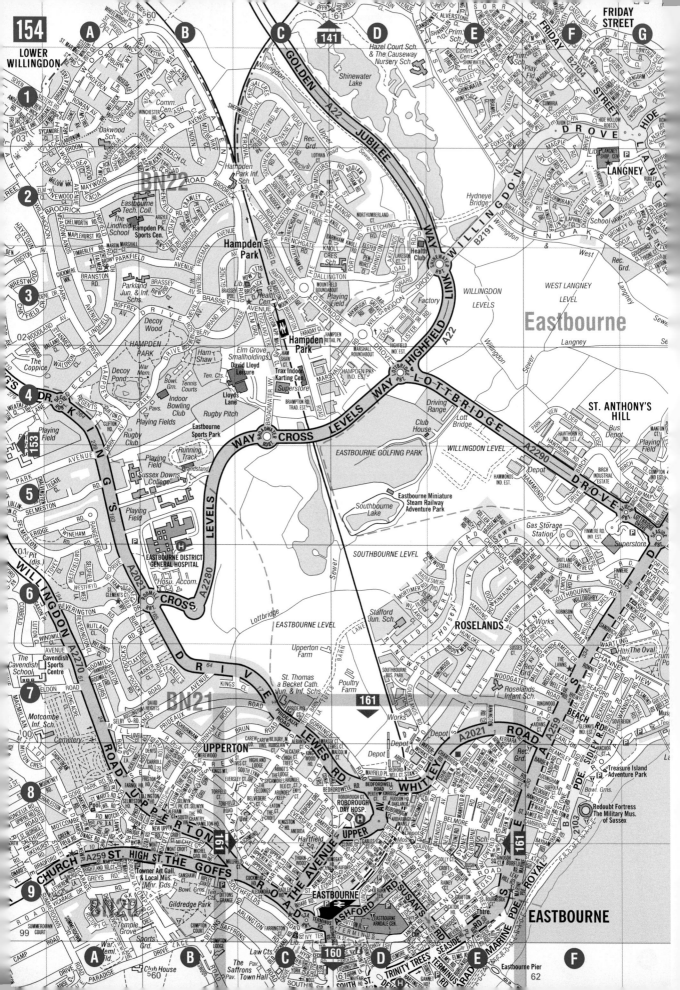

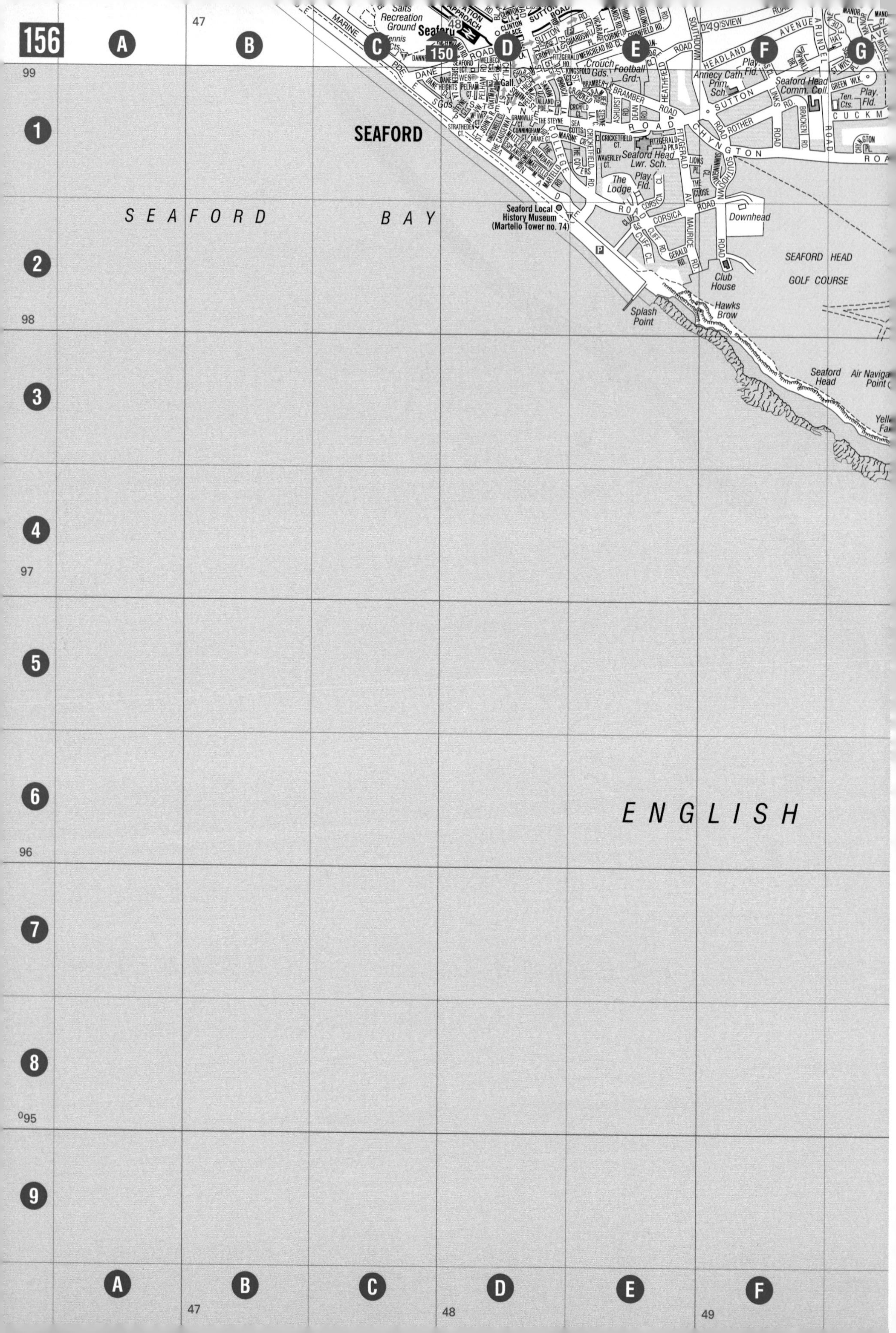

A　　B　　C　　D　　E　　F　　G

47

99

SEAFORD

SEAFORD **BAY**

Salts
Recreation
Ground
Tennis

Seaford

150
48

Crouch
Gds.

Football
Grd.

Play.
Fld.

Annecy Cath.
Prim. Sch.

Seaford Head
Comm. Coll.

Play.
Fld.

Seaford Head
Lwr. Sch.

Play.
Fld.

The
Lodge

Seaford Local
History Museum
(Martello Tower no. 74)

Downhead

SEAFORD HEAD

Club
House

GOLF COURSE

98

Splash
Point

Hawks
Brow

Seaford
Head

Air Naviga
Point

3

Yelle
Fa

4

97

5

6

E N G L I S H

96

7

8

⁰95

9

A　　B　　C　　D　　E　　F

47　　　　　　48　　　　　　49

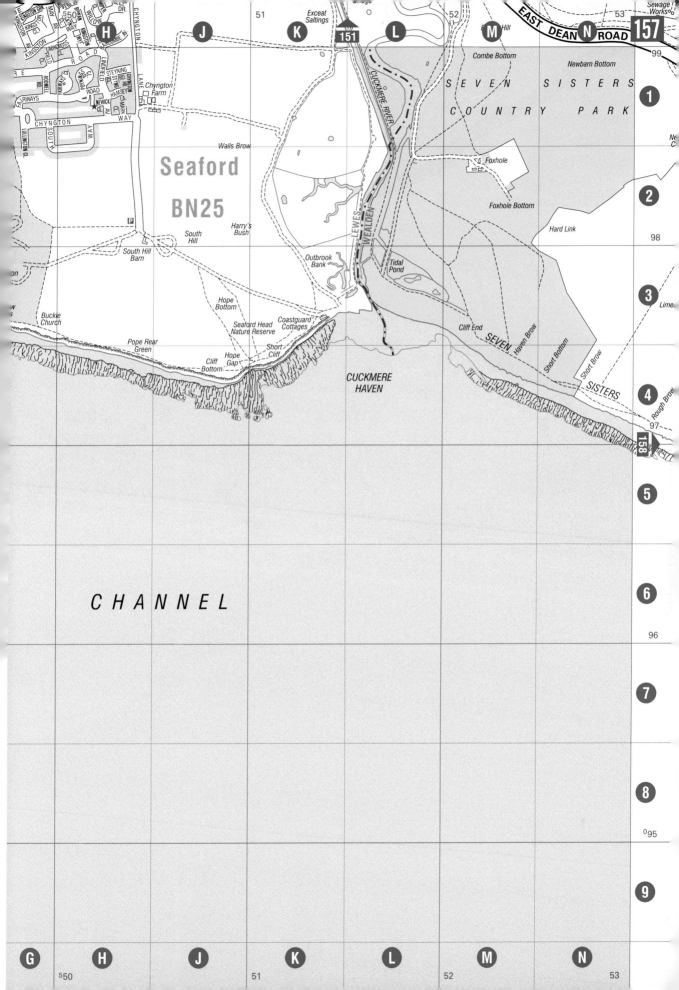

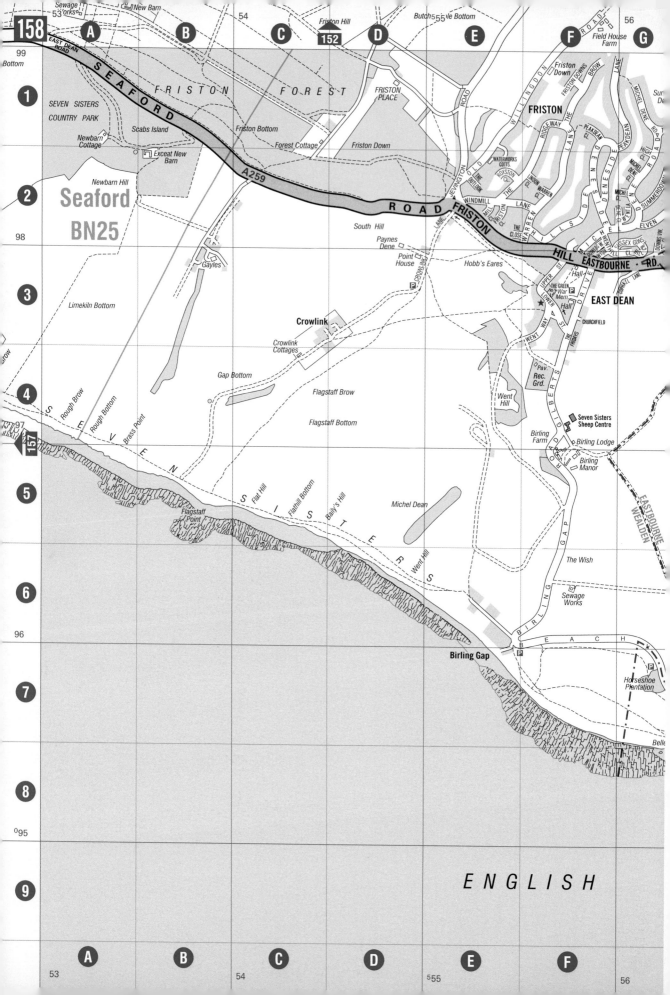

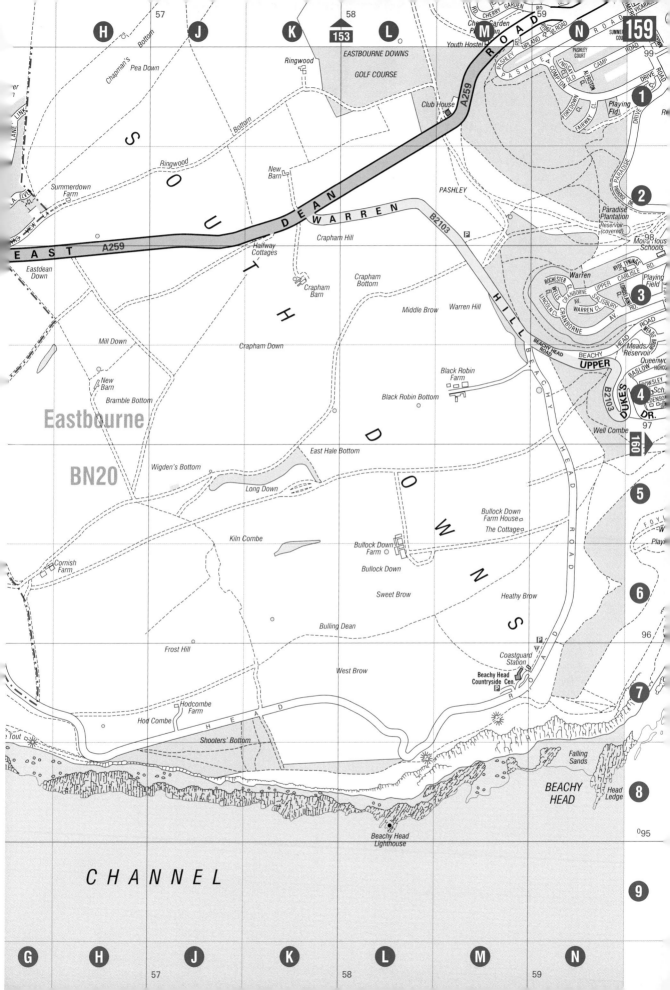

H J K 153 L M N

EASTBOURNE DOWNS
GOLF COURSE

Ringwood

Chapman's Bottom
Pea Down

SOUTH

Ringwood

Bottom

Club House

New Barn

PASHLEY

Youth Hostel

ROAD

CHERRY GARDEN

PASHLEY
UPLAND ROAD
COMPTON
LINDSAY CL
ALDERTON
FOREDOWN CL
FAIRWAY CL

PASHLEY
COURT

CAMP
DRIVE

PARADISE
DRIVE

Playing Fld

1

Summerdown Farm

Eastdean Down

EAST A259

Halfway Cottages

DEAN WARREN

Crapham Hill

Crapham Barn

New Barn

B2103

PASHLEY

Paradise
Plantation

Reservoir
(covered)

Moira Hous Schools

2

Mill Down

New Barn

Bramble Bottom

Crapham Bottom

Crapham Down

Middle Brow

Warren Hill

Black Robin
Farm

Black Robin Bottom

HILL

WARREN

ROCHESTER
WELLS
LINCOLN CL
CRANBORNE

UPPER
CRANBORNE
AV

SALISBURY
LODDISWELL RD

HYDE TYNINGS
CARLISLE RD

Playing
Field

3

Eastbourne

BN20

Wigden's Bottom

Long Down

Kiln Combe

Cornish
Farm

East Hale Bottom

DOWNS

Bullock Down
Farm House

The Cottage

Bullock Down
Farm

Bullock Down

Sweet Brow

Heathy Brow

BEACHY HEAD ROAD

UPPER
Meads
Reservoir

BEACHY
HIGHCO
Queenw

BASLOW
DOWSLEY
HENSON

Sch
Sch

B2103 DUKE'S

DR.

Well Combe

160

5

FOYL
W
Play

6

Bulling Dean

Frost Hill

West Brow

Hodcombe
Farm

Hod Combe

e Tout

Shooters' Bottom

HEAD

Coastguard
Station

Beachy Head
Countryside Cen.

96

7

Falling
Sands

BEACHY
HEAD

Head
Ledge

8

Beachy Head
Lighthouse

095

CHANNEL

9

57 58 59

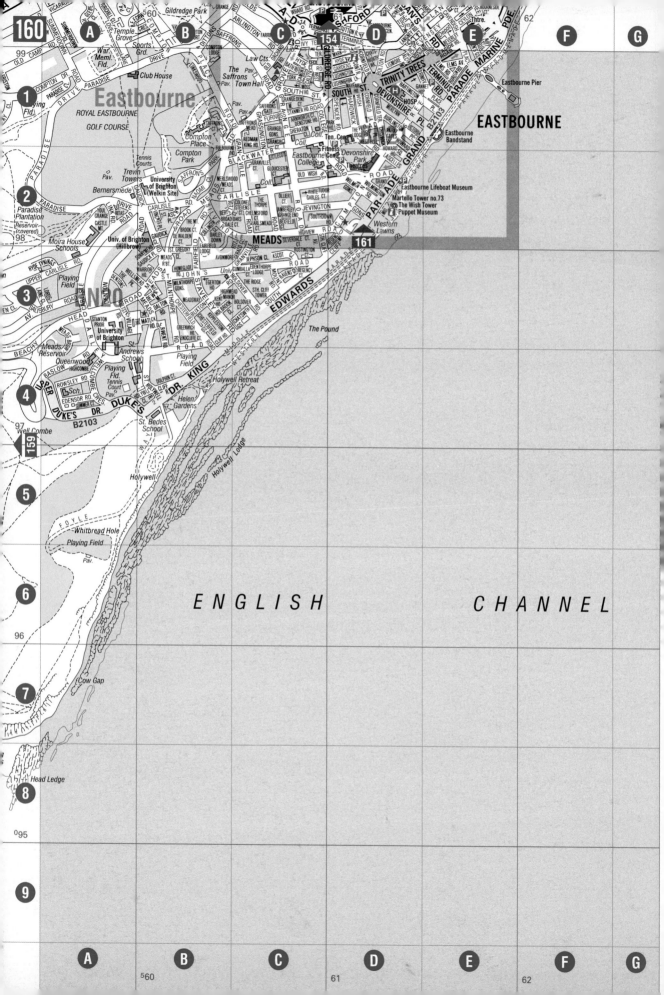

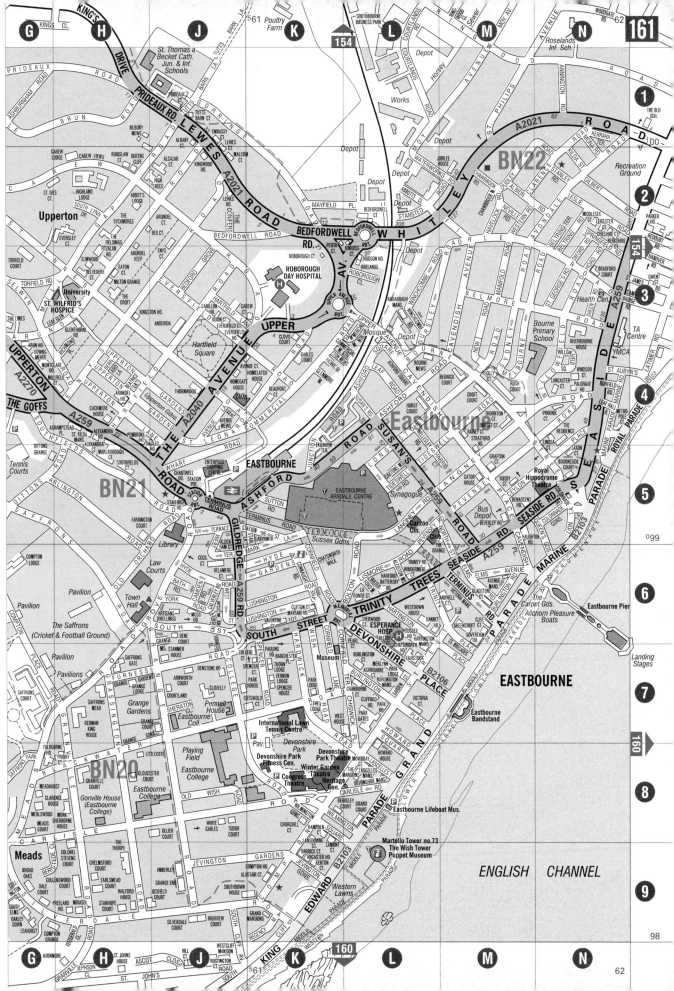

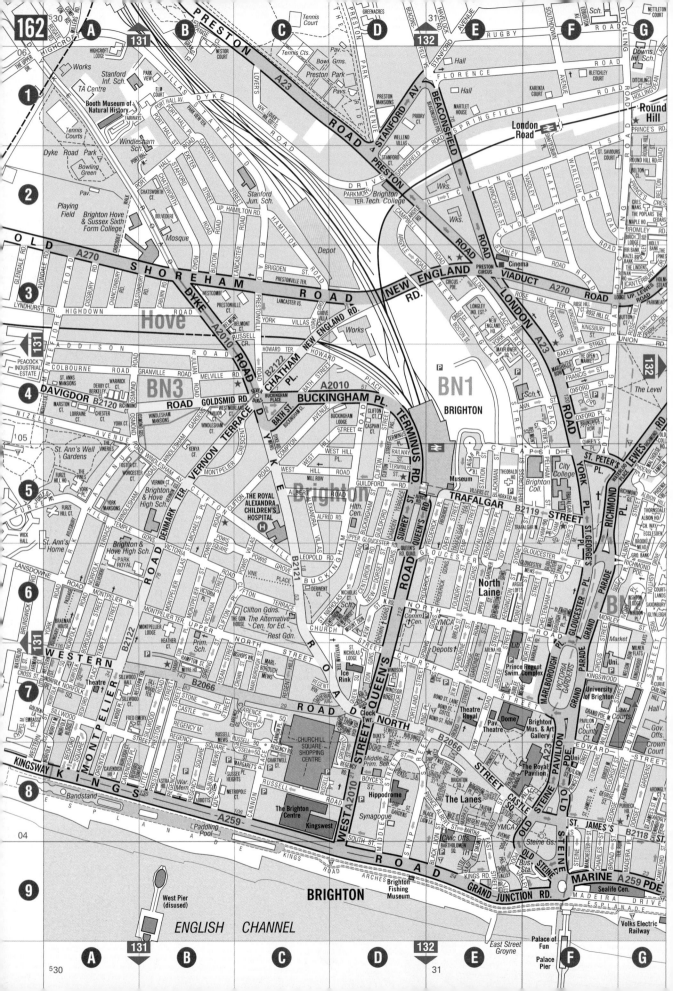

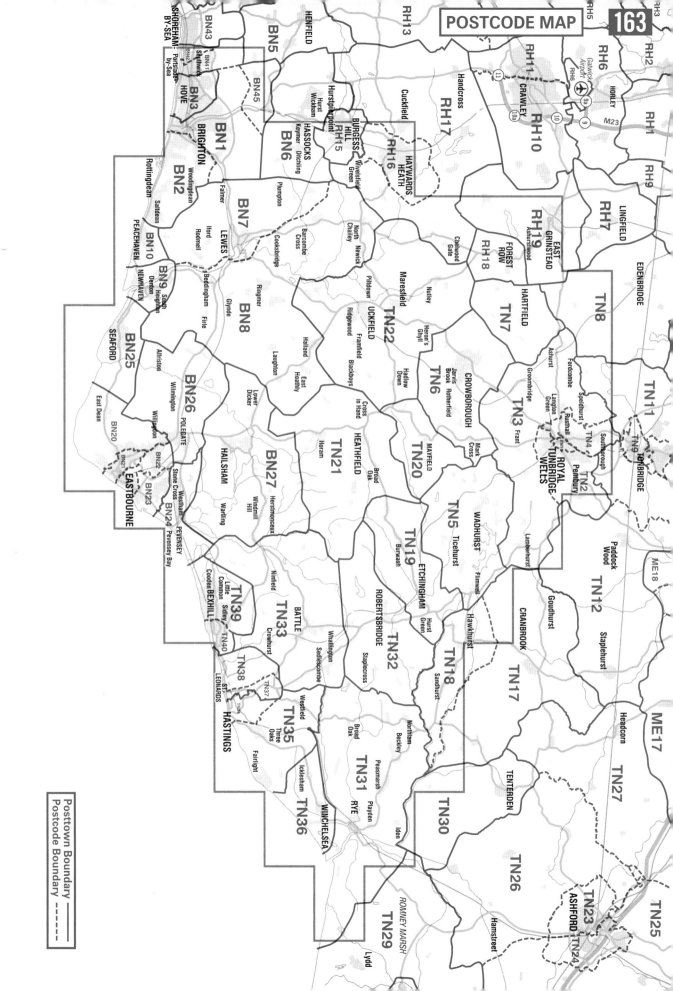

INDEX

Including Streets, Places & Areas, Industrial Estates, Selected Flats & Walkways,
Junction Names, Stations and Selected Places of Interest.

HOW TO USE THIS INDEX

1. Each street name is followed by its Postal District and then by its Locality abbreviation(s) and then by its map reference; e.g. **Abbey Rd.** BN2: Brig . . . .9E **132** is in the Brighton 2 Postal District and the Brighton Locality and is to be found in square 9E on page **132**. The page number is shown in bold type.

2. A strict alphabetical order is followed in which Av., Rd., St., etc. (though abbreviated) are read in full and as part of the street name; e.g. **Abbeyfield Ho.** appears after **Abbey Dr.** but before **Abbey Grn. Rd.**

3. Streets and a selection of flats and walkways too small to be shown on the maps, appear in the index with the thoroughfare to which it is connected shown in brackets; e.g. **Abbeyfield Ho.** BN26: Alfr . . . .1L **151** (off North Rd.)

4. Addresses that are in more than one part are referred to as not continuous.

5. Places and areas are shown in the index in BLUE TYPE and the map reference is to the actual map square in which the town centre or area is located and not to the place name shown on the map; e.g. **ALFRISTON** 1L **151**

6. An example of a selected place of interest is **Adur Indoor Bowls Cen.** 6B **130**

7. An example of a station is **Aldrington Station (Rail)** . . . .5J **131.**

8. Map references shown in brackets; e.g **Abbotts Cl.** BN22: Eastb . . . .8D **154** (2L **161**) refer to entries that also appear on the large scale pages **161** & **162**

GENERAL ABBREVIATIONS

All. : Alley	**Ct.** : Court	**Info.** : Information	**Quad.** : Quadrant
App. : Approach	**Cres.** : Crescent	**Junc.** : Junction	**Ri.** : Rise
Arc. : Arcade	**Cft.** : Croft	**La.** : Lane	**Rd.** : Road
Av. : Avenue	**Dr.** : Drive	**Lit.** : Little	**Rdbt.** : Roundabout
Bri. : Bridge	**E.** : East	**Lwr.** : Lower	**Shop.** : Shopping
Bldg. : Building	**Ent.** : Enterprise	**Mnr.** : Manor	**Sth.** : South
Bldgs. : Buildings	**Est.** : Estate	**Mans.** : Mansions	**Sq.** : Square
Bungs. : Bungalows	**Fld.** : Field	**Mkt.** : Market	**Sta.** : Station
Bus. : Business	**Flds.** : Fields	**Mdw.** : Meadow	**St.** : Street
Cvn. : Caravan	**Gdn.** : Garden	**Mdws.** : Meadows	**Ter.** : Terrace
C'way. : Causeway	**Gdns.** : Gardens	**M.** : Mews	**Twr.** : Tower
Cen. : Centre	**Gth.** : Garth	**Mt.** : Mount	**Trad.** : Trading
Chu. : Church	**Ga.** : Gate	**Mus.** : Museum	**Up.** : Upper
Cir. : Circus	**Gt.** : Great	**Nth.** : North	**Va.** : Vale
Cl. : Close	**Grn.** : Green	**No.** : Number	**Vw.** : View
Comn. : Common	**Gro.** : Grove	**Pde.** : Parade	**Vs.** : Villas
Cnr. : Corner	**Hgts.** : Heights	**Pk.** : Park	**Wlk.** : Walk
Cott. : Cottage	**Ho.** : House	**Pas.** : Passage	**W.** : West
Cotts. : Cottages	**Ind.** : Industrial	**Pl.** : Place	**Yd.** : Yard

LOCALITY ABBREVIATIONS

Alc : **Alciston**	Cuck : **Cuckfield**	Hever : **Hever**	Peace : **Peacehaven**
Alfr : **Alfriston**	Dall : **Dallington**	H Hur : **High Hurstwood**	Peas : **Peasmarsh**
Ard : **Ardingly**	Dane : **Danehill**	Hooe : **Hooe**	Pem : **Pembury**
Arl : **Arlington**	Ditch : **Ditchling**	Horam : **Horam**	P'hrst : **Penhurst**
A'ham : **Ashburnham**	Down : **Downash**	Hors : **Horsmonden**	Pens : **Penshurst**
A'hst : **Ashurst**	Eastb : **Eastbourne**	Hors K : **Horsted Keynes**	Pett : **Pett**
A'hstw : **Ashurstwood**	E Chil : **East Chiltington**	Hove : **Hove**	Pev : **Pevensey**
Barc : **Barcombe**	E Dean : **East Dean**	Hur G : **Hurst Green**	Pev B : **Pevensey Bay**
Barc C : **Barcombe Cross**	E Grin : **East Grinstead**	Ick : **Icklesham**	Pidd : **Piddinghoe**
Barc M : **Barcombe Mills**	E Guld : **East Guldeford**	Iden : **Iden**	Pilt : **Piltdown**
Batt : **Battle**	E Hoath : **East Hoathly**	Ifrd : **Iford**	Play : **Playden**
Bedd : **Beddington**	Eri G : **Eridge Green**	Isf : **Isfield**	Plump : **Plumpton**
Bell G : **Bell's Yew Green**	Etch : **Etchingham**	Jar B : **Jarvis Brook**	Plump G : **Plumpton Green**
Ben : **Benenden**	Ewh G : **Ewhurst Green**	Jev : **Jevington**	Pole : **Polegate**
B'wck : **Berwick**	Exc : **Exceat**	Kiln : **Kilndown**	Ports : **Portslade**
Bex S : **Bexhill-on-Sea**	Fair : **Fairlight**	King L : **Kingston near Lewes**	Poyn : **Poynings**
Bid : **Bidborough**	Falm : **Falmer**	Lamb : **Lamberhurst**	Punn T : **Punnett's Town**
B'stn : **Bishopston**	Filch : **Filching**	Lang : **Langney**	Pye : **Pyecombe**
B'boys : **Blackboys**	Five D : **Five Ash Down**	Lang G : **Langton Green**	Rick : **Rickney**
B'ham : **Blackham**	F Ashes : **Five Ashes**	Laug : **Laughton**	Ring : **Ringmer**
Bod : **Bodium**	Flet : **Fletching**	Lewes : **Lewes**	Ripe : **Ripe**
Bodle G : **Bodle Street Green**	Flim : **Flimwell**	Lind : **Lindfield**	Rob : **Robertsbridge**
Bore S : **Boreham Street**	Folk : **Folkington**	Lit : **Litlington**	Rod : **Rodmell**
Brede : **Brede**	F'cmbe : **Fordcombe**	Lit H : **Little Horsted**	Rolv : **Rolvenden**
Bren : **Brenchley**	F Row : **Forest Row**	Lwr D : **Lower Dicker**	Rolv L : **Rolvenden Layne**
B'lng : **Brightling**	F Wood : **Forest Wood**	Lull : **Lullington**	Roth : **Rotherfield**
Brig : **Brighton**	Fram : **Framfield**	Lydd : **Lydd**	Rott : **Rottingdean**
B Oak : **Broad Oak**	Frant : **Frant**	Lye G : **Lye Green**	Rush G : **Rushlake Green**
Buck : **Buckley**	Fris : **Friston**	Mag D : **Magham Down**	R'hall : **Rusthall**
Burg H : **Burgess Hill**	Fulk : **Fulking**	Mare : **Maresfield**	Rye : **Rye**
B'wsh : **Burwash**	Fur G : **Furner's Green**	M'bch : **Markbeech**	Rye F : **Rye Foreign**
B'wsh C : **Burwash Common**	Glyn : **Glynde**	Mark C : **Mark Cross**	Salt : **Saltdean**
Buxt : **Buxted**	Gold C : **Golden Cross**	Mrle G : **Marle Green**	Sandh : **Sandhurst**
Camb : **Camber**	Goud : **Goudhurst**	Mrsh G : **Marsh Green**	Scay H : **Scaynes Hill**
Cats : **Catsfield**	Groom : **Groombridge**	Mat : **Matfield**	Sea : **Seaford**
Chal : **Chalvington**	Gues T : **Guestling Thorn**	May : **Mayfield**	Sed : **Sedlescombe**
Chel C : **Chelwood Common**	Gun H : **Gun Hill**	May G : **Maynard's Green**	Selm : **Selmeston**
Chel G : **Chelwood Gate**	Had D : **Hadlow Down**	Milt S : **Milton Street**	Sharp : **Sharpthorne**
C'gly : **Chiddingly**	Hails : **Hailsham**	Mount : **Mountfield**	Shef P : **Sheffield Park**
Chid : **Chiddingstone**	Hall : **Halland**	Neth : **Netherfield**	Shor S : **Shoreham-by-Sea**
Chid H : **Chiddingstone Hoath**	Hamm : **Hammerwood**	N'den : **Newenden**	S'bri : **Shortbridge**
Clay : **Clayton**	H'sey : **Hamsey**	N'hvn : **Newhaven**	Short : **Shortgate**
Cole H : **Coleman's Hatch**	Hank : **Hankham**	N'wck : **Newick**	South : **Southborough**
Cooks : **Cooksbridge**	Hart : **Hartfield**	Newt : **Newtimber**	S Chai : **South Chailey**
Copt : **Copthorne**	Hass : **Hassocks**	Nin : **Ninfield**	S Heig : **South Heighton**
Cous W : **Cousley Wood**	Hast : **Hastings**	Nor B : **Norman's Bay**	S'wck : **Southwick**
Cowb : **Cowbeech**	Hawk : **Hawkhurst**	N Cha : **North Chailey**	Speld : **Speldhurst**
C'den : **Cowden**	Hay H : **Haywards Heath**	North : **Northiam**	Stan : **Stanmer**
Cran : **Cranbrook**	H'fld : **Heathfield**	Nort : **Norton**	Staple : **Staplecross**
Cross H : **Cross-in-Hand**	Hell : **Hellingly**	Nut : **Nutley**	St Leo : **St. Leonards-on-Sea**
Crow : **Crowborough**	Her G : **Heron's Ghyll**	Off : **Offham**	Sto C : **Stone Cross**
C'hrst : **Crowhurst**	Herst : **Herstmonceux**	Oving : **Ovingdean**	S'gate : **Stonegate**

Streat : Streat
S Rgh : Streeter's Rough
Tarr N : Tarring Neville
Tels C : Telscombe Cliffs
T Oaks : Three Oaks
Tice : Ticehurst
Tide : Tidebrook
Tonb : Tonbridge
Town R : Town Row
Tude : Tudeley
Tun W : Tunbridge Wells
Uck : Uckfield
Udim : Udimore
Up D : Upper Dicker
Up H : Upper Hartfield
Vine C : Vine's Cross
Wadh : Wadhurst
Wald : Waldron
Wals : Walstead
Warb : Warbleton
Wart : Wartling
W Dean : West Dean
W'fld : Westfield
W Firle : West Firle
W'ham : Westham
W'ton : Westmeston
What : Whatlington
White : Whitesmith
Will : Willingdon
Wilm : Wilmington
Winch : Winchelsea
Withy : Withyham
Witter : Wittersham
Wivel : Wivelsfield
Wivel G : Wivelsfield Green
W'dean : Woodingdean
Wych C : Wych Cross

A

Abbey Cl. BN10: Peace . . . 3C 148
Abbey Ct. TN4: Tun W . . . 8D 8
TN33: Batt . . . 3L 103
Abbey Dr. TN38: Bex S . . . 9B 126
Abbeyfield Ho. BN26: Alfr . . . 1L 151
(off North Rd.)
Abbey Grn. Rd. TN33: Batt . . . 3L 103
Abbey M. RH19: A'hstw . . . 6M 11
TN32: Rob . . . 5J 61
Abbey Path BN27: Hails . . . 4F 120
Abbey Rd. BN2: Brig . . . 9E 132
BN20: Eastb . . . 7M 153
Abbey Vw. TN40: Bex S . . . 8L 125
Abbey Way TN33: Batt . . . 2L 103
Abbotsbury Cl. BN2: Salt . . . 3J 147
Abbots Cl. BN6: Hass . . . 3A 90
TN33: Batt . . . 4N 103
Abbotsfield Cl. TN34: Hast . . . 3M 127
Abbot's Wood . . . 1N 139
Abbotts BN1: Brig . . . 8N 131 (8B 162)
Abbotts Cl. BN22: Eastb . . . 8D 154 (2L 161)
Abbott's Lodge
BN21: Eastb . . . 8C 154 (2H 161)
Aberdale Rd. BN26: Pole . . . 7F 140
Aberdeen Rd. BN2: Brig . . . 5D 132
Abergavenny Ho. BN3: Hove . . . 7M 131
(off Holland Rd.)
Abergavenny Rd. BN7: Lewes . . . 5H 115
Abigail Ho. RH16: Hay H . . . 5F 48
(off Hazelgrove Rd.)
Abinger Ct. BN41: Ports . . . 5D 130
(off Abinger Rd.)
Abinger Pl. BN7: Lewes . . . 5J 115
Abinger Rd. BN2: W'dean . . . 7M 133
BN41: Ports . . . 5D 130
Acacia Av. BN3: Hove . . . 4H 131
Acacia Ct. BN1: Brig . . . 3A 132
Acacia Rd. BN9: N'hvn . . . 2L 149
BN22: Eastb . . . 2A 154
Acer Av. TN2: Tun W . . . 4F 16
Acerlands BN8: N'wck . . . 9J 51
Acorn Cl. RH19: E Grin . . . 4E 10
TN37: St Leo . . . 2J 127
Acorn Grn. BN27: Hails . . . 5E 120
Acorns, The BN27: Hails . . . 7G 120
TN5: S'gate . . . 4H 41
Acorn Way TN19: Hur G . . . 7H 43
Acre Cl. RH16: Hay H . . . 7E 48
Acres Ri. TN5: Tice . . . 1N 41
Adam Cl. TN6: Crow . . . 4E 36
TN38: St Leo . . . 2F 126
Adams Cl. BN1: Brig . . . 3C 132
BN26: Pole . . . 7C 140
Adams La. TN31: North . . . 8J 63
Adastra Av. BN6: Hass . . . 3B 90
Addingham Rd.
BN22: Eastb . . . 8F 154 (2N 161)
Addington Cl. TN38: St Leo . . . 7F 126
Addison Rd. BN3: Hove . . . 6N 131 (4A 162)
Adelaide Cl. BN25: Sea . . . 7D 150
Adelaide Cres. BN3: Hove . . . 8L 131
Adelaide Mans. BN3: Hove . . . 8L 131
Adelaide Rd. TN38: St Leo . . . 3H 127
Ades Fld. BN26: Wilm . . . 7K 139
Admiral's Bri. La. RH19: E Grin . . . 1C 20
Admiral Steps TN34: Hast . . . 5N 127
(off Nelson Rd.)
Admiralty Ct. BN23: Eastb . . . 3L 155
Admiralty Cres. BN23: Eastb . . . 2L 155
Admiralty Way BN23: Eastb . . . 3L 155
Adur Dr. BN24: Sto C . . . 8K 141
Adur Indoor Bowls Cen. . . . 6B 130
Adur Rd. RH15: Burg H . . . 4D 68
Agincourt Cl. TN37: St Leo . . . 8F 104
Agnes St. BN2: Brig . . . 6D 132
Ailsworth La. TN31: Rye . . . 2G 86
(off Landgate)
Ainsworth Av. BN2: Oving . . . 1E 146
Ainsworth Cl. BN2: Oving . . . 9L 133
Ainsworth Ho. BN2: Brig . . . 6D 132
Airlie Ho. BN3: Hove . . . 7L 131
(off Grand Av.)
Air St. BN1: Brig . . . 8A 132 (7D 162)
Airy Rd. BN27: Herst . . . 5D 122
Akehurst Fld. TN33: A'ham . . . 4K 101
Alamein Cl. TN6: Crow . . . 2E 36
Alan Way BN2: Brig . . . 7G 133
Alastair Ct. BN21: Eastb . . . 9J 161
Albany Ct. BN21: Eastb . . . 7C 154 (1J 161)
TN34: Hast . . . 7M 127
(off Robertson Ter.)
TN40: Bex S . . . 2K 145
(off Albany Rd.)
Albany Hill TN2: Tun W . . . 8F 8
Albany Mans. TN38: St Leo . . . 6H 127
TN40: Bex S . . . 2K 145
(off Marina)
Albany M. BN3: Hove . . . 7K 131
Albany Rd. BN25: Sea . . . 9B 150
TN38: St Leo . . . 6G 127
TN40: Bex S . . . 2K 145
Albany Towers BN3: Hove . . . 8K 131
(off St Catherine's Ter.)
Albany Vs. BN3: Hove . . . 8K 131
Albemarle Mans. BN3: Hove . . . 8K 131
(off Medina Ter.)
Albemarle, The BN2: Brig . . . 9F 162
Albert Cl. RH16: Hay H . . . 5H 49
Albert Cotts. TN1: Tun W . . . 9F 8
Albert Ct. TN2: Tun W . . . 9G 8
Albert Dr. RH15: Burg H . . . 6A 68
Albert Mans. BN3: Hove . . . 7L 131
(off Church Rd.)
Albert M. BN3: Hove . . . 7L 131
Albert Pde. BN21: Eastb . . . 7N 153
Albert Pl. BN26: Pole . . . 6D 140
Albert Rd. BN1: Brig . . . 7A 132 (5C 162)
BN26: Pole . . . 6C 140
BN42: S'wck . . . 6A 130
TN22: Uck . . . 2J 73
TN34: Hast . . . 7M 127
TN40: Bex S . . . 2K 145
Albert St. TN1: Tun W . . . 9E 8
Albert Ter. BN21: Eastb . . . 7N 153
Albion Ct. BN2: Brig . . . 8G 162
RH15: Burg H . . . 6A 68
Albion Hill BN2: Brig . . . 7C 132 (5G 162)
Albion Ho. BN2: Brig . . . 5G 162
BN42: S'wck . . . 6B 130
Albion La. TN34: Hast . . . 7N 127
Albion Rd. BN22: Eastb . . . 8E 154 (2M 161)
TN1: Tun W . . . 8E 8
Albion Row TN1: Tun W . . . 8F 8
(off Albion Rd.)
Albion St. BN2: Brig . . . 7C 132 (6G 162)
BN7: Lewes . . . 5K 115
BN41: Ports . . . 6D 130
BN42: S'wck . . . 6A 130
Albourne Cl. BN2: Brig . . . 6F 132
TN38: St Leo . . . 6F 126
Alcazar Ct. BN21: Eastb . . . 8C 154 (2J 161)
Alces Pl. BN25: Sea . . . 7D 150
ALCISTON . . . 5B 138
Alciston M. BN21: Eastb . . . 1D 160 (6L 161)
Aldborough Rd. TN37: St Leo . . . 5J 127
Aldenham Ct. BN21: Eastb . . . 5J 161
ALDERBROOK . . . 4D 36
Alderbrook Cl. TN6: Crow . . . 4E 36
Alderbrook Cotts. TN6: Crow . . . 3E 36
Alderbrook Path TN6: Crow . . . 4E 36
(off Alderbrook Cl.)
Alderbrook Way TN6: Crow . . . 4E 36
Alder Cl. BN23: Eastb . . . 4F 154
TN4: South . . . 4F 8
TN21: H'fld . . . 3D 76
TN37: St Leo . . . 1J 127
Alder La. TN17: Rolv . . . 1A 46
Alders Av. RH19: E Grin . . . 1D 10
Alders Vw. Dr. RH19: E Grin . . . 1E 10
Alderton Ct. TN39: Bex S . . . 2J 145
Aldervale Cotts. TN6: Crow . . . 3E 36
Aldrich Cl. BN2: Brig . . . 7G 133
ALDRINGTON . . . 6H 131
Aldrington Av. BN3: Hove . . . 5J 131
Aldrington Cl. BN3: Hove . . . 6F 130
ALDRINGTON HOUSE DAY HOSPITAL
. . . 7H 131
Aldrington Pl. BN3: Hove . . . 5F 130
Aldrington Station (Rail) . . . 5J 131
Alexander Ct. TN39: Bex S . . . 9E 124
Alexander Dr. TN39: Bex S . . . 1F 144
Alexander Mead BN8: N'wck . . . 9K 51
Alexandra Cl. BN25: Sea . . . 7D 150
Alexandra Ct. BN3: Hove . . . 3H 131
BN21: Eastb . . . 9C 154 (4H 161)
Alexandra Ho. BN21: Eastb . . . 4H 161
Alexandra Pde. TN34: Hast . . . 3K 127
(off Park Av.)
Alexandra Pk. Mans. TN34: Hast . . . 4L 127
Alexandra Rd. BN22: Eastb . . . 6G 155
RH15: Burg H . . . 6D 68
TN20: May . . . 7F 38
TN21: H'fld . . . 2E 76
TN22: Uck . . . 2J 73
TN37: St Leo . . . 6J 127
Alexandra Ter. TN20: May . . . 7F 38
(off Alexandra Rd.)
Alexandra, The TN37: St Leo . . . 7K 127
Alexandra Vs. BN1: Brig . . . 7A 132 (5C 162)
Alfa Ct. BN10: Tels C . . . 5A 148
Alford Way TN40: Bex S . . . 8M 125
Alfray Rd. TN40: Bex S . . . 9A 126
Alfred Davey Ct. BN1: Brig . . . 6E 162
Alfred Rd. BN1: Brig . . . 7A 132 (5C 162)
BN23: Eastb . . . 4J 155
TN35: Hast . . . 3B 128
Alfred St. TN38: St Leo . . . 7J 127
ALFRISTON . . . 1L 151
Alfriston Camping Pk. BN26: Alfr . . . 2L 151
Alfriston Clergy House . . . 2M 151
Alfriston Cl. BN2: Brig . . . 7G 132
BN20: Eastb . . . 1N 159
TN39: Bex S . . . 8D 124
Alfriston Pk. BN25: Sea . . . 7H 151
Alfriston Rd. BN25: Sea . . . 8F 150
BN26: Alfr, B'wck . . . 9E 138
Alice Bright La. TN6: Crow . . . 3D 36
Alice Cl. BN3: Hove . . . 8M 131
Alice St. BN3: Hove . . . 8M 131
Allan Cl. TN4: R'hall . . . 9N 7
Allandale Rd. TN2: Tun W . . . 7G 9
Allards TN35: Gues T . . . 7H 107
Allchorn Pleasure Boats . . . 1E 160
(off Lower Pde.)
Allen Rd. RH16: Hay H . . . 4H 49
Allen's Cl. RH19: A'hstw . . . 6K 11
Allen Way TN40: Bex S . . . 7N 125
Allesley BN20: Eastb . . . 2B 160
(off Meads Rd.)
Allfrey Rd. BN22: Eastb . . . 6G 154
Allfreys La. TN6: Crow . . . 4B 36
Allington Cres. BN8: N'wck . . . 1J 71
Allington La. BN7: Cooks, Off . . . 9C 92
Allington Rd. BN8: N'wck . . . 2H 71
All Saints Arts & Youth Cen. . . . 5K 115
(off Friar's Wlk.)
All Saints Cres. TN35: Hast . . . 6A 128
All Saints Gdns. TN21: H'fld . . . 1C 76
All Saints La. TN39: Bex S . . . 7J 125
All Saints Ri. TN4: Tun W . . . 7D 8
All Saints Rd. TN4: Tun W . . . 7D 8
TN18: Hawk . . . 1A 44
All Saints' St. TN34: Hast . . . 6A 128
Allwood Cres. RH17: Wivel G . . . 4K 69
Alma Rd. RH16: Lind . . . 1J 49
Alma Ter. TN37: St Leo . . . 4J 127
Alma Vs. TN37: St Leo . . . 4J 127
Almhouses, The RH16: Hay H . . . 6D 48
(off Heyworth Ride)
Almonry Flds. TN33: Batt . . . 3J 103
Almonry, The . . . 2L 103
(off High St.)
Alpine Rd. BN3: Hove . . . 5H 131
TN34: Hast . . . 6N 127
Alverstone Cl. BN23: Lang . . . 9L 141
Amanda Cl. TN40: Bex S . . . 7N 125
Ambassadors, The BN3: Hove . . . 7L 131
(off Wilbury Rd.)
Amber Ct. BN3: Hove . . . 6M 131
(Holland Rd.)
BN3: Hove . . . 7L 131
(Salisbury Rd.)
Amberleaze Dr. TN2: Pem . . . 7N 9
Amberley BN21: Eastb . . . 2C 160 (9J 161)
Amberley Cl. BN3: Hove . . . 2G 131
RH15: Burg H . . . 4B 68
RH16: Hay H . . . 5E 48
Amberley Ct. TN4: Tun W . . . 5F 8
Amberley Dr. BN3: Hove . . . 3G 131
Amberley Lodge BN2: Brig . . . 7G 132
(off Whitehawk Way)
Amberley Rd. BN22: Will . . . 3N 153
AMBERSTONE . . . 3H 121
Amberstone Cl. TN34: Hast . . . 2N 127
AMBERSTONE HOSPITAL . . . 2H 121
Amberstone Vw. BN27: Hails . . . 3F 120
Ambleside Av. BN10: Tels C . . . 5A 148
Ambleside Ct. BN10: Tels C . . . 5A 148
America La. RH16: Hay H . . . 4H 49
(not continuous)
Amesbury Cres. BN3: Hove . . . 6G 131
Amherst Cl. TN34: Hast . . . 5K 127
Amherst Cres. BN3: Hove . . . 5H 131
Amherst Gdns. TN34: Hast . . . 5K 127
Amherst Rd. TN4: Tun W . . . 8D 8
TN34: Hast . . . 5J 127
TN40: Bex S . . . 1K 145
Amhurst Rd. BN10: Tels C . . . 5N 147
Ancaster Ho. BN21: Eastb . . . 9K 161
Anchorage Way BN23: Eastb . . . 2L 155
Anchor Ct. BN22: Eastb. . . . 7F 154
Anchor Fld. BN8: Ring . . . 1C 116
Anchor Hill RH17: Scay H . . . 7A 50
Anchor La. BN8: Barc . . . 1N 93
(Dallas La.)
BN8: Barc, Barc M . . . 4N 93
(Crink Hill)
Anderida BN21: Eastb . . . 8C 154 (3J 161)
Anderida Ct. TN39: Bex S . . . 1D 144
Anderida Rd. BN22: Eastb, Will . . . 1M 153
Anderida Roman Fort . . . 7C 142
Anderson Cl. BN9: N'hvn . . . 5H 149
Andrew Rd. TN4: Tun W . . . 5F 8
Andrews Cl. TN2: Tun W . . . 8G 8
TN32: Rob . . . 4K 61
Andwell Ct. BN21: Eastb . . . 6M 161
Angela Cl. TN40: Bex S . . . 7N 125
Angel Ter. TN18: Sandh . . . 4H 45
Anglesea Ter. TN38: St Leo . . . 6J 127
Anglesey Av. BN27: Hails . . . 4D 120
Angmering Ct. BN1: Brig . . . 9G 112
(off Newick Rd.)
Anguilla Ct. BN23: Eastb . . . 5K 155
Angus Cl. BN20: Will . . . 3M 153
Ann Cl. BN6: Hass . . . 2B 90
Anne of Cleves House . . . 6J 115
(off Southover High St.)
Annes Path BN7: Lewes . . . 7J 115
Annington Rd.
BN22: Eastb . . . 7E 154 (1N 161)
Ann St. BN1: Brig . . . 6B 132 (4E 162)
TN34: Hast . . . 4A 128
Anscome RH16: Hay H . . . 3E 48
(off Great Heathmead)
Anson Cl. BN23: Eastb . . . 5H 155
Anson Ho. BN10: Peace . . . 3C 148
Ansty Cl. BN2: Brig . . . 8F 132
Antares Path BN27: Hails . . . 7H 121
Anthony Cl. BN25: Sea . . . 6A 150
Antigua Cl. BN23: Eastb . . . 4J 155
Antioch St. BN7: Lewes . . . 6J 115
Antrim Ct. BN23: Lang . . . 3G 154
Antrona Cl. TN39: Bex S . . . 2D 144
Anvil Cl. BN41: Ports . . . 3D 130
TN22: Uck . . . 2G 73
Anvil Ct. TN37: St Leo . . . 1J 127
Anzac Cl. BN10: Peace . . . 3C 148
Apex Pk. BN27: Hails . . . 7D 120
(not continuous)
Apex Way BN27: Hails . . . 7D 120
Appledene Corner BN8: S Chai . . . 9E 70
Appledore Cl. BN23: Lang . . . 2G 155
Appledore Ct. RH16: Lind . . . 2H 49
Appledore Gdns. RH16: Lind . . . 3H 49
Appledore Rd. BN2: Brig . . . 1G 132
Applesham Av. BN3: Hove . . . 3G 130
Applesham Way BN41: Ports . . . 4C 130
Apple Tree La. TN2: Tun W . . . 5G 8
Applewalk RH15: Burg H . . . 4B 68
Applewood Cl. TN37: St Leo . . . 1H 127
Approach, The BN1: Brig . . . 2N 131
April Pl. TN40: Bex S . . . 1K 145
Aqua Ct. BN10: Tels C . . . 5N 147
Aquarius Cl. BN10: Peace . . . 6C 148
Aquila Pk. BN25: Sea . . . 9F 150
Arbor Ct. RH16: Hay H . . . 4F 48
Arbourvale TN38: St Leo . . . 5G 126
Archer Ct. RH15: Burg H . . . 5B 68
Archery Ct. BN22: Eastb . . . 6F 154
(off Willoughby Cres.)
TN38: St Leo . . . 8H 127
Archery La. BN22: Eastb . . . 6G 154
Archery Rd. TN38: St Leo . . . 7H 127
Archery Wlk. BN27: Hails . . . 7F 120
Archie Ct. TN38: St Leo . . . 8H 127
(off Marina)
Ardarragh Mans.
BN22: Eastb . . . 8D 154 (3L 161)
Ardingly Ct. BN2: Brig . . . 8G 162
Ardingly Rd. BN2: Salt . . . 4L 147
RH17: Cuck . . . 2A 48

Ardingly St.—Bardown Rd.

Ardingly St. BN2: Brig 8C 132 (8G 162)
Arena Ho. BN1: Brig 7E 162
Arequipa Reef BN23: Eastb 4K 155
Argent Cl. BN25: Sea 7F 150
ARGOS HILL 5A 38
Argos Hill Rd. TN6: May 7N 37
TN20: May 7N 37
Argos Lofts BN1: Brig 6E 162
Argyle Ct. BN22: Eastb 2B 154
Argyle Rd. BN1: Brig 5A 132 (2D 162)
TN4: South 3D 8
Argyle Vs. BN1: Brig 2D 162
Argyll Ct. TN39: Bex S 1H 145
(off Eridge Cl.)
Arena Ho. BN1: Brig 6E 162
Arkwright Rd. BN23: Eastb 3D 154
ARLINGTON 2K 139
Arlington Ct. RH16: Hay H 4F 48
Arlington Cres. BN1: Brig 9F 112
Arlington Eagles Rdbt.
BN27: Hails 9C 120
Arlington Gdns. BN2: Salt 1L 147
Arlington Ho. BN21: Eastb 8B 154
(off Upperton Rd.)
Arlington Lodge BN21: Eastb 6L 161
Arlington M. BN2: Brig 9E 132
(off Eastern Rd.)
Arlington Rd.
BN21: Eastb 9C 154 (5H 161)
Arlington Rd. E. BN27: Hails 8D 120
Arlington Rd. W. BN27: Hails 8B 120
Arlington Stadium (Speedway) 8A 120
Armitage Pl. TN18: Hawk 9N 31
Armstrong Cl. TN38: St Leo 2E 126
Arnbury M. TN38: St Leo 8E 126
Arnold St. BN2: Brig 6D 132
Arnside Rd. TN38: St Leo 8E 126
Arnworth Ct. BN21: Eastb 1C 160 (7J 161)
Arran Cl. BN27: Hails 4D 120
Arthur Rd. TN39: Bex S 1J 145
Arthur St. BN3: Hove 5J 131
Artisans Dwellings BN21: Eastb 6J 161
Arts Rd. BN1: Falm 7J 113
Arun Cl. BN24: Sto C 8J 141
(off Arun Way)
Arundel Cl. BN24: Pev B 7H 143
BN27: Hails 4F 120
Arundel Ct. BN1: Brig 9L 111
(off Mill Ri.)
BN2: Brig 9F 132
BN21: Eastb 8C 154 (2J 161)
RH15: Burg H 4A 68
(off West St.)
Arundel Dr. E. BN2: Salt 3K 147
Arundel Dr. W. BN2: Salt 3J 147
Arundel Grn. BN7: Lewes 4H 115
Arundel Ho. BN21: Eastb 4H 161
BN21: Eastb 8B 154
(off Michel Gro.)
Arundel Keep
BN21: Eastb 8C 154 (3H 161)
Arundel M RH16: Hay H 7G 48
Arundel M. BN2: Brig 9F 132
(off Arundel Pl.)
Arundel Pl. BN2: Brig 9F 132
Arundel Rd. BN2: Brig 9F 132
BN9: N'hvn 3L 149
BN10: Peace 5B 148
(not continuous)
BN21: Eastb 8C 154 (3G 161)
BN25: Sea 9F 150
TN1: Tun W 2E 16
Arundel Rd. W. BN10: Peace 4A 148
Arundel St. BN2: Brig 9F 132
Arundel Ter. BN2: Brig 9F 132
Arun Ho. BN21: Eastb 9B 154 (3G 161)
Arun Path TN22: Uck 8K 53
Arun Way BN24: Sto C 8J 141
Ascham Pl. BN20: Eastb 2B 160
Ascot Cl. BN20: Eastb 3C 160 (9H 161)
Ascot M. TN38: St Leo 6G 127
Ashampstead Pl. BN21: Eastb 4H 161
Ashbourne Ct. BN21: Eastb 7L 161
Ashbrook Rd. TN37: St Leo 2H 127
ASHBURNHAM 2M 101
Ashburnham Cl. BN1: Brig 9E 112
Ashburnham Dr. BN1: Brig 8E 112
Ashburnham Gdns.
BN21: Eastb 7B 154
Ashburnham Pl. BN27: Hails 4D 120
Ashburnham Rd.
BN21: Eastb 8B 154 (1G 161)
TN35: Hast 5A 128
Ashby Cl. TN39: Bex S 6H 125
Ash Cl. BN3: Hove 2L 131
BN22: Eastb 1B 154
TN2: Tun W 4G 16
Ashcombe Dr. TN39: Bex S 2E 144
Ashcombe Hollow
BN7: King L, Lewes 7E 114
Ashcombe La. BN7: King L 8E 114
Ash Ct. BN27: Hails 7D 120
BN42: S'wck 4B 130
RH19: E Grin 1E 10
Ashcroft Cl. BN8: Ring 1C 116
Ashdown BN3: Hove 7L 131
Ashdown Av. BN2: Salt 3J 147
Ashdown Chase TN22: Nut 5B 34
Ashdown Cl. RH16: Hay H 5J 49
RH18: F Row 1N 21
TN4: Tun W 9C 8
TN38: St Leo 4E 126
Ashdown Ct. RH19: E Grin 2E 10
(off Tower Cl.)
TN6: Crow 9C 24
(off Mill La.)
TN22: Uck 2J 73
(off Vernon Rd.)
Ashdown Forest 3F 34
Ashdown Forest Cen., The 6N 21
Ashdown Forest Llama Farm 7L 21
Ashdown Ga. RH19: E Grin 2D 10
Ashdown Pl. RH18: F Row 3L 21
TN21: H'fld 2E 76
Ashdown Rd. BN2: Brig 5C 132
RH18: F Row 1M 21
TN40: Bex S 1L 145
Ashdown Vw. RH19: E Grin 5E 10
TN22: Nut 4C 34
Ash Dr. BN25: Sea 9H 151
Ashenden Wlk. TN2: Tun W 5H 9
Ashendon Av. TN31: Rye 3E 86
Ashenground Cl. RH16: Hay H 6F 48
Ashenground Rd. RH16: Hay H 6E 48
Asher Reeds TN3: Lang G 9L 7
Ashford Cl. BN27: Hails 7F 120
Ashford Rd. BN1: Brig 3B 132
BN21: Eastb 9D 154 (5K 161)
TN34: Hast 4L 127
Ashford Sq. BN21: Eastb 9D 154 (4L 161)
Ashford Way TN34: Hast 4L 127
Ashgate Rd. BN23: Lang 2H 155
Ash Gro. BN24: W'ham 7N 141
RH16: Hay H 6E 48
Ashington Ct. BN2: Brig 7G 132
(off Whitehawk Way)
Ashington Gdns. BN10: Peace 6E 148
Ashington Rd. BN22: Eastb 3D 154
Ashlands TN6: Crow 1F 36
Ashleigh Gdns. TN6: Crow 7C 24
Ashleigh Glegg Ho. BN25: Sea 8C 150
(off Grosvenor Rd.)
Ashley Cl. BN1: Brig 7N 111
Ashley Ct. TN37: St Leo 7J 127
(off Terrace Rd.)
Ashley Gdns. BN22: Eastb 6F 154
(off Willoughby Cres.)
BN27: Hails 3F 120
TN4: R'hall 9N 7
TN20: May 8D 38
Ashley Ho. BN3: Hove 8K 131
Ashley Pk. TN4: R'hall 8N 7
Ashley Pk. Cl. TN4: R'hall 8N 7
Ashley Rd. TN6: Town R 1A 38
Ashlings Way BN3: Hove 3G 130
Ashmore Cl. BN10: Peace 2D 148
Ashtead Towers TN40: Bex S 1M 145
ASHTON GREEN 1F 116
Ashton Lodge BN2: Brig 6G 162
Ashton Ri. BN2: Brig 7C 132 (6G 162)
Ashtonville Cl. BN8: Ring 1D 116
Ash Tree Cl. TN21: H'fld 1D 76
ASHURST 2C 14
Ashurst Av. BN2: Salt 4M 147
Ashurst Hill TN3: A'hst 2B 14
Ashurst La. BN6: Plump, Streat 4K 91
BN7: Plump 4K 91
Ashurst Pl. RH16: Hay H 4F 48
Ashurst Rd. BN2: Brig 9G 113
BN25: Sea 1E 156
TN3: A'hst, F'cmbe 1D 14
Ashurst Station (Rail) 2B 14
ASHURSTWOOD 6K 11
Ash Wlk. BN9: N'hvn 5H 149
Ash Way RH15: Burg H 6B 68
Ashwyn Bus. Cen. RH15: Burg H 3A 68
Aspen Cl. RH16: Hay H 5J 49
Aspen Rd. BN22: Eastb 2B 154
Aspen Wlk. RH16: Hay H 5J 49
TN21: H'fld 3E 76
Aspen Way TN4: South 4F 8
TN39: Bex S 1D 144
Aspley St. TN4: R'hall 9A 8
Assembly Hall Theatre, The 9E 8
Assisi Ct. RH16: Hay H 7G 49
Astaire Av. BN22: Eastb 7E 154
Asten Cl. TN38: St Leo 7E 126
Asten Flds. TN33: Batt 2K 103
Astra Ho. BN1: Brig 8B 162
Athelstan Cl. BN23: Eastb 3J 155
Athelston Rd. TN35: Hast 4C 128
Athenaeum, The BN3: Hove 7L 131
Atlantic Dr. BN23: Eastb 4J 155
Atlingworth Ct. BN2: Brig 9C 132
(off Atlingworth St.)
Atlingworth St. BN2: Brig 9C 132
Atrium Ho. BN1: Brig 6E 162
(off Regent St.)
Atrium, The 3E 10
Attfield Wlk. BN22: Eastb 1C 154
(not continuous)
Attree Ct. BN2: Brig 7D 132
Attree Dr. BN2: Brig 7D 132
Auckland Dr. BN2: Brig 4G 133
Auckland Ho. TN40: Bex S 7K 125
Auckland Quay BN23: Eastb 3K 155
Auckland Rd. TN1: Tun W 7F 8
Audrey Cl. BN1: Brig 9N 111
BN25: Sea 7C 150
Audrey Sturley Ct. TN4: R'hall 9A 8
Augustines Way RH16: Hay H 5G 48
Augustus Way TN37: St Leo 9F 104
Aultmore Ct. TN2: Tun W 1F 16
Austen Cl. RH19: E Grin 3B 10
Austen Wlk. BN23: Lang 2G 155
Austen Way TN35: Hast 1C 128
Avard Cres. BN20: Eastb 6M 153
Avards Cl. TN18: Hawk 2M 43
Avenue BN1: Brig 8E 162
Avenue Ct. BN3: Hove 7L 131
(off Palmeira Av.)
BN21: Eastb 4J 161
Avenue La. BN21: Eastb 9C 154 (4J 161)
Avenue Mans. BN21: Eastb 6M 161
Avenue M. BN21: Eastb 4J 161
Avenue Pl. BN21: Eastb 4J 161
Avenue, The BN2: Brig 3E 132
(not continuous)
BN7: King L 9D 114
BN7: Lewes 5H 115
BN21: Eastb 9C 154 (5J 161)
BN27: Hails 8E 120
TN20: May 8E 38
TN21: H'fld 2E 76
TN21: Horam 8C 76
TN35: Fair 2L 129
Avery Cl. BN41: Ports 1B 130
Aviemore Rd. TN6: Crow 9B 24
Avis Cl. BN9: N'hvn 3L 149
Avis Pde. Shops BN9: N'hvn 3L 149
(off Avis Rd.)
Avis Rd. BN9: N'hvn 3K 149
(not continuous)
Avis Way BN9: N'hvn 3L 149
Avis Way Ind. Est. BN9: N'hvn 3K 149
Avocet BN27: Hails 7D 120
Avocet Trad. Est. RH15: Burg H 6A 68
Avon Ct. BN2: Brig 8C 132
(off Mt. Pleasant)
BN23: Lang 1F 154
Avondale Ct. BN25: Sea 9D 150
(off Avondale Rd.)
Avondale Rd. BN3: Hove 6M 131 (3A 162)
BN22: Eastb 8E 154 (2N 161)
BN25: Sea 9D 150
TN38: St Leo 5G 126
Avonhurst RH15: Burg H 5C 68
Avonmore BN20: Eastb 3B 160 (9G 161)
Avon St. TN1: Tun W 8F 8
Awbrook Cl. RH17: Scay H 6N 49
Aylesbury BN3: Hove 7N 131 (5A 162)
Aylesbury Av. BN23: Eastb 4H 155
Aymer Ho. BN3: Hove 7J 131
Aymer Rd. BN3: Hove 7J 131
Aynsley Ct. BN3: Hove 5L 131
Ayscue Cl. BN23: Eastb 5J 155
Ayscue Ct. BN23: Eastb 5J 155

B

Babylon BN20: Jev 4H 153
Babylon Way BN20: Will 4M 153
BACHELOR'S BUMP 9D 106
Back La. BN26: Milt S 9G 139
TN21: Cross H, Wald 9N 55
(St Olive's Cl.)
TN21: Rush G 8N 77
(Marklye La.)
TN22: Nut 8G 35
TN36: Winch 9C 86
Back Rd. TN18: Sandh 5H 45
Backwoods Cl. RH16: Lind 3J 49
Backwoods La. RH16: Lind 3H 49
Baden Rd. BN2: Brig 4E 132
Badens Cl. BN8: N'wck 2J 71
Badger Cl. BN41: Ports 3D 130
Badger Dr. RH16: Hay H 4D 48
Badger Ga. TN31: Rye 3E 86
Badgers Brow BN20: Will 4M 153
Badgers Cl. TN6: Crow 8C 24
Badgers Copse BN25: Sea 9H 151
Badgers Dene BN7: Rod 5K 135
Badgers Fld. BN10: Peace 3C 148
Badgers Holt TN2: Tun W 8H 9
Badgers Mt. TN39: Bex S 9F 124
Badgers Wlk. BN27: Chal 3G 118
RH15: Burg H 6D 68
Badger's Way RH19: E Grin 2F 10
Badgers Way TN34: Hast 1K 127
Badger Way BN1: Brig 8F 112
Badlesmere Rd. BN22: Eastb 6D 154
Bagham La. BN27: Herst 9A 100
Bahram Rd. BN26: Pole 7C 140
Bailey Cres. BN22: Will 1M 153
Baillie Av. BN22: Eastb 7F 154
Bainbridge Cl. BN25: Sea 9E 150
Bainden Cl. TN6: Town R 1A 38
Baird Dr. TN34: Hast 3L 127
Baird Ho. TN37: St Leo 6J 127
Baker Ct. TN22: Uck 1H 73
Bakers Farm Pk. Homes
BN27: Hails 3D 120
Bakers La. TN21: Dall 4G 78
Bakers Rd. BN21: Eastb 9A 154
Baker St. BN1: Brig 6B 132 (4F 162)
BN9: N'hvn 5L 149
TN22: Uck 2J 73
Bakery M. BN2: Brig 4D 132
Bakery Pl. TN32: Rob 5J 61
Bakewell Rd. BN21: Eastb 8A 154
Balaclava La. TN5: Wadh 4B 28
Balcombe Ct. BN10: Peace 4B 148
Balcombe Grn. TN33: Sed 7E 82
Balcombe La. RH17: Sharp 8D 20
RH19: Hors K, Sharp 8D 20
Balcombe Rd. BN10: Peace 4B 148
RH16: Hay H 1E 48
Baldock Rd. TN5: Wadh 7A 28
BALDSLOW 8H 105
Baldslow Down TN37: St Leo 6J 105
Baldslow Rd. TN34: Hast 4M 127
Baldwin Av. BN21: Eastb 6N 153
Baldwins Fld. RH19: E Grin 1D 10
BALDWINS HILL 1D 10
Baldwins La. TN4: Tun W 5F 8
Bale Cl. TN39: Bex S 9F 124
Bal Edmund TN37: St Leo 2H 127
Balfour Gdns. RH18: F Row 3L 21
Balfour Rd. BN1: Brig 3A 132
Balfour Vs. BN1: Brig 3B 132
Ballard Dr. BN8: Ring 7E 94
Ballards Hill TN31: North 9B 46
TN33: C'hrst 2N 125
BALL'S GREEN 7N 13
Ball's Grn. TN7: Withy 7N 13
Ballsocks La. TN21: Vine C 8F 76
Balmoral RH19: E Grin 4G 10
Balmoral Cl. BN25: Sea 6F 150
Balmoral Ct. BN3: Hove 2J 131
Balneath La.
BN8: Cooks, S Chai 8G 70
BALSDEAN 8B 134
Balsdean Rd. BN2: W'dean 4L 133
Baltic Ho. TN1: Tun W 9E 8
(off Goods Sta. Rd.)
Baltimore Ct. BN3: Hove 6L 131
Bamford Cl. BN2: Brig 3H 133
Bampfield St. BN41: Ports 5D 130
Bancroft Ho. TN39: Bex S 9J 125
Bancroft Rd. TN39: Bex S 9J 125
Bank Bldgs. TN21: Horam 9C 76
(off High St.)
TN34: Hast 7M 127
(off Queen's Rd.)
Bank Rd. TN39: Bex S 7K 125
Bankside BN1: Brig 9L 111
BN6: Hass 2A 90
TN5: Wadh 6A 28
TN31: Rye 2E 86
Bankside Ct. BN1: Brig 9L 111
(off Bankside)
Banks Rd. BN8: N Cha 8E 50
Bannatyne Health Club 2D 154
Banner Farm Rd. TN2: Tun W 2E 16
Banner Way BN24: Sto C 7L 141
Bannings Va. BN2: Salt 4L 147
Bannisters Fld. BN8: N'wck 1L 71
Bannister Way RH16: Hay H 3E 48
Baranscraig Av. BN1: Brig 7B 112
Barbados TN40: Bex S 2M 145
Barber Ct. BN7: Lewes 6H 115
(off St Pancras Rd.)
Barbican House Mus. 5J 115
Barbuda Quay BN23: Eastb 5K 155
Barchester Pl. BN21: Eastb 7K 161
Barclay Ho. BN2: Brig 6C 132
BARCOMBE 5L 93
Barcombe Av. BN25: Sea 9H 151
Barcombe Cl. BN20: Eastb 9N 153
BN25: Sea 9H 151
BARCOMBE CROSS 3L 93
BARCOMBE MILLS 4N 93
Barcombe Mills Rd.
BN8: Barc, Barc C, Barc M 3L 93
(not continuous)
Barcombe Pl. BN1: Brig 9G 113
BN8: Barc C 3L 93
TN6: Crow 8D 24
Barcombe Rd. BN1: Brig 1F 132
Barcombe Wlk. BN20: Eastb 9N 153
Barden Rd. BN22: Eastb 8F 154
TN3: Bid, Speld 3K 7
BARDOWN 3G 41
Bardown Rd. TN5: S'gate, Tice 2F 40

Barford Ct.—Beltry Ct.

Barford Ct. *TN22: Uck* *1H* ***73***
(off Grange Rd.)
Barganny TN40: Bex S 2L **145**
Bargate Cl. TN39: Bex S 7K **125**
Barham Cl. TN34: Hast 2K **127**
Barkdale RH15: Burg H 3E **68**
Barkham Manor Vineyard 9A **52**
Barley Av. TN35: Hast 5B **128**
Barley Cl. BN10: Tels C 2B **148**
Barley Fld. Cotts. BN7: Rod 4K **135**
Barley Grattens *TN33: Neth* *6D* ***80***
(off Netherfield Rd.)
Barley La. TN35: Hast 5B **128**
Barley Mow La. TN21: Punn T 4L **77**
Barming Cl. BN23: Lang 2G **154**
Barnard Ga. RH16: Hay H 2F **48**
Barn Cl. BN7: King L 9E **114**
BN24: Sto C 7K **141**
BN25: Sea .7F **150**
BN27: Hails 5F **120**
TN37: St Leo 1J **127**
Barn Cottage La.
RH16: Hay H 4H **49**
Barn Cotts. BN25: Sea 9F **150**
Barnes Rd. BN41: Ports 5D **130**
Barnett Rd. BN1: Brig 3C **132**
Barnetts Cl. TN4: South 4F **8**
Barnetts Hill TN31: Peas 6K **65**
Barnetts Way TN4: South 4F **8**
Barnett Way TN22: Uck 1J **73**
Barnet Way BN3: Hove 2G **130**
Barnfield BN7: Plump G 2M **91**
TN2: Tun W 5C **16**
TN6: Crow .9E **24**
Barnfield Cl. TN34: Hast 6K **127**
Barnfield Gdns. BN2: Brig 7D **132**
BN6: Ditch .4F **90**
Barnham Cl. BN22: Eastb 2D **154**
Barnhams, The TN39: Bex S 2F **144**
Barn Hatch Cl. BN7: Lewes 6G **114**
Barnholme Mnr. Farm Cvn. Pk.
TN39: Bex S 1C **144**
Barnhorn Cl. TN39: Bex S 1D **144**
Barnhorn Rd. TN33: Bex S 1M **143**
TN39: Bex S 1M **143**
Barn Ho., The BN25: Sea 7D **150**
Barn La. TN22: Fram 9B **54**
Barnmead RH16: Hay H 2E **48**
Barn Ri. BN1: Brig 9M **111**
BN25: Sea .7F **150**
Barn Rd. BN7: Lewes 3L **115**
Barnsgate Manor Vineyard 5K **35**
Barnside Av. RH15: Burg H 7D **68**
Barons Cl. BN25: Sea 7B **150**
Barons Ct. RH15: Burg H 6C **68**
TN4: Tun W .8D **8**
Barons Down Rd. BN7: Lewes 6G **114**
Barons Wlk. BN7: Lewes 6G **115**
Barons Way BN26: Pole 8C **140**
Barrack rd. TN40: Bex S 9K **125**
Barrack Sq. TN36: Winch 9D **86**
Barrack Yd. BN1: Brig 7F **162**
Barrhill Av. BN1: Brig 7A **112**
Barrie Cl. BN23: Lang 2H **155**
Barrier Reef Way BN23: Eastb 2K **155**
Barrington Cl. RH16: Lind 1H **49**
Barrington Rd. RH16: Lind 1G **49**
Barrington Wood RH16: Lind 1G **49**
Barrow Cl. BN1: Brig 3D **132**
Barrowfield RH17: Cuck 2A **48**
Barrowfield Cl. BN3: Hove 2L **131**
Barrowfield Dr. BN3: Hove 3L **131**
Barrowfield Lodge BN3: Hove 3L **131**
Barrow Hill BN1: Brig 3D **132**
Barrow La. TN3: Lang G 2K **15**
Barrow Ri. TN37: St Leo 1J **127**
Barry Wlk. BN2: Brig 7D **132**
Bartholomews BN1: Brig 8B **132** (8E **162**)
Bartholomew Sq. BN1: Brig 9E **162**
Bartley Mill Cl. BN24: Sto C 8L **141**
Bartley Mill La. TN3: Lamb 8A **18**
Bartley Mill Rd.
TN3: Lamb, Wadh 8A **18**
TN5: Cous W, Wadh 1B **28**
Barton Cres. RH19: E Grin 4G **11**
Basin Rd. Nth. BN41: Ports 7E **130**
Basin Rd. Sth. BN42: S'wck 7A **130**
Baslow Rd. BN20: Eastb 4A **160**
Bassett's Forge TN5: Wadh 6A **28**
Bassetts La. TN8: Chid H 6N **5**
TN20: May .5C **38**
TN20: Wadh 8H **27**
Batchelor Cres. TN6: Crow 8D **24**
Batchelors TN2: Pem 5N **9**
Batchelor Way TN22: Uck 1F **72**
Bateman's 5J **59**
Bateman's La. TN19: B'wsh 4H **59**
Batemans Rd. BN2: W'dean 6M **133**
Bates Rd. BN1: Brig 3A **132**
Bath Ct. *BN3: Hove* *8K* ***131***
(off King's Esplanade)
Bathford Cl. BN23: Lang 2G **155**
Bath Rd. BN21: Eastb 1C **160** (6J **161**)
Bath St. BN1: Brig 6A **132** (4C **162**)
Battenhurst Rd.
TN5: Etch, S'gate 5K **41**
TN19: Etch .5K **41**
Battery Hill TN35: Fair 1H **129**
BATTLE 3L **103**
Battle Abbey 3L **103**
Battle Area Sports Cen. 3J **103**
Battle Cl. BN25: Sea 7H **151**
Battle Cres. BN27: Hails 6E **120**
TN37: St Leo 2H **127**
Battle Gates TN33: Batt 3J **103**
Battle Hill TN33: Batt 4M **103**
Battle Mus. *2L* ***103***
(off High St.)
Battle Rd. BN27: Hails 6E **120**
TN21: Dall 5J **79**
TN32: Mount, Rob 7J **61**
TN32: Staple, What 3A **82**
TN33: Dall, Neth 5N **79**
TN37: Hast, St Leo 8F **104**
TN38: St Leo 7F **104**
Battle Station (Rail) 3M **103**
Batts Bri. Rd.
TN22: Mare, Pilt 6D **52**
Batts Bri. Rdbt. TN22: Mare 5E **52**
Bavant Rd. BN1: Brig 3N **131**
Baxter Rd. BN7: Lewes 4H **115**
Baxters La. RH17: Chel C 4J **33**
Baxter St. BN2: Brig 6D **132**
Bay Av. BN24: Pev B 8G **142**
Bay Cotts. BN24: Nor B 6L **143**
Bayden Cotts. *BN27: Bore S* *1D* ***122***
(off Victoria Rd.)
Bayencourt Nth. TN40: Bex S 9K **125**
Bayencourt Sth. TN40: Bex S 9K **125**
Bayeux Ct. *TN40: Bex S* *2L* ***145***
(off Middlesex Rd.)
Bayhall Rd. TN2: Tun W 1F **16**
Bayham Abbey 7E **18**
Bayham Rd. BN22: Eastb 8F **154**
BN27: Hails 7F **120**
TN2: Tun W 4E **16**
TN3: Bell G .7J **17**
Bayhams Fld. RH19: Sharp 5A **20**
Bayley's La. BN26: Arl 2L **139**
Bay Pond Rd. BN21: Eastb 8A **154**
Bay Rd. BN24: Pev B 9F **142**
Bay Ter. *BN24: Pev B* *8F* ***142***
(off Marine Ter.)
Baytree Cl. TN21: H'fld 3E **76**
Bay Tree La. BN26: Pole 5C **140**
Bay Tree La. Link BN26: Pole 5C **140**
Bay Vw. Camping & Caravanning Pk.
BN24: Pev B 2L **155**
Bayview Rd. BN10: Peace 7E **148**
Bay Vue Rd. BN9: N'hvn 5J **149**
Baywood Gdns. BN2: W'dean 5K **133**
Bazehill Rd. BN2: Rott 2G **147**
Beach Cl. BN9: N'hvn 6L **149**
BN25: Sea .9C **150**
Beach Cotts. BN25: Sea 8B **150**
Beachings, The BN24: Pev B 9E **142**
BEACHLANDS 7H **143**
Beachlands Way BN24: Pev B 7H **143**
Beach M. BN9: N'hvn 5L **149**
Beach Rd. BN9: N'hvn 5L **149**
BN22: Eastb 7F **154**
Beach Rd. Ind. Est. BN9: N'hvn 6L **149**
Beach Towers *TN39: Bex S* *2J* ***145***
(off West Pde.)
BEACHY HEAD 7N **159**
Beachy Head Countryside Cen. 7M **159**
Beachy Head Rd.
BN20: E Dean, Eastb 6F **158**
BN20: Eastb 3N **159**
Beachy Head Vw. TN38: St Leo 8F **104**
Beacon Bus. Pk. TN6: Jar B 2G **36**
Beacon Cl. BN1: Brig 3B **132**
BN25: Sea .7C **150**
TN6: Crow .9C **24**
Beacon Ct. BN2: Oving 9L **133**
BEACON DOWN 1L **75**
Beacon Dr. BN25: Sea 7C **150**
Beaconfield Ho. TN6: Crow 8C **24**
Beacon Gdns. TN6: Crow 8C **24**
Beacon Hill BN2: Oving 1F **146**
TN39: Bex S 6G **125**
Beacon Ho. *BN3: Hove* *6F* ***130***
(off Erroll Rd.)
Beaconhurst BN6: Hass 4C **90**
Beacon La. TN31: North 2N **63**
TN32: Staple 9E **62**
Beacon Rd. BN6: Ditch 5E **90**
BN25: Sea .8C **150**
(Hawth Way)
BN25: Sea .8C **150**
(Kingsway)
TN6: Crow .2A **36**
TN35: Hast 2D **128**
Beacon Rd. W. TN6: Crow 9B **24**
Beaconsfield Pde. BN1: Brig 1E **162**
Beaconsfield Rd.
BN1: Brig 5B **132** (1E **162**)
BN41: Ports 5D **130**
Beaconsfield Rd. RH17: Chel G 1J **33**
TN34: Hast 4M **127**
TN40: Bex S 8K **125**
Beaconsfield Ter. *TN21: Cross H* *9M* ***55***
(off Firgrove Rd.)
Beaconsfield Vs.
BN1: Brig 3A **132** (1D **162**)
Beaconsville Ct. BN1: Brig 4A **132**
Beagles Wood Rd. TN2: Pem 6N **9**
(not continuous)
Beal Cres. BN1: Brig 3C **132**
Beales La. TN31: North 3A **64**
Beale St. RH15: Burg H 7A **68**
BEAL'S GREEN 7N **31**
Beame Ct. BN25: Sea 9C **150**
Beamsley Hall *BN22: Eastb* *8F* ***154***
(off Beamsley Rd.)
Beamsley Rd. BN22: Eastb 8F **154**
Beaney's La. TN34: Hast 9L **105**
TN34: Hast, W'fld 8L **105**
TN35: Hast 8L **105**
Bear Rd. BN2: Brig 5D **132**
Bear Yd. BN7: Lewes 5K **115**
Beatrice La. BN21: Eastb . . .9C **154** (4H **161**)
Beatrice Wlk. TN39: Bex S 8H **125**
Beatty Av. BN1: Brig 7E **112**
Beatty Rd. BN23: Eastb 6H **155**
Beauchamp Rd. TN38: St Leo 3G **126**
Beauford Rd. TN21: Horam 9C **76**
Beaufort Ct. BN21: Eastb 9D **154** (4K **161**)
TN37: St Leo 4J **127**
Beaufort Cres. TN37: St Leo 4J **127**
Beaufort Home Farm Cl.
TN37: St Leo 9G **104**
Beaufort Rd. TN37: St Leo 4J **127**
Beaufort Ter. BN2: Brig 7D **132**
Beauharrow Rd. TN37: St Leo 9G **104**
Beau Ho. BN1: Brig 4C **162**
Beaulieu Ct. TN40: Bex S 9N **125**
Beaulieu Dr. BN24: Sto C 8K **141**
Beaulieu Gdns. TN37: St Leo 9J **105**
Beaulieu Rd. TN39: Bex S 3D **144**
BEAUPORT 8E **104**
Beauport Gdns. TN37: St Leo 8G **104**
Beauport Pk. Holiday Village
TN37: St Leo 7G **105**
Beaver Cl. TN6: Crow 1E **36**
Beckenham Cl. BN27: Hails 3E **120**
Becket Cl. TN34: Hast 5N **127**
Beckets Fld. TN11: Pens 2E **6**
Beckets Way TN22: Fram 3N **73**
Beckett Way BN7: Lewes 3J **115**
RH19: E Grin 4F **10**
BECKLEY 4G **65**
Beckley Cl. BN2: Brig 8F **132**
TN38: St Leo 4D **126**
BECKLEY FURNACE 1C **84**
Beckley Rd. TN31: North 7A **64**
Beckworth Cl. RH16: Lind 3H **49**
Beckworth La. RH16: Lind 3H **49**
Bedales Hill RH16: Hay H 4L **49**
BEDDINGHAM 1C **136**
Beddingham Gdns. BN8: Glyn 9E **116**
Bedelands Cl. RH15: Burg H 3C **68**
Bedford Av. TN40: Bex S 2L **145**
Bedford Ct. TN22: Uck 9H **53**
Bedford Gro. BN21: Eastb . . .8C **154** (3J **161**)
Bedford Pl. BN1: Brig 8N **131** (7A **162**)
Bedford Rd. TN4: South 4C **8**
TN35: Hast 4B **128**
Bedford Sq. BN1: Brig 8N **131** (8A **162**)
Bedford St. BN2: Brig 9D **132**
Bedford Ter. TN1: Tun W 2D **16**
Bedford Towers BN1: Brig 8A **162**
Bedfordwell Ct.
BN22: Eastb 8D **154** (2L **161**)
Bedfordwell Rd.
BN21: Eastb 8C **154** (2J **161**)
Bedfordwell Rdbt. BN21: Eastb 2L **161**
Bedgebury Cl. TN38: St Leo 4E **126**
BEDGEBURY CROSS 1D **30**
Bedgebury National Pinetum 3E **30**
Bedgebury Pk. TN17: Goud 1E **30**
Bedgebury Rd. TN17: Goud 1E **30**
Bedlam Grn. BN27: Herst 9A **100**
Beecham Pl. TN38: St Leo 2F **126**
Beech Av. BN27: Chal 3G **118**
(not continuous)
Beech Cl. BN41: Ports 2B **130**
RH19: E Grin 2D **10**
TN33: Batt .9K **81**
TN39: Bex S 8D **124**
Beech Ct. *BN26: Pole* *7D* ***140***
(off Walnut Wlk.)
RH19: E Grin 2D **10**
Beech Ct. TN2: Tun W 9G **9**
Beeches Cl. TN21: H'fld 9E **56**
TN22: Uck .9J **53**
Beeches Farm Rd. TN6: Crow 1E **36**
Beeches La. RH19: A'hstw 6K **11**
Beeches Rd. BN41: Ports 2B **130**
TN6: Crow .1F **36**
Beeches, The BN1: Brig 2M **131**
TN2: Tun W .8G **9**
Beeches, The *TN6: Crow* *1F* ***36***
(off Luxford Rd.)
TN18: Hawk 3M **43**
TN38: St Leo 9F **104**
Beech Farm Rd. TN32: Staple 3D **82**
Beechfield Cl. BN24: Sto C 8L **141**
Beech Flds. RH19: E Grin 1F **10**
Beech Grn. La. TN7: Withy 2L **13**
Beech Gro. BN2: Brig 2F **132**
Beech Hill RH16: Hay H 5J **49**
TN5: Wadh .8J **27**
Beech Ho. La. TN32: Rob 1K **61**
Beech Hurst TN2: Pem 6N **9**
Beech Hurst Cl. RH16: Hay H 5D **48**
Beech Hurst Gardens 5D **48**
Beeching Cl. TN39: Bex S 1J **145**
Beeching Pk. Ind. Est.
TN39: Bex S 1J **145**
Beeching Rd. TN39: Bex S 1J **145**
Beeching Way RH19: E Grin 3E **10**
Beech La. TN12: Mat 1E **18**
Beech Rd. TN18: N'den 7B **46**
Beech St. TN1: Tun W 9E **8**
Beechwood BN1: Brig 2N **131**
Beechwood Av. BN1: Brig 1A **132**
Beechwood Cl. BN1: Brig 1A **132**
BN27: Hails 9E **120**
TN19: B'wsh 2K **59**
Beechwood Cres. BN20: Eastb 9A **154**
Beechwood Gdns. TN37: St Leo 1K **127**
Beechwood La. BN7: Cooks 6E **92**
TN21: H'fld .3E **76**
Beechwoods RH15: Burg H 7B **68**
Beechy Av. BN20: Eastb 8M **153**
Beechy Gdns. BN20: Eastb 8M **153**
Beechy Rd. TN22: B'boys 7C **74**
Beeding Av. BN3: Hove 2H **131**
Beeding Ct. *BN1: Brig* *9L* ***111***
(off Mill Ri.)
Bee Rd. BN10: Peace 4C **148**
Beggar's La. BN24: Sto C 8M **141**
Beggars Wood Rd. BN8: N Cha 2B **70**
Belbourne Ct. BN1: Brig 6E **162**
Belfast St. BN3: Hove 6K **131**
Belfield Rd. TN2: Pem 7N **9**
Belfry Orchard TN22: Uck 3J **73**
Belfry, The BN27: Hails 6D **120**
Belgrave Ct. *TN40: Bex S* *2L* ***145***
(off De La Warr Pde.)
Belgrave Cres. BN25: Sea 7E **150**
Belgrave Pl. BN2: Brig 9E **132**
Belgrave Rd. BN25: Sea 8C **150**
TN1: Tun W .9E **8**
Belgrave St. BN2: Brig 7C **132**
Belgrove TN1: Tun W 2D **16**
Bell Alley Rd. TN19: B'wsh 3K **59**
Bellbanks Rd. BN27: Hails 7F **120**
Bellbrook Ind. Est. TN22: Uck 2G **72**
(Bell La.)
TN22: Uck .2F **72**
(Bolton Cl.)
Belle Hill TN40: Bex S 9K **125**
(Chantry La.)
TN40: Bex S 9J **125**
(London Rd.)
Belle Vue Cotts. BN2: Brig 5G **132**
Bellevue Ct. BN1: Brig 4A **132**
Belle Vue Ct. BN2: Brig 8E **132**
BN22: Eastb *7F* ***154***
(off Belle Vue Rd.)
Belle Vue Gdns. BN2: Brig 8D **132**
Belle Vue Rd. BN22: Eastb 7F **154**
Bellfarm La. TN22: Uck 1H **73**
Bellfarm Rd. TN22: Uck 2F **72**
Bell Hammer RH19: E Grin 4E **10**
Bellhurst Rd. TN32: Rob 5H **61**
Bellingham Cl. TN37: St Leo 2H **127**
Bellingham Cres. BN3: Hove 5F **130**
Bell La. BN7: Lewes 6H **115**
TN22: Nut 7N **33**
TN22: Uck .2G **72**
Bellmead BN3: Hove 6M **131**
BELL'S YEW GREEN 7J **17**
Bells Yew Grn. Rd. TN3: Frant 8F **16**
Bell Twr. Ind. Est. BN2: Brig 9F **132**
Bell Wlk. TN22: Uck 2H **73**
Belmaine Ct. *TN39: Bex S* *1G* ***145***
(off Collington La. E.)
BELMONT 5B **128**
Belmont BN1: Brig 6N **131** (3B **162**)
TN39: Bex S 2J **145**
Belmont Ct. BN1: Brig 3C **162**
BN27: Hails 7E **120**
Belmont Rd. TN22: Uck 1G **73**
TN35: Hast 5B **128**
Belmont St. BN1: Brig 6B **132** (4F **162**)
Belmore Rd.
BN22: Eastb 8E **154** (3M **161**)
Belton Cl. BN2: Brig 2G **162**
Belton Rd. BN2: Brig 5C **132** (2G **162**)
Beltring Rd. BN22: Eastb 8E **154** (3N **161**)
TN4: Tun W .7D **8**
Beltring Ter. BN22: Eastb . . .8E **154** (2N **161**)
Beltry Ct. BN21: Eastb 6L **161**

Belvedere—Boscobel Rd.

Belvedere BN1: Brig 5N 131 (2B 162)
BN23: Eastb 3K 155
Belvedere Ct.
BN21: Eastb 8C 154 (3H 161)
Belvedere Gdns. BN25: Sea 7F 150
TN6: Crow 1E 36
Belvedere Pk. TN38: St Leo 6G 127
Belvedere Ter. BN1: Brig 6A 162
Belvedere Wlk. RH16: Hay H 6D 48
Bembridge Rd. BN23: Lang 1E 154
Bembridge St. BN2: Brig 5D 132
Bembrook Rd. TN34: Hast 5A 128
Bemzells La. BN27: Cowb, Herst 5N 99
Benbow Av. BN23: Eastb 6H 155
Benbow Ho. TN39: Bex S 1F 144
Benchfield Cl. RH19: E Grin 4H 11
Bending Cres. TN40: Bex S 9K 125
(off St George's Rd.)
Benenden Cl. BN25: Sea 8F 150
Benenden Ri. TN34: Hast 3L 127
Benett Av. BN3: Hove 3K 131
Benett Dr. BN3: Hove 3K 131
Benfield Cl. BN41: Ports 4E 130
Benfield Ct. BN41: Ports 5E 130
Benfield Cres. BN41: Ports 4E 130
Benfield Way BN41: Ports 5E 130
Bengairn Av. BN1: Brig 7B 112
Benhall Mill Rd. TN2: Tun W 4F 16
TN3: Tun W 4H 17
Benham Ct. BN3: Hove 8K 131
(off King's Esplanade)
Benjamin Cl. BN22: Eastb 2C 154
Benjamin Lodge RH15: Burg H 5E 68
(off Kings Way)
Bennett Rd. BN2: Brig 9F 132
Benson Ct. BN3: Hove 6G 130
Bentham Hill TN3: South 4A 8
Bentham Rd. BN2: Brig 6D 132
Bentley House 3L 95
Bentley Motor Mus. 2K 95
Bentley Wildfowl Reserve 3L 95
Bentswood Cres. RH16: Hay H 4H 49
Bentswood Rd. RH16: Hay H 4G 48
Beresford Cl. TN17: Kiln 1A 30
Beresford Ct. BN3: Hove 6M 131
Beresford Ho. BN10: Peace 3C 148
Beresford La. BN8: N Cha, Plump G . . .7N 69
Beresford Rd. BN2: Brig 8E 132
BN9: N'hvn 3L 149
Beristede Cl.
BN20: Eastb 2B 160 (9G 161)
Berkeley Cl. TN2: Pem 6N 9
Berkeley Ct. BN3: Hove 4A 162
BN21: Eastb 8K 161
Berkeley Mans. TN40: Bex S 2L 145
(off Knole Rd.)
Berkeley Pl. TN1: Tun W 2D 16
Berkeley Rd. TN1: Tun W 2D 16
TN20: May 9B 38
Berkeley Row BN7: Lewes 6G 115
Berkeley Wlk. BN23: Lang 2H 155
(off Close Seventeen)
Berkshire Ct. BN22: Eastb 2N 161
Berlin Rd. TN35: Hast 4B 128
Bermuda Pl. BN23: Eastb 4K 155
Bernard La. BN21: Eastb 9C 154 (4H 161)
Bernard Pl. BN2: Brig 6D 132
Bernard Rd. BN2: Brig 6D 132
Bernard Sunley Outdoor Education Cen.,
The Hindleap Warren 6K 21
BERNER'S HILL 9B 30
Berners Hill TN5: Flim, Tice 9B 30
Bernhard Gdns. BN26: Pole 8C 140
Berriedale Av. BN3: Hove 7G 131
Berriedale Ho. BN3: Hove 7G 131
Berry Cl. BN10: Tels C 3A 148
RH15: Burg H 3B 68
BERWICK 6D 138
Berwick Cl. BN22: Eastb 1N 153
BN25: Sea 8C 150
TN39: Bex S 8D 124
Berwick Ct. BN21: Eastb 4M 161
Berwick Rd. BN2: Salt 1L 147
Berwick Station (Rail) 3F 138
BEST BEECH HILL 8L 27
Betchley Cl. RH19: E Grin 1E 10
Bethune Rd. TN40: Bex S 2M 145
Bethune Way TN34: Hast 5M 127
Beulah Rd. TN1: Tun W 8E 8
Beuzeville Av. BN27: Hails 6E 120
BEVENDEAN 4H 133
Bevendean Av. BN2: Salt 3L 147
Bevendean Cres. BN2: Brig 3F 132
Bevendean Rd. BN2: Brig 5E 132
Beverington Cl. BN21: Eastb 6A 154
Beverington Rd. BN21: Eastb 6A 154
Beverley Ct. BN3: Hove 6F 130
BN20: Eastb 3C 160
(off South Cliff)
Beverley Ho.
BN21: Eastb 9E 154 (5M 161)
Beverley Wlk. TN34: Hast 4N 127
Bevern Bri. Cotts. BN8: S Chai 3F 92
BEWLBRIDGE 2M 29
Bewl Bri. Cl. TN5: Flim 8C 30
Bewl Bri. La. TN3: Lamb 2K 29
Bewlbridge La. TN5: Lamb 3G 29
Bewl Water Boat Trips 3K 29
Bewl Water Outdoor Cen. 3K 29
Bewl Water Sailing Club 3J 29
Bewl Water Visitor Cen. 3K 29
Bex Ct. BN21: Eastb 8C 154 (2J 161)
Bexfield Ct. BN20: Eastb 2C 160 (9J 161)
BEXHILL 2K 145
BEXHILL HOSPITAL 8K 125
Bexhill Leisure Cen. 9J 125
Bexhill Mus. of Costume & Social History
. . . . .1L 145
Bexhill-on-Sea Mus. 2J 145
Bexhill Rd. BN2: W'dean 4L 133
BN22: Eastb 7F 154
BN24: Pev 6D 142
TN33: Nin 1C 124
TN38: Bex S, St Leo 9B 126
Bexhill Station (Rail) 1K 145
Bexleigh Av. TN38: Bex S 9B 126
Bexley Cl. BN27: Hails 4E 120
Bex, The TN40: Bex S 2L 145
Bicton Gdns. TN39: Bex S 1F 144
BIDBOROUGH 1N 7
Bidborough Ct. TN3: Bid 2M 7
Bidborough Ridge TN3: Bid 1N 7
TN4: Bid 1A 8
Biddenden Cl. BN23: Lang 2G 155
Bidwell Av. TN39: Bex S 8H 125
Big All. TN8: Mrsh G 1A 4
Bigwood Av. BN3: Hove 6M 131
Bilbury M. BN21: Eastb 7C 154 (1H 161)
Billam Ho. BN2: Brig 7C 132
(off Belgrave St.)
Billam Ter. BN2: Brig 7C 132
(off Belgrave St.)
Billingham La. TN31: Udim 4H 85
Billington Ct. RH19: E Grin 2E 10
Binsted Cl. BN22: Eastb 2B 154
Biology Rd. BN1: Falm 8J 113
Birch Av. RH17: Hay H 6H 49
Birch Cl. BN23: Eastb 5G 154
RH17: Hay H 6J 49
TN2: Tun W 6G 8
TN22: Uck 9K 53
Birch Ct. BN42: S'wck 4C 130
BIRCHDEN 6H 15
Birchen La. RH16: Hay H 1F 48
Birches Cl. TN6: Crow 7D 24
Birches Ind. Est. RH19: E Grin 1A 10
Birchetts Av. TN3: Lang G 1J 15
BIRCHETT'S GREEN 8H 29
Birchetts Grn. La. TN5: Tice, Wadh 8G 29
BIRCH GROVE 1G 32
Birch Gro. Cres. BN1: Brig 9B 112
Birchgrove La. RH17: Hors K 1E 32
Birchgrove Rd. RH17: Hors K 5D 32
Birch Ho. RH19: E Grin 2D 10
Birch Ind. Est. BN23: Eastb 5F 154
Birchington Cl. TN39: Bex S 1E 144
Birch Lodge BN2: Brig 2G 162
Birch Path TN22: Uck 9J 53
(off Birch Cl.)
Birch Rd. BN23: Eastb 5F 154
Birch Rdbt. BN22: Eastb 5G 154
Birch Ter. TN21: Horam 6A 76
Birch Vw. TN39: Bex S 8K 125
Birch Way BN27: Hails 8E 120
RH17: Hay H 7H 49
TN2: Tun W 6G 9
TN21: H'fld 3D 76
TN34: Hast 3L 127
Birchwood Av. TN4: South 2B 8
Birchwood Gro. Rd. RH15: Burg H 7C 68
Birdcage Wlk. TN1: Tun W 1E 16
Birdham Pl. BN2: Brig 2F 132
Birdham Rd. BN2: Brig 2F 132
Bird in Eye Hill TN22: Fram 2K 73
Bird in Hand St. TN3: Groom 4F 14
Bird La. TN5: Wadh 7K 27
Birdshole La. BN8: Barc, Cooks 2H 93
Birkdale TN1: Tun W 7E 8
TN39: Bex S 1E 144
Birken Rd. TN2: Tun W 7G 9
Birling Cl. BN2: Brig 4E 132
BN25: Sea 8C 150
Birling Dr. TN2: Tun W 3D 16
BIRLING GAP 6E 158
Birling Gap Rd.
BN20: E Dean 6F 158
Birling Pk. Av. TN2: Tun W 4E 16
Birling Rd. TN2: Tun W 4D 16
Birling St. BN21: Eastb 8N 153
Birling Way TN22: Uck 9K 53
(off Nevill Rd.)
Biscay Av. BN23: Eastb 4H 155
Bishop's Cl. BN8: Ring 9D 94
Bishops Cl. BN25: Sea 8B 150
Bishop's Ct. TN4: Tun W 1B 16
Bishop's Down TN4: Tun W 1B 16
Bishop's Down Pk. Rd. TN4: Tun W 9B 8
Bishop's Down Rd. TN4: Tun W 1B 16
Bishops Dr. BN7: Lewes 6G 115
Bishop's La. BN8: Ring 9C 94
Bishops La. TN17: Cran 1M 31
Bishop's La. TN32: Rob 6H 61
Bishops Rd. BN3: Hove 4L 131
BISHOPSTONE 5B 150
Bishopstone Dr. BN2: Salt 2J 147
Bishopstone Rd.
BN25: B'stn, Nort, Sea 4B 150
Bishopstone Station (Rail) 8A 150
Bishops Wlk. BN1: Brig 8A 132 (7C 162)
Bishop's Wlk. TN40: Bex S 8N 125
Bisky Bar TN31: Peas 7N 65
(off School La.)
Bixlea Pde. TN39: Bex S 1E 144
(off Lit. Common Rd.)
Bixley La. TN31: Buck 8F 64
BLACKBOYS .3E 74
Blackbrook La.
BN8: N Cha, Scay H, Shef P 7E 50
RH17: Scay H, Shef P 7E 50
Black Brooks TN33: Sed 1E 104
Blackdon Hill TN3: Eri G 6M 25
Blackdown BN2: Brig 6G 132
Blackdown Rd. TN21: Punn T 2N 77
Black Down Rdbt. TN22: Uck 6G 53
Blackfields Av. TN39: Bex S 9G 124
BLACKHAM 9M 5
BLACK HILL .9J 23
Black Hill RH16: Lind 2H 49
Blackhorse M. TN2: Pem 7M 9
Blackhouse La. RH15: Burg H 4C 68
Blackhurst La. TN2: Tun W 8H 9
BLACKLANDS 4M 127
Blacklands TN33: Sed 7F 82
Blacklands Cres. RH18: F Row 1M 21
Blacklands Dr. TN34: Hast 4M 127
Black Lion La. BN1: Brig 8A 132 (8D 162)
Black Lion St. BN1: Brig 9B 132 (9E 162)
Blackman Av. TN38: St Leo 4G 126
Blackman St. BN1: Brig 7B 132 (5E 162)
Blackmans Yd. BN27: Hails 7F 120
(off Market St.)
Blackmill Cl. TN39: Bex S 6H 125
Blackmores RH17: Wivel 3H 69
BLACKNESS
Crowborough 1E 36
Stone Cross 7K 141
Blackness Rd. TN6: Crow 1D 36
Blackness Vs. TN6: Crow 2E 36
(off Blackness Rd.)
Black Path BN26: Pole 7D 140
BLACK ROCK 1A 146
Blacksmiths Copse BN27: Hails 8D 120
Blacksmiths Fld. TN32: Bod 9C 44
TN33: C'hrst 2A 126
Blacksmith's La. TN5: Wadh 6C 28
Blacksmiths La. TN33: Cats 7F 102
(off Green, The)
Blackstone Way RH15: Burg H 3B 68
Blackthorn Av. TN4: South 4F 8
Blackthorn Cl. BN1: Brig 2M 131
BN22: Eastb 2B 154
BN41: Ports 3D 130
TN37: St Leo 2J 127
Blackthorns RH16: Lind 2H 49
Blackthorns Cl. RH16: Lind 3H 49
Blackthorns, The RH15: Burg H 3C 68
Blackthorn Way TN35: Fair 2L 129
Blackwater Rd.
BN20: Eastb 2C 160 (8G 161)
BN21: Eastb 2C 160 (7J 161)
BLACKWELL .2F 10
Blackwell Farm Rd. RH19: E Grin 1F 10
Blackwell Hollow RH19: E Grin 2F 10
Blackwell Rd. RH19: E Grin 2F 10
Blake Ct. BN2: Brig 5G 162
Blakeney Av. BN10: Peace 6G 148
Blaker St. BN2: Brig 8C 132
Blakes Way BN23: Eastb 6J 155
Blakeway TN2: Tun W 6G 8
Blatchington Cl. BN25: Sea 8E 150
Blatchington Hill BN25: Sea 8D 150
Blatchington Hill Flats BN25: Sea 7E 150
(off Up. Belgrave Rd.)
Blatchington Mill Dr. BN24: Sto C 8L 141
Blatchington Rd. BN3: Hove 6J 131
BN25: Sea 9D 150
TN2: Tun W 3E 16
Blatchington Rd. Ind. Est.
BN25: Sea 9D 150
Blenheim Cl. RH19: E Grin 1G 11
Blenheim Ct. BN3: Hove 7J 131
(off New Chu. Rd.)
TN32: Rob 6J 61
Blenheim Flds. RH18: F Row 9L 11
Blenheim M. RH16: Hay H 7G 48
Blenheim Pl. BN1: Brig 7B 132 (6F 162)
Blenheim Way BN26: Pole 7G 140
TN5: Flim .8D 30
Bletchinglye La. TN6: Town R 1B 38
Bletchley Ct. BN1: Brig 5B 132 (1F 162)
Bligh Ter. BN8: Ring 1C 116
Blind La. BN8: N'wck 2L 71
Blois Rd. BN7: Lewes 3G 115
Blomfield Rd. TN37: St Leo 6K 127
Bloomsbury Pl. BN2: Brig 9D 132
Bloomsbury St. BN2: Brig 9D 132
Blossom Wlk. BN27: Hails 5E 120
Blount Av. RH19: E Grin 3C 10
Bluebell Cl. RH16: Hay H 5G 48
RH19: E Grin 3B 10
Bluebell Glade BN27: Ripe 3F 118
Bluebell Holiday Pk. 5M 95
Bluebell La. RH19: Sharp 5A 20
Bluebell Railway
RH19 . . . . .9A 10
TN22 . . . . .3E 50
Bluebell Walk & Farm Trail 1L 139
Bluebird Ct. BN3: Hove 7J 131
Blue Haze Av. BN25: Sea 8G 150
Bluemans La. TN33: Sed 4G 104
Bluestone Cl. TN38: St Leo 4F 126
Blunden Dr. RH17: Cuck 1A 48
Blunts La. BN8: Barc 9A 72
Blunts Wood Cres. RH16: Hay H 3C 48
Blunts Wood Rd. RH16: Hay H 3C 48
Blytons, The RH19: E Grin 3B 10
Boarders La. TN5: Tice 8K 29
Boardwalk BN2: Brig 1A 146
BOARSHEAD .5G 24
Boarshead Rd. TN6: Crow 5G 25
Boarshead Rdbt. TN6: Crow 6G 24
Boast La. BN8: Barc 2L 93
Boathouse, The TN31: Rye 3G 86
Boatyard, The BN2: Brig 1B 146
Bocking Cl. TN5: Wadh 7A 28
Boddingtons La. BN6: Ditch 4D 90
(not continuous)
BODIAM 1E 62
Bodiam Av. BN2: Brig 4J 133
TN40: Bex S 8L 125
Bodiam Bus. Pk. TN32: Bod 1C 62
Bodiam Castle 1E 62
Bodiam Cl. BN2: Brig 3J 133
BN25: Sea 8H 151
Bodiam Cres. BN22: Eastb 2D 154
Bodiam Dr. TN38: St Leo 3D 126
Bodiam Ferry Company 7C 46
Bodiam Rd. TN18: Sandh 6F 44
TN32: Bod 1E 62
Bodiam Station
Kent & East Sussex Railway 2E 62
Bodiham Ho. BN3: Hove 6M 131
(off Davigdor Rd.)
Bodle Cres. TN39: Bex S 7J 125
BODLE STREET GREEN 6E 100
Bodmin Cl. BN20: Eastb 9N 153
Bogey La. TN4: Tun W 9C 8
BOHEMIA 5J 127
Bohemia Rd. TN34: Hast 7K 127
TN37: St Leo 5J 127
Boiler Ho. Hill BN1: Falm 7J 113
Bolding Way RH16: Hay H 7E 48
Bolebroke Castle 4H 13
Bolebrooke Rd. TN40: Bex S 2L 145
Bolney Av. BN10: Peace 6C 148
(not continuous)
Bolney Rd. BN2: Brig 1G 132
Bolnore Rd. RH16: Hay H 5D 48
BOLNORE VILLAGE 6D 48
Bolsover Rd. BN3: Hove 6G 131
BN20: Eastb 3C 160
Bolton Cl. TN22: Uck 2F 72
Bolton Rd. BN21: Eastb 1D 160 (6L 161)
Boltro Rd. RH16: Hay H 4E 48
Bonchurch Rd. BN2: Brig 5D 132
Bondfield Cl. TN4: South 4D 8
Bond St. BN1: Brig 8B 132 (7E 162)
Bond St. Cotts. BN1: Brig 7E 162
Bond St. Laine BN1: Brig 7E 162
Bond St. Row BN1: Brig 7E 162
Bonfire La. RH17: Hors K 6C 32
Boniface Cl. BN24: Sto C 7M 141
Bonny Wood Rd. BN6: Hass 4A 90
Booker Cl. TN6: Crow 1E 36
Bookgate La. TN18: Hawk 1H 43
TN19: Hawk 1H 43
Booth Mus. of Natural History
. . . . .5N 131 (1A 162)
Bopeep Bostal BN8: Alc 6M 137
BN26: Alc 6M 137
Bopeep La. BN26: Alc 5N 137
BORDE HILL .1B 48
Borde Hill La. RH16: Hay H 1D 48
Border Ct. RH19: E Grin 2F 10
Borders La. TN19: Etch 2N 59
Boreham Hill BN27: Bore S 3H 123
TN33: Nin 3H 123
Boreham La. BN27: Bore S, Wart 7F 122
BOREHAM STREET 2G 123
Borodales TN39: Bex S 1F 144
Borough La. BN20: Eastb 9A 154
Borough St. BN1: Brig 7N 131 (7A 162)
Borrowdale Cl. BN23: Lang 9M 141
Borrow King Cl. BN2: Brig 4E 132
Boscawen Cl. BN23: Eastb 5J 155
Boscobel Rd. TN38: St Leo 7G 127

168 A-Z East Sussex Atlas

Boship Cl.—Brook Ter.

Boship Cl. BN23: Lang 9K 141
Boship Rdbt. BN27: Lwr D 3B 120
Bostal Rd. BN8: W Firle 1G 136
BN45: Poyn 4D 110
Boston Cl. BN23: Eastb 5J 155
Boston Ct. RH16: Hay H 4H 49
(off Allan Rd.)
Boston Rd. RH16: Hay H 4H 49
Boston St. BN1: Brig 6B 132 (3E 162)
Boswell Wlk. BN23: Lang 2H 155
Bough Beeches RH15: Burg H 7D 68
Boughey Pl. BN7: Lewes 3J 115
Boulevard Ho. BN1: Brig 7E 162
(off Regent St.)
Boulevard, The BN24: Pev B 7G 143
Boundary Pas. BN1: Brig 6A 162
Boundary Rd. BN2: Brig 9F 132
BN3: Hove 7E 130
TN2: Tun W 3G 16
Boundary, The BN25: Sea 1D 156
TN3: Lang G 1M 15
Bounds Oak Way TN4: South 2B 8
Boundsway TN22: Uck 9K 53
Bourg-de-Peage Av. RH19: E Grin 3G 10
Bourne Ct. BN1: Brig 1M 131
TN34: Hast 6A 128
(off Bourne, The)
Bourne La. TN18: Sandh 6E 44
TN32: Rob 2M 61
Bourne M. BN21: Eastb 4L 161
Bourne Pas. TN34: Hast 6A 128
(off Bourne, The)
Bourneside Ct.
BN21: Eastb 9E 154 (5N 161)
Bourne St. BN21: Eastb 9D 154 (4L 161)
Bourne, The BN6: Hass 2A 90
TN34: Hast 6A 128
Bowden Ri. BN25: Sea 6D 150
Bowen Ct. BN3: Hove 7L 131
Bowen Rd. TN4: R'hall 8M 7
Bower Cl. TN37: St Leo 2H 127
Bowerhill Cotts. RH19: F Row 5F 20
Bower, The RH16: Hay H 4E 48
BOWLERS TOWN 8E 66
Bowles Outdoor Cen. 5H 25
Bowley Rd. BN27: Hails 7F 120
Bowlplex
Brighton Marina Village 1A 146
Bowlplex Bowling Alley
Tunbridge Wells 5J 9
Bowmans Dr. TN33: Batt 2L 103
Bowood Av. BN22: Eastb 6E 154
Bowrey Pl. TN40: Bex S 9K 125
Bowring Way BN2: Brig 9E 132
Bowsprit M. TN38: St Leo 8E 104
Boxes La. RH17: Chel C 4J 33
RH17: Hors K 5C 32
Boxgate TN6: Crow 7B 24
Boxgrove Cl. TN40: Bex S 1N 145
Box La. RH19: A'hstw 6L 11
Boyce's St. BN1: Brig 8A 132 (8D 162)
Boyles La. BN2: Brig 9F 132
Boyne Pk. TN4: Tun W 9C 8
Boyne Rd. TN35: Hast 5B 128
Brackenbury Cl. BN41: Ports 3D 130
Bracken Cl. TN2: Tun W 8H 9
TN6: Jar B 1G 37
Brackendale TN35: Hast 4C 128
Brackenhill TN7: Up H 2F 22
Bracken Rd. BN20: Eastb 7M 153
(not continuous)
BN25: Sea 1F 156
(not continuous)
TN2: Tun W 8H 9
Bracken Way TN21: B Oak 8H 57
Brackern Cl. TN39: Bex S 3D 144
Bradford Ct. BN22: Eastb 3N 161
Bradford Rd. BN7: Lewes 5H 115
Bradford St. BN21: Eastb 9N 153
Brading Cl. BN23: Lang 9L 141
TN34: Hast 4L 127
Brading Rd. BN2: Brig 6D 132
Bradley La. TN3: B'ham, Pens 7A 6
Bradley Rd. BN27: Herst 5E 122
Braemar Ct. TN39: Bex S 1H 145
(off Eridge Cl.)
Braemar Ho. BN1: Brig 6A 162
Braemore Ct. BN3: Hove 7H 131
Braemore Rd. BN3: Hove 7G 131
Braeside Av. BN1: Brig 7A 112
Brainsmead RH17: Cuck 2A 48
Brakes Coppice Pk. TN33: C'hrst 8A 104
Bramber Av. BN3: Hove 2H 131
BN10: Peace 6C 148
(not continuous)
Bramber Av. Nth. BN10: Peace 4C 148
Bramber Cl. BN10: Peace 4C 148
BN25: Sea 1E 156
RH16: Hay H 5E 48
Bramber Ct. BN3: Hove 6K 131
Bramber Ho. BN21: Eastb 8B 154
(off Michel Gro.)
Bramber La. BN25: Sea 1E 156
Bramber Rd. BN25: Sea 1E 156
Bramber Way RH15: Burg H 4B 68
Bramble Cl. BN23: Lang 1E 154
Bramble Ct. TN21: H'fld 1D 76
(off Station Rd.)
Bramble Cft. TN6: Crow 9E 24
Brambledean Rd. BN41: Ports 6D 130
Bramble Dr. BN27: Hails 7D 120
Bramble Ri. BN1: Brig 9L 111
Brambles BN6: Hass 2A 90
Brambleside TN22: Uck 2F 72
Brambles, The RH17: Cuck 3B 48
Bramble Twitten RH19: E Grin 3G 10
Brambletye La. RH18: F Row 8K 11
Brambletyne Av. BN2: Salt 3L 147
Bramble Wlk. TN2: Tun W 6G 9
Bramble Way BN1: Brig 8D 112
TN35: Fair 2L 129
Bramley Rd. BN26: Pole 7F 140
Bramleys BN7: King L 9E 114
Bramley Wlk. BN27: Bore S 1D 122
Brampton Av. TN39: Bex S 1G 144
Brampton Ct. TN39: Bex S 1G 145
Brampton Rd. BN22: Eastb 3C 154
Brampton Rd. Trad. Est.
BN22: Eastb 4C 154
Brampton Vs. BN21: Eastb 8B 154
(off Watts La.)
Brand Rd. BN22: Eastb 3B 154
Brands Cl. BN9: S Heig 2K 149
Brangwyn Av. BN1: Brig 8N 111
Brangwyn Ct. BN1: Brig 9M 111
Brangwyn Cres. BN1: Brig 8M 111
Brangwyn Dr. BN1: Brig 8M 111
Brangwyns Acre BN6: Ditch 4E 90
Brangwyn Way BN1: Brig 9N 111
Branksome Rd. TN38: St Leo 6G 126
Branston Rd. BN22: Eastb 3A 154
Brassey Av. BN22: Eastb 3B 154
Brassey Pde. BN22: Eastb 3B 154
Brassey Rd. TN40: Bex S 2L 145
Brassey Steps TN34: Hast 7L 162
(off Cambridge Rd.)
Brasslands Dr. BN41: Ports 3B 130
Braybon Av. BN1: Brig 1A 132
Braybon Bus. Pk. RH15: Burg H 6A 68
Braybrooke Cl. TN34: Hast 6L 127
Braybrooke Rd. TN34: Hast 6L 127
Braybrooke Ter. TN34: Hast 6L 127
Braycastle Wlk. TN34: Hast 5N 127
(off St Mary's Rd.)
Braypool La. BN1: Brig 6M 111
BRAY'S HILL 6J 101
Brazen Cl. BN9: N'hvn 5G 149
Breach Rd. BN7: King L 1D 134
Breadsell La. TN38: St Leo 9D 104
Bread St. BN1: Brig 7B 132 (6E 162)
Breaky Bottom Vineyard 6G 135
Brecon Ct. BN3: Hove 6L 131
Brecon Ter. TN6: Roth 2L 37
BREDE 7A 84
Brede Cl. BN2: Brig 8F 132
BN22: Eastb 6G 155
TN37: St Leo 8F 104
Brede Hill TN31: Brede 7A 84
Brede La. TN31: Sed 6H 83
TN33: Sed 7E 82
Brede Rd. TN35: W'fld 1N 105
Brede Valley Vw. TN36: Ick 2K 107
Breedon Av. TN4: South 4C 8
Breeds Pl. TN34: Hast 7M 127
Brendon Cl. BN23: Lang 9A 142
TN2: Tun W 8G 8
Brendon Ri. TN34: Hast 3A 128
Brentwood Cl. BN1: Brig 2C 132
Brentwood Cres. BN1: Brig 2C 132
Brentwood Rd. BN1: Brig 2C 132
Bretland Rd. TN4: R'hall 9A 8
Brett Dr. TN40: Bex S 9N 125
Brett Dr. Ind. Est. TN40: Bex S 1N 145
Bretts Cotts. TN22: Fram 1N 73
Bretts Fld. BN10: Peace 2C 148
Brewers Gro. TN20: May 8E 38
Brewer St. BN2: Brig 6C 132
TN3: Lamb 7J 19
Brian Cres. TN4: South 5E 8
Briar Cl. BN2: W'dean 5L 133
TN35: Fair 1M 129
Briarcroft Rd. BN2: W'dean 6L 133
Briar Pl. BN23: Lang 1E 154
Briary, The TN40: Bex S 9L 125
Brick Kiln La. TN22: Had D 3G 55
Brickyard Cotts. TN6: Mark C 7D 26
Brickyard La. BN8: S Chai 9E 70
TN6: Mark C, Town R 7A 26
Bricky, The BN10: Peace 4C 148
Bridge Cl. RH15: Burg H 4A 68
TN21: Horam 9D 76
Bridge Ct. BN9: N'hvn 5K 149
(off Bridge St.)
Bridge End BN24: Pev 6D 142
Bridge Farm TN22: Uck 2H 73
Bridge Ho. TN4: Tun W 8E 8
Bridgelands BN8: Barc C 3K 93
Bridgemere Rd. BN22: Eastb 6D 154
Bridge Pl. TN31: Rye 2G 87
Bridge Rd. RH16: Hay H 2F 48
Bridge Rd. Bus. Pk. RH16: Hay H 2G 48
Bridge Rd. Ind. Est. RH16: Hay H 3G 48
Bridgersmill RH16: Hay H 2E 48
Bridger Way TN6: Crow 1D 36
Bridge St. BN9: N'hvn 5K 149
Bridge Way TN38: St Leo 8C 126
Bridgewick Cl. BN7: Lewes 3K 115
Bridle Way BN10: Tels C 3A 148
Briers Av. TN34: Hast 3J 127
Briers Gdns. TN34: Hast 3J 127
Briers, The TN37: St Leo 2J 127
Brigden St. BN1: Brig 6A 132 (3C 162)
Brighthelm BN1: Falm 6J 113
Brightland Rd. BN20: Eastb 9A 154
BRIGHTLING 2M 79
Brightling Av. TN35: Hast 2C 128
Brightling Needle 1J 79
Brightling Rd. BN26: Pole 8D 140
TN21: Dall 4H 79
TN32: B'lng, Rob 9N 59
BRIGHTON 8C 132 (7E 162)
Brighton & Hove Albion F.C.
(Withdean Stadium) 2M 131
Brighton & Hove Stadium
(Greyhound) 4K 131
Brighton & Hove Stadium Health Club
4J 131
(off Brighton & Hove Stadium)
Brighton By-Pass BN1: Brig 8L 111
BN3: Hove 1A 130
BN41: Ports 1A 130
Brighton Cen., The 8A 132 (8C 162)
Brighton Dome 8B 132 (7E 162)
Brighton Fishing Mus. 9A 132 (9D 162)
Brighton Fringe Theatre 6E 162
(off Argus Lofts)
BRIGHTON GENERAL HOSPITAL 6E 132
Brighton Health & Racquet Club, The
9H 113
Brighton Hippodrome 8A 132 (8D 162)
Brighton Ice Rink 7D 162
Brighton Marina BN2: Brig 2A 146
BRIGHTON MARINA VILLAGE 1A 146
Brighton Mus. & Art Gallery
8B 132 (7F 162)
Brighton Pl. BN1: Brig 8E 162
Brighton Race Course 6F 132
Brighton Rd. BN7: Falm, Lewes 1L 113
(not continuous)
BN9: N'hvn, Peace 6G 148
Brighton Sq. BN1: Brig 8E 162
Brighton Station (Rail) 7B 132 (5E 162)
Bright Ridge TN4: South 5B 8
Brightwell Ind. Est.
BN9: N'hvn 6L 149
Brills La. BN1: Brig 9B 132 (9E 162)
Brincliffe TN6: Crow 8C 24
Brinker's La. TN5: Wadh 1B 40
Brisbane Quay BN23: Eastb 2K 155
Briscoe's Wlk. TN34: Hast 5K 127
Bristol Ct. BN2: Brig 9E 132
(off Marine Pde.)
Bristol Gdns. BN2: Brig 9F 132
Bristol Ga. BN2: Brig 9E 132
Bristol M. BN2: Brig 9F 132
Bristol Pl. BN2: Brig 9F 132
Bristol Ri. BN2: Brig 9E 132
(off Bowring Way)
Bristol Rd. BN2: Brig 9D 132
TN38: St Leo 3G 126
Bristol St. BN2: Brig 9F 132
Bristol Way TN38: St Leo 3G 127
Britannia Ct. BN2: Brig 1B 146
Britannia Ent. Cen. TN34: Hast 5M 127
(off Waterworks Rd.)
British Engineerium, The 3K 131
Britland Est. BN22: Eastb 6F 154
Brittany Ct. BN3: Hove 6F 130
TN39: Bex S 1H 145
(off Sutherland Av.)
Brittany M. TN38: St Leo 7H 127
Brittany Rd. BN3: Hove 7F 130
TN38: St Leo 7H 127
Britten Cl. BN23: Lang 1G 155
Brittenden La. TN21: Wald 3J 75
Britts Farm Rd. TN22: Buxt 6A 54
Britts Orchard TN22: Buxt 6A 54
Broadcroft TN2: Tun W 4C 16
Broadfields BN2: Brig 2F 132
Broadfields Rd. BN2: Brig 2F 132
Broad Grn. BN2: W'dean 7M 133
Broadgreen Av. RH15: Burg H 6D 68
Broadgrove TN2: Tun W 3D 16
Broadhill Cl. TN21: B Oak 8H 57
Broadhurst Manor Rd.
RH17: Hors K, Sharp 1D 32
BROADLAND ROW 5C 84
Broadlands RH15: Burg H 8C 68
TN35: Hast 2C 128
Broad La. TN3: A'hst 1E 14
Broadley Vw. TN33: Cats 7F 102
Broadmead TN2: Tun W 4B 16
Broadmead Av. TN2: Tun W 4C 16
BROAD OAK
TN21 8H 57
TN31 4A 84
Broad Oak TN3: Groom 6G 14
TN22: Buxt 6A 54
Broadoak Cl. BN23: Lang 9K 141
TN2: Tun W 3C 16
Broad Oak Cl. TN31: B Oak 4A 84
(off Northiam Rd.)
Broadoak Coppice TN39: Bex S 9E 124
Broadoak La. TN39: Bex S 9F 124
(not continuous)
Broad Oaks BN20: Eastb 2B 160 (9G 161)
Broad Rig Av. BN3: Hove 1F 130
Broad Rd. BN20: Will 9C 140
Broadstone RH18: F Row 1N 21
BROAD STREET 1H 107
Broad St. BN2: Brig 9B 132 (9F 162)
BN25: Sea 9D 150
RH17: Cuck 3A 48
TN36: Ick 1H 107
BROADSTREET GREEN 7N 123
Broad Vw. TN21: B Oak 8H 57
TN39: Bex S 8G 125
Broadview Cl. BN20: Will 1K 153
Broadwalk, The TN39: Bex S 1C 144
Broadwater Ct. TN2: Tun W 4B 16
BROADWATER DOWN 3C 16
Broadwater Down TN2: Tun W 4B 16
Broadwater Forest La.
TN3: Groom, Tun W 6J 15
Broadwater La. TN2: Tun W 3C 16
Broadwater M. BN26: Pole 1J 153
Broadwater Ri. TN2: Tun W 3C 16
Broadwater Rdbt. BN22: Eastb 4C 154
Broadwater Way BN22: Eastb 4C 154
Broadway TN35: Fair 1L 129
Broadway, The BN2: Brig 9G 132
BN22: Eastb 3A 154
BN26: Alfr 1L 151
BN42: S'wck 5B 130
RH16: Hay H 4F 48
TN3: Lamb 7K 19
TN6: Crow 8D 24
TN35: Hast 2C 128
Brock Ct. BN25: Sea 8H 151
Brockhurst BN2: Brig 5G 132
Brockhurst Ga. TN40: Bex S 9N 125
Brockley Rd. TN39: Bex S 2H 145
Brocks Gyhll BN20: Will 1L 153
Brodie Pl. BN21: Eastb 8A 154
Brodrick Cl. BN22: Eastb 3C 154
Brodrick Rd. BN22: Eastb 2A 154
Brokes Way TN4: South 5E 8
Bromley Cl. BN6: Hass 3B 90
BN23: Lang 2F 154
Bromley Rd. BN1: Brig 6C 132 (2G 162)
BN25: Sea 8F 150
Brompton Cl. BN1: Brig 8N 111
Brontes, The RH19: E Grin 3D 10
Brook Av. BN6: Hass 4A 90
Brook Cl. RH19: E Grin 3H 11
TN6: Jar B 1H 37
Brook Ct. BN20: Eastb 2B 160
Brooke Mead BN2: Brig 5G 162
Brooker Pl. BN3: Hove 6J 131
Brooker St. BN3: Hove 6K 131
Brookfield TN18: Sandh 4H 45
Brookfield Ct. TN4: South 4D 8
TN40: Bex S 1M 145
(off Lionel Rd.)
Brookfield Rd. TN40: Bex S 1M 145
Brook Ho. TN39: Bex S 8J 125
Brookhouse Bottom RH17: Fur G 5J 33
TN22: Fur G 7J 33
Brookhouse Rd. TN22: Fram 5M 73
Brookhurst Gdns. TN4: South 2B 8
Brookland Cl. BN24: Pev B 7G 143
TN34: Hast 4M 127
Brooklands TN2: Tun W 6G 8
Brooklands Av. TN6: Crow 3D 36
Brooklands Farm Cl. TN3: F'cmbe 7E 6
Brooklands Way RH19: E Grin 4D 10
Brook La. BN8: Glyn 8N 115
RH16: Hay H 1F 48
Brooklyn Rd. BN25: Sea 9D 150
Brookmead Cl. BN22: Eastb 7E 154
Brook Rd. TN2: Tun W 6F 8
Brooks Cl. BN7: Lewes 4K 115
BN9: N'hvn 6K 149
Brooks Gdns. BN8: N'wck 2K 71
Brookside BN6: Hass 4A 90
BN9: Pidd 1G 149
TN22: Uck 2F 72
Brookside Av. BN26: Pole 6C 140
Brookside Cotts. TN2: Tun W 8J 9
Brooks Rd. BN7: Lewes 4L 115
Brook St. BN7: Lewes 5K 115
BN26: Pole 7C 140
RH17: Cuck 1A 48
TN34: Hast 6M 127
Brook Ter. TN6: Crow 7B 24
(off Coopers La.)

Cantelupe M.—Chatsworth Sq.

Cantelupe M. *RH19: E Grin* 3F 10
(*off Cantelupe Rd.*)
Cantelupe Rd. RH19: E Grin 3F 10
TN40: Bex S 2L 145
Canterbury Cl. BN22: Will 2M 153
Canterbury Dr. BN2: Brig 6C 132 (3G 162)
Canterbury Ri. TN34: Hast 3L 127
Canterbury Rd. TN2: Pem 7N 9
Cantercrow Hill BN9: N'hvn 2M 149
Canton *RH16: Hay H* 3E 48
(*off Great Heathmead*)
Cants Cl. RH15: Burg H 5D 68
Cants La. RH15: Burg H 4D 68
Canute Cl. BN23: Eastb 4J 155
Canute Rd. TN35: Hast 3C 128
Cape, The BN2: Rott 3G 147
Capel Av. BN10: Peace 6C 148
(not continuous)
Capella Path BN27: Hails 7G 121
Capenors RH15: Burg H 7A 68
Caple Ct. TN38: St Leo 6H 127
Caple Gdns. TN38: St Leo 7H 127
Carbury *BN20: Eastb* 2B 160
(*off Fairfield Rd.*)
Carden Av. BN1: Brig 1N 131
Carden Cl. BN1: Brig 8B 112
Carden Cres. BN1: Brig 8B 112
Carden Hill BN1: Brig 8C 112
Carden Pde. BN1: Brig 8C 112
Card Hill RH18: F Row 2M 21
Cardiff Rd. TN38: St Leo 7J 127
Cardigan Vs. BN42: S'wck 6A 130
Cardinals Cl. TN40: Bex S 8N 125
Carew Ct. BN21: Eastb 3J 161
BN27: Hails 3F 120
(*off Hawkswood Rd.*)
Carew Lodge
BN21: Eastb 7C 154 (2H 161)
Carew Rd. BN21: Eastb 8B 154 (2G 161)
Carew Views
BN21: Eastb 7C 154 (2H 161)
Carey Down BN10: Tels C 3B 148
Carfax Cl. TN39: Bex S 6J 125
Carillon Ho. BN21: Eastb 3J 161
Carinus Gdns. TN37: St Leo 1G 126
Carisbrooke Cl. BN23: Lang 9L 141
Carisbrooke Rd. BN2: Brig 6E 132
TN38: St Leo 7H 127
Carlisle Pde. TN34: Hast 7L 127
Carlisle Rd. BN3: Hove 7H 131
BN20: Eastb 3A 160 (8G 161)
(not continuous)
Carlton Cl. BN25: Sea 8D 150
Carlton Ct. BN41: Ports 5E 130
TN40: Bex S 2L 145
(*off Knole Rd.*)
Carlton Cres. TN1: Tun W 9F 8
Carlton Hill BN2: Brig 8C 132 (7G 162)
Carlton Ho. BN1: Brig 3N 131
Carlton Mt. *BN2: Brig* 8C 132
(*off Carlton Pl.*)
Carlton Pl. BN2: Brig 8C 132
Carlton Rd. BN22: Eastb 7F 154
BN25: Sea 7C 150
TN1: Tun W 9F 8
Carlton Ter. BN41: Ports 5E 130
TN6: Crow 2D 36
(*off Queens Rd.*)
Carlyle Av. BN2: Brig 4E 132
Carlyle St. BN2: Brig 6D 132
Carmel Cl. TN39: Bex S 2E 144
Carmel Ho. BN3: Hove 6J 131
Carmelstead Cl.
RH16: Hay H 6H 49
Carmen Ct. BN20: Will 1L 153
Carn Ct. *BN2: Brig* 7D 132
(*off North Dr.*)
Carnoustie Cl. TN38: St Leo 7F 126
Carnoustie Ct. *RH16: Hay H* 5F 48
(*off Caxton Way*)
TN39: Bex S 1H 145
(*off Eridge Cl.*)
Carol Cl. BN1: Brig 8A 112
Caroline Cl. BN25: Sea 7C 150
Caroline Way BN23: Eastb 3L 155
Carpenter Dr. TN38: St Leo 2F 126
Carpenters Cft. BN8: E Hoath 2E 96
Carpenters Way BN27: Hails 8D 120
Carpet Gardens, The 1E 160
(*off Grand Pde.*)
CARRICK'S HILL 4F 78
Carriers Path BN27: Hails 6E 120
Carriers Pl. TN3: B'ham 9N 5
Carroll Ho. BN21: Eastb 8B 154
Carroll Wlk. BN23: Lang 2H 155
Carrs Cnr. TN1: Tun W 9E 8
CARTERS CORNER 9J 99
Carters Farm Cvn. Pk. TN35: Pett 6N 107
Carvel Ct. TN38: St Leo 8E 104
Carville Av. TN4: South 4C 8
Cashman Lodge BN1: Brig 9C 112
Caspian Ct. BN1: Brig 4D 162
Caspian Sq. BN2: Rott 3G 147
Castle Banks BN7: Lewes 5J 115
Castle Bolton BN23: Lang 9M 141
Castle Ct. *BN7: Lewes* 4K 115
(*off Spences La.*)
Castle Ditch La. BN7: Lewes 5J 115
Castledown Av. TN34: Hast 6N 127
Castledown Ter. *TN34: Hast* 6M 127
(*off Castle Hill Rd.*)
Castle Dr. BN24: Pev B 9E 142
Castle Farm Cotts. TN7: Hart 8K 13
Castlefields TN7: Hart 8K 13
Castle Gdns. TN34: Hast 7M 127
Castle Ga. BN7: Lewes 5J 115
CASTLEHAM 1E 126
Castleham Ind. Est. TN38: St Leo 1F 126
Castleham Rd. TN38: St Leo 1F 126
CASTLE HILL 5L 37
Castle Hill TN6: Roth 5L 37
Castle Hill Nature Reserve 7K 149
Castle Hill Pas. TN34: Hast 6M 127
Castle Hill Rd. TN34: Hast 7M 127
Castle Ho. BN2: W'dean 4L 133
Castle Hurst TN32: Bod 1B 62
Castle La. BN7: Lewes 5J 115
Castle Mt. BN20: Eastb 2A 160
Castle Precincts BN7: Lewes 5J 115
Castle Ri. *BN7: Lewes* 5J 115
(*off Castle Banks*)
TN22: Uck 4J 73
Castle Rd. BN24: Pev 7C 142
TN4: Tun W 2D 16
Castleross Rd. BN24: Pev B 9E 142
Castle Sq. BN1: Brig 8B 132 (8E 162)
Castle St. BN1: Brig 8N 131 (7B 162)
TN1: Tun W 2D 16
TN4: South 3C 8
TN34: Hast 7M 127
(*off Wellington Pl.*)
TN36: Winch 9D 86
Castle Ter. *BN7: Lewes* 5J 115
(*off New Rd.*)
TN18: Hawk 8N 31
Castle Vw. Cvn. & Camping Site
BN24: Pev B 1L 155
Castle Vw. Gdns. BN24: W'ham 7A 142
Castleview M. *TN34: Hast* 6N 127
(*off Castledown Av.*)
Castle Wlk. TN5: Wadh 7A 28
Castle Way TN22: Uck 4J 73
Cathedral Wlk. BN27: Chal 3F 118
Catherine Pl. TN1: Tun W 9E 8
Catherine Va. BN2: W'dean 5M 133
Catkin Way RH16: Hay H 5J 49
Catley Ct. TN39: Bex S 1H 145
Cator Ho. BN21: Eastb 9E 154 (5M 161)
CATSFIELD 7F 102
Catsfield Cl. BN23: Lang 9K 141
TN38: St Leo 4D 126
Catsfield Rd. TN33: Batt, Cats 3E 102
TN33: C'hrst 1L 125
TN33: Cats, Nin 1C 124
CATSFIELD STREAM 8E 102
Cat St. TN7: Cole H, Up H 3E 22
Catts Cnr. Cotts. *TN6: Town R* 1A 38
(*off Catts Hill*)
Catts Hill TN6: Mark C, Town R 1A 38
Causeway, The BN2: Brig 7E 132
BN25: Sea 1D 156
Cavalier Way RH19: E Grin 5F 10
Cavalry Cres. BN20: Eastb 7M 153
Cavell Av. BN10: Peace 6B 148
(not continuous)
Cavell Av. Nth. BN10: Peace 4C 148
Cavell Ct. *BN10: Peace* 5B 148
(*off Cavell Av.*)
Cavendish Av.
BN22: Eastb 8E 154 (3M 161)
TN38: St Leo 7G 126
Cavendish Cl. BN10: Tels C 3B 148
Cavendish Ct. *TN40: Bex S* 2L 145
(*off De La Warr Pde.*)
Cavendish Dr. TN2: Tun W 2E 16
Cavendish Ho. BN1: Brig 8A 162
BN10: Peace 3C 148
RH16: Hay H 7G 48
Cavendish M. *BN3: Hove* 8M 131
(*off Ivy Pl.*)
Cavendish Pl. BN1: Brig 8N 131 (8A 162)
BN21: Eastb 9D 154 (4L 161)
TN34: Hast 6N 127
(*off Croft Rd.*)
Cavendish Sports Cen. 7A 154
Cavendish St. BN2: Brig 8C 132 (8G 162)
Caveridge La. BN8: S Chai 8E 70
Caves Rd. TN38: St Leo 8G 126
Cavix Fld. TN31: North 2A 64
Caxtons M. BN21: Eastb 9D 154 (5L 161)
Caxton Way RH16: Hay H 5F 48
Cecil Burns Lodge TN2: Tun W 2G 17
Cecil Ct. BN21: Eastb 1C 160 (6J 161)
Cecil Kidby Ho. TN2: Tun W 7J 9
Cedar Cl. BN22: Eastb 2A 154
RH15: Burg H 3C 68
TN37: St Leo 1K 127
Cedar Ct. TN4: Tun W 8D 8
Cedar Gables Camping
TN5: Flim 3N 29
Cedar Lodge TN4: Tun W 1C 16
Cedar Ridge TN2: Tun W 7G 9
Cedars Cl. TN22: Uck 9H 53
Cedars Gdns. BN1: Brig 2M 131
Cedars, The BN1: Brig 2M 131
BN2: Brig 2G 162
BN10: Peace 3C 148
BN27: Hails 5E 120
RH16: Hay H 2E 48
TN22: Uck 9J 53
Cedar Way RH16: Hay H 5J 49
Cedarwell Cl. BN9: Pidd 2H 149
Cedarwood *BN1: Brig* 2N 131
(*off Curwen Pl.*)
Celandine Dr. TN38: St Leo 5G 126
Cello Ct. *BN2: Brig* 8D 132
(*off Western Rd.*)
Centenary Ho. *BN1: Brig* 3N 131
(*off Cumberland Rd.*)
Centenary Ind. Est. BN2: Brig 5C 132
Central Av. BN10: Tels C 5A 148
BN20: Eastb 7M 153
BN26: Pole 6E 140
Central Ct. BN10: Tels C 5A 148
Central Pde. *TN5: Wadh* 7B 28
(*off High St.*)
Centre, The BN26: Pole 7D 140
Centurion Ri. TN34: Hast 2N 127
Centurion Rd.
BN1: Brig 7A 132 (6D 162)
BN1: Brig 6C 162
Ceylon Pl. BN21: Eastb 9E 154 (5M 161)
BN22: Eastb 9E 154 (5M 161)
Ceylon Way TN39: Bex S 2F 144
Chadborn Cl. BN2: Brig 9E 132
Chaffinch Rd. BN23: Lang 2F 154
Chaffinch Wlk. TN22: Uck 3J 73
Chafford La. TN3: F'cmbe 7C 6
CHAILEY 5E 70
Chailey Av. BN2: Rott 2H 147
Chailey Cl. BN23: Lang 3H 155
TN34: Hast 1M 127
Chailey Common 9D 50
Chailey Ct. *BN1: Brig* 9L 111
(*off Mill Ri.*)
RH16: Hay H 6G 48
(*off Whitelands*)
Chailey Cres. BN2: Salt 3M 147
Chailey La.
BN8: N'wck, N Cha 3H 71
Chailey Rd. BN1: Brig 1F 132
Chailey Windmill 1D 70
Chain La. TN33: Batt 2K 103
Chalden Pl. TN39: Bex S 8D 124
Chalfont Dr. BN3: Hove 2L 131
Chalket La. TN2: Pem 8M 9
Chalk Farm Cl. BN20: Will 3M 153
Chalkland Ri. BN2: W'dean 5M 133
Chalklin Bus. Pk. TN2: Tun W 4H 9
Chalky Rd. BN41: Ports 2B 130
Challoners RH17: Hors K 6C 32
Challoners Cl. BN2: Rott 2G 147
Challoners M. BN2: Rott 2G 147
Chaloner Cl. RH16: Lind 2J 49
Chaloner Rd. RH16: Lind 2J 49
CHALVINGTON 7E 118
Chalvington Cl. BN1: Brig 8F 112
BN25: Sea 6E 150
Chalvington Dr. TN37: St Leo 9J 105
Chalvington Ho. *BN21: Eastb* 8A 154
(*off Ocklynge Rd.*)
Chalvington Rd. BN21: Eastb 5N 153
BN27: Chal, Gold C 1H 119
Chamberlaines La. BN8: Ring 9E 94
Chamberlain Rd. BN21: Eastb 8N 153
Chambers Cres. TN38: St Leo 3F 126
Chambers Rd. TN38: St Leo 3F 126
Champions Row BN3: Hove 5L 131
Chancellor Ho. TN4: Tun W 1C 16
Chancellors Pk. BN6: Hass 3A 90
Chanctonbury Dr. TN34: Hast 9L 105
Chanctonbury Rd.
BN3: Hove 6N 131 (3A 162)
RH15: Burg H 7A 68
Chandler Rd. TN39: Bex S 1H 145
Chandlers Mead BN8: Cooks 8G 92
Chandos Ct. *TN40: Bex S* 2K 145
(*off Marina*)
Chandos Rd. TN1: Tun W 8F 8
Channel Grange BN10: Tels C 5A 148
Channel Vw. *BN42: S'wck* 6A 130
(*off Whiterock Pl.*)
TN40: Bex S 2K 145
Channel Vw. E. TN40: Bex S 2K 145
Channel Vw. Rd. BN2: W'dean 5J 133
BN22: Eastb 7F 154
BN24: Pev B 8G 142
Channel Vw. W. TN40: Bex S 2K 145
Channel Way TN35: Fair 3K 129
Channers La. BN8: Ripe 5B 118
Channings BN3: Hove 7H 131
Chant La. TN6: Roth 1N 37
Chantlers Cl. RH19: E Grin 2C 10
Chantlers Mead TN8: C'den 8F 4
Chantry Av. TN40: Bex S 8K 125
Chantry La. TN40: Bex S 9K 125
Chantry, The BN21: Eastb 8B 154
Chapel Barn Cl. BN27: Hails 7F 120
Chapel Cl. BN25: Sea 8D 150
RH15: Burg H 4A 68
Chapel Cotts. TN31: Buck 5F 64
CHAPEL CROSS 3L 77
Chapel Fld. TN31: North 2N 63
Chapelfields RH17: Cuck 1A 48
CHAPEL GREEN 9D 24
Chapel Hill BN7: Lewes 5L 115
BN26: Lull 2N 151
TN33: C'hrst 2N 125
TN33: Sed 9E 82
Chapel Ho. *BN2: Brig* 8C 132
(*off Chapel St.*)
Chapel La. BN7: E Chil 4A 92
RH17: Hors K 5C 32
RH18: F Row 2M 21
RH19: A'hstw 6K 11
TN22: B'boys 1F 74
TN35: Gues T 7F 106
TN35: W'fld 3L 105
Chapel M. BN3: Hove 8M 131 (7A 162)
Chapel Pk. Rd. TN37: St Leo 6J 127
Chapel Path *TN40: Bex S* 9K 125
(*off London Rd.*)
Chapel Pl. BN41: Ports 6D 130
TN4: Tun W 2D 16
TN31: North 3N 63
Chapel Rd. BN7: Plump G 9M 69
BN41: Ports 6C 130
CHAPEL ROW 1B 122
Chapel Row BN27: Herst 3B 122
Chapel St. BN2: Brig 8C 132
BN9: N'hvn 5K 149
(not continuous)
Chapel Ter. BN2: Brig 9E 132
Chapel Ter. M. BN2: Brig 9E 132
Chapel Wlk. TN40: Bex S 8M 125
Chapman's La. RH19: E Grin 3B 10
(not continuous)
CHAPMAN'S TOWN 6L 77
Chapmans Town Rd. TN21: Rush G 5L 77
Chapman Way TN2: Tun W 5F 8
Charis Ct. *BN3: Hove* 6L 131
(*off Eaton Rd.*)
Charity Farm Way TN6: Crow 8E 24
Charles Bennet Ct. RH16: Hay H 5H 49
Charles Cl. BN3: Hove 2J 131
BN25: Sea 7C 150
Charles Kingston Gdns. BN1: Brig 9N 111
Charles Moore Ct. BN26: Pole 6D 140
Charles Rd. TN38: St Leo 6H 127
Charles Rd. W. TN38: St Leo 6H 127
Charles St. BN2: Brig 9B 132 (9F 162)
TN4: South 5D 8
Charleston 3M 137
Charleston Rd. BN21: Eastb 8N 153
Charlesworth Pk. RH16: Hay H 5K 49
Charlotte St. BN2: Brig 9C 132
Charlston Av. BN9: N'hvn 7G 149
Charlton Gdns. BN6: Ditch 4E 90
Charltons, The BN1: Brig 8E 112
Charlton's Way TN4: Tun W 3B 16
CHARLWOOD 2E 20
Charlwood Gdns. RH15: Burg H 3D 68
Charlwood Rd. RH15: Burg H 2D 68
Charlwoods Bus. Cen.
RH19: E Grin 1D 10
Charlwoods Pl. RH19: E Grin 1E 10
Charlwoods Rd. RH19: E Grin 2D 10
Charter Ga. RH16: Hay H 4E 48
Chartfield BN3: Hove 3J 131
Chartfield Way *BN3: Hove* 3J 131
(*off Woodland Dr.*)
Chartness *BN1: Brig* 8A 112
(*off Warmdene Rd.*)
Chartres TN40: Bex S 8L 125
Chartres Cl. TN40: Bex S 8L 125
Chartwell Cl. BN25: Sea 6D 150
Chartwell Ct. BN1: Brig 8C 162
Chartwell Ho. BN21: Eastb 5J 161
Chase, The TN2: Tun W 2E 16
Chates Farm Ct. BN2: Brig 7C 132
Chatfield Cl. TN38: St Leo 2F 126
Chatfield Cres. BN22: Will 3N 153
Chatfield Rd. RH17: Cuck 3B 48
Chatham Grn. BN23: Eastb 3L 155
Chatham Pl. BN1: Brig 6A 132 (4C 162)
BN25: Sea 1D 156
Chatham Rd. TN37: St Leo 4H 127
Chatsworth Av. BN10: Tels C 3A 148
Chatsworth Cl. BN10: Tels C 4A 148
Chatsworth Ct. BN1: Brig 2B 162
Chatsworth Gdns. BN20: Eastb 3C 160
Chatsworth Ho. BN21: Eastb 7L 161
Chatsworth Pk. BN10: Tels C 3B 148
Chatsworth Rd.
BN1: Brig 5N 131 (2B 162)
Chatsworth Sq. BN3: Hove 6M 131

Chatsworth Wlk.—Clayton Rd.

Chatsworth Wlk.
BN21: Eastb 1D 160 (6K 161)
Chaucer Av. RH19: E Grin 4C 10
Chaucer Ct. RH16: Hay H 4E 48
(off Winnals Pk.)
Chaucer Ind. Est. BN26: Pole 7G 140
Chaucer Wlk. BN23: Lang 1H 155
(off Close Seventeen)
Chawbrook M.
BN22: Eastb 8E 154 (2M 161)
Chawbrook Rd.
BN22: Eastb 8E 154 (2M 161)
Cheapside BN1: Brig 7B 132 (5E 162)
Cheeleys RH17: Hors K 5C 32
Chelgates TN39: Bex S 3D 144
Chelmsford Ct.
BN20: Eastb 2C 160 (9H 161)
Chelsea Arc. RH16: Hay H 4F 48
Chelsea Cl. TN40: Bex S 1L 145
Chelston Av. BN3: Hove 6F 130
Cheltenham Pl.
BN1: Brig 7B 132 (6F 162)
Chelwood Cl. BN1: Brig 8D 112
CHELWOOD COMMON 4K 33
CHELWOOD GATE 1J 33
Chelwood Ga. Rd. RH17: Chel G 3L 33
TN22: Nut 4N 33
Chelworth Rd. BN22: Eastb 2A 154
Chene Rd. BN10: Peace 6F 148
Chenies Cl. TN2: Tun W 4D 16
Chepstow Ct. BN1: Brig 9F 112
Chequer Grange RH18: F Row 2L 21
Chequer Mead Theatre & Arts Cen.
3F 10
Chequer Rd. RH19: E Grin 3F 10
Chequers Cl. TN6: Crow 9E 24
Chequers Way TN6: Crow 9E 24
Cherith Cotts. TN21: H'fld 2D 76
Cheriton Ct. BN21: Eastb 8N 153
Cherry Clack TN21: Punn T 2N 77
Cherry Cotts. TN22: Flet 5M 51
Cherrycroft BN1: Brig 9A 112
(off Warmdene Rd.)
Cherry Garden Hill TN31: North 5C 64
Cherry Gdn. Rd. BN20: Eastb 9M 153
Cherry Gdns. TN21: H'fld 3E 76
TN22: H Hur 1N 53
Cherry Gdns. Hill TN3: Groom 9D 14
TN6: Lye G 9C 14
Cherry Side BN27: Hails 6D 120
Cherry Tree Cl. TN37: St Leo 6K 127
Cherry Tree Ct. TN21: Horam 9C 76
Cherry Tree Gdns. TN40: Bex S 8N 125
Cherry Tree Rd. TN2: Tun W 3B 16
Cherrywood BN1: Brig 2N 131
(off Curwen Pl.)
Cherwell Cl. BN24: Sto C 8J 141
Cherwell Ct. TN21: H'fld 9D 56
(off Cherwell Rd.)
Cherwell Rd. TN21: H'fld 9D 56
Chesham Mans. BN2: Brig 9E 132
(off Eaton Pl.)
Chesham Pl. BN2: Brig 9E 132
Chesham Rd. BN2: Brig 9E 132
Chesham St. BN2: Brig 9E 132
Cheshire Ct. BN22: Eastb 2N 161
Chester Av. TN2: Tun W 2G 17
Chester Ct. BN3: Hove 4A 162
Chesterfield Ct. BN2: Brig 8C 132
(off Marine Vw.)
Chesterfield Gdns. BN20: Eastb 3B 160
Chesterfield Rd. BN20: Eastb 3B 160
Chester Ter. BN1: Brig 3B 132
Chesterton Av. BN25: Sea 9G 151
Chesterton Cl. RH19: E Grin 5F 10
Chesterton Dr. BN25: Sea 9G 151
Chestnut Av. BN27: Chal 2F 118
TN4: South 5D 8
Chestnut Cl. BN22: Eastb 2A 154
BN27: Hails 5D 120
BN27: Herst 9A 100
RH15: Burg H 3C 68
RH19: E Grin 3G 11
TN4: South 5E 8
TN31: B Oak 3A 84
Chestnut Cotts. TN22: Flet 6M 51
Chestnut Dr. BN26: Pole 7D 140
Chestnut Pl. TN8: C'den 7F 4
Chestnuts Cl. RH16: Lind 2H 49
Chestnuts, The BN2: Brig 5C 132
(off Prince's Cres.)
RH16: Lind 2G 49
TN18: Hawk 2M 43
Chestnut Wlk. TN39: Bex S 9D 124
Chestnut Way BN9: N'hvn 5H 149
Chetnole RH19: E Grin 2D 10
Cheviot Cl. BN23: Lang 1F 154
Cheviots Cl., The TN34: Hast 2B 128
Chichester Cl. BN2: Brig 9E 132
(off Chichester Pl.)
BN2: Salt 3K 147
BN3: Hove 1G 130
BN10: Peace 5F 148
BN22: Will 2M 153
Chichester Cl. BN25: Sea 8D 150
TN39: Bex S 8J 125
Chichester Ct. BN25: Sea 9D 150
(off Pelham Rd.)
TN39: Bex S 2D 144
Chichester Dr. E. BN2: Salt 3K 147
Chichester Dr. W. BN2: Salt 3J 147
Chichester Ho. TN40: Bex S 1L 145
Chichester Lodge BN25: Sea 9D 150
Chichester Pl. BN2: Brig 9E 132
Chichester Rd. BN25: Sea 9D 150
TN38: St Leo 4H 127
Chichester Ter. BN2: Brig 9E 132
Chichester Way RH15: Burg H 3D 68
Chick Hill TN35: Pett 7N 107
Chicks La. TN17: Kiln 1A 30
CHIDDINGLY 6J 97
Chiddingly Cl. BN2: Brig 8G 132
Chiddingly Ho. BN3: Hove 6M 131
(off Chatsworth Sq.)
Chiddingly Rd. TN21: Horam 3A 98
CHIDDINGSTONE HOATH 4N 5
Chieveley Dr. TN2: Tun W 3G 16
Chilcomb RH15: Burg H 7D 68
Chilgrove BN1: Brig 8A 112
(off Warmdene Rd.)
Chilham Cl. BN23: Lang 2G 154
Chillies La. TN6: H Hur 4N 35
TN22: H Hur 9M 35
Chilling St. RH19: Sharp 6C 20
Chillis Wood Rd. RH16: Hay H 4D 48
CHILSHAM 7B 100
Chilsham La. BN27: Herst 8N 99
Chilston Cl. TN4: Tun W 8D 8
Chilston Rd. TN4: Tun W 8D 8
Chiltern Cl. BN23: Lang 9N 141
Chiltern Ct. BN26: Pole 6D 140
Chiltern Dr. TN34: Hast 3A 128
Chiltern Wlk. TN2: Tun W 9G 8
CHILTINGTON 4C 92
Chiltington Cl. BN2: Salt 2K 147
RH15: Burg H 3A 68
Chiltington La. BN7: E Chil 4C 92
Chiltington Way BN2: Salt 2K 147
Chilver Bri. Rd. BN26: Arl, B'wck 4F 138
Chiswick Pl. BN21: Eastb 1D 160 (7L 161)
CHITCOMBE 2L 83
Chitcombe Rd. TN31: B Oak 2J 83
Chitcombe Wlk. TN34: Hast 1N 127
(off De Chardin Dr.)
Chorley Av. BN2: Salt 2J 147
Chownes Mead La. RH16: Hay H 5C 48
Chown's Hill TN35: Hast 1N 127
Chrisdory Rd. BN41: Ports 2B 130
Christ Chu. Av. TN1: Tun W 1D 16
Christ Chu. Ct. BN9: N'hvn 5K 149
Christchurch Ho. BN1: Brig 7A 162
Christchurch Pl. BN23: Eastb 3K 155
Christie Av. BN8: Ring 9C 94
Christie Rd. BN7: Lewes 5G 115
Christies RH19: E Grin 4D 10
Christine Cl. TN40: Bex S 7A 126
Christopher Rd. RH19: E Grin 3E 10
CHUCK HATCH 4H 23
Church Acre Drove
BN27: Pev, Wart 3B 142
Church App. TN22: Fram 3N 73
Church Av. BN24: W'ham 7C 142
RH16: Hay H 3F 48
Church Bailey BN24: W'ham 8C 142
Church Cl. BN1: Brig 9A 112
BN20: Will 9D 140
RH15: Burg H 5B 68
Church Ct. BN3: Hove 4H 131
RH16: Hay H 5F 48
Church Cres. BN8: Ring 1C 116
Churchdale Av. BN22: Eastb 6F 154
Churchdale Pl. BN22: Eastb 6E 154
Churchdale Rd. BN22: Eastb 5E 154
CHURCHES GREEN 9D 78
Churches Grn. TN21: Dall 1C 100
Church Farm Cl. TN19: Etch 9D 42
Church Farm La. BN27: Chal 7D 118
Churchfield BN20: E Dean 3F 158
TN35: W'fld 4K 105
Church Flds. TN22: Nut 6B 34
Churchfields Ind. Est.
TN38: St Leo 2D 126
CHURCH HILL 5M 23
Church Hill BN1: Brig 8N 111
BN8: Ring 9C 94
BN9: N'hvn 5J 149
TN19: Etch 8C 42
TN33: Sed 6D 82
TN39: Bex S 1D 144
Church Hill Pl. TN39: Bex S 1E 144
(off Hillborough Cl.)
Church Ho. Cl. BN42: S'wck 4B 130
Churchill Av. TN35: Hast 1C 128
Churchill Cl. BN20: Eastb 9A 154
Churchill Ct. BN21: Eastb 8K 161
TN38: St Leo 3H 127
Churchill Ho. BN3: Hove 3F 130
BN25: Sea 8H 151
Churchill Rd. BN7: Lewes 3G 115
BN25: Sea 7C 150
TN21: H'fld 2E 76
Churchill Sq. Shop. Cen.
BN1: Brig 8A 132 (7C 162)
Churchill Way RH15: Burg H 6D 68
Church in the Wood La.
TN38: St Leo 3F 126
Churchland La. TN33: Sed 6E 82
Church La. BN6: Ditch 4E 90
BN7: King L 9D 114
BN7: Lewes 6H 115
(High St.)
BN7: Lewes 4J 115
(St Michael's Ter.)
BN8: Laug 9A 96
BN8: Ripe 5C 118
BN21: Eastb 9A 154
BN24: Pev 7D 142
BN25: Sea 1D 156
BN26: Jev 5G 152
BN27: Hell 9D 98
Church La. BN42: S'wck 6A 130
BN45: Pye 1L 111
RH17: Dane 7G 33
RH17: Hors K 5C 32
RH17: Wivel 2G 69
RH19: E Grin 3F 10
TN3: Frant 8E 16
TN19: Etch 9D 42
TN22: Buxt 4A 54
TN31: Buck 5D 64
TN31: Iden 5F 66
TN31: Peas 9M 65
TN32: Rob 4K 61
TN33: Cats 7F 102
TN33: Hooe 7L 123
TN33: Nin 1C 124
TN35: Gues T 6F 106
TN35: W'fld 4L 105
Church Marks La. BN8: E Hoath 2D 96
Church Mead BN6: Hass 4B 90
Church M. BN20: Will 3M 153
Church of Scientology 8C 10
Church Pas. TN34: Hast 6N 127
(off Croft Rd.)
TN34: Hast 6N 127
(off High St.)
Church Path BN27: Hell 1D 120
TN33: Nin 1B 124
(not continuous)
Church Pl. BN2: Brig 9F 132
Church Rd. BN3: Hove 7J 131
BN8: Barc 6K 93
BN8: N'wck 1K 71
BN24: Pev 7D 142
(off High St.)
BN26: Pole 7D 140
BN27: Hell 1C 120
BN27: Herst 4C 122
BN41: Ports 6D 130
RH15: Burg H 6B 68
RH16: Hay H 5F 48
RH17: Scay H 6N 49
TN1: Tun W 1C 16
TN2: Pem 4N 9
TN3: Lamb 6K 19
TN4: South 3C 8
TN5: Flim, Kiln 2N 29
TN6: Crow 9C 24
TN17: Kiln 2N 29
TN18: Sandh 6F 44
TN22: Buxt 6N 53
TN32: Mount 3H 81
TN33: A'ham 3L 101
TN33: Cats 7F 102
TN37: St Leo 6J 127
Church Row BN7: Lewes 5K 115
Churchsettle La. TN5: Wadh 4C 40
Church Sq. TN31: Rye 3G 86
Church St. BN1: Brig 7A 132 (6C 162)
BN20: Will 3M 153
BN21: Eastb 9A 154
BN22: Will 2N 153
BN25: Sea 9D 150
BN41: Ports 6D 130
RH17: Cuck 3A 48
TN5: Tice 3M 41
TN5: Wadh 7C 28
TN6: Roth 2L 37
TN7: Hart 8J 13
TN8: C'den 8G 4
TN21: H'fld 3G 76
TN22: Uck 9H 53
TN35: Hast 3B 128
TN40: Bex S 9L 125
Church Twitten BN7: Lewes 5K 115
Church Va. Rd. TN40: Bex S 9K 125
Church Vs. BN8: Ring 1C 116
(off Church Hill)
Church Wlk. RH15: Burg H 5B 68
TN18: Hawk 1A 44
TN22: Uck 3H 73
(off High St.)
Church Way BN2: Brig 5G 162
Chu. Wood Dr. TN38: St Leo 4E 126
Churchwood Way TN38: St Leo 4F 126
Chyngton Av. BN25: Sea 8G 151
Chyngton Cl. BN23: Lang 9K 141
Chyngton Gdns. BN25: Sea 8G 151
Chyngton Ho. BN25: Sea 1H 157
Chyngton La. BN25: Sea 9H 151
Chyngton La. Nth. BN25: Sea 8H 151
Chyngton Pl. BN25: Sea 1G 156
Chyngton Rd. BN25: Sea 1F 156
Chyngton Way BN25: Sea 1G 157
Cider Hollow BN27: Bore S 1D 122
Cider Ho. Wlk. BN8: E Hoath 2E 96
(off Buttsfield La.)
Cinderford La. BN27: Hell 7H 99
CINDER HILL 2B 32
Cinder Hill BN8: N Cha 5F 70
RH19: Sharp 1B 32
Cinder Hill La. RH17: Hors K 4A 32
Cinque Foil BN10: Peace 4C 148
Cinque Ports St. TN31: Rye 3F 86
Cinque Ports Way BN25: Sea 8H 151
TN38: St Leo 8E 126
Circus Pde. BN1: Brig 3E 162
Circus St. BN2: Brig 8B 132 (7F 162)
Circus, The BN23: Eastb 4G 155
Cissbury Av. BN10: Peace 6E 148
Cissbury Cres. BN2: Salt 3M 147
Cissbury Rd. BN3: Hove 6N 131 (3A 162)
RH15: Burg H 4A 68
Civic App. TN22: Uck 1H 73
Civic Way RH15: Burg H 6B 68
TN1: Tun W 1E 16
Clackhams La. TN6: Jar B 3H 37
Clair Ct. RH16: Hay H 4F 48
Clair Rd. RH16: Hay H 3F 48
Clambers Play Cen. 7L 127
Clanricarde Gdns. TN1: Tun W 1D 16
Clanricarde Rd. TN1: Tun W 1D 16
Clapham La. BN26: Lit 4M 151
Claphatch La. TN5: Wadh 5J 29
Clappers La. BN5: Fulk 2B 110
Clappers, The TN32: Rob 5J 61
CLAPWATER 2A 52
Claremont TN34: Hast 7L 127
(off Robertson St.)
Claremont Ct. BN25: Sea 9C 150
(off Claremont Rd.)
Claremont Ct. TN4: Tun W 6F 8
(off Nth. Farm Rd.)
Claremont Gdns. TN2: Tun W 2E 16
Claremont Quays BN25: Sea 9D 150
(off Claremont Rd.)
Claremont Ri. TN22: Uck 8H 53
Claremont Rd. BN9: N'hvn 3M 149
BN25: Sea 9B 150
TN1: Tun W 2E 16
TN39: Bex S 7J 125
Clarence Ct. BN24: Pev B 1M 155
Clarence Dr. RH19: E Grin 5F 10
Clarence Gdns. BN1: Brig 7B 162
Clarence Ho. BN20: Eastb 8G 161
Clarence M. BN25: Sea 9D 150
(off Richmond Rd.)
Clarence Rd.
BN22: Eastb 8E 154 (2M 161)
TN1: Tun W 1D 16
TN37: St Leo 5J 127
Clarence Row TN1: Tun W 1D 16
Clarence Sq. BN1: Brig 8A 132 (7C 162)
Clarence Yd. BN1: Brig 8B 132 (8E 162)
Clarendon Cl. TN37: St Leo 2H 127
Clarendon Ct. BN20: Eastb 3C 160
(off Bolsover Rd.)
Clarendon Gdns. TN2: Tun W 3D 16
Clarendon Ho. BN3: Hove 6K 131
Clarendon Pl. BN2: Brig 9D 132
BN41: Ports 7E 130
Clarendon Rd. BN3: Hove 6K 131
Clarendon Ter. BN2: Brig 9E 132
Clarendon Vs. BN3: Hove 6J 131
Clarendon Way TN2: Tun W 3C 16
Clare Rd. BN7: Lewes 4G 115
Clare Wlk. BN2: Brig 8E 132
Clarke Av. BN3: Hove 3G 131
Clarke Ct. BN3: Hove 7H 131
Clarks Ind. Est. BN3: Hove 5K 131
Clarks Yd. TN5: Flim 8B 30
Claverham Cl. TN33: Batt 3J 103
Claverham Way TN33: Batt 3J 103
Clavering Wlk. TN39: Bex S 3C 144
Claxton Cl. BN21: Eastb 7A 154
Claxton Rd. TN40: Bex S 9A 126
Clayfields BN10: Peace 4B 148
CLAYHILL 6D 64
Clay Hill Rd. TN3: Lamb 3E 18
Clays Cl. RH19: E Grin 4E 10
Clayton Av. BN6: Hass 4A 90
Clayton Dr. RH15: Burg H 7A 68
Clayton Hill BN45: Pye 1L 111
Clayton Mill Rd. BN24: Sto C 8L 141
Clayton Rd. BN2: Brig 6E 132
BN6: Ditch 5D 90

Clayton's La.—Coombe Rd.

Clayton's La. TN3: A'hst .3C 14
Clayton Way BN3: Hove .2H 131
Clayton Windmills (Jill & Jack) .8A 90
Clearwater La. RH17: Scay H .6A 50
Clearwaters La. RH16: Hay H .9D 48
Cleeve Av. TN2: Tun W .2G 17
Cleevelands BN22: Will .2M 153
Clement Hill TN34: Hast .3A 128
Clementine Av. BN25: Sea .7B 150
Clement La. BN26: Pole .8D 140
Clerks Acre BN6: Hass .3B 90
(not continuous)
Clermont Ct. BN1: Brig .3N 131
Clermont Rd. BN1: Brig .3N 131
Clermont Ter. BN1: Brig .3N 131
Cleve Cl. TN22: Fram .3N 73
Clevedean Rd. TN39: Bex S .8H 125
Clevedown BN7: Lewes .6G 115
Cleveland TN2: Tun W .9G 8
Cleveland Cl. BN23: Lang .1F 154
Cleveland Gdns.
RH15: Burg H .6C 68
Cleveland Rd. BN1: Brig .3B 132
Clevelands *RH16: Hay H* .3F 48
(off Perrymount Rd.)
Cleve Ter. BN7: Lewes .6H 115
Cliff App. BN2: Brig .9G 133
Cliff Av. BN10: Peace .7E 148
Cliff Cl. BN25: Sea .2E 156
Cliff Ct. BN2: Rott .3G 147
CLIFFE .5L 115
Cliffe Bus. Cen. *BN7: Lewes* .5L 115
(off Cliffe High St.)
Cliffe High St. BN7: Lewes .5K 115
Cliffe Ind. Est. BN8: Lewes .6M 115
Cliffe Leas *BN7: Lewes* .5L 115
(off Foundry La.)
CLIFF END .8N 107
Cliff End La. TN35: Pett .8N 107
Cliff Gdns. BN10: Tels C .4N 147
BN25: Sea .2E 156
Cliff Ho. BN20: Eastb .3B 160
Clifford Av. BN21: Eastb .6N 153
Clifford Ct. TN6: Crow .9D 24
TN40: Bex S .1K 145
Clifford Ho. BN21: Eastb .7L 161
Clifford Rd. TN40: Bex S .1K 145
Cliff Pk. Cl. BN10: Peace .5F 148
Cliff Rd. BN2: Brig .9G 132
BN20: Eastb .4B 160
BN25: Sea .2E 156
Cliff, The BN2: Brig .9G 133
Cliff Way TN35: Fair .1L 129
Clifton Cl. BN22: Eastb .4A 154
Clifton Cotts. TN2: Tun W .5G 8
Clifton Ct. BN1: Brig .4D 162
BN21: Eastb .6K 161
TN34: Hast .6L 127
Clifton Hill BN1: Brig .7N 131 (5B 162)
Clifton Ho. BN22: Eastb .4A 154
Clifton M. BN1: Brig .5C 162
Clifton Pl. BN1: Brig .7N 131 (6B 162)
TN1: Tun W .2E 16
Clifton Ri. TN40: Bex S .9N 125
Clifton Rd. BN1: Brig .7A 132 (5B 162)
BN9: N'hvn .5K 149
TN2: Tun W .6F 8
TN35: Hast .3B 128
Clifton St. BN1: Brig .7A 132 (5D 162)
Clifton St. Pas. BN1: Brig .5D 162
Clifton Ter. BN1: Brig .7A 132 (6C 162)
Cliftonville Ct. BN3: Hove .6K 131
Cliftonville Rd. TN38: St Leo .8D 126
Cliftonville Way TN38: St Leo .8D 126
Clifton Way BN10: Tels C .4A 148
Climping Cl. RH16: Hay H .5E 48
Clinch Grn. Av. TN39: Bex S .6G 125
Clinton Cres. TN38: St Leo .6H 127
Clinton La. BN25: Sea .9D 150
Clinton Pl. BN25: Sea .9D 150
Clinton Way TN35: Fair .1L 129
Clive Av. TN35: Hast .4B 128
Clive Ct. BN21: Eastb .6M 161
Cliveden Cl. BN1: Brig .2N 131
Cliveden Ct. BN1: Brig .3N 131
CLIVE VALE .4C 128
Clive Vs. *TN33: Batt* .4M 103
(off Battle Hill)
Clockhouse TN2: Tun W .7J 9
Clock Ho. La. TN22: Nut .6B 34
Clock Tower .8A 132 (7D 162)
Clock Twr. Ct. TN39: Bex S .2J 145
Cloister Ct. *TN40: Bex S* .2L 145
(off Brassey Rd.)
Cloisters BN9: N'hvn .5J 149
Cloisters, The BN22: Will .2N 153
TN33: Batt .1L 103
TN37: St Leo .7K 127
Close Eight BN23: Lang .1H 155
Close Eighteen BN23: Lang .2H 155
Close Eleven BN23: Lang .1H 155
Close Fifteen BN23: Lang .2H 155
Close Five BN23: Lang .1H 155
Close Four BN23: Lang .2H 155
Close Fourteen BN23: Lang .1H 155
Close Nine BN23: Lang .2H 155
Close Nineteen BN23: Lang .2H 155
Close One BN23: Lang .2G 155
Close Seven BN23: Lang .1H 155
Close Seventeen BN23: Lang .2H 155
Close Six BN23: Lang .1H 155
Close Sixteen BN23: Lang .2H 155
Close Ten BN23: Lang .2H 155
Close, The BN1: Brig .9M 111
BN6: Hass .3A 90
BN9: N'hvn .2M 149
BN20: Fris .2E 158
BN20: Will .4M 153
BN22: Eastb .2N 153
BN25: Sea .1E 156
RH15: Burg H .4D 68
RH19: E Grin .4D 10
TN3: Groom .6G 14
TN4: Tun W .5F 8
TN6: Crow .8C 24
TN22: B'boys .2F 74
TN31: Rye .2E 86
TN35: Fair .2H 129
Close Three BN23: Lang .2G 155
Close Twelve BN23: Lang .2H 155
Close Twenty BN23: Lang .2H 155
Close Twentyfive BN23: Lang .2G 155
Close Twentyfour BN23: Lang .2H 155
Close Two BN23: Lang .2G 155
Cloudesley Rd. TN37: St Leo .6J 127
Clovelly BN21: Eastb .7J 161
Clovelly Ho. BN26: Pole .6C 140
Clover Ct. RH16: Hay H .5F 48
Clover Lea TN34: Hast .1L 127
Clovers End BN1: Brig .7C 112
Clover Way BN41: Ports .3D 130
Clovis Ct. BN21: Eastb .9D 154 (3K 161)
Cluny St. BN7: Lewes .6J 115
Clyde Pk. BN27: Hails .7G 120
Clyde Rd. BN1: Brig .5B 132 (2E 162)
TN38: St Leo .7J 127
Coach And Horses La. RH17: Chel C .4J 33
Coach & Horses Pas. *TN2: Tun W* .2D 16
(off Pantiles, The)
Coach La. RH17: Chel C .4J 33
Coach Rd. TN4: R'hall .9N 7
Coastal Counties Ho. *BN2: Brig* .7C 132
(off Sussex St.)
Coastguard Cl. BN24: Nor B .5M 143
Coastguard Cotts. BN24: Nor B .5M 143
TN31: Camb .6A 88
Coastguard La. TN35: Fair .2G 129
Coastguard Sq. *BN22: Eastb* .8F 154
(off Latimer Rd.)
TN31: Rye .5L 87
Coast Rd. BN24: Nor B .6K 143
BN24: Pev B .8F 142
Coates Ct. BN42: S'wck .6A 130
Cobald Rd. BN24: Pev B .8G 143
COBBARN .9J 15
Cobbetts Mead RH16: Hay H .6J 49
Cobbett's Ride TN2: Tun W .3C 16
Cobblers Fld. TN19: B'wsh C .6C 58
Cobbold Av. BN21: Eastb .6N 153
Cobbs Hill Farm Camping & Cvn. Pk.
TN39: Bex S .4J 125
Cobden Rd. BN2: Brig .6D 132
Cobdown La. TN22: Mare .5H 53
Cobhams TN3: Speld .5L 7
Cobham Towers TN40: Bex S .1N 145
Cobourg Flats *TN34: Hast* .6N 127
(off Croft Rd.)
Cobton Dr. BN3: Hove .2J 131
Coburg Pl. *TN34: Hast* .6N 127
(off Croft Rd.)
Coburn Pl. *BN27: Hails* .7F 120
(off Station Rd.)
Cochrane Cl. BN23: Eastb .5H 155
Cockcrow Wood TN37: St Leo .1K 127
Cockfield La. BN8: N Cha, S Chai .5H 71
COCK MARLING .6M 85
Cockmount La. TN5: Wadh .6B 28
COCKSHOT .1N 43
Cockshut Rd. BN7: Lewes .6J 115
COGGER'S CROSS .4C 98
Cogger's La. TN21: Horam .4C 98
COGGINS MILL .6H 39
Coggins Mill La. TN20: May .7F 38
COGHURST .9B 106
Coghurst Hall Holiday Village
TN35: Hast .7A 106
Coghurst Rd. TN35: Hast .2B 128
Colbourne Av. BN2: Brig .3E 132
Colbourne Rd.
BN3: Hove .6N 131 (4A 162)
Colchester Va. RH18: F Row .1L 21
Colchins RH15: Burg H .7A 68
COLDEAN .8E 112
Coldean La. BN1: Brig .7E 112
Coldharbour Cl. TN6: Crow .1E 36
Coldharbour La. BN8: N Cha .1G 70
TN21: Punn T .3M 77
TN31: Iden, Rye F .7C 66
Coldharbour Rd.
BN27: Lwr D, Up D .6L 119
TN8: Chid H .5B 6
TN11: Chid H, Pens .5B 6
Coldstream Ho. *BN25: Sea* .1E 156
(off Bramber La.)
Coldthorne La. BN27: Hails .1D 140
Coldwaltham La. RH15: Burg H .6E 68
Colebrooke Rd. TN39: Bex S .1H 145
Colebrook Ind. Est. TN2: Tun W .4H 9
Colebrook Rd. BN1: Brig .1M 131
BN42: S'wck .6B 130
TN4: Tun W .6F 8
Coleman Av. BN3: Hove .6G 131
COLEMAN'S HATCH .4D 22
Colemans Hatch Rd.
RH18: Cole H, Wych C .6L 21
TN7: Cole H .6A 22
Coleman St. BN2: Brig .7C 132
Coleridge St. BN3: Hove .5J 131
Coleridge Wlk. *BN23: Lang* .2H 155
(off Close Fifteen)
Coles Ct. TN2: Tun W .1F 16
Colgate Cl. BN2: Brig .7G 132
College Cl. BN41: Ports .2B 130
RH19: E Grin .3F 10
College Ct. *BN2: Brig* .8D 132
(off Eastern Rd.)
BN21: Eastb .7J 161
College Dr. TN2: Tun W .9G 8
College Gdns. BN2: Brig .9D 132
College Grn. BN21: Eastb .8B 154
College La. RH19: E Grin .3F 10
College Pl. BN2: Brig .9D 132
College Rd. BN2: Brig .9D 132
BN21: Eastb .1C 160 (7J 161)
BN25: Sea .1D 156
RH16: Hay H .2F 48
TN40: Bex S .1M 145
College St. BN2: Brig .9D 132
College Ter. BN2: Brig .8D 132
Coller M. TN6: Jar B .2H 37
Collett Cl. TN38: St Leo .1F 126
Colley Cnr. TN39: Bex S .9G 125
Collier Cl. BN22: Eastb .5E 154
Collier Rd. BN24: Pev B .9F 142
TN34: Hast .6N 127
COLLIER'S GREEN .8G 62
Collingford La. RH17: Dane .6H 33
Collington *BN1: Brig* .8A 112
(off Warmdene Rd.)
Collington Av. TN39: Bex S .2G 144
Collington Cl.
BN20: Eastb .2B 160 (9G 161)
Collington Ho. TN39: Bex S .1F 144
Collington La. E. TN39: Bex S .1F 144
Collington La. W. TN39: Bex S .1E 144
Collington Mans. *TN39: Bex S* .2H 145
(off Collington Av.)
Collington Park Cres.
TN39: Bex S .1G 144
Collington Ri. TN39: Bex S .1F 144
Collington Station (Rail) .2H 145
Collingwood Av. TN21: H'fld .1D 76
Collingwood Cl. BN10: Peace .3C 148
BN23: Eastb .6H 155
RH19: E Grin .5F 10
Collingwood Ct. BN2: Brig .1B 146
Collingwood Ri. TN21: H'fld .1D 76
Collinstone Rd. TN38: St Leo .7G 126
Collinswood Dr. TN38: St Leo .7F 126
Collongton Gro. TN39: Bex S .1F 144
Collwell Cl. RH16: Hay H .6G 49
Colmer Ct. RH15: Burg H .5A 68
Colmer Pl. RH15: Burg H .5A 68
Colonade, The TN18: Hawk .9N 31
Colonel Stevens Ct.
BN20: Eastb .2C 160 (9H 161)
Colonels Way TN4: South .3D 8
Colonnade Gdns.
BN21: Eastb .9E 154 (5N 161)
Colonnade Rd.
BN21: Eastb .9E 154 (5N 161)
Colonnades, The BN1: Brig .8E 162
Coltstocks Rd. BN20: Eastb .3A 160
Columbus Dr. BN23: Eastb .5J 155
Colville Ct. *BN21: Eastb* .8B 154
(off Selwyn Rd.)
Colwell Gdns. RH16: Hay H .6G 48
Colwell La. RH17: Hay H .8G 49
Colwell Rd. RH16: Hay H .7F 48
Colwood Cres. BN20: Eastb .7M 153
Combe Haven Holiday Pk.
TN38: St Leo .7D 126
Combe La. BN20: Eastb .4A 160
Combe Ri. BN20: Will .2L 153
Combermere Rd. TN38: St Leo .6H 127
Combe, The BN20: Will .5L 153
Commanders Wlk. TN35: Fair .2K 129
Command Rd. BN20: Eastb .7M 153
Commercial M. Nth.
BN21: Eastb .8D 154 (3L 161)
Commercial M. Sth.
BN21: Eastb .9D 154 (3K 161)
Commercial Rd.
BN21: Eastb .9D 154 (4K 161)
RH15: Burg H .5A 68
TN1: Tun W .8E 8
Commercial Sq. *BN7: Lewes* .5J 115
(off Mt. Pleasant)
RH16: Hay H .3F 48
Common La. BN6: Ditch .2E 90
BN8: Laug .8M 95
BN26: Selm .3B 138
Common Rd. TN4: R'hall .9N 7
Common Wood Ri. TN6: Crow .7D 24
Compass Ct. BN41: Ports .2A 130
Compasses La. TN32: Staple .2C 82
Compass La. TN33: A'ham .7N 101
Compass Point BN23: Eastb .5J 155
Comphurst La. BN27: Bore S .2D 122
Comp La. BN26: B'wck .7C 138
Comp, The BN8: Alfr .3F 150
Compton Av. BN1: Brig .7A 132 (5C 162)
Compton Cl. TN40: Bex S .9M 125
Compton Ct. BN21: Eastb .9B 154
Compton Dr. BN20: Eastb .1N 159
Compton Grange BN20: Eastb .9G 161
Compton Ho. BN21: Eastb .9K 161
Compton Ind. Est. BN23: Eastb .5G 154
Compton Lodge
BN21: Eastb .9B 154 (6G 161)
Compton Pl. Rd. BN20: Eastb .9B 154
BN21: Eastb .1B 160 (6G 161)
Compton Rd. BN1: Brig .4M 131 (1A 162)
RH16: Lind .1J 49
Compton St. BN21: Eastb .2D 160 (9K 161)
Compton Ter. BN27: Hails .8F 120
Compts, The BN10: Peace .3B 148
Conan Doyle Ct. *TN6: Crow* .9C 24
(off Goldsmiths Av.)
Concord Cl. TN2: Tun W .9F 8
Concorde Cl. TN39: Bex S .8G 124
Conduit Hill TN31: Rye .2G 86
Coneyburrow Gdns. TN38: St Leo .2E 126
Coneyburrow La. TN39: Bex S .1A 144
Coneyburrow Rd. TN2: Tun W .8H 9
Coney Furlong BN10: Peace .3D 148
Conghurst La. TN18: Hawk .5A 44
Congress Theatre .2D 160 (8K 161)
Conifer Cl. TN34: Hast .3M 127
Conifers, The
BN21: Eastb .8C 154 (2J 161)
Coniston Av. TN4: Tun W .8B 8
Coniston Ct. BN3: Hove .6M 131
Coniston Ho. BN3: Hove .6M 131
Coniston Rd. BN23: Lang .9M 141
Connaught Pl. TN2: Tun W. .3C 16
Connaught Rd. BN3: Hove .7J 131
BN21: Eastb .1D 160 (6K 161)
BN25: Sea .9B 150
Connaught Ter. BN3: Hove .6K 131
Connaught Way TN4: Tun W .8C 8
Connell Dr. BN2: W'dean .6M 133
Conqueror Ind. Est. TN38: St Leo .9F 104
Conqueror Rd. TN38: St Leo .7E 126
Conqueror Ter. TN33: Sed .7F 82
CONQUEST HOSPITAL .9K 105
Conquest Ho. TN39: Bex S .1G 145
Constable Rd. BN23: Lang .3G 155
Constable Way TN40: Bex S .8M 125
Constitutional Hill Rd. TN4: South .4B 8
Conway Ct. *BN3: Hove* .6K 131
(off Clarendon Rd.)
TN38: St Leo .8H 127
(off Marina)
Conway Pl. BN3: Hove .5K 131
Conway St. BN3: Hove .6K 131
COODEN .2D 144
Cooden Beach Station (Rail) .3C 144
Cooden Cl. TN39: Bex S .2D 144
Cooden Dr. TN39: Bex S .3D 144
Cooden Ledge TN38: St Leo .8E 104
Cooden Sea Rd. TN39: Bex S .3C 144
Cook Av. BN23: Eastb .6H 155
Cookham Dene TN40: Bex S .1K 145
COOKSBRIDGE .8G 92
Cooksbridge Rd. BN2: Brig .7F 132
Cooksbridge Station (Rail) .7G 92
Cookson Gdns. TN35: Hast .3B 128
Cookstown Cl. TN33: Nin .9A 102
Coolham Dr. BN2: Brig .7F 132
(not continuous)
Coolwater Pk. BN1: Brig .1M 131
Coombe Cl. BN27: Bore S .1D 122
Coombe End TN6: Crow .2D 36
Coombe Hall Pk. RH19: E Grin. .6d 10
COOMBE HILL .8A 102
Coombe Hill Rd. RH19: E Grin .6C 10
Coombe La. TN5: Wadh .4M 39
TN33: Nin .9A 102
Coombe Lea BN3: Hove .7L 131
Coombe Lodge BN25: Sea .9B 150
Coombe Mdw. BN2: Salt .1M 147
Coombe Ri. BN2: Salt .1L 147
Coombe Rd. BN2: Brig .4D 132
BN7: Lewes .4K 115
BN20: Eastb .8N 153

Coombers La.—Crowne Ho.

Coombers La. RH16: Hay H ... 4J 49
Coombe Shaw TN33: Nin ... 9B 102
Coombe Ter. BN2: Brig ... 4D 132
Coombe Va. BN2: Salt ... 1L 147
Coombs Cl. TN31: Buck ... 4H 65
Coombs Cotts. TN31: Buck ... 4H 65
Cooper Dr. TN39: Bex S ... 6J 125
Cooper Ri. TN37: St Leo ... 1G 126
Cooper Rd. TN31: Rye ... 3E 86
Coopers Cl. RH15: Burg H ... 3C 68
COOPER'S CORNER ... 6H 43
Coopers Cotts. BN27: Up D ... 6L 119
(off Coldharbour Rd.)
COOPER'S CROFT ... 1M 121
Coopers Cft. BN20: Will ... 2M 153
COOPER'S GREEN ... 6J 53
Coopers Hill BN20: Will ... 2M 153
Coopers La. TN3: F'cmbe ... 6G 6
TN6: Crow ... 7B 24
TN11: F'cmbe, Pens ... 6G 6
Coopers Row TN22: Mare ... 5J 53
Coopers Way BN27: Hails ... 8D 120
Coopers Wood TN6: Crow ... 7B 24
Copenhagen Ct. BN2: Brig ... 2B 146
Copestake Dr. RH15: Burg H ... 5E 68
Cophall La. BN20: E Dean ... 3G 158
Coplands La. TN31: North ... 2A 64
Coplands Plat TN31: North ... 2A 64
(off Station Rd.)
Coplands Ri. TN31: North ... 2A 64
Coppards Cl. RH17: Wivel G ... 4K 69
Coppards La. TN31: North ... 1B 64
Coppards La. Ind. Est. TN31: North ... 1C 64
Copper Beeches BN1: Brig ... 4N 131
TN37: St Leo ... 2J 127
Copperfields TN2: Tun W ... 4E 16
Coppers Ct. TN4: South ... 5D 8
Copper's Hill TN19: B'wsh ... 4G 58
Coppice Av. BN20: Will ... 9D 140
Coppice Cl. BN20: Will ... 9D 140
Coppice, The RH17: Scay H ... 6N 49
TN2: Pem ... 6N 9
TN33: Batt ... 4A 104
TN34: Hast ... 5L 127
Coppice Vw. TN21: H'fld ... 2E 76
Coppice Way RH16: Hay H ... 6E 48
Copse Cl. RH19: E Grin ... 1G 10
TN38: St Leo ... 3D 126
Copse Hill BN1: Brig ... 9M 111
Copse Rd. TN39: Bex S ... 1F 144
Copse, The RH16: Hay H ... 4J 49
Copthall Av. TN18: Hawk ... 1A 44
Copthorne Ct. BN3: Hove ... 7L 131
Copthorne Ho. BN21: Eastb ... 9B 154
(off Michel Gro.)
Copthorne Rd. RH10: Copt ... 1A 10
Copwood Av. TN22: Uck ... 1G 72
Copwood Rdbt. TN22: Uck ... 2F 72
Copyhold La. RH17: Cuck ... 6A 48
Copyhold Rd. RH19: E Grin ... 4D 10
Coral Reef Cl. BN23: Eastb ... 3K 155
Cordons BN7: King L ... 9D 114
Cord's Wlk. BN45: Poyn ... 1E 110
Cormorant Cl. BN23: Lang ... 2F 154
Cornelius Av. BN9: N'hvn ... 7G 149
Corner Grn. BN8: Ring ... 1C 116
(off Church Hill)
Corn Exchange TN2: Tun W ... 2D 16
Cornfield Cl. BN25: Sea ... 9E 150
Cornfield Grn. BN27: Hails ... 5F 120
Cornfield La.
BN21: Eastb ... 1D 160 (6K 161)
Cornfield Rd.
BN21: Eastb ... 1D 160 (6K 161)
BN25: Sea ... 9E 150
Cornfield Ter.
BN21: Eastb ... 1D 160 (6K 161)
TN37: St Leo ... 5J 127
Cornford Cl. BN41: Ports ... 3D 130
RH15: Burg H ... 3A 68
TN2: Pem ... 7M 9
TN6: Crow ... 1E 36
Cornford La. TN2: Pem, Tun W ... 9H 9
Cornford Pk. TN2: Pem ... 7M 9
Cornish Cl. BN23: Lang ... 9L 141
Cornmill Gdns. BN26: Pole ... 9B 140
Cornwall Av. BN10: Peace ... 7E 148
(not continuous)
Cornwall Ct. BN3: Hove ... 6L 131
BN20: Eastb ... 7N 153
Cornwall Gdns. BN1: Brig ... 2N 131
RH19: E Grin ... 4F 10
Cornwall Ho. BN1: Brig ... 3A 132
Cornwallis Cl. BN23: Eastb ... 5J 155
Cornwallis Gdns. TN34: Hast ... 6L 127
Cornwallis St. TN34: Hast ... 6M 127
Cornwallis Ter. TN34: Hast ... 6L 127
Cornwall Rd. TN39: Bex S ... 2J 145
CORNWELL'S BANK ... 3J 71
Coronation Cotts. TN5: Tice ... 9A 30
TN32: Rob ... 4K 61
Coronation Gdns. TN19: Hur G ... 7G 43
TN33: Batt ... 3N 103
Coronation Rd. RH19: E Grin ... 5E 10
Coronation St. BN2: Brig ... 6D 132
Corporation Yd. TN39: Bex S ... 9J 125
(off London Rd.)
Corseley Rd. TN3: Groom, Lye G ... 6F 14
TN6: Lye G ... 9D 14
Corsica Cl. BN25: Sea ... 2E 156
Corsica Rd. BN25: Sea ... 2E 156
Costells Edge RH17: Scay H ... 6N 49
Cotchford Hill TN7: Hart ... 2J 23
Cotchford La. TN7: Hart, Up H ... 1G 22
Cotswold Cl. BN23: Lang ... 9M 141
BN23: Lang ... 9M 141
TN34: Hast ... 2A 128
Cotswold Ct. BN21: Eastb ... 7K 161
Cotswold Pl. BN2: Brig ... 8G 132
(off Findon Rd.)
Cotswolds, The BN42: S'wck ... 6A 130
Cottage Cl. BN9: N'hvn ... 3K 149
Cottage Hill TN6: Roth ... 5L 37
Cottage Homes BN6: Ditch ... 1F 90
Cottage La. BN24: Hank ... 4H 141
TN33: Sed, W'fld ... 9E 82
TN35: W'fld ... 9F 82
COTTENDEN ... 5K 41
Cottenden Rd. TN5: S'gate ... 4H 41
County Oak Av. BN1: Brig ... 8C 112
Courcels BN2: Brig ... 9F 132
(off Arundel Rd.)
Course, The BN7: Lewes ... 6J 115
Court Cl. BN1: Brig ... 7N 111
RH19: E Grin ... 3F 10
Court Cres. RH19: E Grin ... 3F 10
Courtenay Ga. BN3: Hove ... 8K 131
Courtenay Ter. BN3: Hove ... 8K 131
Courtenwell TN3: Lang G ... 7J 7
Ct. Farm Cl. BN9: Pidd ... 2G 149
Court Farm Rd. BN2: Rott ... 1F 146
Ct. Farm Rd. BN3: Hove ... 3H 131
BN9: N'hvn ... 7J 149
Courthope Av. TN5: Wadh ... 7B 28
Courthope Dr. TN39: Bex S ... 9F 124
Courthouse St. TN34: Hast ... 6A 128
Courtland BN21: Eastb ... 7J 161
Courtland Rd. BN26: Pole ... 8D 140
Courtlands BN2: Brig ... 6G 162
BN9: N'hvn ... 5J 149
RH16: Hay H ... 6F 48
TN22: Nut ... 8C 34
Courtlands TN38: St Leo ... 8H 127
(off W. Hill Rd.)
Courtlands Pl. TN6: Crow ... 1C 36
Courtlands Rd.
BN22: Eastb ... 7D 154 (1L 161)
Court La. TN22: Five D ... 5J 53
Court Leet BN25: Sea ... 1D 156
(off Steyne Rd.)
Court Mdw. TN6: Roth ... 2M 37
Court Mdw. Cl. TN6: Roth ... 3L 37
Courtmead Rd. RH17: Cuck ... 3A 48
Courtney King Ho. BN2: Brig ... 9E 132
Court Ord Cotts. BN2: Rott ... 1G 146
Court Ord Rd. BN2: Rott ... 1F 146
Court Rd. BN7: Lewes ... 5K 115
BN22: Eastb ... 2C 154
TN4: Tun W ... 9B 8
Court, The BN20: Will ... 3M 153
Courtyard, The
Sheffield Pk. House ... 4J 51
Courtyard, The BN1: Falm ... 8K 113
RH19: E Grin ... 3H 11
TN34: Hast ... 5L 127
Courtyard, The BN3: Hove ... 5K 131
COUSLEY WOOD ... 4D 28
Cousley Wood Rd.
TN5: Cous W, Lamb, Wadh ... 5B 28
TN5: Lamb ... 3E 28
Coventry Ct. BN22: Eastb ... 6G 154
(off Allfrey Rd.)
Coventry Rd. TN38: St Leo ... 3H 127
Coventry St. BN1: Brig ... 5N 131 (1B 162)
Coverdale Av. TN39: Bex S ... 2D 144
Coverdale Ct. RH19: E Grin ... 1C 10
Covers, The BN25: Sea ... 1E 156
Covert, The TN39: Bex S ... 3D 144
COWBEECH ... 6L 99
COWBEECH HILL ... 8K 99
Cowbeech Rd. BN27: Cowb ... 2L 99
TN21: Cowb, Rush G ... 2L 99
COWDEN ... 7F 4
Cowden Cl. TN18: Hawk ... 3M 43
Cowden Hall La. TN21: Vine C ... 3F 98
Cowden La. TN18: Hawk ... 3M 43
Cowden M. TN8: C'den ... 8F 4
COWDEN POUND ... 3F 4
Cowden Pound Rd.
TN8: C'den, M'bch ... 3F 4
Cowden Rd. BN2: Salt ... 4L 147
Cowdens Cl. BN3: Hove ... 1F 130
Cowden Station (Rail) ... 5J 5
Cowden Wlk. TN38: St Leo ... 4G 127
Cowdown La. BN45: Pye ... 1J 111
Cowdray Cl. TN39: Bex S ... 8E 124
Cowdray Ct. BN3: Hove ... 6L 131
Cowdray Pk. Rd. TN39: Bex S ... 8D 124
Cowfold Rd. BN2: Brig ... 8F 132
Cow La. BN26: Alfr ... 4L 151
TN8: M'bch ... 3J 5
Cowley Dr. BN2: W'dean ... 7M 133
Cownwy Ct. BN2: Rott ... 3G 147
Cowper St. BN3: Hove ... 6J 131
Cox Gro. RH15: Burg H ... 3A 68
Coxheath Cl. TN38: St Leo ... 8E 104
Coxswain Gdns. TN38: St Leo. ... 8F 104
Crabtree Av. BN1: Brig ... 9B 112
Crabtree Ho. TN38: St Leo ... 7H 127
Cradle Hill Ind. Est. BN25: Sea ... 6G 150
Cradle Hill Rd. BN25: Sea ... 6F 150
Craig Cl. TN33: C'hrst ... 9A 104
Craigmore Hall TN6: Crow ... 1E 36
(off Crowborough Hill)
Craignair Av. BN1: Brig ... 7A 112
Cranborne Av. BN20: Eastb ... 3N 159
Cranborne Ct. BN21: Eastb ... 7L 161
Cranbourne St. BN1: Brig ... 8A 132 (7D 162)
Cranbrook BN2: Brig ... 7C 132
(off John St.)
Cranbrook Rd. TN18: Hawk ... 9N 31
TN37: St Leo ... 5J 127
Cranedown BN7: Lewes ... 7G 115
Cranfield Rd. TN40: Bex S ... 1K 145
Cranleigh Av. BN2: Rott ... 3J 147
Cranleigh Cl. TN39: Bex S ... 1H 145
Cranley Ct. BN3: Hove ... 6F 130
Cranmer Av. BN3: Hove ... 4H 131
Cranmer Cl. BN7: Lewes ... 4K 115
Cranston Cl. TN39: Bex S ... 1G 145
Cranston Ri. TN39: Bex S ... 1G 144
Cranston Rd. RH19: E Grin ... 2E 10
Cranwell Rd. TN4: R'hall ... 9N 7
Crates Yd. TN4: Tun W ... 8D 8
Craven Ct. RH19: E Grin ... 2F 10
(off Badger's Way)
Craven Path BN2: Brig ... 7E 132
Craven Pl. BN2: Brig ... 8E 132
Craven Rd. BN2: Brig ... 7E 132
Crawfurd Way RH19: E Grin ... 2E 10
Crawley Cres. BN22: Eastb ... 2B 154
Crawley Rd. BN1: Brig ... 8E 112
Crayford Rd. BN2: Brig ... 4E 132
Crazy La. TN33: Sed ... 1E 104
Crazy Lane Tourist Pk. TN33: Sed ... 1E 104
Crecy Cl. TN37: St Leo ... 8F 104
Crendon Pk. TN4: South ... 4D 8
Crescent Cl. BN2: W'dean ... 5M 133
RH15: Burg H ... 5C 68
Crescent Ct. BN2: Brig ... 6C 132
(off Park Cres. Ter.)
Crescent Dr. Nth. BN2: W'dean ... 5L 133
Crescent Dr. Sth. BN2: W'dean ... 7L 133
Crescent Mans. BN2: Brig ... 2G 162
Crescent Pl. BN2: Brig ... 9D 132
Crescent Rd. BN2: Brig ... 5C 132
RH15: Burg H ... 5B 68
RH19: E Grin ... 3D 10
TN1: Tun W ... 1E 16
Crescent, The BN2: Brig ... 3F 132
BN6: Hass ... 4C 90
BN9: N'hvn ... 3M 149
BN20: Eastb ... 7M 153
BN20: Will ... 1L 153
BN42: S'wck ... 5B 130
TN4: South ... 1B 8
TN34: Hast ... 3J 127
Crescent Way RH15: Burg H ... 5B 68
Crespin Way BN1: Brig ... 3D 132
Cresta Cl. BN26: Pole ... 6D 140
Cresta Ct. BN10: Peace ... 5C 148
(off Sth. Coast Rd.)
Cresta Rd. BN9: Peace ... 6G 148
Crest Rd. BN9: N'hvn ... 3M 149
Crest Way BN41: Ports ... 2D 130
Crestway Pde. BN1: Brig ... 3D 132
(off Crestway, The)
Crestway, The BN1: Brig ... 3D 132
Cricket Ct. RH19: E Grin ... 1E 10
Cricketers Cl. TN3: Bell G ... 7K 17
Cricketers Fld. TN32: Staple ... 8E 62
Cricketfield BN8: N'wck ... 9K 51
Cricketfield Ct. BN25: Sea ... 1E 156
Cricketfield Rd. BN25: Sea ... 1E 156
Cricketing La. BN27: Herst ... 1M 121
Criers La. TN20: F Ashes ... 2K 55
TN22: F Ashes ... 2K 55
Crink Hill BN8: Barc ... 4M 93
Cripland Cl. RH16: Hay H ... 3J 49
Cripps Av. BN10: Peace ... 3D 148
CRIPP'S CORNER ... 1D 82
Crispin Ct. TN40: Bex S ... 1L 145
(off Up. Sea Rd.)
Crisp Rd. BN7: Lewes ... 3G 115
Crittle's Ct. TN5: Wadh ... 7B 28
Crockendale Fld. BN8: Ring ... 9D 94
Crockers La. TN31: North ... 1A 64
Crocks Dean BN10: Peace ... 2D 148
Crocodile Wlk. BN3: Hove ... 5N 131 (3A 162)
Crodon Cotts. TN6: Crow ... 8D 24
(off Park Rd.)
Croft Av. BN42: S'wck ... 6A 130
Croft Cl. BN26: Pole ... 9C 140
Croft Ct. BN21: Eastb ... 9E 154 (4M 161)
(Bourne St.)
BN21: Eastb ... 8B 154
(Moat Cft. Rd.)
BN25: Sea ... 9D 150
Croft Dr. BN41: Ports ... 2C 130
Crofton Pk. Av. TN39: Bex S ... 2F 144
Croft Rd. BN1: Brig ... 1M 131
TN6: Crow ... 1D 36
TN34: Hast ... 5N 127
Croft Ter. TN34: Hast ... 6N 127
(off Croft Rd.)
Croft, The BN6: Hass ... 2A 90
BN20: Will ... 3M 153
BN21: Eastb ... 8C 154 (3H 161)
BN27: Lwr D ... 2M 119
BN42: S'wck ... 5A 130
TN34: Hast ... 6N 127
TN39: Bex S ... 1H 145
Croft Works BN27: Hails ... 7E 120
Croham Rd. TN6: Crow ... 8D 24
Cromarty Wlk. BN23: Eastb ... 4J 155
Cromer Wlk. TN34: Hast ... 5M 127
Cromer Way BN27: Hails ... 4D 120
Cromleigh Way BN42: S'wck ... 3A 130
Cromwell Ct. BN3: Hove ... 6L 131
Cromwell M. RH15: Burg H ... 4A 68
Cromwell Pl. BN7: Lew ... 5H 115
Cromwell Pl. RH19: E Grin ... 5F 10
Cromwell Rd. BN3: Hove ... 6L 131
RH15: Burg H ... 5A 68
TN2: Tun W ... 1F 16
Cromwell St. BN2: Brig ... 6D 132
Crooked La. BN25: Sea ... 1E 156
Crossbush Rd. BN2: Brig ... 7F 132
CROSS-IN-HAND ... 9M 55
Cross In Hand Rd. TN21: H'fld ... 1B 76
Cross La. TN5: Tice ... 1M 41
Cross La. Gdn. TN5: Tice ... 1M 41
Cross Levels Way BN21: Eastb ... 6B 154
BN22: Eastb ... 4C 154
BN23: Eastb ... 4C 154
Cross Rd. BN42: S'wck ... 5A 130
Cross Rd. Cl. BN42: S'wck ... 5A 130
Cross St. BN1: Brig ... 6B 132 (3E 162)
BN3: Hove ... 8M 131 (7A 162)
BN26: Pole ... 7D 140
TN37: St Leo ... 7J 127
Cross, The TN6: Crow ... 8D 24
Cross Way BN7: Lewes ... 5G 114
Crossways BN8: W Firle ... 1G 136
Crossways Av. RH19: E Grin ... 3C 10
Crossways, The BN24: Sto C ... 7K 141
Crossway, The BN1: Brig ... 3C 132
BN41: Ports ... 3C 130
TN4: Tun W ... 2A 16
Crouch Cl. BN20: Will ... 3M 153
Crouchfield Cl. BN25: Sea ... 1E 156
Crouchlands Farm RH17: Cuck ... 1A 48
Crouch La. BN25: Sea ... 1D 156
TN17: Sandh ... 3L 45
TN18: Sandh ... 5K 45
(not continuous)
TN33: Nin ... 2C 124
Crouch, The BN25: Sea ... 1D 156
(off Crouch La.)
CROWBOROUGH ... 8D 24
Crowborough Camping & Cvn. Site
TN6: Crow ... 7E 24
Crowborough Ct. TN6: Crow ... 8D 24
(off Eridge Rd.)
Crowborough Hill TN6: Crow, Jar B ... 9D 24
Crowborough M. TN6: Crow ... 9C 24
Crowborough Rd. BN2: Salt ... 3L 147
TN22: Nut ... 5B 34
TN35: Hast ... 2D 128
Crowborough Station (Rail) ... 2G 37
Crowborough Tennis & Squash Club
... 9C 24
CROWBOROUGH WAR MEMORIAL HOSPITAL
... 1C 36
CROWBOROUGH WARREN ... 9A 24
Crowders La. TN33: Batt ... 4D 102
CROWHURST ... 1N 125
Crowhurst Cl. BN23: Lang ... 9K 141
Crowhurst La. TN39: Bex S ... 7K 125
Crowhurst Pk. Holiday Homes Pk.
TN33: Batt ... 7C 104
Crowhurst Rd. BN1: Brig ... 7C 112
TN33: Cats ... 1J 125
TN38: St Leo ... 4D 126
TN38: St Leo ... 3A 126
Crowhurst Station (Rail) ... 9A 104
CROWLINK ... 3C 158
Crowlink La. BN20: Fris ... 3D 158
Crowmere Av. TN40: Bex S ... 9K 125
Crowmere Ter. TN40: Bex S ... 9K 125
Crown Cl. BN3: Hove ... 7M 131
(off Palmeira Av.)
BN27: Hails ... 7D 120
TN22: Uck ... 9H 53
Crowne Ho. BN21: Eastb ... 8B 154
(off Star Rd.)

E. Slope Flats—Fairview La.

E. Slope Flats BN1: Falm 7J **113**
East St. BN1: Brig 8B **132** (8E **162**)
BN1: Falm 8K **113**
BN7: Lewes 5K **115**
BN25: Sea 9D **150**
BN41: Ports 6E **130**
TN20: May 7F **38**
TN31: Rye 3G **86**
TN34: Hast 7N **127**
East Sussex Gliding Club 6K **95**
East Sussex National Golf Course 7F **72**
East Vw. Flds. BN7: Plump G 2M **91**
East Vw. Ter. TN33: Sed 7F **82**
East Way BN7: Lewes 4F **114**
Eastway TN39: Bex S 1D **144**
E. Well Pl. BN27: Hails 6E **120**
East Wick RH16: Lind 2K **49**
Eastwick Cl. BN1: Brig 7C **112**
Eastwood Rd. TN39: Bex S 1H **145**
Eatenden La. TN32: Mount 6F **80**
TN33: Mount, Neth 6F **80**
Eaton Ct. *BN2: Brig 9E* ***132***
(off Eaton Pl.)
BN3: Hove 6K ***131***
(off Eaton Gdns.)
BN21: Eastb 8C **154** (3H **161**)
Eaton Gdns. BN3: Hove 6L **131**
Eaton Gdns. Mans. *BN3: Hove 6L* ***131***
(off Eaton Gdns.)
Eaton Ga. BN3: Hove 6L **131**
Eaton Gro. BN3: Hove 6L **131**
Eaton Hall BN3: Hove 6K **131**
Eaton Mnr. BN3: Hove 6L **131**
Eaton Pl. BN2: Brig 9E **132**
Eaton Rd. BN3: Hove 6K **131**
Eaton Vs. BN3: Hove 6K **131**
Eaton Wlk. TN33: Sed 7D **82**
Ebdens Hill TN33: Batt, St Leo 6H **105**
TN37: St Leo 6H **105**
Ebenezer Rd. TN34: Hast 6A **128**
Ecclesden BN2: Brig 5G **162**
ECKINGTON CORNER 6D **118**
Ecmod Rd. BN22: Eastb 6F **154**
Edburton Av. BN1: Brig 3B **132** (1F **162**)
Edburton Rd. BN5: Fulk 3A **110**
Edenbridge Rd. TN7: Hart 2J **13**
Eden Cl. BN24: Sto C 8K **141**
Eden Ct. TN18: Hawk 9N **31**
Eden Dr. TN39: Bex S 1F **144**
Eden Rd. TN1: Tun W 2D **16**
Edensor Rd. BN20: Eastb 4A **160**
Edenthorpe Lodge BN20: Eastb 3C **160**
Eden Va. RH19: E Grin 1D **10**
(not continuous)
Eden Wlk. TN1: Tun W 2D **16**
Edgar Rd. TN35: Hast 4B **128**
Edgehill Cl. TN21: H'fld 1C **76**
Edgehill Way BN41: Ports 3B **130**
Edgeland Ter. BN22: Eastb 3C **154**
Edinburgh Ct. *BN20: Eastb 7N* ***153***
(off Central Av.)
BN25: Sea 9C **150**
Edinburgh Rd. BN2: Brig 5C **132**
BN25: Sea 9C **150**
TN38: St Leo 7E **126**
TN40: Bex S 9K **125**
Edinburgh Way RH19: E Grin 5F **10**
Edison Rd. BN23: Eastb 3D **154**
Edith Av. BN10: Peace 6B **148**
(not continuous)
Edith Av. Nth. BN10: Peace 4C **148**
Edith Rd. TN35: Hast 3C **128**
Edmonton Rd. TN39: Bex S 7J **125**
Edmund Cl. BN23: Eastb 4H **155**
Edmund Rd. TN35: Hast 4B **128**
Edser Ct. *BN41: Ports 2B* ***130***
(off Mile Oak Rd.)
Edward Av. BN2: Salt 1L **147**
BN3: Hove 2J **131**
Edward Cl. BN3: Hove 2J **131**
BN25: Sea 6N **149**
Edward Ct. BN3: Hove 7H **131**
Edward Rd. BN23: Eastb 3D **154**
Edward Rd. RH16: Hay H 6F **48**
TN37: St Leo 7K **127**
Edward St. BN2: Brig 8B **132** (8F **162**)
BN7: Lewes 5K **115**
TN4: R'hall 9M **7**
TN4: South 4C **8**
Edward Ter. TN38: St Leo 2G **126**
Edwin Rd. TN35: Hast 4B **128**
Effingham Cl. BN2: Salt 2K **147**
Effingham Dr. TN39: Bex S 2E **144**
Egbert Cl. BN23: Eastb 4H **155**
Egerton Ho. BN20: Eastb 3B **160**
Egerton Park 2J **145**
Egerton Rd. TN39: Bex S 2J **145**
Egginton Cl. BN2: Brig 9H **113**
Egginton Rd. BN2: Brig 9G **113**
Egles Gro. TN22: Uck 9G **52**
Egmont Rd. BN3: Hove 4F **130**
Egremont Pl. BN2: Brig 8C **132**
TN34: Hast 4A **128**
Eight Acre La. TN35: T Oaks 6C **106**
Eight Bells Cl. TN22: Buxt 5A **54**
Eighteen Pounder La. TN35: Hast 5N **105**
Eileen Av. BN2: Salt 3J **147**
Eisenhower Dr. TN38: St Leo 9F **104**
Elder Cl. BN41: Ports 3D **130**
Elder Pl. BN1: Brig 6B **132** (3E **162**)
Elderwood Cl. BN22: Eastb 2A **154**
TN39: Bex S 7K **125**
Eldon Rd. BN21: Eastb 7N **153**
Eldred Av. BN1: Brig 8M **111**
Eleanor Cl. BN7: Lewes 4H **115**
BN25: Sea 7C **150**
Eley Cres. BN2: Rott 1F **146**
Eley Dr. BN2: Rott 9M **133**
Elford St. TN34: Hast 6M **127**
Elgar Way BN23: Lang 1H **155**
Elgin Gdns. BN25: Sea 8H **151**
Elim Ct. BN2: Brig 6C **132**
Elim Pk. *TN34: Hast 4M* ***127***
(off Elphinstone Av.)
Elizabethan Cl. TN33: Hooe 4A **124**
Elizabeth Av. BN3: Hove 2J **131**
Elizabeth Cl. BN3: Hove 2J **131**
BN25: Sea 6N **149**
Elizabeth Ct. *BN3: Hove 6L* ***131***
(off Wilbury Rd.)
BN20: Eastb 7N **153**
BN26: Pole 7D **140**
BN27: Hails 7F **120**
Elizabeth Cres. RH19: E Grin 1F **10**
Elizabeth Garlick Ct. *TN1: Tun W 9E* ***8***
(off Goods Station Rd.)
Elizabeth Rd. TN38: St Leo 4G **127**
Ellen Ho. BN3: Hove 6K **131**
Ellenslea Rd. TN37: St Leo 7J **127**
Ellen St. BN3: Hove 6K **131**
BN41: Ports 6E **130**
Ellenwhorne La. TN32: Staple 2F **82**
Ellerslie La. TN39: Bex S 7G **124**
Elliots Way TN21: H'fld 9D **56**
Ellis Cl. TN34: Hast 7L **127**
Ellis Gordon Ct. BN9: N'hvn 5H **149**
Ellison Cl. TN6: Crow 7C **24**
Ellis Way TN22: Uck 1F **72**
Elm Av. BN27: Chal 3G **118**
(not continuous)
Elm Cl. BN3: Hove 3L **131**
BN8: Laug 8A **96**
BN25: Sea 9H **151**
Elm Cotts. BN27: Up D 6L **119**
Elm Ct. BN1: Brig 5N **131** (1B **162**)
BN9: N'hvn 5H **149**
BN26: Pole 7D ***140***
(off Walnut Wlk.)
BN41: Ports 5D ***130***
(off Elm Rd.)
RH19: E Grin 2D **10**
Elm Ct. Gdns. TN6: Crow 7C **24**
Elm Dr. BN3: Hove 4G **130**
RH19: E Grin 3G **10**
Elm Grn. BN27: Hails 5E **120**
Elm Gro. BN2: Brig 6C **132**
BN7: Lewes 6J **115**
BN22: Eastb 3C **154**
Elmhurst Av. TN2: Pem 5N **9**
Elm Lodge BN2: Brig 3G **162**
Elmore Rd. BN2: Brig 7C **132**
Elm Rd. BN41: Ports 5D **130**
TN4: South 4C **8**
Elms Av. BN21: Eastb 1E **160** (6M **161**)
Elmsdown Pl. BN27: Hails 7F **120**
Elms La. TN35: Pett 6L **107**
Elms Lea Av. BN1: Brig 3N **131**
Elmsmead TN31: Iden 5F **66**
Elms Rd. BN21: Eastb 1E **160** (6M **161**)
Elmstead Rd. TN40: Bex S 9M **125**
Elms, The BN8: Ring 1B **116**
Elm Way TN21: H'fld 2E **76**
Elmwood BN21: Eastb 3H **161**
Elmwood Cl. BN23: Lang 9M **141**
Elmwood Gdns. BN23: Lang 9M **141**
Elphick Pl. TN6: Crow 8D **24**
Elphick Rd. BN8: Ring 8E **94**
BN9: N'hvn 4J **149**
Elphick's Pl. TN2: Tun W 4E **16**
Elphinstone Av. TN34: Hast 4M **127**
Elphinstone Gdns. TN34: Hast 3M **127**
Elphinstone Rd. TN34: Hast 4M **127**
Elrington Rd. BN3: Hove 4L **131**
Elsted Cl. BN22: Eastb 2D **154**
Elsted Cres. BN1: Brig 8D **112**
Elsted Rd. TN39: Bex S 3D **144**
Elven Cl. BN20: E Dean 2G **159**
Elven La. BN20: E Dean 2G **158**
Elvin Cres. BN2: Rott 9M **133**
Elwood Cl. RH15: Burg H 7A **68**
Elwyn Jones Ct. BN1: Brig 9N **111**
Ely Ct. TN1: Tun W 9E **8**
ELY GRANGE 7F **16**
Ely La. TN1: Tun W 9E **8**
Embassey Ct. *RH16: Hay H 3F* ***48***
(off Sydney Rd.)
Embassy Ct. BN1: Brig 7A **162**
BN21: Eastb 7C **154** (1J **161**)
Emmanuel Rd. TN34: Hast 5N **127**
Encore Ho. *TN21: H'fld 9C* ***56***
(off Streatfield Rd.)
Endcliffe Ct. BN20: Eastb 3B **160**
Endwell Rd. TN40: Bex S 2K **145**
Engalee RH19: E Grin 2C **10**
English Bus. Pk. BN3: Hove. 5G **131**
English Cl. BN3: Hove 5G **131**
English Pas. BN7: Lewes 5K **115**
English Wine Cen. 6E **138**
Enholms La. RH17: Dane 6G **32**
Ensenada Reef BN23: Eastb 3L **155**
Ensign Ct. TN38: St Leo 8G **127**
Enterprise Est. BN1: Brig 7D **112**
Enterprise Shop. Cen.
BN21: Eastb 5J **161**
Enys Ct. BN21: Eastb 8C **154** (3J **161**)
Enys Rd. BN21: Eastb 9C **154** (4H **161**)
E Plan Est. BN9: N'hvn 3K **149**
Epsom Cl. TN38: St Leo 6G **127**
Epsom Ct. *TN40: Bex S 1M* ***145***
(off Sutton Pl.)
Erica Cl. BN23: Lang 2E **154**
Eridge Cl. TN39: Bex S 1H **145**
Eridge Dr. TN6: Crow 8D **24**
Eridge Gdns. TN6: Crow 8E **24**
ERIDGE GREEN 8M **15**
Eridge Grn. BN7: Lewes 3H **115**
Eridge La. TN6: Roth 1M **37**
Eridge Rd. BN3: Hove 3J **131**
BN21: Eastb 5N **153**
TN3: Eri G 9L **15**
(Eridge Grn.)
TN3: Eri G, Groom 6H **15**
(Birchden)
TN4: Tun W 4B **16**
TN6: Crow 8D **24**
Eridge Station (Rail) 1J **25**
Erroll Mans. BN3: Hove 6F **130**
Erroll Rd. BN3: Hove 7E **130**
Ersham Rd. BN27: Hails 9E **120**
Ersham Way BN27: Hails 8E **120**
Erskine Pk. Rd. TN4: R'hall 9M **7**
Esher Cl. BN25: Sea 8E **150**
Eshton Rd. BN22: Eastb 7F **154**
Eskbank Av. BN1: Brig 7B **112**
Eskdale Cl. BN23: Lang 9L **141**
ESPERANCE BMI HOSPITAL, THE
. . . . .1D **160** (6L **161**)
Esplanade BN2: Brig 9F **132**
(Duke's Mound)
BN2: Brig 9B **132** (9F **162**)
(Madeira Dr.)
BN3: Hove 8M **131** (8A **162**)
BN25: Sea 1C **156**
Esplanade M. BN25: Sea 1D **156**
Esplanade, The BN10: Tels C 5N **147**
Esporta Health & Fitness Cen. 5J **9**
Essenden Rd. TN38: St Leo 8G **126**
Essex Cl. TN2: Tun W 4C **16**
Essex Cotts. *BN2: Brig 9D* ***132***
(off Essex St.)
Essex Ct. BN20: Eastb 6M **153**
Essex M. *BN9: N'hvn 5J* ***149***
(off Essex Pl.)
Essex Pl. *BN2: Brig 9D* ***132***
(off Montague St.)
BN9: N'hvn 5J **149**
Essex Rd. TN38: St Leo 2G **126**
Essex St. BN2: Brig 9D **132**
Estate Rd. BN9: N'hvn 3K **149**
(Nth. Quay Rd.)
BN9: N'hvn 5L **149**
(Railway Rd.)
Estcots Dr. RH19: E Grin 3F **10**
ETCHINGHAM 9C **42**
Etchingham Rd. BN23: Lang 3H **155**
TN19: B'wsh, Etch 3K **59**
Etchingham Station (Rail) 9D **42**
ETCHINGWOOD 7A **54**
Ethelred Cl. BN23: Eastb 4H **155**
Ethel St. BN3: Hove 6K **131**
Etherington Hill
TN3: South, Speld, Tun W 5M **7**
Etherton Way BN25: Sea 8F **150**
ETHNAM 7L **45**
Ethnam La. TN18: Sandh 7L **45**
Eton Cl. BN25: Sea 8F **150**
Eton M. BN21: Eastb 9D **154** (4K **161**)
Eugene Way BN23: Eastb 3L **155**
Euro Bus. Pk. BN9: N'hvn 4K **149**
Evelyn Av. BN9: N'hvn 5J **149**
Evelyn Ct. BN41: Ports 4D **130**
Evelyn Glennie Ct. *BN2: Brig 8D* ***132***
(off Somerset St.)
Evelyn Rd. BN7: Lewes 4H **115**
Evelyn Ter. BN2: Brig 8D **132**
Everest Ho. BN3: Hove 6H **131**
EVERSFIELD CENTRE 8G **126**
Eversfield Ct. BN21: Eastb 3J **161**
TN40: Bex S 2K ***145***
(off Wilton Rd.)
Eversfield Ho. BN21: Eastb 3J **161**
Eversfield M. Sth. *TN37: St Leo 7J* ***127***
(off Western Rd.)
Eversfield Pl. TN37: St Leo 8K **127**
(not continuous)
Eversfield Rd.
BN21: Eastb 8C **154** (3J **161**)
Evershed Ct. BN10: Tels C 5N **147**
Eversley Cl. TN37: St Leo 4J **127**
Eversley Ct. BN21: Eastb 8B **154** (2H **161**)
Eversley Cres. TN37: St Leo 4J **127**
Eversley Rd. TN37: St Leo 4J **127**
TN40: Bex S 2K **145**
Evolution Indoor Climbing Cen. 1C **24**
Ewart St. BN2: Brig 7C **132**
Ewehurst La. TN3: Speld 7K **7**
Ewell Ct. TN40: Bex S 1M **145**
Ewhurst Cl. TN34: Hast 2M **127**
EWHURST GREEN 4H **63**
Ewhurst La. TN31: North 5M **63**
Ewhurst Rd. BN2: Brig 5D **132**
EXCEAT 8L **151**
Exceat Cl. BN2: Brig 7F **132**
BN23: Lang 9K **141**
Excelsior, The BN1: Brig 1M **131**
Exeter Cl. BN22: Will 2M **153**
Exeter St. BN1: Brig 5N **131** (2B **162**)
Exmouth Pl. TN34: Hast 6N **127**

F

Factory La. BN27: Hails 7D **120**
Fairbanks RH16: Hay H 5F **48**
Fairbridge Way RH15: Burg H 3A **68**
Faircrouch La. TN5: Wadh 4L **27**
Fairdene BN42: S'wck 4B **130**
Fairfax Av. TN38: St Leo 8F **104**
Fairfield BN10: Peace 5B **148**
BN27: Herst 9A **100**
Fairfield Av. TN2: Tun W 8F **8**
Fairfield Chase TN39: Bex S 1G **144**
Fairfield Cl. RH15: Burg H 4A **68**
Fairfield Gdns. BN41: Ports 4D **130**
RH15: Burg H 4A ***68***
(off Fairfield Rd.)
Fairfield Lodge BN20: Eastb 2B **160**
Fairfield Rd. BN20: Eastb 3B **160**
RH15: Burg H 5A **68**
RH19: E Grin 4F **10**
TN37: St Leo 9J **105**
Fairfields Farm Cvn. Pk.
BN24: W'ham 8B **142**
Fairfield Way RH16: Hay H 1E **48**
Fairford Cl. RH16: Hay H 4F **48**
Fairglen Cotts. TN5: Wadh 8L **27**
Fairglen Rd. TN5: Wadh 8L **27**
Fairhaven BN7: Plump 6M **91**
Fairholme *BN7: Lewes 6J* ***115***
(off Southover High St.)
Fairholme Ct. *TN6: Crow 1D* ***36***
(off Queen Rd.)
Fairholme Rd. BN9: N'hvn 3M **149**
Fairhurst BN10: Tels C 5N **147**
Fair Isle Cl. BN23: Eastb 4H **155**
Fairisle Cl. BN27: Hails 4D **120**
Fair La. TN32: Rob 5J **61**
(not continuous)
Fairlawn *RH16: Hay H 5F* ***48***
(off Oathill Rd.)
Fairlawn Cres. RH19: E Grin 2B **10**
Fairlawn Dr. RH19: E Grin 2B **10**
Fairlawns BN3: Hove 7H **131**
Fairlawns Dr. BN27: Herst 9A **100**
Fairlea Cl. RH15: Burg H 4A **68**
Fairlie Gdns. BN1: Brig 2N **131**
FAIRLIGHT .2H **129**
Fairlight TN22: Uck 8K **53**
Fairlight Av. BN10: Tels C 5N **147**
TN35: Hast 3C **128**
Fairlight Cl. BN26: Pole 7D **140**
TN4: South 3D **8**
TN40: Bex S 9A **126**
Fairlight Ct. BN10: Tels C 4N **147**
FAIRLIGHT COVE 1K **129**
Fairlight Fld. BN8: Ring 1C **116**
Fairlight Gdns. TN35: Fair 2L **129**
Fairlight Pl. *BN2: Brig 5D* ***132***
(off Pevensey Rd.)
Fairlight Rd. BN22: Eastb 7F **154**
TN35: Hast 3C **128**
Fairlight Wood Cvn. Club Site
TN35: Gues T 6J **107**
Fair Mdw. TN31: Rye 1G **86**
Fairmile Rd. TN2: Tun W 8H **9**
Fairmount Rd. TN40: Bex S 9L **125**
Fair Oak Cl. TN21: H'fld 1D **76**
Fairoaks BN26: Pole 7F **140**
Fairplace RH17: Wivel G 4K **69**
Fairstone Cl. TN35: Hast 2D **128**
Fairview TN18: Hawk 9N **31**
Fairview Cotts. TN5: Wadh 5C **28**
Fairview La. TN3: Tun W 4M **15**
TN6: Crow 7C **24**

A-Z East Sussex Atlas 177

Fairview Ri.—Forward Cl.

Fairview Ri. BN1: Brig 9M 111
FAIRWARP 8G 35
Fairway Bus. Cen. BN2: Brig 1F 132
Fairway Cl. BN20: Eastb 1N 159
Fairway Cres. BN41: Ports 3E 130
Fairways BN1: Brig 5N 131 (1A 162)
Fairways Cl. BN25: Sea 1H 157
Fairways Rd. BN25: Sea 1G 157
Fairways, The TN4: South 6D 8
Fairway, The BN9: N'hvn 5G 149
TN38: St Leo 6F 126
TN39: Bex S 8G 125
Fairway Trad. Est. BN2: Brig 1F 132
Falaise Fitness Cen. 7L 127
Falaise Rd. BN9: N'hvn 3M 149
TN34: Hast 7K 127
Falconbury Dr. TN39: Bex S 2E 144
Falcon Ct. *BN2: Brig 6G 132*
(off Swanborough Pl.)
Falconer Dr. TN33: Batt 3N 103
Falcon Way BN27: Hails 3E 120
Fallowfield Cl. BN3: Hove 3H 131
Fallowfield Cres. BN3: Hove 3G 131
FALMER 8K 113
Falmer Av. BN2: Salt 1J 147
Falmer Cl. BN20: Eastb 5M 153
BN22: Eastb 3A 154
Falmer Ct. *TN22: Uck 9J 53*
(off London Rd.)
Falmer Gdns. BN2: W'dean 5L 133
Falmer Hill BN1: Falm 8J 113
Falmer Ho. Rd. BN1: Falm 8J 113
Falmer Rd.
BN2: Brig, Falm, W'dean 1L 133
BN2: Rott, W'dean 5L 133
Falmer Sports Complex 7K 113
Falmer Station (Rail) 8J 113
Falmouth Cl. BN23: Eastb 4J 155
Faraday Av. RH19: E Grin 6F 10
Faraday Cl. BN22: Eastb 3C 154
Farlaine Rd. BN21: Eastb 5N 153
Farley Bank TN35: Hast 4A 128
Farleys Way TN31: Peas 7N 65
Farley Way TN35: Fair 1K 129
Farlington Av. RH16: Hay H 4G 48
Farlington Cl. RH16: Hay H 4G 48
Farman St. BN3: Hove 8M 131 (7A 162)
Farm Cl. BN25: Sea 8G 151
BN41: Ports 3C 130
RH19: E Grin 4H 11
Farmcombe Cl. TN2: Tun W 2E 16
Farmcombe La. TN2: Tun W 2E 16
Farmcombe Rd. TN2: Tun W 2E 16
Farm Cotts. *RH16: Hay H 6D 48*
(off Parkfield Way)
Farm Ct. TN4: Tun W 4B 16
Farmet Ct. *RH19: E Grin 1C 10*
(off Halsford La.)
Farm Gdns. TN31: Peas 7A 66
Farm Hill BN2: W'dean 5K 133
Farmlands Av. BN26: Pole 9C 140
Farmlands Cl. BN26: Pole 9D 140
TN37: St Leo 1J 127
Farmlands Ct. BN26: Pole 9D 140
Farmlands Way BN26: Pole 8C 140
Farmland Way BN27: Hails 5F 120
Farm La. BN6: Ditch 4F 90
TN31: Camb 5A 88
Farm M. BN3: Hove 7M 131
Farm Rd. BN3: Hove 7M 131
Farm Way BN42: S'wck 6C 130
RH15: Burg H 7E 68
Farmway Cl. BN3: Hove 3F 130
Farm World (Great Knelle Farm) 1F 64
Farm Yd. BN1: Brig 7D 162
Farncombe Cl. RH17: Wivel G 4L 69
Farncombe Rd. *BN7: Lewes 5L 115*
(off Foundry La.)
Farne Cl. BN27: Hails 4C 120
Farnham Av. BN6: Hass 2B 90
Farnham Beeches TN3: Lang G 9L 7
Farnham Cl. TN3: Lang G 1L 15
Farnham La. TN3: Lang G, R'hall 1L 15
TN4: R'hall 8L 7
Farnham Pl. TN3: Lang G 1L 15
Farningham Rd. TN6: Jar B 3G 36
Farnlea RH15: Burg H 3E 68
Farnol Ho. BN21: Eastb 8A 154
Farrance Ct. TN1: Tun W 9E 8
Farr Cl. RH17: Cuck 1A 48
Farriers Pl. BN8: Ring 1C 116
Farriers Wlk. TN22: Uck 2H 73
Farrington Ct.
BN21: Eastb 9C 154 (5H 161)
Farthing Hill TN5: Tice 1N 41
Farthing La. BN27: A'ham 2F 100
TN33: A'ham 3G 101
Farthings La. TN33: Batt, Cats 5G 102
Farthings, The TN6: Crow 8E 24
Fastnet Cl. BN23: Eastb 4H 155
Faulkners Way RH15: Burg H 3B 68
Faversham Rd. BN23: Lang 2G 154
Faygate Cl. TN39: Bex S 6J 125
Faygate Ct. BN2: Brig 7F 132
Faygate Rd. BN22: Eastb 2B 154
Fayre Mdw. TN32: Rob 5J 61
Fazan Ct. TN5: Wadh 7B 28
Fearon Rd. TN34: Hast 4M 127
Felbridge Cen., The RH19: E Grin 1A 10
Felbridge Cl. RH19: E Grin 1C 10
Feld, The RH19: E Grin 1A 10
Fellows Rd. TN34: Hast 3N 127
Felride RH16: Hay H 6F 48
Felwater Ct. RH19: E Grin 1A 10
Fen Ct. TN38: St Leo 5E 126
Fennell's Cl. BN21: Eastb 7B 154
Fenn La. TN36: Winch 9C 86
Ferbies TN3: Speld 6L 7
Ferbies Cl. TN3: Speld 6L 7
Ferdinand Ter. *TN3: Groom 5G 14*
(off Corseley Rd.)
Ferguson Rd. TN31: Lydd 6N 89
Fermor Rd. TN6: Crow 3D 36
Fermor Row TN6: Crow 2D 36
Fermor Way TN6: Crow 2D 36
Fernbank Shop. Cen. TN6: Crow 8D 24
Fern Cl. BN23: Lang 1F 154
FERNDALE 8F 8
Ferndale TN2: Tun W 9F 8
Ferndale Cl. TN2: Tun W 9F 8
Ferndale Gdns. TN2: Tun W 9F 8
Ferndale Point TN2: Tun W 9F 8
Ferndale Rd. BN3: Hove 6M 131
RH15: Burg H 7C 68
Fern Grn. BN27: Hails 5E 120
Fernhurst Cl. BN1: Brig 8C 112
Fernhurst Cres. BN1: Brig 9C 112
TN4: South 3D 8
Fernlea Cl. TN35: W'fld 3L 105
Fernleigh Ct. TN39: Bex S 1H 145
Fern Rd. TN38: St Leo 5F 126
Fernside Av. TN38: St Leo 6F 126
Ferns, The TN1: Tun W 9F 8
Fernwood Ri. BN1: Brig 8M 111
Ferrers Rd. BN7: Lewes 4H 115
Ferring Cl. TN31: Rye 2E 86
Ferring Ct. *BN1: Brig 9G 112*
(off Newick Rd.)
Ferringham TN4: Tun W 9C 8
Ferryfields Pk. TN36: Winch 8C 86
Ferry Hill TN36: Winch 8C 86
Ferry Rd. TN31: Rye 3F 86
Festival Gdns. TN39: Bex S 7K 125
Fidley Cl. BN23: Eastb 5H 155
Field Cl. BN25: Sea 1G 157
Field End TN22: Mare 5F 52
Fielden La. TN6: Crow 2B 36
Fielden Rd. TN6: Crow 9A 24
FIELD GREEN 2E 44
Fieldings, The
BN21: Eastb 8C 154 (2H 161)
Fields End Cl. RH16: Hay H 5G 48
Fieldway BN6: Ditch 4E 90
RH16: Lind 1G 49
TN31: B Oak 3A 84
Field Way TN38: St Leo 6E 126
Fieldways TN18: Hawk 1A 44
Fiennes Rd. BN27: Herst 9A 100
Fife Ct. BN22: Eastb 2D 154
Figg La. TN6: Crow 2D 36
FILCHING 2H 153
Filching Cl. BN26: Pole 1J 153
Filching Ct. BN20: Eastb 7M 153
Filching Manor & Motor Mus. 2H 153
Filching Rd. BN20: Eastb 7M 153
Filder Cl. BN22: Eastb 6D 154
(not continuous)
FILSHAM 6E 126
Filsham Dr. TN40: Bex S 8A 126
Filsham Rd. TN38: St Leo 8E 126
Filsham Valley TN38: St Leo 7F 126
Finch Ct. BN10: Tels C 5A 148
Finches Ct. RH16: Lind 1H 49
Finches Gdns. RH16: Lind 1H 49
Finches La. RH16: Lind 1H 49
Finches M. RH16: Lind 1H 49
Finches Pk. Rd. RH16: Lind 1H 49
Finches, The TN38: St Leo 1G 126
TN40: Bex S 1M 145
Findon Av. BN2: Salt 3M 147
Findon Cl. BN3: Hove 2H 131
BN25: Sea 9H 151
TN39: Bex S 2F 144
Findon Rd. BN2: Brig 8G 132
Finistere Av. BN23: Eastb 4H 155
Finmere Cl. BN22: Eastb 6F 154
Finmere Ct. BN22: Eastb 6F 154
Finmere Rd. BN22: Eastb 6F 154
Finmere Rd. Ind. Est. BN22: Eastb 5F 154
Finsbury Lodge *BN2: Brig 7D 132*
(off Finsbury Rd.)
Finsbury Rd. BN2: Brig 7C 132
Fir Bank BN2: Brig 3G 162
Firbank Way RH19: E Grin 3D 10
Fir Cl. BN2: W'dean 6N 133
Fircroft Cl. BN1: Brig 2N 131
FIRE HILLS 3J 129
Firgrove Rd. TN21: Cross H 2K 75
Firlands RH16: Hay H 5G 49
FIRLE 1G 136
Firle Bostal BN8: W Firle 3G 136
Firle Cl. BN25: Sea 7D 150
TN35: Hast 2D 128
Firle Cres. BN7: Lewes 4F 114
Firle Dr. BN25: Sea 7D 150
Firle Grange BN25: Sea 7D 150
Firle Grn. TN22: Uck 8K 53
Firle Place 2H 137
Firle Rd. BN2: Brig 7E 132
BN8: Ripe 8N 117
BN10: Peace, Tels C 3B 148
BN22: Eastb 8E 154 (2M 161)
BN25: Sea 7D 150
TN39: Bex S 1E 144
Firle Ter. BN9: S Heig 2K 149
Firs Ct. TN4: Tun W 7C 8
First Av. BN3: Hove 8L 131
BN9: N'hvn 6J 149
TN31: Camb 6C 88
TN40: Bex S 9N 125
Firs, The *TN35: Hast 5B 128*
(off Barley La.)
Firstone Ho. *TN20: May 8C 38*
(off Stone Cross)
First St. TN3: Lang G 1K 15
Firtoft Cl. RH15: Burg H 5C 68
Fir Toll Cl. TN20: May 8C 38
Fir Toll Rd. TN20: May 8N 37
Fir Tree Cl. BN27: Hails 5F 120
TN39: Bex S 2D 144
Fir Tree Rd. TN4: Tun W 1C 16
TN34: Hast 4N 127
Fir Tree Way BN6: Hass 3B 90
Firwood Cl. BN22: Eastb 3B 154
TN21: H'fld 9D 56
Firwood Ri. TN21: H'fld 9D 56
Fisher Cl. BN23: Eastb 5J 155
Fisherman's Mus. 7A 128
FISHER'S GATE
TN7 3M 23
FISHERSGATE
BN41 6C 130
Fishersgate Cl. BN41: Ports 6C 130
Fisher's Ga. Cotts. TN7: Withy 3M 23
Fishersgate Station (Rail) 6C 130
Fishersgate Ter. BN41: Ports 6C 130
Fisher St. BN7: Lewes 5K 115
Fishmarket Rd. TN31: Rye 3G 87
Fishponds La. TN35: W'fld 4L 105
Fitch Dr. BN2: Brig 4F 132
Fitzalan Ct. *BN10: Peace 5B 148*
(off Cavell Av.)
Fitzalan Ho. BN21: Eastb 3H 161
Fitzgerald Av. BN25: Sea 1E 156
Fitzgerald Cl.
BN20: Eastb 2C 160 (9H 161)
Fitzgerald Ho. BN25: Sea 9D 150
Fitzgerald Pk. BN25: Sea 1E 156
Fitzgerald Rd. BN7: Lewes 3K 115
Fitzherbert Ct. *BN2: Brig 5E 132*
(off Fitzherbert Dr.)
Fitzherbert Dr. BN2: Brig 5E 132
Fitzjohn Ct. BN6: Hass 4A 90
Fitzjohn's Rd. BN7: Lewes 4G 115
Fitzmaurice Av. BN22: Eastb 7E 154
Fitzroy Rd. BN7: Lewes 3H 115
Five Acre Wlk. TN34: Hast 5K 127
FIVE ASH DOWN 5J 53
FIVE ASHES 3M 55
Five Ashes Rd. TN6: Roth 5L 37
TN20: May 7N 37
Five Chimneys La. TN22: Had D 4E 54
Five Ho's. *TN36: Winch 8C 86*
(off North St.)
Five Ways BN1: Brig 3B 132
FLACKLEY ASH 6M 65
Flag Ct. BN3: Hove 8K 131
Flamstead Rd. BN27: Herst 5C 122
Flaxmore Pk. TN4: South 3D 8
Fleetway Ct. TN31: Camb 6C 88
Fleetwood Cl. TN37: St Leo 9H 105
Fleming Cl. BN23: Lang 2J 155
Fleming Wlk. RH19: E Grin 6F 10
Fletcher Av. TN37: St Leo 8F 104
Fletcher Cl. BN27: Hails 7F 120
FLETCHING 6M 51
Fletching Cl. BN2: Brig 7G 132
FLETCHING COMMON 8H 51
Fletching Rd. BN22: Eastb 2D 154
Fletching St. TN20: May 7E 38
FLIMWELL 8D 30
Flimwell Bird Pk. 9E 30
Flimwell Cl. BN2: Brig 8F 132
(not continuous)
BN23: Lang 9K 141
TN5: Flim 7E 30
TN38: St Leo 4D 126
Flint Cl. BN25: Sea 6D 150
BN41: Ports 3D 130
Flints, The BN7: King L 9E 114
Flitterbrook La.
TN21: Punn T, Rush G 3M 77
Floral Clock *7L 131*
(off Western Rd.)
Florance La. TN3: Groom 6F 14
Florence Av. BN3: Hove 5F 130
Florence Ct. *BN1: Brig 3A 132*
(off Gordon Rd.)
Florence Pl. BN1: Brig 4C 132 (1G 162)
Florence Rd. BN1: Brig 5B 132 (1E 162)
FLOWERS GREEN 3B 122
Floyd Cl. TN4: Tun W 6D 8
Folders Cl. RH15: Burg H 7E 68
Folders Grange RH15: Burg H 7D 68
Folders La. RH15: Burg H 7C 68
Folders Vs. RH15: Burg H 7F 68
Foley Cl. BN23: Eastb 5H 155
Folkestone Cl. BN25: Sea 7H 151
Folkestone Rd. TN31: E Guld 9J 67
FOLKINGTON 9M 139
Folkington Gdns. TN37: St Leo 1J 127
Folkington La. BN26: Folk 9M 139
Folly Fld. BN9: N'hvn 5J 149
Fonthill Rd. BN3: Hove 5K 131
Fontridge La. TN19: B'wsh, Etch 7M 59
Fontwell Av. TN39: Bex S 9D 124
Foords La. BN24: Hank 6L 141
TN21: Vine C 8F 76
Footland Wood 3A 82
Foot's La. TN19: B'wsh C 6D 58
Fordbrook Hill TN6: H Hur 8C 36
FORDCOMBE 8F 6
Fordcombe La. TN3: F'cmbe 8F 6
Fordcombe Rd. TN3: F'cmbe 8F 6
TN11: Pens 3E 6
Ford Rd. TN38: St Leo 4F 126
FORD'S GREEN 7C 34
Foredown Cl. BN20: Eastb 1N 159
BN41: Ports 3D 130
Foredown Dr. BN41: Ports 4D 130
Foredown Rd. BN41: Ports 1C 130
(not continuous)
Foredown Tower Countryside Cen.
2D 130
Forest Dene TN6: Jar B 1H 37
Forest Fold Cotts. TN6: Crow 6B 24
Forest La. TN21: Punn T 3N 77
Forest Lodge RH19: E Grin 4F 10
Forest Pk. TN6: Crow 9B 24
TN22: Mare 4E 52
Forest Pl. TN21: Cross H 2K 75
Forest Ridge RH19: Sharp 5A 20
Forest Ri. TN6: Jar B 1H 37
Forest Rd. BN1: Brig 9F 112
RH18: F Row 2A 22
TN2: Tun W 4D 16
FOREST ROW 1M 21
Forest Row Bus. Pk. RH18: F Row 9M 11
Forest Vw. BN27: Hails 6D 120
TN22: Nut 7B 34
Forest Vw. Rd. RH19: E Grin 6E 10
Forest Way 5G 11
Forest Way BN27: Chal 3G 118
RH18: F Row 8J 11
RH19: E Grin, F Row 7H 11
TN2: Pem 5N 9
TN2: Tun W 3F 16
TN7: Up H 9C 12
Forest Way TN34: Hast 5L 127
Forewood La. TN33: Batt, C'hrst 9N 103
Forewood Ri. TN33: C'hrst 9N 103
Forge Cl. BN41: Ports 3D 130
TN11: Pens 1F 6
TN22: Uck 2H 73
TN32: Staple 8E 62
Forge Cotts. *BN26: Alfr 1L 151*
(off West St.)
Forgefield TN5: S'gate 4H 41
Forgefield Cotts. TN18: Sandh 6G 44
Forge La. TN32: Staple 8E 62
TN33: A'ham 3M 101
Forge La. Cotts. TN22: Nut 1F 52
Forge M. TN31: Rye 3F 86
Forge Ri. TN22: Uck 2G 73
Forge Rd. TN3: Eri G, Groom 9F 14
TN4: South 4C 8
Forge Way *RH15: Burg H 4A 68*
(off Packman Way)
RH15: Burg H 4A 68
(off Maple Dr.)
TN37: St Leo 1J 127
Formula Fun Go-Karts
Fort Fun 7H 155
Forstall TN3: Lang G 9L 7
Forstall, The TN3: Eri G 9J 15
Forstal, The TN2: Pem 5N 9
Fort Cl. TN2: Tun W 1F 16
Fort Fun BN22: Eastb 7H 155
Fort Ga. BN9: N'hvn 7L 149
Fort La. BN22: Eastb 6G 154
Fort Ri. BN9: N'hvn 7K 149
Fort Rd. BN9: N'hvn 5K 149
BN22: Eastb 6G 154
Fort Vw. BN9: S Heig 2L 149
Forum, The 2D 16
Forward Cl. BN9: S Heig 2L 149

Glenfalls Av.—Greystones Ct.

Glenfalls Av. BN1: Brig 7B 112
Glenfergus RH16: Hay H 3F 48
Glengorse TN33: Batt 4N 103
Glenleigh Av. TN39: Bex S 8G 125
GLENLEIGH PARK 8H 125
Glenleigh Pk. Rd. TN39: Bex S 8G 125
Glenleigh Wlk. TN32: Rob 5H 61
Glenmore M.
BN21: Eastb 9D 154 (4K 161)
Glenmore Pk. TN2: Tun W 4C 16
Glenmore Rd. TN6: Crow 8A 24
Glenmore Rd. E. TN6: Crow 8B 24
Glennys Ind. Est. BN22: Eastb 7F 154
Glen Ri. BN1: Brig 9K 111
Glen Ri. Cl. BN1: Brig 9K 111
Glen, The TN22: Uck 8J 53
Glenthorne Ho. BN21: Eastb 3H 161
Glenthorn Rd. TN39: Bex S 1H 145
Glenview Cl. TN35: Hast 5C 128
Glen Vue RH19: E Grin 3E 10
Glessing Rd. BN24: Sto C 7L 141
Gleton Av. BN3: Hove 3F 130
Gloucester Av. TN40: Bex S 9A 126
Gloucester Cl. BN22: Will 2N 153
RH19: E Grin 4G 10
Gloucester Cotts. *TN34: Hast 6N 127*
(off Croft Rd.)
Gloucester Ct.
BN20: Eastb 2C 160 (8H 161)
BN23: Lang 3H 155
Gloucester M. BN1: Brig 6F 162
Gloucester Pas. BN1: Brig 6F 162
Gloucester Pl. BN1: Brig 7B 132 (6F 162)
TN5: Wadh 5B 28
(off Gloucester Rd.)
Gloucester Pl. TN2: Tun W. 3D 16
Gloucester Rd. BN1: Brig . . .7B 132 (6E 162)
(not continuous)
RH15: Burg H 5A 68
TN5: Wadh 5B 28
Gloucester St. BN1: Brig 7B 132 (6F 162)
Gloucester Yd. BN1: Brig 6F 162
Glovers La. TN39: Bex S 7K 125
Glover's Yd. BN1: Brig 4A 132
GLYNDE 8E 116
Glynde Av. BN2: Salt 2L 147
BN22: Eastb 3B 154
GLYNDEBOURNE 4D 116
Glyndebourne Av. BN2: Salt 2K 147
Glyndebourne Gdns. TN37: St Leo 9J 105
Glyndebourne Opera House 4D 116
Glynde Cl. BN9: N'hvn 2K 149
Glynde Ct. TN39: Bex S 2D 144
Glynde Ho. BN3: Hove 7M 131
Glynde Place 7E 116
Glynde Rd. BN2: Brig 7E 132
Glynde Station (Rail) 8E 116
Glyndley Mnr. Cottage Est.
BN24: Hank 3J 141
Glyne Ascent TN40: Bex S 9N 125
Glyne Barn Cl. TN40: Bex S 9A 126
Glyne Dr. TN40: Bex S 9A 126
GLYNE GAP 9B 126
Glyne Hall TN40: Bex S 2L 145
Glynleigh BN2: Brig 6G 162
Glynleigh Dr. BN26: Pole 6F 140
Glynleigh Rd. BN24: Hails, Hank 3F 140
Glynn Ri. BN10: Peace 3B 148
Glynn Rd. BN10: Peace 3C 148
Glynn Rd. W. BN10: Peace 3C 148
GOAT CROSS ROAD 5G 20
GOATHAM GREEN 3L 83
Goatham La. TN31: B Oak 5K 83
Gochers Ct. *BN2: Brig 6D 132*
(off Islingword Rd.)
Godden Rd. BN8: N'wck 1J 71
Goddens Cl. TN31: North 2A 64
Goddensfield TN5: Wadh 6A 28
Goddens Gill TN31: North 2A 64
Godfrey Cl. BN7: Lewes 3J 115
GODLEYS GREEN 3A 70
Godwin Rd. BN3: Hove 4F 130
TN35: Hast 5B 128
Goffs, The BN21: Eastb 9B 154 (4G 161)
Golby Ct. BN10: Tels C 5A 148
Goldbridge Rd. BN8: N'wck 1L 71
Goldcrest Dr. TN22: Uck 3J 73
GOLDEN CROSS
Golden Cross 9H 97
Herstmonceux 3A 122
Golden Cross Inn Holiday Cvn. Site
BN27: Gold C 1H 119
Golden Ga. Way BN23: Eastb 3K 155
Golden Hill RH15: Burg H 5E 68
Golden Jubilee Way
BN22: Eastb 8H 141
BN24: Sto C 8H 141
Golden La. BN1: Brig 8M 131 (7A 162)
Golden Miller La. BN26: Pole 7B 140
Goldhurst Grn. TN36: Ick 2K 107
Golding Rd. BN23: Lang 2J 155
Gold La. BN10: Peace 2C 148
Goldsmid M. *BN3: Hove 7M 131*
(off Farm M.)
Goldsmid Rd. BN3: Hove . . .6N 131 (4B 162)
Goldsmith Cl. BN23: Lang 1H 155
Goldsmiths Av. TN6: Crow 8B 24
Goldsmiths Leisure Cen. 7D 24
Goldstone Cl. BN3: Hove 3J 131
Goldstone Ct. BN3: Hove 2J 131
Goldstone Cres. BN3: Hove 2J 131
Goldstone Ho. *BN3: Hove 6K 131*
(off Clarendon Rd.)
Goldstone La. BN3: Hove 5K 131
Goldstone Retail Pk. BN3: Hove 5K 131
Goldstone Rd. BN3: Hove 6K 131
Goldstone St. BN3: Hove 6K 131
(not continuous)
Goldstone Vs. BN3: Hove 6K 131
Goldstone Way BN3: Hove 2J 131
Golf Dr. BN1: Brig 2C 132
Goods Sta. Rd. TN1: Tun W 9D 8
Goodtrees La. TN8: C'den 2G 13
Goodwin Cl. BN27: Hails 4D 120
Goodwins Cl. RH19: E Grin 1D 10
Goodwins, The TN2: Tun W 3C 16
Goodwood Cl. BN20: Will 2M 153
TN40: Bex S 8L 125
Goodwood Ct. BN3: Hove 6M 131
Goodwood Way BN2: Brig 2F 132
Gooseberry La. TN31: North 6N 63
Gordon Cl. RH16: Hay H 3F 48
Gordon Ho. BN21: Eastb 2J 161
Gordon Pl. TN39: Bex S 8J 125
Gordon Rd. BN1: Brig 3A 132
BN27: Hails 7E 120
BN41: Ports 6E 130
BN41: Ports 6C 130
RH15: Burg H 4D 68
RH16: Hay H 3F 48
TN4: Tun W 6F 8
TN6: Crow 9D 24
TN22: Buxt 6N 53
TN34: Hast 6N 127
Gore Pk. Av. BN21: Eastb 8A 154
Gore Pk. Rd. BN21: Eastb 8A 154
Gorseide La. RH17: Cuck 1A 48
Gorham Av. BN2: Rott 2H 147
Gorham Cl. BN2: Rott 2H 147
Gorham Ct. BN10: Tels C 4M 147
Gorham Way BN10: Tels C 4M 147
Goring Ct. BN1: Brig 9G 113
Gorringe Cl. BN20: Will 1L 153
Gorringe Dr. BN20: Will 1L 153
Gorringe Rd.
BN21: Eastb 7C 154 (1J 161)
BN22: Eastb 7C 154 (1J 161)
Gorringe Valley Rd. BN20: Will 1L 153
Gorse Cl. BN20: Eastb 7M 153
BN41: Ports 1B 130
Gorse Dr. BN25: Sea 6E 150
Gorse Hill TN21: B Oak 7H 57
Gorselands TN33: Sed 7E 82
Gorse Rd. TN2: Tun W 8H 9
Gorses, The TN39: Bex S 3D 144
Gorsethorn Way TN35: Fair 2K 129
Gorseway, The TN39: Bex S 9D 124
Gosford Way BN26: Pole 7C 140
Gote La. BN8: Ring 2B 116
GOTHAM 7C 124
Goudhurst Cl. BN23: Lang 3G 154
Goudhurst Rd. TN3: Lamb 5K 19
Gower Rd. RH16: Hay H 5F 48
Gows Cft. BN7: King L 9E 114
Gradwell End BN8: S Chai 9D 70
Graffham Cl. BN2: Brig 7F 132
Grafton Ct. BN21: Eastb 9E 154 (5M 161)
Grafton St. BN2: Brig 9C 132
Graham Av. BN1: Brig 1N 131
BN41: Ports 1B 130
Graham Cl. BN41: Ports 1B 130
Graham Cres. BN41: Ports 1B 130
Grampian Cl. BN23: Lang 1F 154
TN2: Tun W 8G 9
Granary Rural Bus. Cen., The
BN27: Hell 9C 98
Grand Av. BN3: Hove 8L 131
BN6: Hass 3A 90
BN25: Sea 7B 150
TN40: Bex S 8A 126
Grand Av. Mans. *BN3: Hove 7L 131*
(off Grand Av.)
Grand Ct. BN21: Eastb 2D 160 (8L 161)
Grand Cres. BN2: Rott 3H 147
Grand Junc. Rd.
BN1: Brig 9B 132 (9E 162)
Grand Mans. BN20: Eastb 9K 161
Grand Pde. BN2: Brig 8B 132 (7F 162)
BN21: Eastb 2D 160 (8L 161)
BN26: Pole 7C 140
TN37: St Leo 8J 127
TN38: St Leo 8J 127
Grand Pde. M. BN2: Brig 8B 132 (7F 162)
Grange Av. TN34: Hast 2K 127
Grange Cl. BN1: Brig 4N 131 (1B 162)
RH15: Burg H 3D 68
TN6: Crow 1B 36
TN21: Horam 1C 98
Grange Ct. *BN3: Hove 5H 131*
(off Payne Av.)
BN7: Lewes 6J 115
BN21: Eastb 1C 160 (7H 161)
BN42: S'wck 6A 130
Grange Ct. Dr. TN39: Bex S 8J 125
Grange End BN21: Eastb 2C 160 (9J 161)
Grange Farm Cotts. *BN2: Oving 9L 133*
(off Greenways)
Grange Gdns.
BN20: Eastb 1C 160 (7H 161)
(Blackwater Rd.)
BN20: Eastb 1C 160 (7H 161)
(Furness Rd.)
TN4: R'hall 9A 8
Grange Ind. Est., The
BN42: S'wck 6A 130
Grange Lodge BN20: Eastb 7H 161
Grange M. BN21: Eastb 1C 160 (6J 161)
Grange Rd. BN3: Hove 6G 131
BN7: Lewes 6J 115
BN8: Barc C 3K 93
BN21: Eastb 1C 160 (6J 161)
BN42: S'wck 6A 130
TN4: R'hall 9A 8
TN22: Uck 1H 73
TN34: Hast 1L 127
Grange, The 2H 147
Grange, The BN2: Salt 4L 147
BN8: Barc C 3K 93
BN21: Eastb 6L 161
TN33: Nin 1A 124
Grange Wlk. BN1: Brig 9N 111
Grangeways BN1: Brig 9N 111
Granham Bank BN8: Barc C 3L 93
Grantham Cl. BN8: S Chai 9E 70
Grantham Rd. BN1: Brig 4B 132
Grants Hill Ho. TN22: Uck 1H 73
Grant St. BN2: Brig 6C 132
Granville Ct. *BN3: Hove 6K 131*
(off Denmark Vs.)
BN20: Eastb 2C 160 (8H 161)
BN25: Sea 1D 156
Granville Crest BN20: Eastb 3B 160
Granville Rd. BN3: Hove 6N 131 (4B 162)
BN20: Eastb 1C 160 (7H 161)
TN1: Tun W 8F 8
Graperies, The BN2: Brig 8D 132
Grasmere Cl. BN23: Lang 9L 141
Grassington Rd.
BN20: Eastb 1C 160 (7H 161)
Grassmere Av. BN10: Tels C 4N 147
Grassmere Ct. BN10: Tels C 4A 148
Gratton Ct. TN39: Bex S 2H 145
Gravelye Cl. RH16: Hay H 4J 49
Gravelye La. RH16: Hay H 6H 49
(not continuous)
Gravett Cl. RH15: Burg H 6A 68
GRAVETYE 1A 20
Graycoats Dr. TN6: Crow 9D 24
Graystone La. TN35: Hast 3B 128
Graywood La. BN8: E Hoath. 1H 97
Graywood Rd. BN8: E Hoath. 1F 96
Grazebrook Cl. TN39: Bex S 2D 144
Gt. Bounds Dr. TN4: South 2B 8
Gt. Brooms Rd. TN4: Tun W 5E 8
Gt. Cliffe Rd. BN23: Lang 3H 155
Gt. College St. BN2: Brig 9D 132
Gt. Courtlands TN3: Lang G 9L 7
Great Dixter House & Gardens 2M 63
Greater Paddock BN8: Ring 9D 94
Gt. Footway TN3: Lang G 1K 15
Gt. Hall Arc. TN1: Tun W 1E 16
Greatham Ct. *BN1: Brig 8N 111*
(off Old London Rd.)
Great Heathmead RH16: Hay H 3E 48
Great Ho. Ct. RH19: E Grin 4F 10
GREAT JOB'S CROSS 2B 46
Gt. Lodge Retail Pk. TN2: Tun W 4H 9
Great Maytham Hall 1E 46
Great Oak TN19: Hur G 7H 43
Great Rough BN8: N'wck 2G 71
GREAT STREELE 9N 53
Gt. Wilkins Halls of Residence
BN1: Falm 9J 113
Grecian Rd. TN1: Tun W 2E 16
Greeba Ct. *TN38: St Leo 8H 127*
(off Marina)
Greenacre BN10: Peace 2D 148
Greenacre Ct. *RH15: Burg H 6B 68*
(off Station Rd.)
Greenacres BN1: Brig 4A 132 (1D 162)
BN10: Tels C 5A 148
TN35: W'fld 4L 105
Greenacres Dr. BN8: Ring 2B 116
BN27: Hails 6F 120
Greenacres Way BN27: Hails 6F 120
Greenbank Av. BN2: Salt 3K 147
Green Cl. BN8: Ring 9D 94
BN42: S'wck 6A 130
Green Ct. *BN42: S'wck 6A 130*
(off Green, The)
Greencroft BN21: Eastb 6M 161
Greene Ct. BN7: Lewes 6H 115
Greenfield Cl. BN1: Brig 9B 112
BN42: S'wck 5A 130
TN4: R'hall 8N 7
Greenfield Cres. BN1: Brig 9A 112
Greenfield Dr. TN22: Uck 4J 73
Greenfield Rd. BN21: Eastb 8A 154
TN19: B'wsh 1L 59
Greenfields BN27: Hails 5D 120
Greenfields Cl. TN37: St Leo 9H 105
Green Ga. BN10: Peace 3C 148
Green Gro. BN27: Hails 6E 120
Green Hedges Av. RH19: E Grin 2D 10
Green Hedges Cl. RH19: E Grin 2D 10
Greenhill Way BN10: Peace 2C 148
RH17: Hay H 7H 49
Greenlands Cl. RH15: Burg H 8C 68
Greenlands Dr. RH15: Burg H 8C 68
Green La. BN2: W'dean 7M 133
BN7: Lewes 6J 115
BN8: Ring 6F 94
BN8: S Chai 7E 70
(not continuous)
BN25: Sea 1D 156
BN26: Jev 3G 152
RH17: Wivel 4J 69
TN6: Crow 9F 24
TN12: Bren 1J 19
TN21: H'fld 2E 76
TN22: B'boys 1E 74
TN39: Bex S 9E 124
Greenleaf Gdns. BN26: Pole 5D 140
Greenleas BN3: Hove 3F 130
TN2: Pem .7M 9
Green Mdws. RH16: Lind 1J 49
Green Pk. Cnr. RH17: Wivel 4H 69
Green Ridge BN1: Brig 9K 111
Green Rd. RH17: Wivel, Wivel G 3H 69
Green Sq. TN5: Wadh 6B 28
Greenstede Av. RH19: E Grin 1F 10
GREEN STREET 2B 126
Green St. BN21: Eastb 8N 153
Green, The BN2: Rott 2G 147
BN3: Hove 3L 131
BN8: N'wck 1K 71
BN20: E Dean 3F 158
BN27: Hails 3F 120
BN42: S'wck 6A 130
RH17: Hors K 5D 32
TN3: Frant 9E 16
TN3: Groom 4G 14
TN3: Lang G 1J 15
TN22: B'boys 2E 74
TN32: Bod 2E 62
TN33: Cats 7F 102
TN33: Nin 9C 102
TN33: Sed 8E 82
TN38: St Leo 5H 127
Green Vw. RH15: Burg H 5A 68
Greenviews Cvn. Pk. TN21: B Oak 9G 56
Green Wlk. BN25: Sea 1G 156
BN27: Hails 5F 120
Green Walk, The BN22: Will 1M 153
Green Wall BN7: Lewes 5K 115
Green Way BN8: Alfr 2F 150
Greenway BN20: Eastb 6M 153
Green Way TN2: Tun W 5H 9
Greenway Ct. BN2: Rott 3H 147
Greenways BN2: Oving 9L 133
BN41: Ports 5D 130
BN42: S'wck 4B 130
RH16: Hay H 3G 48
TN39: Bex S 7G 124
Greenways Cnr. BN2: Oving 9K 133
Greenwell Cl. BN25: Sea 8G 151
Greenwich Ho. BN20: Eastb 3B 160
Greenwich Rd. BN27: Hails 7G 120
Greenwich Way BN10: Peace 5B 148
GREENWOODS 6H 29
Greenwoods La. TN21: Punn T 2N 77
Greggs Wood Rd. TN2: Tun W 7H 9
Gregory La. BN24: W'ham 8B 142
Gregory Wlk. TN33: Sed 8E 82
Grenada TN39: Bex S 2H 145
Grenada Cl. BN23: Eastb 5K 155
TN39: Bex S 1E 144
Grenville Ho. BN10: Peace 3D 148
Grenville Rd. BN24: Pev B 9E 142
Grenville St. BN1: Brig 8A 132 (8D 162)
Gresham BN24: Pev 7D 142
Gresham Cl. BN21: Eastb 6N 153
Gresham Way TN38: St Leo 6G 126
Gresley Rd. TN38: St Leo 1F 126
Greville Rd. TN35: Hast 3B 128
Grey Alders RH16: Hay H 3J 49
Greybury La. TN8: Mrsh G 3A 4
Greyfriars BN3: Hove 5M 131
Greyfriars Ct. BN7: Lewes 5K 115
Greyfriars Pl. TN36: Winch 1F 108
Greyhorses TN39: Bex S 1C 144
Grey Owl's Reach *TN34: Hast 5N 127*
(off Milward Rd.)
Greys Rd. BN20: Eastb 9A 154
Greystones Ct. *TN6: Crow 7B 24*
(off St John's Rd.)

Grey Tower Bungs.—Hassocks

Grey Tower Bungs.
BN24: Pev B 1M 155
Grey Tower Cvn. Site
BN24: Pev B 1L 155
Grey Tower Rd. BN24: Pev B 1L 155
Griffits Path RH18: F Row 1L 21
Grinley Ct. *TN40: Bex S* *1K 145*
(off Cranfield Rd.)
Grinstead La. RH19: F Row 2B 20
Grinstead Mt. BN2: Brig 8G 132
GRISLING COMMON 9A 52
Gromenfield TN3: Groom 5G 14
GROOMBRIDGE 5G 14
Groombridge Hill TN3: Groom 5G 14
TN3: Groom 4G 14
Groombridge La. TN3: Eri G 1J 25
Groombridge Rd.
TN3: A'hst, Groom 3E 14
Groombridge Station
Spa Valley Railway 5G 15
Grosvenor Bri. TN1: Tun W 8E 8
Grosvenor Cl. BN26: Pole 8C 140
Grosvenor Ct. BN1: Brig 2N 131
BN21: Eastb 2J 161
BN25: Sea 9C 150
RH19: E Grin *3D 10*
(off Grosvenor Rd.)
Grosvenor Cres. TN38: St Leo 8F 126
Grosvenor Gdns. TN38: St Leo 8F 126
Grosvenor Mans. BN3: Hove 7K 131
Grosvenor M. BN25: Sea 8C 150
Grosvenor Pk. TN1: Tun W 9D 8
Grosvenor Pl. TN1: Tun W 7E 8
Grosvenor Pl. TN4: Tun W 7F 8
Grosvenor Quay BN23: Eastb 4K 155
Grosvenor Rd. BN25: Sea 9C 150
RH19: E Grin 3D 10
TN1: Tun W 9D 8
Grosvenor St. BN2: Brig 8C 132
Grosvenor Wlk. TN1: Tun W 9D 8
Grove Av. TN1: Tun W 2D 16
Grove Bank BN2: Brig 6G 162
GROVEBRIDGE 5G 99
Grove Ct. BN3: Hove 7L 131
GROVE HILL 6H 99
Grove Hill BN2: Brig 7C 132 (6G 162)
BN27: Hell 5H 99
Grove Hill Gdns. TN1: Tun W 2E 16
Grove Hill Ho. *TN1: Tun W* *1E 16*
(off Grove Hill Rd.)
Grove Hill Rd. TN1: Tun W 1E 16
Grovelands Cl. RH15: Burg H 7A 68
Grovelands Rd. BN27: Hails 5D 120
Grove La. TN31: Iden 5F 66
Grovelye La. TN21: Dall 7D 78
Grove Rd. BN21: Eastb 1C 160 (6H 161)
BN25: Sea 9E 150
RH15: Burg H 6C 68
TN8: Chid H, Pens 4B 6
TN11: Pens 4C 6
TN35: Hast 2C 128
Grover St. TN1: Tun W 9E 8
Grove St. BN2: Brig 7C 132
Grove, The BN9: N'hvn 2L 149
BN20: Will 1K 153
BN20: Will 5M 153
BN27: Hails 8E 120
RH16: Hay H 6J 49
TN2: Pem 5N 9
TN6: Crow 1C 36
TN20: May 7D 38
TN31: Rye 2G 86
TN33: Batt 4N 103
TN39: Bex S 9F 124
Grove Villa BN1: Brig 3C 162
Growers End BN8: N'wck 1K 71
Guardian Ct. BN26: Pole 6C 140
Guardswell Pl. BN25: Sea 9E 150
GUESTLING GREEN 7F 106
Guestling Rd. BN22: Eastb 7G 154
GUESTLING THORN 3F 106
Guildford Rd.
BN1: Brig 7A 132 (5D 162)
TN1: Tun W 1E 16
Guildford St. BN1: Brig 7A 132 (5D 162)
Guinness Ct. BN9: N'hvn 2L 149
Guinness Trust Bungs.
BN9: S Heig *2L 149*
(off Iveagh Cres.)
BN9: S Heig 2L 149
Guldeford Rd. TN31: E Guld 2H 87
Gundreda Rd. BN7: Lewes 4G 115
Gun Garden *3G 87*
(off Church Sq.)
GUN HILL 5N 97
Gun Rd. TN22: B'boys 1E 74
Gunter's La. TN39: Bex S 7H 125
Gurth Rd. TN35: Hast 5B 128
Gwent Ct. BN22: Eastb 3N 161
Gwydyr Mans. BN3: Hove 7M 131
Gwyneth Gro. TN40: Bex S 7N 125
Gwynne Gdns. *BN26: Alfr* *1L 151*
(off North Rd.)
RH19: E Grin 2C 10

H

Hackenden Cl. RH19: E Grin 1E 10
Hackenden Cotts. RH19: E Grin 1E 10
Hackenden La. RH19: E Grin 2E 10
Hackhurst La. BN27: Lwr D 2M 119
Hackhurst La. Ind. Est.
BN27: Lwr D 2M 119
Hackwood TN32: Rob 5F 60
Haddington Cl. BN3: Hove 7K 131
Haddington St. BN3: Hove 6K 131
Hadley Ct. BN26: Pole 8D 140
TN4: Tun W 7C 8
Hadley Ho. BN21: Eastb 9C 154 (4J 161)
Hadlow Av. BN23: Lang 9K 141
Hadlow Cl. BN2: Brig 7E 132
HADLOW DOWN 4G 55
Hadlow Down Rd. TN6: Crow 8D 36
Hadrian Av. BN42: S'wck 5C 130
Hadrian Gdns. TN37: St Leo 9G 104
Haig Av. BN1: Brig 8E 112
HAILSHAM 6E 120
Hailsham Av. BN2: Salt 1L 147
Hailsham Ct. *TN40: Bex S* *2K 145*
(off Marina)
Hailsham Heritage Cen. *7F 120*
(off Blackmans Yd.)
Hailsham Ind. Pk. BN27: Hails 7D 120
Hailsham Rd. BN24: Hank 4H 141
BN26: Pole 6C 140
BN27: Hails 3G 120
BN27: Herst 1M 121
TN21: H'fld 3D 76
Hairpin Cft. BN10: Peace 3C 148
HALE GREEN 5L 97
Half Mile Drove BN8: Ring 9G 95
Half Moon La. TN11: Tude 1N 9
HALLAND 1A 96
Halland Cl. BN22: Will 4A 154
Halland Rd. BN2: Brig 1G 132
BN8: E Hoath 1C 96
Hallands, The *RH15: Burg H* *4D 68*
(off St Andrews Rd.)
Hallett Rd. BN2: Brig 6E 132
Halley Pk. BN27: Hails 7G 121
Halley Rd. BN27: Herst 5D 122
TN21: B Oak 1G 77
Hall La. TN22: Had D 4G 55
HALL'S CROSS 6M 123
Hall's Hole Rd. TN2: Tun W 2G 17
Hallyburton Rd. BN3: Hove 5F 130
Halsford Cft. RH19: E Grin 1B 10
Halsford Grn. RH19: E Grin 1B 10
Halsford La. RH19: E Grin 2B 10
Halsford Pk. Rd. RH19: E Grin 2C 10
HALTON 4A 128
Halton Cres. TN34: Hast 4A 128
Halton Hgts. *TN34: Hast* *4A 128*
(off Priory Rd.)
Halton Pl. TN34: Hast 4A 128
Halton Rd. BN22: Eastb 8F 154
Halton Ter. TN34: Hast 4A 128
Hamble Rd. BN24: Sto C 8J 141
Hambleton Cl. BN23: Lang 1G 155
Hambrook RH15: Burg H 7D 68
Hamelin Ct. *TN22: Uck* *4J 73*
(off Pipers Fld.)
Hamelsham Ct. BN27: Hails 6D 120
HAM GREEN 1A 66
Hamilton Cl. BN41: Ports 2C 130
Hamilton Ct. BN2: Brig 1B 146
TN4: Tun W 8D 8
Hamilton Gdns. TN35: Hast 3C 128
Hamilton Ho. BN21: Eastb 8B 154
BN25: Sea 8D 150
TN4: Tun W 8D 8
Hamilton Mans. BN3: Hove 8K 131
Hamilton Rd. BN1: Brig 5A 132 (2C 162)
Hamilton Ter. TN39: Bex S 1H 145
Hamlands La. BN22: Will 1M 153
Ham La. BN7: Lewes 6K 115
BN8: Ring 8A 94
RH17: Scay H 6M 49
RH17: Wivel 1K 69
TN19: B'wsh 1J 59
Hammer La. BN27: Cowb 3J 99
TN21: Vine C, Warb 1J 99
HAMMERWOOD 1A 12
Hammerwood Park 2B 12
Hammerwood Rd. RH19: A'hstw 6K 11
Hammonds TN18: Hawk 1A 44
Hammonds Dr. BN23: Eastb 5F 154
Hammonds Gdns. RH15: Burg H 7A 68
HAMMOND'S GREEN 2M 73
Hammonds Ind. Est. BN23: Eastb 5E 154
Hammonds Ridge RH15: Burg H 7A 68
Hampden Av. BN22: Eastb 3C 154
Hampden Cl. TN33: Batt 3J 103
Hampden Cl. TN37: St Leo 6J 127
Hampden Ct. BN21: Eastb 8K 161
Hampden Gdns. BN8: Glyn 8E 116
BN9: S Heig 2K 149
Hampden Lodge TN21: H'fld 2D 76
HAMPDEN PARK 3C 154
Hampden Pk. Dr. BN22: Eastb 4A 154
Hampden Pk. Ind. Est.
BN22: Eastb 4D 154
Hampden Pk. Sports Cen. 2B 154
Hampden Park Station (Rail) 3C 154
Hampden Retail Pk. BN22: Eastb 3C 154
Hampden Rd. BN2: Brig 6D 132
Hampden Ter. *BN22: Eastb* *9F 154*
(off Latimer Rd.)
Hampden Va. Cvn. Cen.
BN9: Tarr N 1K 149
Hampshire Ct. BN2: Brig 9C 132
BN23: Lang 3H 155
Hampstead Rd. BN1: Brig 4M 131
Hampton Ho. *BN27: Hails* *7E 120*
(off Summerheath Rd.)
Hampton Pl. BN1: Brig 8N 131 (7B 162)
Hampton St. BN1: Brig 8N 131 (7B 162)
Hampton Ter. BN1: Brig 6B 162
Hampton Way RH19: E Grin 5F 10
HAMSEY 9H 93
Hamsey Cl. BN2: Brig 8G 132
BN20: Eastb 6M 153
Hamsey Cres. BN7: Lewes 4F 114
Hamsey La. BN8: Cooks, H'sey 7G 92
BN25: Sea 1H 157
Hamsey Rd. BN2: Salt 3L 147
BN8: Barc 6K 93
RH19: Sharp 5A 20
Ham Shaw Ct. BN22: Eastb 4C 154
Hamsland RH17: Hors K 6C 32
Hanbury La. RH16: Hay H 4H 49
Hangdown Mead Bus. Pk.
RH19: Sharp 6B 20
Hanging Birch La. TN21: Horam 6A 76
HANGLETON 3G 130
Hangleton Cl. BN3: Hove 3F 130
Hangleton Gdns. BN3: Hove 4F 130
Hangleton La. BN3: Hove 3E 130
BN41: Ports 3D 130
(not continuous)
Hangleton Link Rd. BN41: Ports 2E 130
Hangleton Mnr. Cl. BN3: Hove 3E 130
Hangleton Rd. BN3: Hove 5F 130
Hangleton Valley Dr. BN3: Hove 3E 130
Hangleton Way BN3: Hove 4F 130
HANKHAM 5M 141
Hankham Ct. BN24: Sto C 8K 141
Hankham Hall Rd.
BN24: Hank, W'ham 5L 141
Hankham Rd. BN24: Hank 7L 141
Hankham St. BN24: Hank 6L 141
Hanlye La. RH16: Hay H 1B 48
RH17: Cuck, Hay H 1B 48
Hanover Cl. BN25: Sea 6A 150
TN40: Bex S 9K 125
Hanover Ct. BN2: Brig 6C 132
BN21: Eastb 7A 154
BN27: Hails *6F 120*
(off St Mary's Av.)
RH16: Hay H 5E 48
Hanover Cres. BN2: Brig 6C 132
Hanover Lofts *BN2: Brig* *7C 132*
(off Finsbury Rd.)
Hanover M. BN2: Brig 6C 132
Hanover Pl. *BN2: Brig* *6C 132*
(off Lewes Rd.)
Hanover Rd. BN22: Eastb 8F 154 (3N 161)
TN1: Tun W 9D 8
Hanover St. BN2: Brig 6C 132
Hanover Ter. BN2: Brig 6C 132
Hanson Rd. BN9: N'hvn 6H 149
Harbour Ct. *BN42: S'wck* *6B 130*
(off Whiterock Pl.)
Harbour Farm TN36: Winch 1F 108
HARBOUR HEIGHTS 7H 149
Harbour Quay BN23: Eastb 3K 155
(not continuous)
Harbour Rdbt. BN23: Eastb 3J 155
Harbour's Yd. TN33: Batt 3M 103
Harbour Vw. Cl. BN9: N'hvn 6H 149
BN25: Sea 6A 150
Harbour Vw. Rd. BN9: N'hvn 7H 149
Harbour Way TN38: St Leo 8E 104
Harcourt Cl. TN22: Uck 2H 73
Harcourt Rd. TN22: Uck 2J 73
Harding Av. BN22: Eastb 6E 154
Hardinge Av. TN4: South 2B 8
Hardrada Ri. TN34: Hast 3L 127
Hardwicke Ho. *BN25: Sea* *1D 156*
(off Esplanade)
Hardwicke Rd. TN34: Hast 4A 128
Hardwick Gardens *1D 156*
(off Esplanade)
Hardwick Rd. BN3: Hove 2G 130
BN21: Eastb 1D 160 (6K 161)
Hardwick Way BN3: Hove 2G 130
(not continuous)
Hardy Dr. BN23: Eastb 6J 155
Harebeating Cl. BN27: Hails 4F 120
Harebeating Cres. BN27: Hails 4F 120
Harebeating Dr. BN27: Hails 3E 120
Harebeating Gdns. BN27: Hails 4F 120
Harebeating La. BN27: Hails 4F 120
Harebell Cl. BN23: Lang 1F 154
Harebell Dr. BN41: Ports 2C 130
Harecombe Ri. TN6: Crow 1D 36
Harecombe Rd. TN6: Crow 2D 36
Haremere Hill TN19: Etch 8E 42
Harescroft TN2: Tun W 4C 16
HARESDEAN 1K 111
Hare Way TN37: St Leo 1J 127
Harewood Cl. TN39: Bex S 2H 145
Harewood Ct. BN3: Hove 7L 131
Harfield Cl. BN9: N'hvn 2M 149
Harford Battersby Ho. BN21: Eastb 6L 161
Hargate Cl. TN2: Tun W 5C 16
Hargreaves Rd. BN23: Eastb 3D 154
Harkness Dr. TN34: Hast 1A 128
Harlands Cl. RH16: Hay H 3D 48
Harlands M. TN22: Uck 3J 73
Harlands Rd. RH16: Hay H 3D 48
Harlands Vs. *TN22: Uck* *3J 73*
(off Mallard Dr.)
Harland Way TN4: Bid, South, Tonb 1B 8
Harlequin Gdns. TN37: St Leo 9G 105
Harlequin La. TN6: Crow 1C 36
Harlequin Pl. TN6: Crow 2C 36
Harley La. TN21: H'fld 2D 76
HARLEY SHUTE 7E 126
Harley Shute Rd. TN38: St Leo 8D 126
Harley Way TN38: St Leo 8E 126
Harmans Dr. RH19: E Grin 3H 11
Harmans Mead RH19: E Grin 3H 11
Harmer Ct. TN4: South 3D 8
Harmers Hay Rd. BN27: Hails 4E 120
Harmers Hill BN8: N'wck 1J 71
Harmony St. TN4: R'hall 9A 8
Harmsworth Cres. BN3: Hove 2G 130
Harold Cl. BN24: Pev B 7H 143
Harold Dr. BN23: Eastb 4H 155
Harold M. *TN38: St Leo* *8J 127*
(off Mews Rd.)
Harold Pl. TN34: Hast 7M 127
Harold Rd. TN35: Hast 6A 128
Harold Ter. TN33: Batt 4N 103
Harpers Rd. BN9: N'hvn 5J 149
Harping Hill BN9: Pidd 1G 148
Harrier La. TN33: Batt 3N 103
Harries Rd. TN2: Tun W 6G 9
Harrington Ct. BN1: Brig 3N 131
Harrington Mans. BN1: Brig 3N 131
Harrington Pl. BN1: Brig 3C 132
Harrington Rd. BN1: Brig 3N 131
Harrington Vs. BN1: Brig 3A 132
Harris Ct. BN21: Eastb 9E 154 (5L 161)
Harrison Rd. BN25: Sea 8F 150
Harrisons La. BN8: Ring 1D 116
Harrison's Rocks 8G 14
Harrow Cl. BN25: Sea 8F 150
Harrow La. TN37: St Leo 9H 105
Hart Cl. TN22: Uck 1F 72
HARTFIELD 8J 13
Hartfield Av. BN1: Brig 1B 132
Hartfield Ct. BN3: Hove 7L 131
Hartfield La. BN21: Eastb 8C 154 (3J 161)
Hartfield Mdw. TN38: St Leo 3D 126
Hartfield Rd. BN2: Salt 3L 147
BN21: Eastb 9C 154 (4H 161)
BN25: Sea 9F 150
RH18: F Row 9M 11
TN8: C'den, Hever 1D 4
TN39: Bex S 3E 144
Harting Combe TN38: St Leo 6H 127
Hartington Mans.
BN21: Eastb 6L 161
Hartington Pl. BN2: Brig 5D 132
BN21: Eastb 1D 160 (6L 161)
Hartington Rd. BN2: Brig 5D 132
Hartington Ter. BN2: Brig 5D 132
Hartington Vs. BN3: Hove 5K 131
HARTLEY 1N 31
Hartley Ct. BN1: Brig 4D 162
TN40: Bex S *2L 145*
(off Knole Rd.)
Hartley Rd. TN17: Cran 1N 31
Harts Grn. TN33: Sed 9F 82
Hartwood Lodge *TN40: Bex S* *1K 145*
(off Cranfield Rd.)
Harvard Cl. BN7: Lewes 3J 115
Harvard Rd. BN8: Ring 1C 116
Harvest Cl. BN10: Tels C 2B 148
RH16: Lind 2J 49
Harvesters RH16: Hay H 7E 48
Harvest Hill RH19: E Grin 4E 10
Harvest Way TN37: St Leo 1J 127
Harvey Cl. TN38: St Leo 2F 126
Harveys La. BN8: Ring 4G 95
Harvey's La. TN22: Lit H 4G 95
Harvey's Way BN7: Lewes 5L 115
Harwood Cl. BN23: Eastb 5H 155
Harwoods Cl. RH19: E Grin 5F 10
Harwoods La. RH19: E Grin 5F 10
Haslam Cres. TN40: Bex S 8N 125
Haslemere Ind. Est. TN2: Tun W 5F 8
Hasletts Cl. TN1: Tun W 7E 8
HASSOCKS 3A 90

Hassocks Cl.—High St.

Hassocks Cl. BN23: Lang . . . 9J 141
Hassocks Ct. BN6: Hass . . . 3A 90
Hassocks Lodge BN6: Hass . . . 4A 90
Hassocks Station (Rail) . . . 3A 90
Hastingford La. TN6: Had D . . . 8D 36
TN22: Had D . . . 8D 36
HASTINGS . . . 7M 127
Hastings Av. BN25: Sea . . . 7H 151
HASTINGS BUPA HOSPITAL . . . 9K 105
Hastings Castle . . . 7N 127
Hastings Cl. BN26: Pole . . . 6E 140
Hastings Country Pk. . . . 5C 128
Hastings Ct. TN40: Bex S . . . 9M 125
(off Hastings Rd.)
Hastings Crematorium TN35: Hast . . . 1N 127
Hastings Embroidery . . . 6M 127
(off Queen's Rd.)
Hastings Indoor Bowls Club . . . 7K 127
Hastings Mus. & Art Gallery . . . 7L 127
Hastings Pier . . . 8L 127
Hastings Rd. TN17: Rolv . . . 2B 46
BN2: Brig . . . 5D 132
TN2: Pem . . . 7N 9
TN3: Kiln, Lamb . . . 9K 19
TN5: Flim . . . 8E 30
TN18: Hawk . . . 3N 43
TN18: N'den . . . 6A 46
TN31: B Oak, North . . . 8N 63
TN33: Batt, St Leo . . . 4N 103
TN36: Winch . . . 1A 108
TN38: Bex S . . . 9A 126
TN40: Bex S . . . 9L 125
(not continuous)
Hastings Station (Rail) . . . 6L 127
Hastings United F.C. (Pilot Field, The)
. . . 2N 127
Hatch End RH18: F Row . . . 1M 21
Hatchgate Cl. RH17: Cuck . . . 3B 48
Hatchgate La. RH17: Cuck . . . 3B 48
Hatchings, The BN26: Pole . . . 8D 140
Hatchlands RH17: Cuck . . . 3A 48
Hatherley Rd. TN37: St Leo . . . 7J 127
Hatters Hill TN17: Rolv L . . . 6J 47
Haughton Ho. BN21: Eastb . . . 5M 161
Havana Ct. BN23: Eastb . . . 4J 155
Havelock Rd. BN1: Brig . . . 3A 132 (1E 162)
BN22: Eastb . . . 8E 154 (2M 161)
TN34: Hast . . . 6M 127
TN40: Bex S . . . 8K 125
Haven Brow BN25: Sea . . . 8F 150
Haven Cl. BN22: Will . . . 1M 153
BN24: Pev B . . . 7G 143
Haven Rd. TN38: St Leo . . . 8D 126
Haven Way BN9: N'hvn . . . 6H 149
Havering Cl. TN2: Tun W . . . 7J 9
HAWKENBURY . . . 2G 17
Hawkenbury Cl. TN2: Tun W . . . 2G 16
Hawkenbury Mead TN2: Tun W . . . 3G 16
Hawkenbury Rd. TN2: Tun W . . . 2G 16
Hawkenbury Way BN7: Lewes . . . 5G 114
HAWKHURST . . . 1A 44
Hawkhurst Cl. BN23: Lang . . . 2F 154
HAWKHURST COMMON . . . 7F 74
HAWKHURST COTTAGE HOSPITAL . . . 9L 31
Hawkhurst Golf & Squash Club . . . 9M 31
Hawkhurst La. BN8: E Hoath . . . 7F 74
TN21: Wald . . . 5H 75
Hawkhurst Pl. BN1: Brig . . . 8E 112
Hawkhurst Rd. BN1: Brig . . . 7E 112
TN17: Cran . . . 5N 31
TN18: Cran, Hawk . . . 5N 31
TN32: Sed . . . 4D 82
TN33: Sed . . . 4D 82
Hawkhurst Way TN39: Bex S . . . 3E 144
Hawkins Way BN27: Hails . . . 6E 120
Hawksbridge Cl. BN22: Will . . . 1M 153
Hawks Farm Cl. BN27: Hails . . . 4E 120
Hawks Rd. BN27: Hails . . . 5E 120
Hawkstown Cl. BN27: Hails . . . 3E 120
Hawks Town Cres. BN27: Hails . . . 4E 120
Hawkstown Gdns. BN27: Hails . . . 3E 120
Hawkstown View BN27: Hails . . . 3E 120
Hawkswood Dr. BN27: Hails . . . 3F 120
Hawkswood Rd. BN27: Hails . . . 3E 120
Hawth Cl. BN25: Sea . . . 8B 150
Hawth Cres. BN25: Sea . . . 8B 150
Hawth Gro. BN25: Sea . . . 7B 150
Hawth Hill BN25: Sea . . . 7A 150
Hawthorn Av. TN39: Bex S . . . 2E 144
Hawthorn Bank BN2: Brig . . . 1G 132
Hawthorn Cl. BN2: Salt . . . 2K 147
RH15: Burg H . . . 3E 68
Hawthorn Ct. BN26: Pole . . . 7D 140
Hawthorne Cl. TN21: H'fld . . . 2E 76
Hawthorn Est. BN9: N'hvn . . . 4L 149
Hawthornes, The TN31: B Oak . . . 4A 84
Hawthorn Ri. BN9: N'hvn . . . 5H 149
Hawthorn Rd. BN23: Eastb . . . 4F 154
TN35: Hast . . . 4C 128
Hawthorn Rd. Ind. Est.
BN23: Eastb . . . 4F 154
Hawthorns, The BN27: Hails . . . 7D 120
RH15: Burg H . . . 3B 68
Hawthorn Wlk. TN2: Tun W . . . 5H 9
Hawthorn Way BN41: Ports . . . 2C 130
Hawth Pk. Rd. BN25: Sea . . . 7B 150
Hawth Pl. BN25: Sea . . . 8B 150
Hawth Ri. BN25: Sea . . . 7B 150
Hawth Valley Ct. BN25: Sea . . . 8B 150
Hawth Way BN25: Sea . . . 8C 150
Hawthylands Cres. BN27: Hails . . . 4E 120
Hawthylands Dr. BN27: Hails . . . 4E 120
Hawthylands Rd. BN27: Hails . . . 4E 120
Haybourne Cl. BN2: Brig . . . 6F 132
Haybourne Rd. BN2: Brig . . . 6F 132
Hayes Cl. BN8: Ring . . . 1C 116
BN41: Ports . . . 5E 130
Hayesden La. TN11: Bid . . . 1L 7
Hayes La. TN31: Peas . . . 3F 84
Hayes Plat TN31: North . . . 4B 64
Hayland Grn. BN27: Hails . . . 5F 120
Hayland Ind. Est. TN38: St Leo . . . 1F 126
Haylind Rd. RH16: Hay H . . . 4J 49
Hayreed La. BN26: Wilm . . . 4L 139
Haystoun Cl. BN22: Will . . . 2N 153
Haystoun Pk. BN22: Will . . . 2N 153
Hayward Rd. BN7: Lewes . . . 3G 115
HAYWARDS HEATH . . . 5F 48
HAYWARDS HEATH NUFFIELD HOSPITAL
. . . 3E 48
Haywards Heath Rd. BN8: N Cha . . . 1A 70
RH17: N Cha . . . 9A 50
Haywards Heath Station (Rail) . . . 3F 48
Haywards Rd. BN1: Brig . . . 8B 112
RH16: Hay H . . . 6F 48
Haywards Vs. RH16: Hay H . . . 6G 48
Haywood Way TN35: Hast . . . 2B 128
HAZARD'S GREEN . . . 1M 123
Hazel Bank BN2: Brig . . . 3G 162
Hazelbank TN3: Lang G . . . 1K 15
Hazel Cl. BN9: N'hvn . . . 5H 149
BN41: Ports . . . 2E 130
Hazeldene BN25: Sea . . . 9G 150
Hazeldene La. BN8: N Cha . . . 1F 70
Hazeldene Meads BN1: Brig . . . 2M 131
Hazel Gro. BN20: Will . . . 1L 153
RH15: Burg H . . . 7C 68
Hazelgrove Gdns. RH16: Hay H . . . 5F 48
Hazelgrove Rd. RH16: Hay H . . . 5F 48
Hazel Holt BN41: Ports . . . 2B 130
HAZEL STREET . . . 1N 19
Hazelwood BN1: Brig . . . 2M 131
(off Curwen Pl.)
Hazelwood Av. BN22: Eastb . . . 1A 154
Hazelwood Cl. TN2: Tun W . . . 5G 9
TN39: Bex S . . . 2D 144
Hazelwood Gdns. TN37: St Leo . . . 1K 127
Headland Av. BN25: Sea . . . 9F 150
Headland Cl. BN10: Peace . . . 5E 148
Headland Cnr. BN25: Sea . . . 1F 156
(off Headland Av.)
Headland Way BN10: Peace . . . 6E 148
Heartenoak Rd. TN18: Hawk . . . 7N 31
Hease Wood RH16: Hay H . . . 6D 48
Heath Cl. RH16: Hay H . . . 5F 48
Heathcote Dr. RH19: E Grin . . . 2B 10
Heath Ct. RH16: Hay H . . . 4F 48
Heathdown Cl. BN10: Peace . . . 2D 148
Heatherbank RH16: Hay H . . . 4D 48
Heather Cl. BN23: Lang . . . 1E 154
Heather Ct. BN1: Brig . . . 7N 131 (6B 162)
Heatherdune Rd. TN39: Bex S . . . 9H 125
Heather Wlk. TN6: Jar B . . . 1H 37
Heather Way TN35: Fair . . . 2L 129
HEATHFIELD . . . 2E 76
Heathfield Av. BN2: Salt . . . 2L 147
Heathfield Cl. TN34: Hast . . . 1M 127
Heathfield Cres. BN41: Ports . . . 1B 130
Heathfield Dr. BN41: Ports . . . 2B 130
Heathfield Gdns. TN32: Rob . . . 6J 61
Heathfield Leisure Cen. . . . 1G 77
Heathfield Pk. TN21: H'fld . . . 1F 76
Heathfield Rd. BN25: Sea . . . 1E 156
TN19: B'wsh C . . . 6A 58
Heathfields TN2: Tun W . . . 9G 8
Heath Hill Av. BN2: Brig . . . 3G 132
Heathlands TN35: W'fld . . . 4L 105
Heath Rd. RH16: Hay H . . . 4F 48
Heath Sq. RH16: Hay H . . . 4E 48
HEATHY BROW . . . 2B 148
Heathy Brow BN10: Peace, Tels C . . . 3B 148
Heavegate Rd. TN6: Crow . . . 2A 36
(Fielden Rd.)
TN6: Crow . . . 1A 36
(Warren Rd.)
Heaven Farm . . . 9H 33
Hebrides Wlk. BN23: Eastb . . . 5H 155
Hectors La. RH19: E Grin . . . 5J 11
Hedge Barton Countryside Home Pk.
TN3: F'cmbe . . . 8D 6
Heighton Cl. TN39: Bex S . . . 2E 144
Heighton Cres. BN9: N'hvn . . . 2K 149
Heighton Rd. BN9: N'hvn, S Heig . . . 2K 149
HEIGHTON STREET . . . 2J 137
Heights, The BN1: Brig . . . 9K 111
RH16: Hay H . . . 5F 48
(off Church Rd.)
TN35: Hast . . . 2D 128
Helena Cl. BN41: Ports . . . 3E 130
Helena Rd. BN2: W'dean . . . 4K 133
Helen Gardens . . . 4B 160
Helensdene Wlk. TN37: St Leo . . . 6K 127
(off Church Rd.)
HELLINGLY . . . 1D 120
Hellingly Cl. BN2: Brig . . . 8G 132
HELLINGLY HOSPITAL . . . 1G 121
Helsman Ri. TN38: St. Leo . . . 8F 104
Helvellyn Dr. BN23: Lang . . . 9M 141
Hempstead Gdns. TN22: Uck . . . 1J 73
Hempstead La. BN27: Hails . . . 6B 120
TN22: Uck . . . 1J 73
Hempstead Ri. TN22: Uck . . . 1H 73
Hempstead Rd. BN2: Salt . . . 2L 147
TN22: Uck . . . 1H 73
Hemsley Ho. TN21: H'fld . . . 9C 56
(off Streatfield Rd.)
Hendal Hill TN3: Groom . . . 6E 14
Henderson Cl. TN34: Hast . . . 3M 127
Hendon St. BN2: Brig . . . 8E 132
Henfield Cl. BN2: Brig . . . 8G 132
Henfield Rd. BN22: Eastb . . . 2B 154
Henfield Way BN3: Hove . . . 2H 131
Henge Way BN41: Ports . . . 3D 130
Hengist Cl. BN23: Eastb . . . 4H 155
Henleaze BN21: Eastb . . . 9B 154
Henley Cl. TN2: Tun W . . . 8F 8
TN31: Rye . . . 2E 86
Henley Ct. BN2: Brig . . . 9G 132
Henley Rd. BN2: Brig . . . 9G 132
HENLEY'S DOWN . . . 1H 125
Henleys Hill BN27: Bodle G . . . 7H 101
TN33: Bodle G . . . 7H 101
Henshill La. TN18: Hawk . . . 2M 43
HENWOOD GREEN . . . 7N 9
Henwood Grn. Rd. TN2: Pem . . . 6N 9
Henwoods Cres. TN2: Pem . . . 7N 9
Herbert Rd. BN1: Brig . . . 3A 132
Herbrand Wlk. TN39: Bex S . . . 4A 144
Hereford Ct. BN2: Brig . . . 8D 132
BN3: Hove . . . 6L 131
BN23: Lang . . . 3H 155
Hereford St. BN2: Brig . . . 8C 132
Hereward Rd. BN23: Eastb . . . 3J 155
Hereward Way BN7: Lewes . . . 3K 115
Herman Hill TN31: North . . . 3N 63
Hermitage La. RH19: E Grin . . . 4F 10
Hermitage Rd. RH19: E Grin . . . 1D 10
Hermitage, The TN34: Hast . . . 6L 127
(off Holmesdale Gdns.)
Herne Down TN6: Crow . . . 3D 36
Herne Rd. TN6: Crow . . . 2D 36
Heron Cl. BN23: Lang . . . 2F 154
TN22: Uck . . . 3J 73
TN38: St Leo . . . 6E 126
Heron Ct. BN2: Brig . . . 6G 132
(off Swanborough Pl.)
Heron Pl. RH19: E Grin . . . 4F 10
Heron Ridge BN26: Pole . . . 7E 140
Heronsdale Rd. BN2: W'dean . . . 5N 133
HERON'S GHYLL . . . 7J 35
Heron's Tye BN6: Hass . . . 4A 90
Herons Way BN27: Chal . . . 2F 118
TN2: Pem . . . 5N 9
Herontye Dr. RH19: E Grin . . . 4F 10
Herontye Ho. RH19: E Grin . . . 5F 10
Herring La. TN21: Cross H . . . 9A 56
Herring's Rd. TN21: A'ham, Dall . . . 7G 79
TN33: A'ham . . . 7G 79
HERSTMONCEUX . . . 9A 100
Herstmonceux Castle . . . 5D 122
Hertford Cl. TN38: St Leo . . . 2G 126
Hertford Rd. BN1: Brig . . . 3C 132
Heskett Pk. TN2: Pem . . . 6N 9
Heston Av. BN1: Brig . . . 7A 112
Hever Cl. BN23: Lang . . . 2G 154
Hever Cr. TN39: Bex S . . . 9G 125
Hever La. TN8: C'den, Hever . . . 2F 4
Heyshott Lodge BN2: Brig . . . 7F 132
(off Crossbush Rd.)
Heyworth Cl. BN2: W'dean . . . 5N 133
Heyworth Ride RH16: Hay H . . . 6D 48
Hickling Cl. BN23: Lang . . . 9L 141
Hickmans Cl. RH16: Lind . . . 1J 49
Hickman's La. RH16: Lind . . . 1H 49
(not continuous)
Hickman Way TN34: Hast . . . 2K 127
Hide Hollow BN23: Lang . . . 1G 154
BN24: Lang, W'ham . . . 9A 142
Hide Hollow Rdbts. BN23: Lang . . . 1F 154
Higglers Cl. TN22: Buxt . . . 6A 54
Higham Gdns. TN35: Gues T . . . 7F 106
Higham La. TN31: North . . . 2N 63
TN32: Rob . . . 2M 61
Highbank BN1: Brig . . . 9L 111
High Bank Cl. TN35: Hast . . . 3B 128
High Beach Ho. BN25: Sea . . . 9B 150
High Beech Chalet Pk.
TN38: St Leo . . . 9F 104
High Beech Cl. TN38: St Leo . . . 9F 104
High Beeches TN2: Tun W . . . 7G 8
High Beeches La. BN45: Newt . . . 1F 110
BN45: Poyn . . . 1F 110
High Beech La. RH16: Hay H . . . 1G 49
High Branches TN39: Bex S . . . 1F 144
Highbridge La. BN7: E Chil . . . 2B 92
Highbrook Cl. BN2: Brig . . . 3E 132
High Broom La. TN6: Crow . . . 3C 36
High Broom Rd. TN6: Crow . . . 3C 36
HIGH BROOMS . . . 5F 8
High Brooms Rd. TN4: Tun W . . . 5E 8
High Brooms Station (Rail) . . . 6F 8
Highcliff Ct. BN2: Rott . . . 3H 147
High Cl. BN20: E Dean . . . 1G 158
BN41: Ports . . . 4C 130
Highcombe BN20: Eastb . . . 4A 160
Highcroft Cres. TN21: H'fld . . . 1D 76
Highcroft Lodge
BN1: Brig . . . 5N 131 (1A 162)
Highcroft M. BN1: Brig . . . 4M 131 (1A 162)
Highcroft Rd. RH19: Sharp . . . 6A 20
Highcroft Vs. BN1: Brig . . . 5N 131 (1A 162)
HIGH CROSS . . . 4N 37
High Cross Flds. TN6: Crow . . . 8D 24
Highden BN2: Brig . . . 7D 132
Highdown BN42: S'wck . . . 4B 130
Highdown Cl. BN42: S'wck . . . 4B 130
Highdown Ct. BN1: Brig . . . 2N 131
Highdown Rd.
BN3: Hove . . . 6N 131 (3A 162)
BN7: Lewes . . . 4F 114
Highfield Bus. Pk. TN38: St Leo . . . 2D 126
Highfield Cl. TN2: Pem . . . 7N 9
TN18: Hawk . . . 1A 44
Highfield Ct. RH16: Hay H . . . 5F 48
(off Church Rd.)
Highfield Cres. BN1: Brig . . . 9B 112
Highfield Dr. TN38: St Leo . . . 3D 126
Highfield Ind. Est.
BN23: Eastb . . . 3D 154
Highfield Link BN23: Eastb . . . 4D 154
Highfield Rd. RH19: E Grin . . . 1D 10
TN4: Tun W . . . 6F 8
TN21: Horam . . . 9C 76
Highfields BN1: Brig . . . 9F 112
RH18: F Row . . . 1M 21
TN19: B'wsh . . . 3J 59
TN31: Rye . . . 1F 86
Highfields Gdns. TN39: Bex S . . . 7K 125
High Fords TN36: Ick . . . 2K 107
Highfords Cl. TN36: Ick . . . 1K 107
HIGHGATE
Forest Row . . . 2M 21
Hawkhurst . . . 1B 44
Highgate Flats TN6: Roth . . . 1M 37
Highgate Hill TN18: Hawk . . . 1N 43
Highgate Rd. RH18: F Row . . . 2L 21
Highgate Works RH18: F Row . . . 2L 21
HIGH GROVE . . . 5B 10
Highgrove TN2: Tun W . . . 4D 16
TN33: Batt . . . 3J 103
High Hurst Cl. BN8: N'wck . . . 1K 71
HIGH HURSTWOOD . . . 9M 35
Highland Ct. RH16: Hay H . . . 5F 48
Highland Lodge
BN21: Eastb . . . 8C 154 (2H 161)
Highland M. TN38: St Leo . . . 8H 127
(off Archery Rd.)
Highland Rd. RH16: Hay H . . . 6G 49
Highlands TN2: Tun W . . . 6G 9
Highlands Av. TN22: Uck . . . 4J 73
Highlands Cl. BN6: Hass . . . 4B 90
TN6: Crow . . . 8C 24
TN39: Bex S . . . 7H 125
Highlands Ct. TN6: Crow . . . 8C 24
(off Beacon Gdns.)
Highlands Dr. RH15: Burg H . . . 4B 68
TN38: St Leo . . . 7H 127
Highlands Gdns. TN38: St Leo . . . 7H 127
Highlands Grange TN6: Crow . . . 8C 24
(off Beacon Rd.)
Highlands Ho. TN1: Tun W . . . 1F 16
Highlands Rd. BN25: Sea . . . 9E 150
BN41: Ports . . . 4D 130
HIGHLANDS, THE . . . 6G 124
Highlands, The RH17: Cuck . . . 1A 48
TN39: Bex S . . . 6G 125
Highlea Cl. TN37: St Leo . . . 1J 127
Highleigh BN2: Brig . . . 7C 132
Highmead Mnr. BN20: Eastb . . . 3B 160
High Mdw. TN31: North . . . 2N 63
High Pk. TN31: North . . . 2N 63
High Pk. Av. BN3: Hove . . . 2G 131
High Pk. Cl. TN31: North . . . 2N 63
High Point RH16: Hay H . . . 6H 49
High Rocks . . . 3M 15
High Rocks Halt Station
Spa Valley Railway . . . 3M 15
High Rocks La. TN3: Tun W . . . 3M 15
Highsted Pk. BN10: Peace . . . 2D 148
High St. BN2: Brig . . . 8C 132
BN2: Rott . . . 3G 147
BN6: Ditch . . . 4E 90
BN7: Lewes . . . 6J 115
BN8: Barc C . . . 3K 93
BN8: E Hoath . . . 2E 96
BN8: N'wck . . . 1K 71

Kenilworth Rd.—Langney Rdbt.

Kenilworth Rd. TN38: St Leo 7H 127
Kenmure Av. BN1: Brig 7B 112
Kennard Ct. RH18: F Row 9L 11
Kennedy Av. RH19: E Grin 1D 10
Kennedy Cl. TN21: H'fld 2E 76
Kennedy Cl. TN38: St Leo 3H 127
Kennedy Rd. TN40: Bex S 1M 145
Kennedy Way BN9: N'hvn 5H 149
Kennel La. TN39: Bex S 1D 144
Kennett Cl. BN24: Sto C 8J 141
Kenrith Ct. TN34: Hast 4L 127
Kensington BN23: Eastb 3K 155
Kensington Cl. TN38: St Leo 3D 126
Kensington Gdns.
BN1: Brig 7B 132 (6E 162)
Kensington Pl. BN1: Brig . . . 7B 132 (6E 162)
Kensington St.
BN1: Brig 7B 132 (6E 162)
Kent & East Sussex Railway
Bodiam 2F 62
Northiam 9N 45
Potman's Heath 5H 47
Kent & Sussex Crematorium
TN2: Tun W 4E 16
KENT & SUSSEX HOSPITAL 9D 8
Kent Cl. TN36: Winch 9C 86
TN40: Bex S 9A 126
Kent Ct. BN20: Eastb 6M 153
Kent Flds. BN7: King L 9E 114
Kent Ho. BN20: Eastb 3B 160
Kentish Gdns. TN2: Tun W 4B 16
Kent La. TN32: B'lng 2N 79
Kenton Cl. TN39: Bex S 9H 125
Kenton Ct. BN21: Eastb 9K 161
Kenton Rd. BN3: Hove 6F 130
Kent Rd. TN4: Tun W 7D 8
TN38: St Leo 2F 126
Kent's La. BN6: Streat 1K 91
Kents Rd. RH16: Hay H 6G 48
KENT STREET 3F 104
Kent St. TN33: Batt, Sed 2E 104
Kenwards BN1: Brig 7E 112
Kenwood Cl. TN34: Hast 2A 128
Kenya Ct. BN1: Brig 5B 162
Keppel Rd. TN34: Hast 4M 127
Kepplestone BN20: Eastb 3B 160
Kerrara Ter. BN22: Eastb 7E 154 (1N 161)
Kerrison M. BN3: Hove 8M 131
(off Lwr. Market St.)
Kerry Ct. BN23: Lang 3G 155
Keston Ho. RH16: Hay H 3F 48
Kestrel Cl. BN3: Hove 5M 131
TN40: Bex S 1M 145
Kestrel Ct. BN2: Brig 6G 132
(off Swanborough Pl.)
Kestrels, The TN38: St Leo 1F 126
Ketches La. RH17: Scay H 1C 50
Ketche's La. TN22: Shef P 2F 50
Kevin Gdns. BN2: W'dean 5M 133
Kewhurst Av. TN39: Bex S 2D 144
Kewhurst Ho. TN39: Bex S 1F 144
Kew St. BN1: Brig 7A 132 (6D 162)
KEYMER 4B 90
Keymer Av. BN10: Peace 6C 148
(not continuous)
Keymer Cl. BN23: Lang 3H 155
TN38: St Leo 8E 126
Keymer Ct. RH15: Burg H 6C 68
(off Station Rd.)
Keymer End RH16: Hay H 6E 48
Keymer Gdns. RH15: Burg H 7C 68
Keymer Ho. BN21: Eastb 9B 154
(off Michel Gro.)
Keymer Pde. RH15: Burg H 6C 68
(off Station Rd.)
Keymer Pk. BN6: Hass 4C 90
Keymer Rd. BN1: Brig 8C 112
BN6: Hass 3A 90
RH15: Burg H 6C 68
Keymer Ter. BN6: Hass 4B 90
Keysford La. RH17: Hors K 6A 32
KEY'S GREEN 1E 18
Key W. BN23: Eastb 5J 155
Kibbles La. TN4: South 4B 8
Kidbrook RH16: Hay H 3J 49
KIDBROOKE PARK 2K 21
Kidbrooke Ri. RH18: F Row 1L 21
Kidd's Hill TN7: Cole H 6E 22
Kilburn Ter. BN21: Eastb 9D 154 (4K 161)
Kildare Cl. TN34: Hast 2A 128
Kildare Ct. BN20: Eastb 9N 153
Kilda St. BN22: Eastb 8E 154 (2N 161)
Kilnbarn Ct. RH16: Hay H 7E 48
(off Kilnbarn Way)
Kilnbarn Way RH16: Hay H 7E 48
Kiln Cl. TN22: Uck 4J 73
KILNDOWN 1B 30
Kiln Dr. TN31: Rye 9F 66
Kiln La. RH16: Hay H 4J 49
TN22: Isf 2D 94
TN33: Hooe 7K 123
Kiln Rd. BN8: Ring 7F 94
Kiln, The RH15: Burg H 5D 68
Kilnwood La. BN8: S Chai 9E 70
Kilpatrick Cl. BN23: Lang 1G 154
Kimberley Ct. TN39: Bex S 8J 125
Kimberley Rd. BN2: Brig 4E 132
BN25: Sea 8B 150
Kindersley Cl. RH19: E Grin 1H 11
Kinfauns Av. BN22: Eastb 6E 154
King Alfred Leisure Cen. 8J 131
King Edward Av. TN34: Hast 2J 127
King Edward Cl. TN34: Hast 3J 127
King Edwards Pde.
BN20: Eastb 4B 160 (9K 161)
BN21: Eastb 4B 160 (9K 161)
Kingfisher Cl. TN22: Uck 3K 73
Kingfisher Ct. BN2: Brig 6G 132
(off Albourne Cl.)
Kingfisher Dr. BN23: Lang 2F 154
Kingfisher Ri. RH19: E Grin 4F 10
King George VI Av. BN3: Hove 2H 131
King George Av. RH19: E Grin 1C 10
King George VI Dr. BN3: Hove 2J 131
King George V Hill TN2: Tun W 8F 8
King George VI Mans. BN3: Hove 3H 131
King Henry's Rd. BN7: Lewes 4H 115
King Offa Way TN40: Bex S 9K 125
King Pl. BN1: Brig 8B 132 (7D 162)
King's Av. BN9: N'hvn 3L 149
BN21: Eastb 7B 154
TN31: Rye 2H 87
KING'S BANK 6F 64
King's Bank La. TN31: Buck 7E 64
Kingsbury Rd. BN1: Brig 6B 132 (3F 162)
Kingsbury St. BN1: Brig 6B 132 (3F 162)
Kings Chase TN6: Crow 8B 24
Kings Cl. BN10: Peace 3B 148
BN21: Eastb 7B 154 (1G 161)
TN40: Bex S 1K 145
Kings Copse RH19: E Grin 4F 10
Kingscote Lodge BN1: Brig 9G 112
(off Ringmer Dr.)
Kingscott Cl. TN39: Bex S 6H 125
Kings Ct. BN1: Brig 7E 162
BN23: Eastb 4J 155
TN6: Crow 9C 24
Kings Ct. Sth. BN23: Eastb 4J 155
Kings Ct. W. BN23: Eastb 4H 155
Kingsdale Cl. TN33: Batt 4N 103
TN37: St Leo 9J 105
Kings Dr. BN6: Hass 3A 90
King's Dr.
BN21: Eastb, Will 4N 153 (1H 161)
King's Esplanade BN3: Hove 8J 131
(not continuous)
Kingsfield Cl. BN42: S'wck 5A 130
Kingsfield Cotts. BN8: Ripe 6C 118
Kingsfold BN2: Brig 8G 132
Kingsfold Ct. BN25: Sea 1E 156
Kingsford BN23: Eastb 5G 155
King's Gdns. BN3: Hove 8K 131
Kings Ga. BN3: Hove 5L 131
RH16: Hay H 3F 48
King's Hill Rd. TN19: B'wsh 5K 59
Kings Leisure Cen. 3E 10
Kingsley Cl. TN37: St Leo 1G 126
Kingsley Ct. BN1: Brig 8A 162
TN5: Wadh 7C 28
Kingsley Rd. BN1: Brig 4M 131
BN7: Lewes 4H 115
Kingsmarsh Cotts. TN20: F Ashes 4M 55
Kingsmead BN25: Sea 7D 150
Kingsmead Cl. BN25: Sea 8D 150
King's Mead La. BN25: Sea 8C 150
Kingsmead La. BN25: Sea 8D 150
Kingsmead Wlk. BN25: Sea 8D 150
Kingsmere BN1: Brig 3N 131
Kingsmere Way BN23: Eastb 4H 155
King's M. BN3: Hove 7L 131
Kings Mt. BN21: Eastb 8B 154
Kings Pde. BN1: Brig 3B 132
Kings Pk. BN23: Eastb 4J 155
(off Kingsmere Way)
TN2: Tun W 1G 16
Kings Ride BN25: Sea 8C 150
BN26: Alfr 2L 151
RH15: Burg H 7E 68
Kings Rd. BN1: Brig 8N 131 (8A 162)
BN42: S'wck 4A 130
RH16: Hay H 6G 48
King's Rd. TN37: St Leo 7J 127
Kings Rd. Arches
BN1: Brig 9A 132 (9C 162)
Kings Row BN8: Laug 7A 96
Kings Standing Bus. Pk. TN2: Tun W . . . 4J 9
Kings St. BN1: Brig 8B 132 (7E 162)
Kingstanding Way TN2: Tun W 3J 9
Kingsthorpe Rd. BN3: Hove 5G 131
KINGSTON 9E 114
Kingston Av. BN25: Sea 9G 151
Kingston Cl. BN1: Brig 8F 112
BN3: Hove 3G 130
BN25: Sea 9G 151
Kingston Grn. BN25: Sea 9G 151
Kingston Ho.
BN21: Eastb 8C 154 (3H 161)
Kingston Quay BN23: Eastb 4J 155
Kingston Ridge BN7: King L 8D 114
Kingston Rd. BN7: Lewes 9G 114
BN22: Eastb 2C 154
Kingston Rdbt. BN7: Lewes 7E 114
Kingston Vs. TN21: Horam 2A 98
Kingston Way BN25: Sea 1G 157
King St. RH19: E Grin 3E 10
King's Wlk. TN34: Hast 6M 127
(off Queen's Rd.)
Kingsway BN3: Hove 7E 130 (8A 162)
BN25: Sea 8C 150
Kings Way RH15: Burg H 7D 68
Kingsway Ct. BN3: Hove 8L 131
BN25: Sea 8C 150
Kings Well Ct. BN25: Sea 1D 156
Kingswest 8A 132 (8C 162)
Kingswood Av. TN39: Bex S 8G 125
Kingswood Cl. TN2: Tun W 1F 16
Kingswood Flats BN2: Brig 7G 162
Kingswood Rd. TN2: Tun W 1F 16
Kingswood St. BN2: Brig 8B 132 (7F 162)
King Wood Hill TN31: Brede, B Oak 5A 84
Kingwood Ho.
BN21: Eastb 8C 154 (2J 161)
Kinross Ct. BN21: Eastb 8D 154 (3L 161)
Kinsale Ct. BN3: Hove 6M 131
Kinver La. TN40: Bex S 8A 126
Kipling Av. BN2: W'dean 5M 133
Kipling Ct. BN2: Rott 3H 147
RH16: Hay H 4E 48
(off Winnals Pk.)
TN40: Bex S 8K 125
(off Hollier's Hill)
Kipling Wlk. BN23: Lang 2H 155
Kipling Way RH19: E Grin 3C 10
Kirby Ct. TN3: Lang G 1L 15
Kirby Dr. BN10: Tels C 3A 148
Kirdford Cl. RH15: Burg H 7D 68
Kirdford Lodge BN2: Brig 7F 132
(off Crossbush Rd.)
Kirkdale Rd. TN1: Tun W 9E 8
Kirkstall Cl. BN22: Eastb 1B 154
Kirk Way BN20: Eastb 7M 153
Kitchenham Rd.
TN33: A'ham, P'hrst 8L 101
Kitchenour La. TN31: Buck, Peas 5J 65
Kite Cl. TN38: St Leo 6E 126
Kites Nest Wlk. TN39: Bex S 1C 144
Kitilear Ct. BN3: Hove 7M 131
Kloofs Cvn. Pk. TN39: Bex S 7C 124
Knebworth Rd. TN39: Bex S 9G 125
Knelle Rd. TN32: Rob 5G 61
Knelle Vw. TN31: North 2A 64
Knepp Cl. BN2: Brig 3G 133
Knightsbridge Cl. TN4: Tun W 8C 8
Knightsbridge Ct. TN4: Tun W 7E 8
Knights Cl. TN2: Pem 5N 9
Knights Garden BN27: Hails 8E 120
Knights Ga. Rd. BN1: Falm 7K 113
Knights Mdw. TN22: Uck 9K 53
TN33: Batt 3N 103
Knights Pk. TN2: Tun W 4J 9
(not continuous)
Knight's Pl. TN2: Pem 6N 9
Knights Ridge TN2: Pem 6N 9
Knights Way TN2: Tun W 5J 9
Knockhatch Adventure Pk. 7B 120
Knole Ct. TN40: Bex S 2L 145
(off Knole Rd.)
Knole Gro. RH19: E Grin 1C 10
Knole Rd. BN2: Rott 3H 147
TN40: Bex S 2L 145
Knoll Bus. Cen., The BN3: Hove 5F 130
Knoll Cl. BN3: Hove 4F 130
Knoll Cres. BN22: Eastb 2D 154
Knoll Ho. BN3: Hove 5G 130
Knoll Pl. RH16: Hay H 4J 49
Knoll Ri. TN38: St Leo 7G 127
Knoll Rd. BN22: Eastb 2D 154
Knowle Cl. TN3: Lang G 1J 15
Knowle Farm Bus. Cen.
TN3: Frant 2H 27
Knowle Hill TN20: May 9D 38
Knowle La. BN8: Hall 9M 73
Knowle Pk. TN6: Crow 9B 24
Knowle Pk. Rd. TN20: May 8D 38
Knowle Pl. TN6: Jar B 2G 37
Knowle Rd. TN35: Fair 1K 129
Knowle, The RH17: Cuck 2A 48
Knowsley Ct. TN37: St Leo 9H 105
Knoyle Rd. BN1: Brig 3N 131
Knyveton Ct. RH15: Burg H 5C 68
Kymer Gdns. BN6: Hass 4B 90

L

Laburnum Av. BN3: Hove 4G 131
Laburnum Gdns. TN40: Bex S 8N 125
Laburnum Grn. BN27: Hails 5E 120
Laburnum Gro. BN1: Brig 2C 132
(off Burstead Cl.)
Laburnum Wlk. BN22: Eastb 1A 154
Laburnum Way RH16: Hay H 5J 49
Labyrinth, The BN21: Eastb 5K 161
Lacy's Hill BN8: Glyn 5D 116
Ladies Mile BN1: Brig 7C 112
TN6: Lye G 8A 14
TN7: Withy 8A 14
Ladies Mile Cl. BN1: Brig 8A 112
Ladies Mile Ct. BN1: Brig 8N 111
Ladies' Mile Rd. BN1: Brig 8N 111
Lady Bee Ind. Est. BN42: S'wck 7A 130
Ladycross Cl. BN25: Sea 9H 151
Ladymead RH15: Burg H 3D 68
Lady Oak La. TN5: Flim 6D 30
TN17: Goud 6D 30
Lady's Gift Rd. TN4: South 5C 8
Ladysmith Rd. BN2: Brig 5D 132
L.A. Fitness 9E 8
Lagoon Leisure Cen. 6F 120
Lagwood Cl. BN6: Hass 4A 90
Laine Cl. BN1: Brig 2N 131
Laines, The BN26: Alfr 1L 151
(off Furlong Rd.)
Lake Dr. BN10: Peace 4B 148
Lake Ho. Cl. TN39: Bex S 1E 144
Lakehurst La. TN33: A'ham 8H 79
Lakelands Cl. BN22: Eastb 3D 154
Lakelands Dr. TN39: Bex S 1E 144
Lakeman Way TN4: Tun W 6E 8
Lake Rd. TN4: Tun W 9B 8
Lakeside TN2: Tun W 7H 9
Lakeside Ct. BN22: Eastb 3D 154
Lake St. TN6: May 1D 38
TN20: May 2F 38
Lakeview BN2: Brig 8D 132
Laleham Cl. BN21: Eastb 8B 154
TN37: St Leo 1J 127
Laleham Ct. BN21: Eastb 8B 154
LAMBERDEN 6N 45
LAMBERHURST 7K 19
Lamberhurst By-Pass TN3: Lamb 9K 19
LAMBERHURST QUARTER 2G 18
Lamberhurst Rd. TN3: Hors, Lamb 4L 19
TN12: Hors 4L 19
Lamberhurst Vineyard Pk. 8J 19
Lambersart Cl. TN4: South 4G 8
Lambert Pl. BN7: Lewes 3J 115
Lambert Rd. BN23: Lang 1H 155
Lamberts Rd. TN2: Tun W 5G 9
Lamb House 3G 86
(off West St.)
Lambourn Av. BN24: Sto C 8K 141
Lambourn Cl. RH19: E Grin 1E 10
Lambourne Cl. BN1: Brig 3D 132
Lambourne Rd. BN1: Brig 3D 132
Lambourn Way TN2: Tun W 3G 16
Lamont Ct. BN21: Eastb 9K 161
Lampham Drove BN27: Pev 2E 142
Lampington Row TN3: Lang G 1J 15
Lampool Rdbt. TN22: Mare 2F 52
Lanark Ct. BN20: Eastb 6M 153
Lancaster Ct. BN3: Hove 8J 131
BN22: Eastb 4N 161
Lancaster Dr. RH19: E Grin 1G 11
Lancaster Ho. Rd. BN1: Falm 7J 113
Lancaster Rd. BN1: Brig . . . 6A 132 (3C 162)
TN38: St Leo 1F 126
Lancaster St. BN7: Lewes 5J 115
Lancaster Vs. BN1: Brig 3C 162
Lancing Cl. TN34: Hast 3K 127
Lancing Ct. BN2: Brig 8G 133
(off Findon Rd.)
Lancing Way BN26: Pole 9C 140
Landgate TN31: Rye 2G 86
Landgate Sq. TN31: Rye 2G 86
LANDPORT 4H 115
Landport Farm Rd. BN7: Lewes 3G 115
Landport Rd. BN7: Lewes 3G 115
(not continuous)
Landsdowne Way TN40: Bex S 9M 125
Landseer Rd. BN3: Hove 5J 131
LANES, THE 8B 132 (8E 162)
Lane, The BN25: W Dean 8M 151
TN3: F'cmbe 8G 6
Langdale Cl. BN23: Lang 9M 141
Langdale Ct. BN3: Hove 7H 131
Langdale Gdns. BN3: Hove 7H 131
Langdale Rd. BN3: Hove 7H 131
Langham Cl. BN8: Ring 1C 116
TN34: Hast 2M 127
Langham Rd. TN32: Rob 5F 60
TN34: Hast 2M 127
Langholm Rd. TN3: Lang G 9K 7
Langhurst BN2: Brig 9F 132
(off Eastern Rd.)
Langley Cl. TN39: Bex S 6J 125
Langley Cres. BN2: W'dean 4L 133
LANGNEY 2F 154
Langney Grn. BN23: Lang 4H 155
Langney Point Roundabouts
BN23: Eastb 5K 155
Langney Rd.
BN21: Eastb 9D 154 (5L 161)
BN22: Eastb 9E 154 (5M 161)
Langney Rdbt. BN23: Eastb 4H 155

A-Z East Sussex Atlas 185

Langney Shop. Cen.—Little London

Langney Shop. Cen. BN23: Lang 2F 154
Langney Sports Club 1J 155
LANGNEY VILLAGE 3H 155
Langridge Cl. TN6: Crow 2B 36
Langridge Dr. BN41: Ports 2D 130
RH19: E Grin 4E 10
Langridge La. RH16: Hay H 4H 49
Langridges Cl. BN8: N'wck 2J 71
Langton Cl. TN33: Batt 3M 103
LANGTON GREEN 1K 15
Langton Ridge TN3: Lang G 1M 15
Langton Rd. TN3: Lang G, R'hall 2H 15
TN3: Speld 8K 7
TN4: R'hall 1N 15
Langtye La. BN8: Ripe, Selm 7B 118
BN26: Selm 7B 118
Lankhurst Oak TN22: B'boys 3C 74
Lansdowne Ct. BN21: Eastb 8K 161
Lansdowne Cres. BN27: Hails 4D 120
Lansdowne Dr. BN27: Hails 3D 120
Lansdowne Gdns. BN27: Hails 4E 120
Lansdowne M. BN3: Hove 7M 131
Lansdowne Pl. BN3: Hove 8M 131
Lansdowne Rd.
BN3: Hove 7L 131 (6A 162)
BN27: Hails 4E 120
TN1: Tun W 9E 8
Lansdowne Sq. BN3: Hove 8M 131
TN1: Tun W 9E 8
Lansdowne St. BN3: Hove 7M 131
Lansdowne Ter. BN21: Eastb 9K 161
Lansdowne Way BN27: Hails 3D 120
Lansdown Pl. BN7: Lewes 6K 115
Lansdown Rd. BN25: Sea 7G 151
Lansdown Ter. *TN21: H'fld 2D 76*
(off Hailsham Rd.)
Lanthorne M. TN1: Tun W 8E 8
Lapierre Rd. BN9: N'hvn 5H 149
Lapwing Cl. BN23: Lang 2F 154
Larch Bank *BN2: Brig 5C 132*
(off Bromley Rd.)
Larch Cl. BN2: W'dean 6N 133
TN21: H'fld 3E 76
TN38: St Leo 5G 127
Larches Ho. RH19: E Grin 1H 11
Larches, The RH19: E Grin 1H 11
Larches, The TN37: St Leo 6J 127
Larch Gdns. BN22: Eastb 1A 154
Larch Way RH16: Hay H 5J 49
Larkfield Cl. TN38: St Leo 3G 127
Larkfield Way BN1: Brig 1B 132
Lark Hill BN3: Hove 2G 130
Larkhill TN40: Bex S 1K 145
Larkspur Dr. BN23: Lang 9K 141
Larnach Cl. TN22: Uck 9J 53
La Ronde Ct. BN21: Eastb 6L 161
Lascelles Mans. BN21: Eastb 8L 161
Lascelles Ter.
BN21: Eastb 2D 160 (8L 161)
La Serena Pl. BN23: Eastb 3L 155
Laser La. *TN37: St Leo 7J 127*
(off King's Rd.)
Lashbrooks Rd. TN22: Uck 1G 72
Latimer Ct. *BN22: Eastb 8F 154*
(off Latimer Rd.)
Latimer Rd.
BN22: Eastb 9F 154 (4N 161)
Laton Rd. TN34: Hast 4L 127
Latymers TN11: Pens 1F 6
LAUGHTON .8A 96
Laughton Cl. BN23: Lang 9K 141
LAUGHTON COMMON 6M 95
LAUGHTON PLACE 3L 117
Laughton Rd. BN2: W'dean 5N 133
BN8: Laug, Ring 9F 94
Laundry La. RH17: S Rgh 2K 33
Laundry La. TN21: Mrle G, Vine C 1E 98
Laurel *RH16: Hay H 3E 48*
(off Great Heathmead)
Laurel Bank TN4: South 6E 8
TN40: Bex S 9M 125
Laurel Cl. RH15: Burg H 3E 68
Laurel Dene RH19: E Grin 3F 10
Laurel La. TN36: Ick 2L 107
Laurel Rd. TN2: Tun W 6G 8
Laurels, The *BN2: Brig 5C 132*
(off Bromley Rd.)
TN22: Uck 9K 53
Laurel Wlk. *TN38: St Leo 3E 126*
(off Juniper Cl.)
Laurel Way TN2: Tun W 6G 8
Laurens Wlk. Shop. Arc.
BN2: Rott 3G 147
(off Nevill Rd.)
Lauriston Rd. BN1: Brig 3N 131
Lavant Cl. TN39: Bex S 8D 124
Lavant Rd. BN24: Sto C 8L 141
Lavender Cl. BN23: Lang 1E 154
BN27: Hails 5C 120
Lavender Ct. TN2: Tun W 3B 16
Lavender Gdns. TN5: Tice 1N 41
Lavender Ho. *BN2: Brig 9C 132*
(off Lavender St.)
Lavender Line, The 8D 72
Lavender St. BN2: Brig 9C 132
Lawes Av. BN9: N'hvn 5J 149
Lawns Av. BN21: Eastb 8A 154
Lawns, The BN20: Will 3M 153
BN22: Eastb 7F 154
BN22: Will 2M 153
BN27: Hails 8F 120
TN38: St Leo 7J 127
Lawnswood RH15: Burg H 4B 68
Lawrence Cl. BN23: Lang 3G 155
Lawrence Ho. *TN22: Uck 1H 73*
(off Hempstead Rd.)
TN39: Bex S 6H 125
Lawrence Rd. BN3: Hove 6H 131
Lawrie La. RH16: Hay H 4J 49
Laylands Ct. *BN41: Ports 6C 130*
(off Chapel Rd.)
Laylands Rd. BN41: Ports 6C 130
Lazonby Ct. TN38: St Leo 6H 127
Lea Av. TN31: Rye 2E 86
Leach Ct. BN2: Brig 8D 132
Leacroft RH19: E Grin 2D 10
Leaf Glen BN21: Eastb 3G 161
Leaf Hill Rd.
BN22: Eastb 9E 154 (4N 161)
Leaf Rd. BN21: Eastb 9D 154 (4L 161)
Lea Ho. BN21: Eastb 8B 154
Leahurst BN20: Eastb 9G 161
Leahurst Ct. BN1: Brig 2M 131
Leahurst Ct. Rd. BN1: Brig 2M 131
Lealands Cl. TN3: Groom 6G 15
Lealands Ct. TN22: Uck 8H 53
Lealands Dr. TN22: Uck 9H 53
Leamland Wlk. *BN27: Hails 7E 120*
(off Lindfield Dr.)
Leap Cross Small Bus. Cen.
BN27: Hails 5D 120
Lea Rd. BN10: Peace 4B 148
Leasam La. TN31: Play 1E 86
Leasingham Gdns. TN39: Bex S 9H 125
Leas, The BN10: Peace 7F 148
RH15: Burg H 4A 68
TN5: Wadh .5C 28
TN38: St Leo 8G 127
Le Brun Rd. BN21: Eastb 7B 154 (1G 161)
Ledgers Mdw. RH17: Cuck 3A 48
Ledsham Av. TN37: St Leo 1H 127
Ledsham Cl. TN37: St Leo 1H 127
Ledsham Pk. TN37: St Leo 1H 127
Ledsham Way TN37: St Leo 1H 127
Lee Bank *BN2: Brig 7C 132*
(off Grove Hill)
Lee Ct. *BN9: N'hvn 4J 149*
(off Elphick Rd.)
Leeds Av. BN23: Eastb 4G 154
Leeds Cl. TN35: Hast 2C 128
Leeds La. TN20: F Ashes 3M 55
Lee Rd. BN7: Lewes 4H 115
Leeves Cl. TN21: H'fld 2D 76
Leeves Way TN21: H'fld 2D 76
Leeward Quay BN23: Eastb 4J 155
Lee Way BN9: N'hvn 4J 149
Leggs La. TN3: Lang G, Speld 8H 7
Legsheath La. RH19: F Row 2C 20
Leicester Ct. BN22: Eastb 2N 161
Leicester Dr. TN2: Tun W 4C 16
Leicester Rd. BN7: Lewes 5H 115
Leicester Sq. TN11: Pens 1F 6
Leicester St. BN2: Brig 8C 132
Leicester Vs. BN3: Hove 6F 130
Leighside Ho. *BN7: Lewes 5K 115*
(off Court Rd.)
Leighton Cl. TN4: Tun W 6D 8
Leighton Rd. BN3: Hove 5J 131
RH17: Hors K 5C 32
Leighton Vs. *RH17: Hors K 5C 32*
(off Leighton Rd.)
Leneda Dr. TN2: Tun W 4B 16
Lenham Av. BN2: Salt 3J 147
Lenham Rd. E. BN2: Rott, Salt 3J 147
Lenham Rd. W. BN2: Rott 3H 147
Lennox Cl. BN20: Eastb 7M 153
Lennox Ct. TN21: H'fld 9E 56
Lennox Rd. BN3: Hove 5H 131
Lennox St. BN2: Brig 8C 132
Leopold Flats *TN39: Bex S 1J 145*
(off Leopold Rd.)
Leopold Rd. BN1: Brig 7A 132 (6C 162)
TN39: Bex S 1J 145
Lepeland BN27: Hails 5D 120
LEPHAM'S BRIDGE 5K 53
Lesley Cl. TN40: Bex S 7N 125
Leslie St. BN22: Eastb 8E 154 (2N 161)
Letheren Pl. BN21: Eastb 9A 154
Leveller End BN8: N'wck 1K 71
Leveller Rd. BN8: N'wck 1K 71
Level, The 6C 132 (4G 162)
Levett Av. BN26: Pole 6F 140
Levett Cl. BN26: Pole 7F 140
Levett Rd. BN26: Pole 7F 140
Levetts La. TN32: Bod 9D 44
Levett Way BN26: Pole 7F 140
LEWES 5K 115
Lewes Athletics Track 6L 115
Lewes Bus. Cen. & Waterside Cen.
BN7: Lewes 4J 115
Lewes Castle 5J 115
Lewes Cl. BN2: Salt 3M 147
TN39: Bex S 8H 125
Lewes Ct. BN1: Falm 6J 113
BN21: Eastb 8D 154 (2K 161)
BN21: Eastb 2J 161
Lewes Cres. BN2: Brig 9F 132
(not continuous)
Lewes F.C. (The Dripping Pan) 6K 115
Lewes Leisure Cen. 6L 115
Lewes Little Theatre 5K 115
Lewes M. *BN2: Brig 9F 132*
(off Arundel Pl.)
Lewes Priory 6J 115
Lewes Rd. BN2: Brig 7C 132 (5G 162)
BN6: Ditch, W'ton 4E 90
BN8: Hall .1A 96
BN8: Laug, White 8M 95
BN8: Ring 2B 116
BN8: Selm, W Firle 1M 137
BN9: N'hvn 3H 149
BN21: Eastb 7C 154 (1J 161)
BN26: Alc, Selm 2A 138
BN26: B'wck, Folk, Milt S, Pole, Wilm
. . . . .6F 138
RH16: Lind .2J 49
RH17: Chel G 2J 33
RH17: Dane 6G 32
RH17: Hay H, Scay H 6H 49
RH17: Hors K 6C 32
RH18: F Row, Wych C 3K 21
RH18: Wych C 8K 21
RH19: A'hstw, E Grin 4F 10
TN22: B'boys 5D 74
TN22: Isf .1D 94
TN22: Uck .5H 73
Lewes Southern By-Pass
BN7: Lewes 7F 114
BN8: Lewes 7L 115
Lewes Station (Rail) 6K 115
Lewes St. BN2: Brig 7C 132
Lewis Av. TN40: Bex S 9A 126
Lewis Cl. BN9: N'hvn 2M 149
Lewis Rd. TN38: St Leo 3G 126
Lewry Cl. BN9: N'hvn 5H 149
Lexden Ct. BN25: Sea 8F 150
Lexden Dr. BN25: Sea 7E 150
Lexden Lodge *TN6: Jar B 2H 37*
(off Crowborough Hill)
Lexden Lodge Ind. Est. TN6: Jar B 2H 37
Lexden Rd. BN25: Sea 6E 150
(not continuous)
Leybourne Cl. BN2: Brig 4H 133
Leybourne Gdns. TN37: St Leo 2J 127
Leybourne Pde. *BN2: Brig 4H 133*
(off Leybourne Rd.)
Leybourne Rd. BN2: Brig 3H 133
Leyland Rd. BN24: Pev B 9F 142
Leylands Pk. RH15: Burg H 3C 68
Leylands Rd. RH15: Burg H 4A 68
LEYSWOOD .9F 14
Leyton Lea RH17: Cuck 3A 48
Library Rd. BN1: Falm 7J 113
Library Way TN22: Uck 1H 73
Lichfield Ct. BN2: Brig 8G 132
LIDHAM HILL 1D 106
Lilac Cl. BN22: Eastb 2A 154
Lilac Ct. BN1: Brig 1M 131
Lillywhite Cl. RH15: Burg H 3A 68
Limden Cl. TN5: S'gate 4H 41
Lime Cl. TN3: Frant 8E 16
TN22: Uck .9J 53
TN38: St Leo 5G 127
Lime Hill Rd. TN1: Tun W 9D 8
Limekiln Forest Rd. TN3: Eri G 7J 25
Lime Pk. BN27: Herst 1B 122
Limes Gro. TN18: Hawk 6N 31
Limes La. TN22: Buxt 6A 54
Limes, The *BN2: Brig 5C 132*
(off Bromley Rd.)
BN21: Eastb 8B 154 (3G 161)
Limetree Av. BN22: Eastb 1A 154
Lime Tree Av. TN22: Uck 1J 73
Lime Tree Gro. RH16: Lind 2K 49
Limeway TN21: H'fld 2E 76
Limney Rd. BN2: Brig 6F 132
Linchmere BN2: Brig 6G 132
Linchmere Av. BN2: Salt 3K 147
Lincoln Av. BN10: Peace 5A 148
Lincoln Av. Sth. BN10: Peace 5A 148
Lincoln Cl. BN20: Eastb 3N 159
TN38: St Leo 2F 126
Lincoln Cotts. BN2: Brig 7C 132
Lincoln Ct. BN3: Hove 5L 131
BN10: Peace 5A 148
BN20: Eastb 5M 153
Lincoln Rd. BN41: Ports 6D 130
Lincoln St. BN2: Brig 7C 132
Lincoln Way TN6: Crow 2E 36
Lincoln Wood RH16: Hay H 4D 48
Linden Av. RH19: E Grin 2C 10
Linden Chase TN22: Uck 1H 73
Linden Cl. BN22: Eastb 1B 154
TN4: Tun W .2D 16
Linden Ct. TN22: Uck 1H 73
Linden Flds. TN2: Tun W 3D 16
Linden Gdns. TN2: Tun W 3C 16
TN21: H'fld .2C 76
Linden Gro. BN27: Hails 3F 120
RH16: Lind .3H 49
Linden Pk. Rd. TN4: Tun W 2D 16
Linden Rd. TN40: Bex S 2K 145
Lindens, The BN2: Brig 3G 162
LINDFIELD .2G 49
Lindfield *BN41: Ports 4D 130*
(off Windlesham Cl.)
Lindfield Av. BN25: Sea 1H 157
Lindfield Cl. BN2: Salt 2J 147
Lindfield Ct. *BN1: Brig 4D 132*
(off Crestway, The)
Lindfield Dr. BN27: Hails 7E 120
Lindfield Ent. Pk. RH16: Lind 3K 49
Lindfield Rd. BN22: Eastb 2A 154
Lindon Cl. BN20: Fris 2F 158
Lindsay Cl. BN20: Eastb 1N 159
Lingfield Rd. RH19: E Grin 1D 10
Linkden Cotts. TN18: Sandh 5L 45
LINKHILL 6K 45
Link Pl. BN1: Brig 4C 132
Link Rd. BN20: Eastb 2A 160
Links Av. BN10: Peace 5G 148
Links Cl. BN25: Sea 9F 150
BN41: Ports 5E 130
TN6: Crow .1B 36
Links Dr. TN40: Bex S 1M 145
Links Rd. BN25: Sea 1F 156
BN41: Ports 5E 130
Links, The TN38: St Leo 6F 126
TN40: Bex S 2L 145
(off Bolebrooke Rd.)
Links Way TN31: Camb 6B 88
Linkswood BN21: Eastb 1B 160
Link, The BN20: E Dean 1G 158
TN31: Rye .3E 86
Linkway BN20: Will 5M 153
Link Way TN2: Tun W 5H 9
Linkway, The BN1: Brig 4C 132
BN24: W'ham 7A 142
Linley Cl. TN34: Hast 3N 127
TN40: Bex S 1L 145
Linley Dr. TN34: Hast 4M 127
Linnet Cl. BN23: Lang 2F 154
Linnet Grn. TN22: Uck 3J 73
Linosa Ct. BN22: Eastb 4N 161
Linthouse Cl. BN10: Peace 2D 148
Linton Cl. TN34: Hast 5L 127
Linton Cres. TN34: Hast 6L 127
Linton Rd. BN3: Hove 5H 131
TN34: Hast 5L 127
Lion Hill BN24: Sto C 8L 141
Lion Ho. Pk. BN27: Hails 8H 121
Lion La. BN21: Eastb 9E 154 (5N 161)
Lion M. BN3: Hove 6H 131
TN22: Uck 2J 73
(off Framfield Rd.)
Lions Ct. BN2: Brig 8F 132
Lions Dene BN1: Brig 1M 131
Lions Gdns. BN1: Brig 3M 131
Lions Ga. BN3: Hove 4G 130
LIONS GREEN 7M 75
Lions Pl. BN25: Sea 1E 156
Lion St. TN31: Rye 3G 86
Liphook Cl. BN1: Brig 4D 132
Lipscombe Rd. TN2: Tun W 7G 8
Liptraps La. TN2: Tun W 6G 8
Liquidambar Av. TN17: Goud 3E 30
Lismore Rd.
BN21: Eastb 1D 160 (6L 161)
Lister Av. RH19: E Grin 6E 10
Lister Rd. BN23: Eastb 3D 154
LITLINGTON 4M 151
Litlington Ct. BN25: Sea 8B 150
Litlington Rd. BN25: Lit, W Dean 6L 151
BN26: Lit .6L 151
Little All. TN8: Mrsh G 1A 4
LITTLE BAYHAM 7B 18
Lit. Bentswood RH16: Hay H 4G 49
Lit. Bentswood Cl. RH16: Hay H 4G 49
Lit. Black Hill RH16: Lind 2J 49
Lit. Boundes Cl. TN4: South 2B 8
LITTLE COMMON 9D 124
Little Common Rd. TN39: Bex S 1E 144
LITTLE CONGHURST 3C 44
Lit. Copse Rd. BN6: Hass 3A 90
Littlecote BN20: Eastb 2C 160 (8H 161)
Little Cres. BN2: Rott 3H 147
Little Dene BN8: Glyn 1E 136
Lit. East St. BN1: Brig 9B 132 (9E 162)
BN7: Lewes 5K 115
Little Footway TN3: Lang G 1K 15
Lit. George St. BN2: Brig 8B 132 (8F 162)
Lit. Horstead Rdbt. TN22: Uck 5H 73
LITTLE HORSTED 7H 73
Lit. King St. RH19: E Grin 3E 10
Lit. Ledgers RH17: Cuck 3A 48
LITTLE LONDON 4B 76

M

Manor Ct.—Meadows, The

Manor Ct. BN25: Sea 9G 150
BN42: S'wck 6C 130
RH15: Burg H 3D 68
TN21: Horam 9C 76
(off High St.)
TN40: Bex S 9L 125
Manor Cres. BN2: Brig 8F 132
Manor Dr. BN10: Tels C 3B 148
RH17: Cuck 2A 48
Manor End TN22: Uck 9H 53
Manor Flds. TN4: South 2C 8
Manor Gdns. BN2: Brig 8F 132
Manor Grn. BN2: Brig 8F 132
Mnr. Hall Rd. BN42: S'wck 5B 130
Manor Hill BN2: Brig 7E 132
Manor Ho. Ct. *TN22: Uck 9H 53*
(off Regency Cl.)
Manor Mobile Home Pk., The
BN27: Hell 2F 120
Manor Paddock BN2: Brig 9F 132
Mnr. Paddock Ho. *BN2: Brig 9F 132*
(off Manor Paddock)
MANOR PARK 8K 53
Manor Pk. TN4: Tun W 1B 16
Manor Pk. Cl. BN27: Hails 3D 120
Manor Pk. Ct. BN26: Pole 7D 140
Manor Pk. Rd. BN27: Hails 3D 120
Manor Pl. BN2: Brig 9F 132
Manor Rd. BN2: Brig 9F 132
BN22: Eastb 2D 154
BN25: Sea 9G 150
BN41: Ports 4D 130
RH15: Burg H 3D 68
RH19: E Grin 2C 10
TN4: R'hall 9N 7
TN4: South 4B 8
TN21: Horam 8C 76
TN34: Hast 5N 127
TN40: Bex S 1L 145
Manor Rd. Nth. BN25: Sea 8G 150
Manor Ter. *BN7: Lewes 6J 115*
(off Course, The)
Manor Vs. *TN5: Wadh 6B 28*
(off Sparrows Grn. Rd.)
Manor Way BN2: Brig 8F 132
BN20: Will 4M 153
BN26: Pole 7D 140
TN6: Crow 2C 36
TN22: Uck 9H 53
Mansell Cl. TN39: Bex S 2D 144
Mansell Ct. RH15: Burg H 5C 68
Mansers La. BN27: Lwr D 3N 119
Mansfield Rd. BN3: Hove 6G 130
Mansion Cl. RH15: Burg H 5E 68
Mansion Ho. M. *TN1: Tun W 1E 16*
(off Grove Hill Rd.)
Mansions, The BN21: Eastb 8L 161
Manston Way TN34: Hast 4L 127
Mantell Cl. BN7: Lewes 2J 115
Mantell Ho. *BN2: Brig 8C 132*
(off Lennox St.)
Manton Ct. BN23: Eastb 4G 154
Manton Rd. BN2: Brig 4F 132
Manvers Rd. BN20: Eastb 9M 153
Maple Av. TN39: Bex S 2D 144
Maple Cl. BN2: W'dean 6M 133
RH15: Burg H 3D 68
RH16: Hay H 6J 49
TN2: Tun W 3D 16
TN22: Mare 5F 52
TN39: Bex S 2D 144
Maple Ct. BN27: Hails 6D 120
Maple Dr. RH15: Burg H 3A 68
RH19: E Grin 3G 11
Maple Gdns. BN3: Hove 4G 131
Maple Hgts. TN37: St Leo 8H 105
Maple Ho. BN2: Brig 2G 162
Maplehurst BN8: S Chai 9D 70
Maplehurst Cl. TN37: St Leo 8H 105
Maplehurst Dr. TN37: St Leo 7J 105
Maplehurst Ri. TN37: St Leo 8J 105
Maplehurst Rd. BN22: Eastb 2A 154
BN41: Ports 4C 130
TN37: St Leo 8H 105
Mapleleaf Cl. BN9: N'hvn 5H 149
Maple Leaf Cotts.
TN22: B'boys 2E 74
Mapleleaf Gdns. BN26: Pole 5D 140
Maple Rd. BN10: Peace 6F 148
BN23: Eastb 5G 154
Maples, The BN8: Ring 9D 94
Maple Wlk. TN39: Bex S 2C 144
Maplewood *BN1: Brig 2N 131*
(off Curwen Pl.)
Marbles Rd. BN8: N'wck 1K 71
Marchants Dr. TN31: Camb 6B 88
Marchants Way RH15: Burg H 3A 68
March Ho. BN3: Hove 4K 131
Marcia Cl. BN20: Will 4L 153
Marcus Gdns. TN37: St Leo 1G 126
Mardan Ct. TN38: St Leo 7H 127
Marden Cl. BN2: W'dean 4M 133
Marden Ct. TN39: Bex S 2H 145
MARDEN'S HILL 6N 23
Marden's Hill TN6: Crow 5N 23
Mare Bay Cl. TN38: St Leo 8E 104
MARESFIELD 4G 52
Maresfield By-Pass TN22: Mare 4E 52
Maresfield Dr. BN24: Pev B 7G 143
MARESFIELD PARK 4F 52
Maresfield Rd. BN2: Brig 8F 132
Margaret Ct. BN10: Peace 5B 148
Margaret St. BN2: Brig 9C 132
Margery Rd. BN3: Hove 5F 130
Marianne Pk. TN35: Hast 5A 128
Marina TN38: St Leo 8G 127
TN40: Bex S 2K 145
Marina Arc. TN40: Bex S 2K 145
Marina Ct. *TN40: Bex S 2K 145*
(off Marina)
Marina Ct. Av. TN40: Bex S 2K 145
Marina Wlk. BN23: Eastb 4H 155
Marina Water Tours *1A 146*
(off Village Sq.)
Marina Way BN2: Brig 9G 132
Marine Av. BN3: Hove 7G 130
BN24: Pev B 7H 143
Marine Cl. BN2: Salt 3J 147
BN24: Pev B 7H 143
Marine Cotts. TN31: Camb 6C 88
Marine Ct. BN2: Salt 4K 147
BN9: N'hvn 6K 149
BN10: Tels C 5N 147
BN24: Pev B 8F 142
(off Terrace, The)
BN25: Sea 9B 150
(off Connaught Rd.)
TN38: St Leo 8J 127
(off Marina)
Marine Cres. BN25: Sea 1D 156
Marine Dr. BN2: Brig 9G 132
BN2: Oving, Rott, Salt 3F 146
BN25: Sea 6N 149
Marine Gdns. BN2: Brig 9C 132
Marine Ga. BN2: Brig 9G 132
Marine Pde. BN2: Brig 9C 132 (9F 162)
BN21: Eastb 1E 160 (6N 161)
BN22: Eastb 9E 154 (5N 161)
BN25: Sea 8A 150
TN34: Hast 7N 127
Marine Path *BN2: Salt 3K 147*
(off Marine Dr.)
Marine Rd. BN22: Eastb 9E 154 (4N 161)
BN24: Pev B 8F 142
Mariners Ga. BN9: N'hvn 7K 149
Mariner's Quay BN2: Brig 1A 146
Marine Sq. BN2: Brig 9D 132
Marine Ter. BN24: Pev B 8F 142
Marine Ter. M. *BN2: Brig 9D 132*
(off Bristol Rd.)
Marine Vw. BN2: Brig 8C 132
BN9: N'hvn 6H 149
(not continuous)
MARKBEECH 3J 5
Mark Cl. BN25: Sea 1H 157
MARK CROSS
RH19 4N 117
TN6 8D 26
Mark Cross La. BN8: Ripe 4A 118
Market La. BN7: Lewes 5K 115
Market Pas. TN34: Hast 7N 127
TN38: St Leo 8J 127
(off Norman Rd.)
Market Pl. BN27: Hails 7F 120
RH15: Burg H 6B 68
RH16: Hay H 3E 48
TN2: Tun W 2D 16
Market Rd. TN31: Rye 3G 86
TN33: Batt 3K 103
Market Sq. *BN27: Hails 7F 120*
(off Market St.)
TN1: Tun W 9E 8
TN33: Batt 2L 103
(off High St.)
Market St. BN1: Brig 8B 132 (8E 162)
BN7: Lewes 5K 115
BN27: Hails 7F 120
TN2: Tun W 2D 16
TN31: Rye 3G 86
TN38: St Leo 8J 127
Market Ter. *TN38: St Leo 8J 127*
(off Market St.)
Markland Way TN22: Uck 1F 72
Mark La. BN21: Eastb 1D 160 (6K 161)
Marklye La. TN21: H'fld 7E 56
TN21: Rush G 5L 77
Markstakes Corner BN8: S Chai 7E 70
Markstakes La.
BN8: N'wck, S Chai 7E 70
Markwick Ter. TN38: St Leo 6H 127
(not continuous)
Marlborough Cl. BN23: Lang 1G 155
TN4: Tun W 9B 8
TN38: St Leo 5G 126
Marlborough Ct. BN3: Hove 6L 131
BN9: N'hvn 5J 149
(off Church Hill)
BN21: Eastb 5H 161
Marlborough Dr. RH15: Burg H 6D 68
Marlborough M.
BN1: Brig 8A 132 (7C 162)
Marlborough Pl. BN1: Brig 6F 162
BN1: Brig 8B 132 (7F 162)
Marlborough St.
BN1: Brig 8A 132 (7C 162)
Marle Av. RH15: Burg H 4B 68
MARLE GREEN 1E 98
Marle Grn. Cotts. TN21: Mrle G 1E 98
Marle Pl. Rd. TN12: Bren 1L 19
Marley Cl. TN33: Batt 3N 103
Marley Gdns. TN33: Batt 3N 103
Marley La. TN33: Batt, Sed 3M 103
Marley Ri. TN33: Batt 3N 103
Marley Rd. TN31: Rye 2E 86
Marline Av. TN38: St Leo 2G 126
Marline Rd. TN38: St Leo 2G 127
Marlings, The RH16: Hay H 6D 48
Marlow Av. BN22: Eastb 6E 154
Marlow Ct. BN2: Brig 6C 132
TN6: Crow 2D 36
Marlow Dr. RH16: Hay H 5K 49
TN37: St Leo 1H 127
Marlowes, The *TN40: Bex S 9M 125*
(off Hastings Rd.)
Marlow Rd. BN2: Brig 9G 132
Marlpit Cl. RH19: E Grin 1E 10
Marlpit Rd. RH19: Sharp 5A 20
MARLPITS
Ninfield 8C 102
Nutley 4C 34
Marlpits La. TN33: Nin 9B 102
Marlpit, The TN5: Wadh 6A 28
Marmion Rd. BN3: Hove 6H 131
Marsden Ct. BN10: Tels C 5A 148
Marsden Rd. BN23: Lang 3H 155
Marshall Ct. BN22: Eastb 2A 154
Marshall La. BN9: N'hvn 5J 149
Marshall Rd. BN22: Eastb 4C 154
Marshall Rdbt. BN23: Eastb 4D 154
Marshalls Row BN1: Brig 6B 132 (4F 162)
Marshall Way BN3: Hove 4H 131
Marshfoot La. BN27: Hails 6F 120
(not continuous)
MARSH GREEN
TN7 3G 22
TN8 1A 4
Marsh Grn. Rd. TN8: Mrsh G 1A 4
Marshlands La. TN21: H'fld 9D 56
Marsh Quarter La.
TN18: Sandh 6J 45
Marston Ct. BN3: Hove 4A 162
Martello Beach Cvn. Pk.
BN24: Pev B 1M 155
Martello Ct. BN9: N'hvn 3K 149
BN24: Pev B 1M 155
(off Grenville Rd.)
Martello Dr. TN31: Rye 4F 86
Martello M. BN25: Sea 1D 156
Martello Rd. BN22: Eastb 6G 154
BN25: Sea 1D 156
Martello Rdbt. BN23: Eastb 2K 155
Martello Tower no. 28 6L 87
Martello Tower no. 30 4F 86
Martello Tower no. 55 6L 143
Martello Tower no. 60 9F 142
Martello Tower no. 61 1M 155
Martello Tower no. 62 1M 155
Martello Tower no. 64 3L 155
Martello Tower no. 66 5K 155
Martello Tower no. 73 2D 160 (8L 161)
Martens Fld. BN7: Rod 4L 135
Martha Gunn Rd. BN2: Brig 4F 132
Martin Ct. BN22: Eastb 2A 154
Martineau La. TN35: Hast 1D 128
Martingdale Cl.
TN37: St Leo 1J 127
Martinique Way BN23: Eastb 5K 155
Martin Rd. BN3: Hove 4F 130
Martins, The BN10: Tels C 3B 148
Martlet Ct. *BN2: Brig 8D 132*
(off Hereford St.)
Martlet Ho. BN1: Brig 5B 132 (1E 162)
BN2: Salt 4L 147
TN39: Bex S 1H 145
Martlets BN22: Will 1M 153
TN40: Bex S 9M 125
Martlets Ct. TN6: Crow 1D 36
MARTLETS HOSPICE, THE 4H 131
Martlets, The BN7: Lewes 3K 115
BN27: Hails 7D 120
RH15: Burg H 5B 68
TN31: B Oak 4B 84
TN34: Hast 4L 127
(off St Helen's Cres.)
Martlet, The BN3: Hove 5M 131
Martletts, The BN8: Ring 9D 94
BN8: S Chai 9D 70
TN19: B'wsh C 6B 58
Martyns Cl. BN2: Oving 9M 133
Martyns Pl. RH19: E Grin 4F 10
Martyns Way TN40: Bex S 8A 126
Maryan Ct. BN27: Hails 6E 120
Mary Burfield Ct. TN21: H'fld 1D 76
Maryland Rd. TN2: Tun W 3G 16
Marylands RH16: Hay H 4G 49
Mary Stamford Grn. TN31: Rye 5L 87
Maskelyne Rd. BN27: Herst 6C 122
Mason Cl. RH19: E Grin 2E 10
Mason Rd. BN25: Sea 8E 150
TN31: Rye 3E 86
Matlock Rd. BN1: Brig 4M 131
BN20: Eastb 3B 160
Matthew Ho. *BN3: Hove 7J 131*
(off Miles Wlk.)
Maunsell Rd. TN38: St Leo 1F 126
Maurice Rd. BN25: Sea 2E 156
Maxfield Cl. BN20: Eastb 7M 153
Maxfield La. TN35: T Oaks 5C 106
May Av. BN25: Sea 9G 151
May Cotts. BN2: Brig 5C 132
Maycroft Pl. *TN20: May 8C 38*
(off Stone Cross)
Mayfair Cl. BN26: Pole 9C 140
Mayfair Ho. BN21: Eastb 1D 160 (6K 161)
Mayfair M. TN40: Bex S 8K 125
MAYFIELD 7E 38
Mayfield Av. BN10: Peace 6D 148
(not continuous)
Mayfield Cl. BN1: Brig 9A 112
TN20: May 8C 38
Mayfield Ct. BN2: Salt 2K 147
RH15: Burg H 5C 68
TN21: B Oak 8H 57
Mayfield Cres. BN1: Brig 9A 112
Mayfield Flat TN21: Cross H 9K 55
Mayfield La. TN5: Wadh 8L 27
TN38: St Leo 4D 126
Mayfield Pk. TN5: Wadh 6N 27
Mayfield Pl. BN22: Eastb 8D 154 (2K 161)
Mayfield Rd. TN3: Frant, Mark C 3D 26
TN4: Tun W 9C 8
TN6: Mark C 4D 26
TN6: Roth 3M 37
TN21: Cross H, F Ashes 7M 55
Mayfield Way TN40: Bex S 9M 125
Mayflower Ct. RH16: Hay H 5G 48
Mayflower Rd. RH16: Hay H 5G 48
Mayflower Sq. BN1: Brig 6B 132 (4E 162)
Mayhew Way BN7: Lewes 4K 115
Mayhouse Rd. RH15: Burg H 7A 68
MAYNARD'S GREEN 6D 76
Mayne Way TN34: Hast 2A 128
Mayo Ct. BN2: Brig 5C 132
BN23: Lang 3G 155
(off Pembury Rd.)
Mayo La. TN39: Bex S 6H 125
Mayor Cotts. TN3: B'ham 8N 5
Mayo Ri. TN39: Bex S 6H 125
Mayo Rd. BN2: Brig 5C 132
Maypole Cotts. TN22: H Hur 1N 53
Maypole Rd. RH19: A'hstw 6L 11
RH19: E Grin 2D 10
May Rd. BN2: Brig 6E 132
Maytham Rd. TN17: Rolv 1E 46
Maytree Cl. *BN3: Hove 5F 130*
(off Dorothy Rd.)
May Tree Gdns. TN40: Bex S 8N 125
May Tree Wlk. BN3: Hove 4G 130
Mayvern Ct. TN6: Crow 8D 24
Mayview Cl. TN21: B Oak 8H 57
Maywood Av. BN22: Eastb 2A 154
Maze Hill TN38: St Leo 7H 127
Maze Hill Ter. TN38: St Leo 7H 127
McWilliam Rd. BN2: W'dean 4K 133
Meachants Ct. BN20: Will 2M 153
Meachants La. BN20: Will 2L 153
Mead Cl. TN35: Fair 2K 129
Meadhurst BN20: Eastb 2B 160 (8G 161)
Meadow Bank TN33: Batt 3N 103
Meadow Cl. BN2: Rott 1F 146
BN3: Hove 2K 131
BN27: Hails 5E 120
BN41: Ports 3D 130
BN42: S'wck 5B 130
TN38: St Leo 2G 126
Meadow Cres. TN39: Bex S 7K 125
Meadowcroft Cl. RH19: E Grin 2C 10
Meadow Dr. RH16: Hay H 3J 49
Meadow Hill Rd. TN1: Tun W 1E 16
Meadowlands Av. BN22: Eastb 2A 154
Meadow La. RH15: Burg H 7A 68
RH16: Lind 3J 49
TN33: Sed 7D 82
Meadow Pde. BN2: Rott 1G 146
Meadow Pl. TN22: Uck 2H 73
Meadow Ri. TN21: Horam 9C 76
Meadow Rd. BN27: Hails 8D 120
TN1: Tun W 9D 8
TN3: Groom 5G 14
TN4: R'hall 9N 7
TN4: South 4C 8
Meadows BN6: Hass 2A 90
Meadows Rd. BN22: Will 2M 153
Meadows, The BN3: Hove 2E 130
BN7: Lewes 3L 115
BN27: Chal 3F 118

Montague Way—Newton Pk.

Montague Way BN24: W'ham 8B 142
Montana Ct. TN38: St Leo 9F 104
Montargis Way TN6: Crow 1D 36
Montclare Ho. BN21: Eastb 4G 161
Montefiore Rd.
BN3: Hove 6N 131 (4A 162)
Monteith Cl. TN3: Lang G 1L 15
Monterey Ct. BN1: Brig 2N 131
Monterey Gdns. TN39: Bex S 2F 144
Montery Cl. TN39: Bex S 2E 144
Montes Hill RH16: Hay H 1N 49
Monteswood La.
RH16: Hay H, Hors K 9A 32
RH17: Hors K 1A 50
Montfort Cl. BN24: W'ham 7B 142
Montfort Rd. BN24: W'ham 7B 142
Montgomery Rd. TN4: Tun W 6E 8
TN35: Hast 1C 128
Montgomery St. BN3: Hove 6H 131
Montgomery Ter. *BN3: Hove* *6J 131*
(off Montgomery St.)
Montpelier Apartments *BN1: Brig* *7A 162*
(off Montpelier Rd.)
Montpelier Cres.
BN1: Brig 7N 131 (5B 162)
Montpelier Pl. BN1: Brig 7N 131 (6A 162)
Montpelier Rd.
BN1: Brig 8N 131 (8A 162)
Montpelier St. BN1: Brig 7N 131 (6B 162)
Montpelier Ter.
BN1: Brig 7N 131 (6B 162)
Montpelier Vs. BN1: Brig 7N 131 (6B 162)
Montpellier Lodge BN1: Brig 6B 162
Montreal Rd. BN2: Brig 7C 132
Monument Vw. BN2: Brig 7E 132
Moonrise Way BN27: Chal 3F 118
MOON'S GREEN 6M 47
Moons Hill TN33: Nin 9B 102
Moons Yd. TN6: Roth 2M 37
Moore Pk. BN27: Hails 7G 120
Moore's La. TN31: Buck 1C 84
Moor Hall Dr. TN33: Nin 9A 102
Moorhen Cl. TN38: St Leo 6E 126
Moor Hill TN18: Hawk 2N 43
Moorhurst Rd. TN38: St Leo 1F 126
Moorings, The *BN7: Lewes* *5L 115*
(off South St.)
BN20: Eastb *3B 160*
(off St John's Rd.)
RH19: E Grin 1A 10
TN18: Sandh 6G 44
Moor La. BN8: Glyn, Ring 5E 116
TN35: W'fld 4L 105
Moor Pl. RH19: E Grin 2D 10
Moorshill La. BN26: Arl, Wilm 3J 139
Moorside TN2: Tun W 9G 8
MOOR, THE 2N 43
Moor, The TN18: Hawk 2N 43
TN35: W'fld 4M 105
Moray Wlk. BN27: Hails 4D 120
Morecambe Rd. BN1: Brig 8B 112
Morestead BN10: Peace 3D 148
Morgan Cl. TN39: Bex S 6J 125
Morgay Wood La. TN35: T Oaks 5D 106
Morlais Pl. TN36: Winch 1F 108
Morlais Ridge TN36: Winch 1F 108
Morland Cl. TN33: Nin 1C 124
Morland Dr. TN3: Lamb 7K 19
Morley Cl. BN7: Lewes 7H 115
Morley Lodge BN2: Brig 6C 132
Morley St. BN2: Brig 7B 132 (6F 162)
Morningside Cl. BN25: Sea 8E 150
Mornington Cres. BN3: Hove 6F 130
Mornington Mans. BN3: Hove 7F 130
Morris Rd. BN7: Lewes 5L 115
Mortain Pk. BN27: Hails 7G 121
Mortain Rd. BN24: W'ham 7B 142
Mortimer Gdns. BN26: Pole 9C 140
Mortimer M. BN3: Hove 5H 131
Mortimer Rd. BN3: Hove 5H 131
BN22: Eastb 6D 154
Morton Ct. BN41: Ports 5D 130
Morton Rd. RH19: E Grin 5E 10
Moscow Rd. TN35: Hast 3B 128
MOSEHAM 8D 28
Moss Dell BN27: Chal 3F 118
Moss Ho. BN21: Eastb 1C 160 (6J 161)
Motcombe Ct. *TN40: Bex S* *2L 145*
(off Bedford Av.)
Motcombe La. BN21: Eastb 8A 154
Motcombe Rd. BN21: Eastb 8A 154
Motcombe Swimming Pool 8A 154
Motte Fld. TN7: Hart 8K 13
Mottins Hill TN6: Jar B 2H 37
Motts Down TN3: Groom 9D 14
MOTTS MILL 9D 14
Moulescoomb Pl. BN2: Brig 3E 132
MOULSECOOMB 3E 132
Moulsecoomb Community Leisure Cen.
2F 132
Moulsecoomb Station (Rail) 3E 132
Moulsecoomb Way BN2: Brig 2F 132
Mountain Ash Cl. BN27: Hails 6D 120
Mountbatten Cl. TN35: Hast 1C 128
Mountbatten Ct. BN3: Hove 5G 131
Mountbatten Dr. BN23: Eastb 5H 155
Mt. Caburn Cres. BN10: Peace 2C 148
Mount Cl. BN9: N'hvn 4M 149
Mount Dr. BN2: Salt 2L 147
Mt. Edgecombe Rd. TN4: Tun W 1D 16
MOUNT EPHRAIM 5L 73
Mt. Ephraim TN1: Tun W 1C 16
Mt. Ephraim Ct. TN4: Tun W 9C 8
Mt. Ephraim Rd. TN1: Tun W 9D 8
MOUNTFIELD 3J 81
Mountfield Ct. *TN1: Tun W* *1E 16*
(off Mountfield Gdns.)
Mountfield Gdns. TN1: Tun W 1E 16
Mountfield La. TN32: Mount 1C 80
Mountfield Rd. BN7: Lewes 6K 115
BN22: Eastb 3C 154
TN1: Tun W 1E 16
Mountfield Rdbt. BN22: Eastb 3C 154
Mountfields BN1: Brig 3D 132
Mountfield Vs. TN32: Mount 3K 81
Mt. Harry Rd. BN7: Lewes 4G 114
Mt. Idol Vw. TN39: Bex S 6H 125
Mt. Joy TN33: Batt 2L 103
Mountney Bri. Bus. Pk.
BN24: W'ham 9B 142
Mountney Dr. BN24: Pev B 7H 143
Mountney Rd. BN21: Eastb 8N 153
Mount Noddy 2E 10
Mount Pl. BN7: Lewes 5J 115
MOUNT PLEASANT
Barcombe 1M 93
Newhaven 3L 149
Mt. Pleasant BN2: Brig 8C 132
BN7: Lewes 5J 115
Mount Pleasant BN8: Barc 1L 93
TN5: Wadh 6A 28
TN6: Crow 2G 36
Mt. Pleasant TN22: B'boys 2E 74
Mount Pleasant *TN22: Mare* *4G 52*
(off Straight Half Mile)
Mt. Pleasant TN22: Uck 2H 73
TN38: St Leo *8J 127*
(off Mercatoria)
Mt. Pleasant Av. TN1: Tun W 1E 16
Mt. Pleasant Ct. *TN34: Hast* *5N 127*
(off Manor Rd.)
Mt. Pleasant Cres. TN34: Hast 5M 127
Mt. Pleasant La. TN3: Lamb 6F 18
Mt. Pleasant Rd. TN1: Tun W 1D 16
TN34: Hast 4M 127
Mountreed TN20: F Ashes 2M 55
Mount Rd. BN9: N'hvn 3M 149
BN20: Eastb 3C 160
TN35: Hast 4B 128
Mt. Sion TN1: Tun W 2D 16
Mounts La. TN17: Rolv, Rolv L 1F 46
Mount St. BN7: Lewes 6J 115
TN33: Batt 2L 103
Mount, The BN20: Eastb 2B 160
BN27: Hails 8F 120
TN5: Flim 8E 30
TN22: Uck 9H 53
TN38: St Leo 7H 127
Mt. View Ter. BN27: Hails 8F 120
Mt. Zion Pl. BN1: Brig 7A 132 (6D 162)
Mowbray Ct. BN21: Eastb 8L 161
Moy Av. BN22: Eastb 7D 154 (1L 161)
Moyne Cl. BN3: Hove 4G 131
MUDDLES GREEN 7J 97
Muirfield Ct. *RH16: Hay H* *5F 48*
(off Caxton Way)
Muirfield Ri. TN38: St Leo 6F 126
Mulberry Cl. BN1: Brig 2A 132
BN22: Eastb 1B 154
TN4: South 4G 8
TN39: Bex S 1D 144
Mulberry Ct. *BN26: Pole* *7D 140*
(off Walnut Wlk.)
Mulberry La. BN6: Ditch 4E 90
Mulberry Pk. TN22: Mare 4G 52
Mulberry Wlk. TN37: St Leo 1K 127
Mulberry Way TN21: H'fld 3E 76
MULBROOKS 2F 140
Munns Dr. RH15: Burg H 4C 68
Munster Grn. BN8: Barc C 3L 93
Murial Ho. BN3: Hove 5G 130
Murray Av. BN9: N'hvn 5J 149
Mus. of Local History 6N 127
Museum of Rural Life 5J 61
Musgrave Av. RH19: E Grin 5E 10
Musgrave Collection 7G 154
Mushroom Fld. BN7: King L 9E 114
Muskerry Ct. TN4: R'hall 9M 7
Muster Ct. RH16: Hay H 5E 48
Muster Grn. Nth. RH16: Hay H 4E 48
Muster Grn. Sth. RH16: Hay H 5E 48
MUTTON HALL 9E 56
Mutton Hall Hill TN21: H'fld 9D 56
Mutton Hall La. TN21: H'fld 9D 56
Myrtle Cotts. *TN6: Crow* *8D 24*
(off Park Rd.)
Myrtle Rd. BN22: Eastb 6G 154
TN6: Crow 1D 36
Mytten Bank RH17: Cuck 3A 48
Mytten Cl. RH17: Cuck 3A 48
Mytten Twitten RH17: Cuck 3A 48

N

Namrik M. BN3: Hove 7J 131
Nanson Rd. BN1: Brig 8E 112
Nan Tucks La. TN22: Buxt 6A 54
Naomi Cl. BN20: Eastb 2B 160
Napier Ho. BN2: Brig 6D 132
Napier Rd. TN2: Tun W 2G 16
TN38: St Leo 1E 126
Nash La. RH17: Scay H 5A 50
NASH STREET 9L 97
Nash St. BN27: Gold C 1K 119
Natal Rd. BN2: Brig 4E 132
Neale Cl. RH19: E Grin 1B 10
Neale Ho. RH19: E Grin 2E 10
Neath Rd. TN31: Camb 7J 89
Neaves La. BN8: Ring 1F 116
Needles Pas. *TN31: Rye* *3F 86*
(off Cinque Ports St.)
Neill's Cl. BN9: N'hvn 5J 149
Neills Rd. TN3: Lamb 2D 28
TN5: Lamb 2D 28
Nellington Ct. TN4: R'hall 9M 7
Nellington Rd. TN4: R'hall 8M 7
Nelson Dr. BN23: Eastb 6H 155
Nelson Ho. TN39: Bex S 1F 144
Nelson Pl. BN2: Brig 6G 162
Nelson Rd. TN2: Tun W 2G 16
TN34: Hast 5N 127
Nelson Row BN2: Brig 8C 132 (7G 162)
Neptune Ct. BN2: Brig 1A 146
Nesbitt Rd. BN2: Brig 4E 132
Nestor Ct. BN1: Brig 4N 131 (1B 162)
NETHERFIELD 6D 80
Netherfield Av. BN23: Lang 2J 155
Netherfield Grn. BN2: W'dean 5N 133
Netherfield Hill TN33: Batt 8H 81
Netherfield Rd. TN33: Batt 1K 103
(Wattle's Wish)
TN33: Batt, Neth 6D 80
(Darvel Down)
Netherfield Way TN33: Neth 6E 80
Nether La. TN22: Nut 7B 34
Netherwood Cl. TN34: Hast 1L 127
Nettlesworth La. TN21: H'fld, Vine C 4G 76
Nettleton Ct. BN1: Brig 4C 132 (1G 162)
Nevill Av. BN3: Hove 3G 131
BN22: Eastb 3B 154
Nevill Bungs. BN6: Ditch 5D 90
Nevill Cl. BN3: Hove 3J 131
TN6: Crow 2A 36
Nevill Cotts. BN6: Ditch 5E 90
Nevill Ct. BN3: Hove 4J 131
TN4: Tun W 2A 16
TN6: Crow 2A 36
Nevill Cres. BN7: Lewes 4G 115
Neville Rd. BN10: Peace 6D 148
BN22: Eastb 8E 154 (2M 161)
Neville Ter. *BN7: Lewes* *5H 115*
(off Nevill Rd.)
Nevill Gdns. BN3: Hove 3J 131
Nevill Ga. TN2: Tun W 3E 16
Nevill Grn. TN22: Uck 8J 53
NEVILL HOSPITAL 4G 131
Nevill Lodge TN2: Tun W 9F 8
Nevill Pk. TN4: R'hall 1A 16
Nevill Pl. BN3: Hove 3J 131
Nevill Ridge TN4: R'hall 1A 16
Nevill Rd. BN2: Rott 3G 146
BN3: Hove 3J 131
BN7: Lewes 4G 115
TN6: Crow 8D 24
TN22: Uck 8J 53
Nevill St. TN2: Tun W 2D 16
Nevill Ter. TN2: Tun W 2C 16
TN6: Crow *8D 24*
(off Nevill Rd.)
Nevill Way BN3: Hove 3J 131
Newark Pl. BN2: Brig 7C 132
New Barn Cl. BN27: Hails 8F 120
BN41: Ports 3D 130
Newbarn Drove BN25: W Dean 9A 152
New Barn La. TN22: Uck 3H 73
New Barn Rd. BN2: Rott 1F 146
NEWBRIDGE 5E 22
Newbury Cotts. TN5: Cous W 3D 28
Newbury La. RH17: Cuck 4A 48
TN5: Cous W 3E 28
New Camden Pk. TN2: Tun W 2F 16
New Chu. Rd. BN3: Hove 6E 130
New Coastguard Cotts.
BN25: Sea 8B 150
TN36: Pett 7A 108
New College Cl. BN23: Lang 9M 141
Newcomen Rd. TN4: Tun W 8D 8
New Cotts. *TN6: Jar B* *2G 37*
(off Victoria Rd.)
TN20: F Ashes 3M 55
NEW CUT 3L 105
New Cut TN32: Mount 3K 81
TN35: W'fld 3K 105
New Derby Ho. BN23: Eastb 5G 155
Newdigate Ho. *TN40: Bex S* *2L 145*
(off Knole Rd.)
New Dorset St. BN1: Brig 6D 162
BN1: Brig 7A 132 (6D 162)
(Up. Gloucester Rd.)
Newells Cl. BN2: W'dean 4M 133
NEWENDEN 7C 46
New England Ho. BN1: Brig 3E 162
New England La. TN31: Play 9G 66
TN33: Sed 2E 104
New England Ri. BN41: Ports 1C 130
New England Rd.
BN1: Brig 6A 132 (4C 162)
RH16: Hay H 5F 48
TN4: Tun W 6D 8
New England St.
BN1: Brig 6B 132 (3E 162)
Newfield La. BN9: N'hvn 5J 149
Newfield Rd. BN9: N'hvn 5J 149
Newgate Rd. TN37: St Leo 5J 127
NEWHAVEN 5J 149
NEWHAVEN DOWNS HOUSE 5J 149
Newhaven Fort 7K 149
Newhaven Harbour Station (Rail) 6K 149
Newhaven Hgts. BN9: N'hvn 7J 149
Newhaven Local & Maritime History Mus.
3K 149
Newhaven Rd. BN7: Rod 5K 135
BN25: Sea 7N 149
Newhaven Sq. *BN9: N'hvn* *5K 149*
(off South La.)
Newhaven St. BN2: Brig 7C 132
Newhaven Town Station (Rail) 5K 149
Newhaven Wlk. TN38: St Leo 3G 127
NEWICK 1K 71
Newick Cl. BN25: Sea 1H 157
Newick Dr. BN8: N'wck 1J 71
Newick Hill BN8: Flet, N'wck 9J 51
Newick La. TN20: H'fld, May 9D 38
TN21: May 3E 56
Newick Rd. BN1: Brig 1F 132
BN20: Eastb 6N 153
Newlands TN3: Lang G 1L 15
Newlands Av. TN39: Bex S 9H 125
Newlands Cl. BN6: Hass 4B 90
TN34: Hast 1L 127
Newlands Cres. RH19: E Grin 2D 10
Newlands Pk. Way BN8: N'wck 1J 71
Newlands Pl. RH18: F Row 9M 11
Newlands Ri. TN4: Tun W 7D 8
Newlands Rd. BN2: Rott 3H 147
TN4: Tun W 7D 8
Newlands Way TN4: Tun W 6E 8
New Langney Ct. BN23: Lang 3H 155
New Lydd Rd. TN31: Camb 6A 88
Newlyn Ct. *TN40: Bex S* *2L 145*
(off Brassey Rd.)
Newmans Way TN35: Hast 2C 128
Newmarket Rd. BN2: Brig 5D 132
Newmarket Ter. BN2: Brig 5D 132
New Moorsite TN35: W'fld 4M 105
Newnham Way TN21: H'fld 2D 76
New Pde. TN21: H'fld 9D 56
New Park Av. TN40: Bex S 1K 145
New Pk. Av. TN40: Bex S 1K 145
New Pl. BN21: Eastb 9A 154
TN22: Uck 3H 73
New Pl. Cl. TN22: Uck 3H 73
New Pond Hill TN21: Cross H 3N 75
New Pond La. TN21: Cross H 3A 76
Newport Rd. RH15: Burg H 5A 68
Newport St. BN2: Brig 6C 132
New Rd. BN1: Brig 8B 132 (8E 162)
BN6: Clay, Hass 6A 90
BN7: Lewes 5J 115
BN8: Glyn, Ring 2B 116
BN9: N'hvn 3K 149
(not continuous)
BN22: Eastb 8E 154 (4M 161)
(not continuous)
BN26: Pole 7E 140
BN27: Hell 2E 120
TN6: Crow 8D 24
TN6: Roth 2M 37
TN11: Pens 3E 6
TN22: Uck 5J 73
TN31: North 6N 63
TN31: Rye 2G 87
TN35: Fair 2J 129
TN35: Hast 4C 128
Newstead BN1: Brig 4D 162
New Steine BN2: Brig 9C 132
New Steine Mans. *BN2: Brig* *8C 132*
(off Devonshire Pl.)
New Steine M. BN2: Brig 8C 132
Newtimber Dr. BN41: Ports 4C 130
Newton Av. RH19: E Grin 6F 10
Newton Cl. RH16: Lind 2J 49
Newton Ct. RH16: Hay H 4F 48
Newton Pk. BN27: Hails 7G 120

Newton Rd.—Ockley La.

Newton Rd. BN7: Lewes 4H 115
BN10: Peace 5C 148
RH16: Lind 2J 49
TN1: Tun W 9E 8
Newton's Hill TN7: Hart 9H 13
Newton Willows TN3: Groom 5G 15
NEW TOWN
Uckfield 2J 73
NEWTOWN
Hever 1J 5
Newtown Rd. BN3: Hove 5K 131
Newts Way TN38: St Leo 5E 126
New Upperton Rd. BN21: Eastb 8B 154
New Venture Theatre 7A 162
New Villas *BN26: Pole* *7E 140*
(off Western Av.)
New Winchelsea Rd. TN31: Rye 6F 86
TN36: Rye 6F 86
Nicholson Ct. BN23: Lang 3H 155
Nightingale Cl. BN23: Lang 2F 154
RH16: Hay H 5G 49
RH19: E Grin 5D 10
Nightingale La. RH15: Burg H 8A 68
Nightingale Ri. TN22: Uck 4J 73
Nightingales, The TN22: Uck 3K 73
Nile St. BN1: Brig 8E 162
NINFIELD 9C 102
Ninfield Pl. BN2: Brig 6F 132
Ninfield Rd TN39: Bex S, Nin 3D 124
Ninfield Rd. TN39: Bex S 4F 124
Nizells Av. BN3: Hove 6M 131 (4A 162)
Nizells La. BN3: Hove 6M 131 (4A 162)
Noah's Ark La. RH16: Lind 2K 49
Noble Ct. BN3: Hove 6G 131
Nodes La. BN27: Mag D 2J 121
Noel Grn. RH15: Burg H 4C 68
Noel Ri. RH15: Burg H 4C 68
Nolan Rd. BN2: W'dean 6M 133
NOOK BEACH 8H 87
Nook Cl. TN35: Hast 3C 128
Nook, The TN22: Uck 4J 73
Noonan's Steps *TN34: Hast* *5N 127*
(off Stonefield Rd.)
Norbury Cl. TN6: Crow 7C 24
Nore Rd. BN9: N'hvn 6H 149
Norfolk Bldgs. BN1: Brig 7A 162
Norfolk Cl. TN39: Bex S 7J 125
Norfolk Ct. BN1: Brig 7A 162
BN22: Eastb *8F 154*
(off Redoubt Rd.)
Norfolk Dr. TN38: St Leo 1F 126
Norfolk Hgts. TN1: Tun W 9D 8
Norfolk M. BN1: Brig 8N 131 (7A 162)
Norfolk Pl. BN1: Brig 7A 162
Norfolk Rd. BN1: Brig 7N 131 (7A 162)
TN1: Tun W 2E 16
Norfolk Sq. BN1: Brig 8N 131 (7A 162)
Norfolk St. BN1: Brig 8N 131 (8A 162)
Norfolk Ter. BN1: Brig 7N 131 (6A 162)
Norfolk Way TN22: Uck 9H 53
NORLINGTON 9C 94
Norlington Ct. BN8: Ring 9C 94
Norlington Flds. BN8: Ring 9B 94
Norlington La. BN8: Ring 9C 94
Norman Cl. BN25: Sea 6A 150
TN33: Batt 3M 103
Norman Ct. TN34: Hast 7L 127
Normandale TN39: Bex S 2G 145
Normandale Ho. *TN39: Bex S* *2G 145*
(off Normandale)
Normandy Cl. RH19: E Grin 4F 10
Normandy Ct. *TN39: Bex S* *2J 145*
(off West Pde.)
Normandy Ho. BN3: Hove 7L 131
Normandy Rd. TN34: Hast 3J 127
Normanhurst *BN2: Brig* *7C 132*
(off Grove Hill)
TN33: Batt 4D 102
Normanhurst Ct. Cvn. Club Site
TN33: Batt 5D 102
Normanhurst Gdns. TN33: Batt 4D 102
Norman Rd. BN3: Hove 7G 130
BN9: N'hvn 5J 149
BN24: Pev B 9F 142
RH15: Burg H 5A 68
TN1: Tun W 9E 8
TN38: St Leo 8J 127
Normans *TN39: Bex S* *2G 145*
(off Normandale)
Normansal Cl. BN25: Sea 6F 150
Normansal Pk. Av. BN25: Sea 7E 150
NORMAN'S BAY 5M 143
Norman's Bay Camping & Caravanning Pk.
BN24: Nor B 6K 143
Normans Bay Cvn. Pk.
BN24: Nor B 5L 143
Norman's Bay Station (Rail) 5L 143
Normans Gdns. RH19: E Grin 3E 10
Normansland TN22: Nut 8G 35
Normans Vs. *TN32: Rob* *5J 61*
(off High St.)
NORMANSWOOD 1E 40
Normanton St. BN2: Brig 6D 132
Norman Vw. TN40: Bex S 1M 145
Norris Cl. TN18: Hawk 1A 44
Norstead Gdns. TN4: South 5E 8
Norsted La. TN22: Isf 9D 72
Northampton Way
TN38: St Leo 2G 126
North Av. BN20: Eastb 7M 153
TN17: Goud 4F 30
Nth. Barnes La.
BN7: E Chil, Plump G 2M 91
Nth. Beeches Rd. TN6: Crow 1E 36
Nth. Boscobel Rd. TN38: St Leo 7G 127
Northbourne Rd. BN22: Eastb 5E 154
NORTHBRIDGE STREET 4J 61
Northbridge St. TN32: Rob 4J 61
Nth. Camp La. BN25: Sea 8E 150
NORTH CHAILEY 1E 70
Northcliffe Cl. BN25: Sea 8E 150
North Cl. BN26: Pole 6E 140
BN41: Ports 3C 130
NORTH COMMON 1D 70
Nth. Common Rd.
BN8: N Cha, Wivel G 4K 69
RH17: Wivel G 4K 69
NORTH CORNER 3F 98
Northcote La. BN10: Tels C 3A 148
North Ct. BN7: Lewes 5L 115
Nth. Crescent Ind. Est.
BN27: Hails 7D 120
Northdown Cl. BN9: N'hvn 6J 149
Northdown Rd. BN9: N'hvn 6H 149
Northdown Ter. RH19: E Grin 1D 10
North Dr. BN2: Brig 7D 132
Northease Cl. BN3: Hove 3F 130
Northease Dr. BN3: Hove 3F 130
Northease Gdns. BN3: Hove 2G 130
Northease Wall BN7: Rod 3J 135
NORTH END
East Grinstead 1B 10
Hamsey 7J 93
North End BN6: Ditch 4E 90
RH19: E Grin 1B 10
Northerlea *BN41: Ports* *4C 130*
(off Drove Rd.)
Northern Av. BN26: Pole 6E 140
Nth. Farm Cotts. *BN41: Ports* *3C 130*
(off North Rd.)
Nth. Farm Ind. Est. TN2: Tun W 4G 9
Nth. Farm La. TN2: Tun W 5G 8
North Farm La. TN2: Tun W 4H 9
Nth. Farm Rd. TN2: Tun W 5F 8
TN4: Tun W 6F 8
Northfield BN26: Pole 8C 140
Northfield Cl. BN25: Sea 7E 150
Northfield Cotts. TN22: Isf 8C 72
Northfield Ri. BN2: Rott 2H 147
BN3: Hove 1F 130
Northfields TN3: Speld 5L 7
Northfields Bus. Pk.
BN27: Lwr D 2L 119
Northfield Way BN1: Brig 1B 132
North Gdns. BN1: Brig 7A 132 (6D 162)
Northgate Cl. BN2: Rott 2G 147
Northgrove Rd. TN18: Hawk 9N 31
Nth. Heath Cl. BN27: Hails 4F 120
Nth. Hill Rd. TN18: Hawk 1K 43
NORTHIAM 3A 64
Northiam Ri. TN38: St Leo 4D 126
Northiam Rd. BN20: Eastb 8N 153
TN31: B Oak 2A 84
TN31: Buck 5D 64
TN32: Staple 8E 62
Northiam Station
Kent & East Sussex Railway 8B 46
North Ind. Est. BN9: N'hvn 3K 149
NORTH LAINE 7B 132 (6E 162)
Northlands TN32: Bod 9C 44
Northlands Av. RH16: Hay H 6H 49
Northlands Cotts. TN32: Bod 9C 44
North La. BN9: N'hvn 5J 149
BN41: Ports 2C 130
TN35: Gues T 2C 106
NORTH MOULSECOOMB 1F 132
North Pl. BN1: Brig 7B 132 (7F 162)
Nth. Quay Rd. BN9: N'hvn 3K 149
North Ridge TN31: North 2N 63
North Rd. BN1: Brig 4N 131
(Home Rd.)
BN1: Brig 7A 132 (6D 162)
(Kew St.)
BN8: Ring 9C 94
BN24: Pev B 9F 142
BN26: Alfr 1K 151
BN27: Bodle G 5E 100
BN41: Ports 3C 130
RH16: Hay H 5H 49
TN37: St Leo 5J 127
TN39: Bex S 7K 125
North Row TN22: Uck 9H 53
North Salts TN31: Rye 2G 87
Nth. South Rd. BN1: Falm 7J 113
North St. BN1: Brig 8A 132 (7D 162)
BN7: Lewes 4K 115
BN21: Eastb 1E 160 (5M 161)
BN26: Alfr 1M 151
North St. BN27: Hails 6E 120
(High St.)
BN27: Hell 1C 120
(Church Rd.)
BN41: Ports 6D 130
TN2: Tun W 1F 16
TN6: Roth 2M 37
TN8: C'den 7F 4
TN20: May 7E 38
TN21: Horam 4C 98
TN21: Punn T 3N 77
TN21: Wald 4K 75
TN36: Winch 8C 86
TN38: St Leo 7J 127
North St. Quad. BN1: Brig 7D 162
North Ter. TN34: Hast 4A 128
Nth. Trade Rd. TN33: Batt 3E 102
Northumberland Ct.
BN22: Eastb 2D 154
North Way BN7: Lewes 5G 114
BN9: N'hvn 5J 149
BN25: Sea 6E 150
Northway RH15: Burg H 4D 68
Northwood Av. BN2: Salt 3M 147
NORTON 4B 150
Norton Cl. BN3: Hove 7K 131
Norton Dr. BN2: W'dean 4L 133
Norton Rd. BN3: Hove 7K 131
BN9: N'hvn 5L 149
TN4: South 4C 8
Norton Ter. BN9: N'hvn 5L 149
Norton Wall BN7: Ifrd 2H 135
Norway Rd. BN22: Eastb 6G 154
Norway St. BN41: Ports 6E 130
Norwich Cl. BN2: Brig 3H 133
Norwich Cres. BN2: Brig 3G 133
Norwich Dr. BN2: Brig 3G 133
Norwich Ho. Rd. BN1: Falm 7H 113
Norwood BN1: Brig 1B 132
Nottidge Rd. TN4: Tun W 3A 16
Novington La. BN7: E Chil 8A 92
Nunnery La. TN11: Pens 6D 6
Nuns Wlk. BN9: N'hvn 5J 149
Nursery Cl. BN26: Pole 7E 140
BN27: Hails 6F 120
BN41: Ports 1A 130
RH16: Hay H 4E 48
TN5: Flim 8C 30
Nursery Fld. TN22: Buxt 5N 53
Nursery La. BN27: Bore S 1D 122
TN21: B'boys 8H 55
TN22: B'boys 8H 55
TN22: Mare, Nut 9G 34
TN22: Nut 6B 34
TN22: Uck 4J 73
Nursery Path BN27: Hails 8E 120
(not continuous)
Nursery Rd. TN4: Tun W 5E 8
Nursery, The RH15: Burg H 4D 68
Nursery Way TN21: H'fld 1B 76
Nutbourne Cl. *BN23: Lang* *2H 155*
(off Spring Lodge Cl.)
Nuthatch Rd. BN23: Lang 2F 154
Nuthurst Cl. BN2: Brig 7G 132
Nuthurst Pl. BN2: Brig 7G 132
NUTLEY 5B 34
Nutley Av. BN2: Salt 3K 147
Nutley Cl. BN3: Hove 2H 131
TN31: Rye 2E 86
Nutley Mill Rd. BN24: Sto C 8L 141
Nutley Windmill 3C 34
Nye Cl. TN6: Crow 1D 36
Nye La. BN6: Ditch 6E 90
(not continuous)
Nye Rd. RH15: Burg H 5C 68
Nyetimber Hill BN2: Brig 3F 132

O

Oakapple Rd. BN42: S'wck 3A 130
Oak Av. BN27: Chal 3G 118
(not continuous)
Oak Bank RH16: Lind 2G 49
Oak Cl. BN1: Brig 2N 131
Oak Cotts. *TN6: Crow* *3D 36*
(off Fermor Rd.)
TN22: Flet 5M 51
Oak Ct. *RH19: E Grin* *2D 10*
(off Newlands Cres.)
Oak Cft. RH19: E Grin 4G 10
Oakdale Rd. RH16: Hay H 6G 49
TN4: Tun W 9C 8
Oakdene RH16: Hay H 4E 48
Oakdene Av. BN41: Ports 2A 130
Oakdene Cl. BN41: Ports 2A 130
Oakdene Cres. BN41: Ports 2A 130
Oakdene Gdns. BN41: Ports 2A 130
Oakdene Ri. BN41: Ports 1A 130
Oakdene Way BN41: Ports 1A 130
Oakend TN18: Hawk 9N 31
Oak End Cl. TN4: South 3D 8
Oakendene BN2: Brig 1G 132
Oakenden La. TN8: Chid H 4N 5
Oakenfield RH15: Burg H 3A 68
Oak Est. BN9: N'hvn 3K 149
Oakfield TN18: Hawk 9N 31
Oakfield Cl. RH16: Lind 2H 49
Oakfield Ct. TN2: Tun W 1F 16
Oakfield Ct. Rd. TN2: Tun W 1F 16
Oakfield Rd. TN35: Hast 3B 128
Oakfield, The TN31: Play 9F 66
Oak Field, The TN35: Pett 6L 107
Oakfield Way RH19: E Grin 1F 10
TN39: Bex S 8D 124
Oak Hall Pk. RH15: Burg H 7C 68
Oakhill Dr. TN31: B Oak 3A 84
Oakhurst RH16: Hay H 1E 48
Oakhurst Cl. TN34: Hast 1L 127
Oakhurst Dr. TN6: Crow 8E 24
Oakhurst Gdns. RH19: E Grin 2C 10
Oakhurst La. RH16: Hay H 1E 48
Oakhurst Rd. TN33: Batt 1L 103
Oakland Dr. TN32: Rob 5E 60
Oaklands BN21: Eastb 8D 154 (3L 161)
BN24: W'ham 7N 141
TN6: Crow 1F 36
Oaklands Av. BN2: Salt 3K 147
Oaklands Cl. BN26: Pole 7E 140
Oaklands Rd. RH16: Hay H 4E 48
TN3: Groom 6F 14
TN18: Hawk 1A 44
Oaklands Way BN27: Hails 8D 120
Oaklea Cl. TN37: St Leo 2J 127
Oakleaf Ct. BN26: Pole 6D 140
Oakleaf Dr. BN26: Pole 6D 140
Oaklea Way TN22: Uck 1G 73
Oak Lees RH16: Lind 1J 49
Oakleigh Dr. TN21: H'fld 2E 76
Oakleigh Rd. TN39: Bex S 1D 144
Oakley Cl. RH19: E Grin 5H 11
Oakley Ct. TN22: Uck 2J 73
Oakley Down
BN20: Eastb 2B 160 (9G 161)
Oakley Ho. *BN2: Brig* *8C 132*
(off Leicester St.)
Oakmead Rd. RH15: Burg H 7A 68
Oakmede Way BN8: Ring 1C 116
Oak Passage *TN34: Hast* *6N 127*
(off High St.)
Oak Rd. TN2: Tun W 6F 8
TN40: Bex S 9K 125
Oakroyd Cl. RH15: Burg H 3E 68
Oaks Cl. TN19: Etch 9C 42
Oaks Forstal TN18: Sandh 5J 45
Oaks, The RH16: Hay H 4H 49
(Jubilee Cl.)
RH16: Hay H 5K 49
(Marlow Dr.)
RH19: E Grin 4G 11
TN21: H'fld 2E 76
TN37: St Leo 1K 127
Oak Ter. TN18: Hawk 9N 31
Oaktree BN8: Barc C 3L 93
Oak Tree Cl. BN23: Lang 9M 141
RH19: E Grin 1C 10
TN2: Tun W 3D 16
Oak Tree Cotts. RH17: Dane 6G 33
Oak Tree Ct. TN22: Uck 9J 53
Oak Tree La. BN23: Lang 9M 141
Oak Tree Way BN27: Hails 4F 120
Oakwood RH16: Hay H 5E 48
Oakwood Av. TN39: Bex S 7J 125
Oakwood Cl. RH15: Burg H 6C 68
TN34: Hast 3M 127
Oakwood Ct. RH16: Hay H 5E 48
Oakwood Dr. TN22: Uck 9K 53
Oakwood Pk. RH18: F Row 1M 21
TN22: Nut 5B 34
Oakwood Ri. TN2: Tun W 5H 9
Oakwood Rd. RH15: Burg H 6C 68
RH16: Hay H 5E 48
Oast Cl. TN2: Tun W 6G 9
Oasthouse Cl. TN37: St Leo 1K 127
Oasthouse Dr. TN31: Rye 4D 86
Oast Ho. Fld. TN36: Ick 1L 107
Oast Ho. Rd. TN36: Ick 2L 107
Oathall Av. RH16: Hay H 3G 48
Oathall Rd. RH16: Hay H 4F 48
Oban Rd. TN37: St Leo 3H 127
Observatory Science Cen., The 5E 122
Observatory Vw. BN27: Hails 7G 121
Ocean Fitness *7J 127*
(off London Rd.)
Oceania *TN39: Bex S* *2J 145*
(off West Pde.)
Ochiltree Cl. TN34: Hast 2N 127
Ochiltree Rd. TN34: Hast 2N 127
Ochorios M. BN23: Eastb 4J 155
Ockenden Lea RH17: Cuck 3A 48
Ockenden Way BN6: Hass 4A 90
OCKHAM 3E 62
OCKLEY 8N 31
Ockley Hill BN6: Hass 1C 90
Ockley La. BN6: Hass 1C 90
RH15: Hass 9C 68
TN18: Hawk 7N 31

A-Z East Sussex Atlas 191

Ockley Rd.—Park Cres.

Ockley Rd. TN18: Hawk ... 9N **31**
Ockley Way BN6: Hass ... 3B **90**
Ocklye Rd. TN6: Crow ... 9A **24**
Ocklynge Av. BN21: Eastb ... 8A **154**
Ocklynge Cl. TN39: Bex S ... 9D **124**
Ocklynge Rd. BN21: Eastb ... 8A **154**
Ockman La. *TN31: Rye* ... *3G **86***
(off East St.)
Octagon, The BN2: Brig ... 1A **146**
Odeon Cinema
Hastings ... *7M **127***
(off Albert Rd.)
Tunbridge Wells ... 5J **9**
Offa Ct. TN40: Bex S ... 1K **145**
Offa Rd. TN35: Hast ... 3C **128**
OFFHAM ... 1G **114**
Offham Cl. BN23: Lang ... 9J **141**
BN25: Sea ... 7E **150**
Offham Ct. BN25: Sea ... 8B **150**
Offham Rd. BN7: Lewes, Off ... 9F **92**
Offham Ter. *BN7: Lewes* ... *5J **115***
(off White Hill)
Office Village, The TN22: Uck ... 1H **73**
Okehurst Rd. BN21: Eastb ... 9N **153**
Oldaker Rd. BN8: N'wck ... 1J **71**
Old Barn Cl. BN20: Will ... 3M **153**
Old Barn Ct. RH16: Hay H ... 7E **48**
Old Barn Way BN42: S'wck ... 6C **130**
Old Boat Wlk. BN1: Brig ... 7C **112**
Old Brewery Yd. TN33: Batt ... 3L **103**
Old Brickyard TN31: Rye ... 3E **86**
Old Camp Rd. BN20: Eastb ... 1N **159**
Old Chu. Rd. TN2: Pem ... 3N **9**
TN38: St Leo ... 1G **126**
Old Coastguard Cotts. BN9: N'hvn ... 6K **149**
TN36: Pett ... 8A **108**
Old College Ho. BN2: Brig ... 4G **162**
Old Convent RH19: E Grin ... 2E **10**
Old Ct. Cl. BN1: Brig ... 1A **132**
Old Drive BN26: Pole ... 7C **140**
Old Drove BN23: Lang ... 1F **154**
Olde Pl. M. BN2: Rott ... 3G **147**
Old Farm Cl. RH16: Hay H ... 7H **49**
Old Farm Rd. BN1: Brig ... 9A **112**
TN39: Bex S ... 8J **125**
Oldfield Av. BN20: Will ... 9D **140**
Oldfield Cres. BN27: Hails ... 5E **120**
BN42: S'wck ... 6A **130**
Oldfield Rd. BN20: Will ... 9D **140**
Old Foord Cl. BN8: S Chai ... 9D **70**
Old Forest La. TN6: Roth ... 2J **37**
Old Forewood La. TN33: C'hrst ... 8N **103**
Old Forge La. TN22: Nut ... 1E **52**
Old Gdns. Cl. TN2: Tun W ... 4E **16**
Old Ghyll Rd. TN21: H'fld ... 3D **76**
Old Harbour Farm La. TN36: Winch ... 1F **108**
Old Harrow Rd. TN37: St Leo ... 3H **127**
Old Heath Cl. BN8: Hall ... 1A **96**
OLD HEATHFIELD ... 3G **77**
Old Hop Gdn., The TN31: Peas ... 7A **66**
Old Ho. Gdns. TN34: Hast ... 2M **127**
Old Ho. La. TN3: F'cmbe ... 9G **7**
TN22: Uck ... 4J **73**
Old Humphrey Av. *TN34: Hast* ... *6A **128***
(off All Saints' St.)
Old Ladies Ct. *TN33: Batt* ... *2L **103***
(off High St.)
OLDLANDS ... 6J **35**
Oldlands Av. BN6: Hass ... 3B **90**
Oldlands Hill TN22: Her G, Nut ... 8H **35**
Oldlands La. BN6: Hass ... 2C **90**
Old La. TN6: Crow ... 1F **36**
(Crowborough Hill)
TN6: Crow ... 8B **24**
(Glenmore Rd.)
TN20: May ... 8D **38**
Old London Rd. BN1: Brig ... 8N **111**
TN34: Hast ... 4B **128**
(North Ter.)
TN34: Hast ... 2C **128**
(Winchelsea Rd.)
TN35: Hast ... 6A **128**
Old Lydd Rd. TN31: Camb ... 6B **88**
Old Malling Way BN7: Lewes ... 3J **115**
Old Manor Cl. TN40: Bex S ... 1L **145**
Old Mansion Cl. BN20: Will ... 4L **153**
Old Martello Rd. BN24: Pev B ... 2L **155**
Old Mill Cvn. Pk., The
BN27: Gold C ... 1H **119**
Old Mill Cl. BN1: Brig ... 9N **111**
BN27: Hails ... 3D **120**
BN41: Ports ... *6C **130***
(off Chapel Rd.)
Old Mill Ct. TN6: Crow ... 9C **24**
Old Mill La. BN26: Pole ... 1J **153**
Old Mill Pk. TN39: Bex S ... 8H **125**
Old Mill Wlk. *TN33: Batt* ... *2L **103***
(off High St.)
Old Motcombe M. BN21: Eastb ... 8A **154**
Old Needle Makers, The ... *5K **115***
(off West St.)
Old Nursery Cl. BN25: Sea ... 7G **151**
Old Orchard TN18: Sandh ... 5H **45**
Old Orchard Pl. BN27: Hails ... 7E **120**
Old Orchard Rd.
BN21: Eastb ... 1C **160** (6H **161**)
Old Parish La. BN2: W'dean ... 5K **133**
Old Pk. Cl. RH17: Cuck ... 3B **48**
Old Patcham M. BN1: Brig ... 8N **111**
Old Place Ct. *BN2: Rott* ... *3G **147***
(off High St.)
Old Racecourse, The BN7: Off ... 3E **114**
Old River Way TN36: Winch ... 9F **86**
Old Rd. BN27: Herst, Mag D ... 2J **121**
RH19: E Grin ... 3F **10**
Old Roar Rd. TN37: St Leo ... 2J **127**
Old School Cl. BN8: Ring ... 9D **94**
Old School Cotts.
BN7: Plump G ... 2M **91**
Old School Ct. RH16: Hay H ... 2J **49**
Old School Path *TN34: Hast* ... *5N **127***
(off Nelson Rd.)
Old School Pl. RH15: Burg H ... 6A **68**
Old School., The BN22: Eastb ... 1N **161**
Old Shoreham Rd.
BN1: Brig ... 6N **131** (2A **162**)
BN3: Hove ... 5F **130** (2A **162**)
BN41: Ports ... 4A **130**
BN42: S'wck ... 4A **130**
Old Station Rd. TN5: Wadh ... 4A **28**
Old Steine BN1: Brig ... 8B **132** (8E **162**)
Old Swan La. BN27: Hails ... 9G **120**
Old Timbers La. TN22: Uck ... 2H **73**
Old Top Rd. TN35: Hast ... 2C **128**
OLD TOWN
BN20 ... 7N **153**
TN34 ... 6A **128**
TN40 ... 9L **125**
Old Tree Pde. *BN25: Sea* ... *9D **150***
(off Broad St.)
Old Viaduct Ct. BN2: Brig ... 5D **132**
Old Wardsdown TN5: Flim ... 8C **30**
Old Wickham La. RH16: Hay H ... 2E **48**
Old Willingdon Rd. BN20: Fris ... 2E **158**
Old Wish Rd.
BN21: Eastb ... 2C **160** (8J **161**)
Oliver Cl. TN6: Crow ... 1E **36**
TN34: Hast ... 7L **127**
Oliver Ho. BN3: Hove ... 8K **131**
Olive Rd. BN3: Hove ... 5F **130**
OLIVER'S HILL ... 8H **79**
Olivers M. TN33: Batt ... 3M **103**
Olives Mdw. TN22: Uck ... 1H **73**
Olives Yd. TN22: Uck ... 1H **73**
Olivier Cl. BN2: Brig ... 8D **132**
Ollier Ct. BN20: Eastb ... 2C **160** (8J **161**)
One O'Clock La. RH15: Burg H ... 6D **68**
Onslow Rd. BN3: Hove ... 4L **131**
Open Mkt., The
BN1: Brig ... 6B **132** (4F **162**)
Orange Row BN1: Brig ... 8B **132** (7E **162**)
Orchard Av. BN3: Hove ... 4J **131**
Orchard Bus. Cen. TN2: Tun W ... 5G **8**
Orchard Cl. BN42: S'wck ... 5B **130**
RH16: Hay H ... 1E **48**
RH17: Scay H ... 6N **49**
TN22: Nut ... 8G **35**
TN34: Hast ... 3M **127**
TN40: Bex S ... *9L **125***
(off Church St.)
Orchard Cnr. RH16: Hay H ... 4J **49**
Orchard Cotts. TN6: Roth ... 2M **37**
Orchard Gdns. BN3: Hove ... 4J **131**
Orchard Grange BN27: Lwr D ... 3N **119**
Orchard Ho. BN3: Hove ... 4K **131**
Orchard La. BN6: Ditch ... 3D **90**
BN6: Hass ... 3A **90**
Orchard M. BN9: N'hvn ... 2M **149**
Orchard Pde. BN20: Will ... 1L **153**
Orchard Ri. TN3: Groom ... 6F **14**
Orchard Rd. BN3: Hove ... 4J **131**
BN7: Lewes ... 4L **115**
RH15: Burg H ... 5A **68**
TN40: Bex S ... 8K **125**
Orchards Shop. Cen. RH16: Hay H ... 5F **48**
Orchards, The *BN2: Brig* ... *2F **132***
(off Moulsecoomb Way)
Orchard Ter. TN31: North ... 3A **64**
Orchard, The BN6: Hass ... 4A **90**
BN20: Will ... *3M **153***
(off Church St.)
TN19: Etch ... 9D **42**
TN22: Nut ... 6B **34**
TN31: B Oak ... 4A **84**
Orchard Valley Ct. BN7: Lewes ... 4L **115**
Orchard Vw. Cvn. Pk.
BN27: Bore S ... 9C **100**
Orchard Way RH15: Burg H ... 5A **68**
RH16: Hay H ... 1E **48**
RH19: E Grin ... 3E **10**
TN31: Peas ... 8A **66**
TN33: Sed ... 7E **82**
Orchid Cl. BN23: Lang ... 1E **154**
Orchidhurst TN2: Tun W ... 6G **9**
Orchid Pk. RH16: Hay H ... 5K **49**
Orchid Vw. BN1: Brig ... 8D **112**
ORE ... 3C **128**
Ore Pl. TN34: Hast ... 2N **127**
Ore Station (Rail) ... 4N **127**
Oriental Pl. BN1: Brig ... 8N **131** (8A **162**)
Orion Cl. BN27: Hails ... 7G **121**
Orion Pde. BN6: Hass ... 4A **90**
Orkney Ct. BN20: Eastb ... 6M **153**
Ormerod Av. TN38: St Leo ... 2G **126**
Ormerod Ct. RH16: Hay H ... 4F **48**
Orpen Rd. BN3: Hove ... 4M **131**
Orwell Cl. BN24: Sto C ... 8L **141**
Osbern Cl. TN39: Bex S ... 2D **144**
Osborne Cl. TN34: Hast ... 4L **127**
Osborne Ho. TN21: Rush G ... 7N **77**
Osborne Rd. BN1: Brig ... 3A **132**
Osborne Vs. BN3: Hove ... 7K **131**
Osbourne Hill TN6: Jar B ... 2G **36**
Osbourne Rd. BN20: Eastb ... 8M **153**
TN6: Jar B ... 2G **36**
Osmers Hill TN5: Wadh ... 4B **28**
Osmond Gdns. BN3: Hove ... 4B **162**
Osmond Rd. BN3: Hove ... 6N **131** (4A **162**)
Osprey Dr. TN22: Uck ... 3K **73**
Osprey Ho. BN1: Brig ... 7A **162**
Ospringe Pl. TN2: Tun W ... 7J **9**
Oswald Ct. TN40: Bex S ... 1K **145**
Otham Ct. La. BN26: Pole ... 5D **140**
Otham Pk. BN27: Hails ... 7G **121**
Otham Rd. BN22: Eastb ... 2D **154**
Ottafield Ct. RH16: Hay H ... 3G **48**
Otteham Cl. BN26: Pole ... 7E **140**
Otterbourne Pl. RH19: E Grin ... 3B **10**
Oulton Cl. BN23: Lang ... 1E **154**
Ousedale Cl. BN7: Lewes ... 5H **115**
Ouse Estuary Nature Reserve ... 5M **149**
Outlook Av. BN10: Peace ... 6F **148**
Outlook, The BN20: Fris ... 2E **158**
Oval Cl. BN10: Peace ... 2C **148**
Overdown Ri. BN41: Ports ... 1B **130**
Overhill BN42: S'wck ... 3A **130**
Overhill Dr. BN1: Brig ... 9N **111**
Overhill Gdns. BN1: Brig ... 9N **111**
Overhill Way BN1: Brig ... 8N **111**
Over St. BN1: Brig ... 7B **132** (6E **162**)
Overton Ct. RH19: E Grin ... 3E **10**
Overton Shaw RH19: E Grin ... 1E **10**
OVINGDEAN ... 9L **133**
Ovingdean Cl. BN2: Oving ... 8L **133**
Ovingdean Rd. BN2: Oving ... 9L **133**
Owen Cl. RH15: Burg H ... 7A **68**
Owl House Gardens ... 5G **19**
Owls Gdns. TN5: S'gate ... 5H **41**
Oxbottom Cl. BN8: N'wck ... 2H **71**
Oxbottom La. BN8: N'wck, N Cha ... 2H **71**
Oxenbridge La. TN19: Etch ... 1C **60**
Oxenbridge Row TN19: Etch ... 1C **60**
Oxendean Gdns. BN22: Will ... 9E **140**
Oxford Cl. BN1: Brig ... 6B **132** (4F **162**)
Oxford M. BN3: Hove ... 6L **131**
Oxford Pl. BN1: Brig ... 6B **132** (4F **162**)
Oxford Rd. BN22: Eastb ... 8E **154** (3N **161**)
TN38: St Leo ... 3G **127**
Oxford St. BN1: Brig ... 6B **132** (4F **162**)
Oxford Ter. *TN34: Hast* ... *6A **128***
(off All Saints' St.)
Ox Lea TN3: Lang G ... 1L **15**
OXLEY'S GREEN ... 9N **59**
Oxshott Ct. TN40: Bex S ... 1N **145**
Oyster Creek TN31: Rye ... 5K **87**

P

Pacific Dr. BN23: Eastb ... 3K **155**
Pacific Hgts. Nth. BN23: Eastb ... 3K **155**
Pacific Hgts. Sth. BN23: Eastb ... 3K **155**
Packer Cl. RH19: E Grin ... 1G **10**
Packman Way RH15: Burg H ... 4A **68**
Paddock Cl. TN3: F'cmbe ... 8F **6**
TN40: Bex S ... 8L **125**
Paddock Ct. BN41: Ports ... 2B **130**
Paddock Dr. TN37: St Leo ... 1J **127**
Paddock Fld. BN1: Falm ... 9J **113**
Paddock Gdns. BN26: Pole ... 9C **140**
RH19: E Grin ... 5E **10**
Paddockhall Rd. RH16: Hay H ... 4E **48**
Paddock La. BN7: Lewes ... 5J **115**
Paddock Rd. BN7: Lewes ... 5J **115**
Paddocks, The BN7: Plump G ... 1M **91**
BN7: Rod ... 5K **135**
BN27: Hails ... 4D **120**
RH16: Hay H ... 6D **48**
TN8: C'den ... 6G **5**
Paddock Ter. *BN7: Lewes* ... *5J **115***
(off New Rd.)
Paddock, The BN3: Hove ... 4L **131**
BN22: Eastb ... 2C **154**
TN2: Pem ... 7M **9**
TN3: F'cmbe ... 8D **6**
TN22: Mare ... 5F **52**
TN31: North ... 2A **64**
Padgham La. TN21: Dall ... 7E **78**
Padua Ho. BN2: W'dean ... 5N **133**
Padua Ho. Flats BN2: W'dean ... 5M **133**
Pages Av. TN39: Bex S ... 3G **144**
Pages Cl. TN21: H'fld ... 1B **76**
Pages Hill TN21: H'fld ... 1B **76**
Pages La. TN39: Bex S ... 2F **144**
Pagets, The BN8: N'wck ... 1K **71**
Pagham Cl. BN23: Lang ... 9L **141**
PAINE'S CORNER ... 5M **57**
Paines Cotts. *TN31: Rye* ... *5L **87***
(off Rye Harbour Rd.)
Paine's Twitten *BN7: Lewes* ... *6J **115***
(off Stewards Inn La.)
Pak Vw. RH16: Hay H ... 3F **48**
Palace of Fun ... 9B **132** (9F **162**)
Palace Pier
Brighton ... 9B **132** (9F **162**)
Palace Pl. BN1: Brig ... 8B **132** (8F **162**)
PALEHOUSE COMMON ... 5M **73**
Palesgate La. TN6: Crow, Jar B ... 8G **24**
Palesgate Way BN20: Eastb ... 7M **153**
Palgrave Ho. BN22: Eastb ... 4N **161**
Palliser Cl. BN23: Eastb ... 6H **155**
Palma Cl. BN26: Pole ... 6D **140**
Palm Ct. BN3: Hove ... 7M **131**
Palmeira Av. BN3: Hove ... 7L **131**
Palmeira Ct. BN3: Hove ... 7M **131**
(Palmeira Sq.)
BN3: Hove ... 8L **131**
(St John's Rd.)
Palmeira Grande *BN3: Hove* ... *7M **131***
(off Holland Rd.)
Palmeira Ho. BN3: Hove ... 6M **131**
Palmeira Mans. *BN3: Hove* ... *7L **131***
(off Church Rd.)
Palmeira Pl. BN3: Hove ... 6M **131**
Palmeira Sq. BN3: Hove ... 8L **131**
(not continuous)
Palmers Row BN27: Hails ... 7E **120**
Palmerston Ho. *RH16: Hay H* ... *3F **48***
(off Sydney Rd.)
Palmerston Rd. BN9: N'hvn ... 3M **149**
Palmyra Pl. BN23: Eastb ... 4K **155**
Pangdene Cl. RH15: Burg H ... 7A **68**
Pankhurst Av. BN2: Brig ... 7D **132**
Pankhurst Cl. TN39: Bex S ... 6H **125**
Pankhurst Ri. TN39: Bex S ... 6H **125**
Pannel La. TN35: Ick, Pett ... 6K **107**
TN36: Pett ... 6K **107**
Pannell Cl. RH19: E Grin ... 4D **10**
Pannett Ho. *RH16: Hay H* ... *7E **48***
(off Pinewood Way)
Pantiles, The TN2: Tun W ... 2D **16**
Parade, The BN1: Brig ... 1L **131**
BN3: Hove ... 3G **130**
BN24: Pev B ... 8F **142**
(Seaville Dr., not continuous)
BN24: Pev B ... 7H **143**
(Westham Dr.)
RH19: E Grin ... 1B **10**
TN6: Crow ... 8D **24**
Paradise Cl. BN20: Eastb ... 1A **160**
Paradise Dr. BN20: Eastb ... 2N **159**
Paradise Pk. & Planet Earth ... 3K **149**
Paragon, The BN20: Will ... 1K **153**
Parham Cl. BN2: Brig ... 8E **132**
Parham Ho. *BN3: Hove* ... *6M **131***
(off Chatsworth Sq.)
Parish Pk. TN33: Nin ... 1C **124**
Park and Ride
Withdean ... 1M **131**
Park Av. BN3: Hove ... 6G **131**
BN6: Hass ... 5B **90**
BN10: Tels C ... 4A **148**
BN21: Eastb ... 5N **153**
TN34: Hast ... 3K **127**
TN39: Bex S ... 2J **145**
Park Cl. BN1: Brig ... 8N **111**
(Old London Rd.)
BN1: Brig ... 9F **112**
(Ridge Vw.)
BN3: Hove ... 2G **131**
BN20: Eastb ... 9A **154**
BN27: Hails ... 8E **120**
BN41: Ports ... 4D **130**
RH15: Burg H ... 5A **68**
TN34: Hast ... 3K **127**
PARK CORNER
BN8 ... 5D **96**
TN3 ... 7H **15**
Park Cotts. TN18: Hawk ... 1A **44**
Park Ct. BN1: Brig ... 8N **111**
(Old London Rd.)
BN1: Brig ... 4A **132**
(Preston Pk. Av.)
BN3: Hove ... *6M **131***
(off Davigdor Rd.)
BN10: Peace ... *5B **148***
(off Roderick Av.)
RH15: Burg H ... 5B **68**
RH16: Hay H ... *5F **48***
(off Church Rd.)
TN4: Tun W ... 8D **8**
Park Cres. BN2: Brig ... 6C **132** (3G **162**)
BN2: Rott ... 3G **147**
(not continuous)
BN41: Ports ... 5C **130**

Piltdown Rd.—Queen's Av.

Piltdown Rd. BN2: Brig 7G 132
Piltdown Way BN23: Lang 9K 141
Pimms Gdns. BN1: Brig 6E 162
Pinders Rd. TN35: Hast 4C 128
Pinders Wlk. TN35: Hast 3C 128
Pine Av. TN34: Hast 3A 128
Pine Cl. BN9: N'hvn 4K 149
Pine Ct. *BN25: Sea 7E 150*
(off Up. Belgrave Rd.)
Pine Gro. RH19: E Grin 1B 10
TN6: Crow 9C 24
Pineham Copse RH16: Hay H 5G 48
Pinehurst RH15: Burg H 7B 68
Pinehurst Wlk. *TN34: Hast 3A 128*
(off Pine Av.)
Pines, The BN2: Brig 3G 162
BN3: Hove 7N 131 (5A 162)
RH16: Hay H 5J 49
Pine Tree Cl. BN9: N'hvn 5J 149
Pine Tree Rd. TN21: H'fld 2D 76
Pine Wlk. TN22: Uck 9J 53
Pine Way BN27: Hails 7D 120
Pine Way Cl. RH19: E Grin 5E 10
Pinewood BN1: Brig 2M 131
Pinewood Chase TN6: Crow 8B 24
Pinewood Cl. BN1: Brig 3N 131
BN22: Eastb 2A 154
BN25: Sea 8E 150
Pinewood Ct. RH16: Hay H 7E 48
TN4: South 4D 8
Pinewood Gdns. TN4: South 4D 8
Pinewood Rd. TN2: Tun W 8G 8
Pinewoods TN39: Bex S 1F 144
Pinewoods Ct. TN39: Bex S 1F 144
Pinewood Way RH16: Hay H 7E 48
TN38: St Leo 3E 126
Pinfold *RH16: Hay H 3E 48*
(off Great Heathmead)
Pinfold Cl. BN2: W'dean 7M 133
Pink All. *TN2: Tun W 2D 16*
(off Nevill St.)
Pinton Hill TN5: Tice 8K 29
Pinwell Rd. BN7: Lewes 6K 115
Pipe Pas. BN7: Lewes 5J 115
Pipers Cl. BN3: Hove 2E 130
TN5: Wadh 7C 28
TN40: Bex S 9K 125
Pipers Fld. TN22: Uck 4J 73
Pipers Ga. TN22: Uck 4J 73
Pipers La. TN32: Rob 5J 61
Pipit Mdw. TN22: Uck 3J 73
Pippin Cl. BN27: Bore S 1D 122
PIPSDEN 1D 44
Pit Ga. TN33: Batt 3N 103
Pitreavie Dr. BN27: Hails 6D 120
Pitt Dr. BN25: Sea 7F 150
Pitt Gdns. BN2: W'dean 5L 133
PIXTON HILL .8A 12
Place La. BN25: Sea 9D 150
Plainfields Av. BN1: Brig 7B 112
Plaistow Cl. BN2: Brig 7G 132
Plashett Pk. Gates TN22: Lit H 2E 94
Plat, The TN31: North 3A 64
PLATT, THE .2E 26
Platt, The RH16: Hay H 4J 49
Plaw Hatch La. RH19: F Row 5C 20
PLAYDEN 9G 66
Playden Cl. BN2: Brig 9F 132
Playden Gdns. TN34: Hast 2A 128
Playden La. TN31: Iden 6F 66
Pleasant Vw. Rd. TN6: Crow 7D 24
Plemont Gdns. TN39: Bex S 8H 125
Pleyden Ri. TN39: Bex S 1A 144
Plough La. TN37: St Leo 1H 127
Plover Cl. BN23: Lang 2F 154
Plover Ct. TN38: St Leo 3E 126
Plovers Barrow TN22: Buxt 5B 54
Plummerden La. RH16: Lind 9A 32
PLUMPTON .8M 91
Plumpton Bostall BN7: Plump 9L 91
Plumpton Cl. BN23: Lang 9K 141
TN40: Bex S 8K 125
PLUMPTON CROSSWAYS 7M 69
PLUMPTON GREEN 1M 91
Plumpton La. BN7: Plump 4M 91
Plumpton Race Course 3M 91
Plumpton Rd. BN2: Brig 7E 132
BN8: N Cha 4A 70
Plumpton Station (Rail) 2M 91
Plum Tree Cotts. TN18: Hawk 2M 43
Plumyfeather Farm TN6: Lye G 1C 24
Plymouth Av. BN2: Brig 4F 132
Plymouth Cl. BN23: Eastb 4J 155
Plynlimmon Rd. TN34: Hast 6N 127
Pocock's Rd. BN21: Eastb 7A 154
Poels Ct. RH19: E Grin 2E 10
Point Hill TN31: Rye 1G 87
POLEGATE .6E 140
Polegate By-Pass BN26: Hank, Pole . . .4C 140
Polegate Rd. BN27: Hails 9D 120
Polegate Station (Rail) 7D 140
Polegate Towermill 8D 140
Polegate Windmill Milling Mus. . . . . *.8D 140*
(off Park Cft.)
Polesden Rd. TN2: Tun W 2G 16
Polestub La. RH17: Cuck 2A 48
Polley Cl. TN2: Pem 6N 9
Pollington Pl. TN6: Crow 9D 24
Pond Cl. TN31: B Oak 3A 84
Pondcroft Rd. RH16: Lind 2J 49
Pondside RH16: Hay H 6D 48
Pondsyde Ct. BN25: Sea 8E 150
PONDTAIL 8C 4
Pond Way RH19: E Grin 3H 11
Ponswood Ind. Est. TN38: St Leo 4H 127
Ponswood Rd. TN38: St Leo 4H 127
Pont Cl. TN21: Punn T 2M 77
PONTS GREEN 3K 101
Pookreed Cl. TN21: H'fld 2C 76
Pook Reed La. TN21: Cross H, H'fld . . .2B 76
Pool Bar Wall BN7: Ifrd 8L 115
Pool Pas. BN1: Brig 9E 162
Pool Valley BN1: Brig 9B 132 (9E 162)
Poona Rd. TN1: Tun W 2E 16
Popes Folly BN2: Brig 4D 132
Poplar Av. BN3: Hove 2G 130
Poplar Cl. BN1: Brig 3A 132
BN3: Hove 2G 130
Poplar La. RH18: F Row 2L 21
Poplars, The BN2: Brig 2G 162
BN6: Hass .4B 90
Poplar Wlk. BN22: Eastb 1A 154
Poppinghole La. TN32: Rob 8K 61
Popps La. TN39: Bex S 2D 144
Porters Way BN26: Pole 7D 140
Portfield Av. BN1: Brig 8B 112
Portfield Cl. TN40: Bex S 9L 125
Port Hall Av. BN1: Brig 5N 131 (1B 162)
Port Hall M. BN1: Brig 5N 131 (2B 162)
Port Hall Pl. BN1: Brig 5N 131 (1B 162)
Port Hall Rd. BN1: Brig 5N 131 (2A 162)
Port Hall St. BN1: Brig 5N 131 (1B 162)
Portland Av. BN3: Hove 6G 130
Portland Bus. Pk. BN3: Hove 5G 130
Portland Cl. BN27: Hails 5D 120
Portland Ga. BN3: Hove 6G 130
Portland La. BN3: Hove 6F 130
Portland M. BN2: Brig 9D 132
Portland Pl. BN2: Brig 9D 132
TN34: Hast 6M 127
Portland Rd. BN3: Hove 5F 130
RH15: Burg H 5A 68
RH19: E Grin 4E 10
Portland Rd. Trad. Est. BN3: Hove 5F 130
Portland Sq. TN21: H'fld 1G 77
Portland Steps *TN34: Hast 6M 127*
(off Portland Pl.)
Portlands, The BN23: Eastb 5J 155
Portland St. BN1: Brig 8A 132 (7D 162)
Portland Ter. BN9: N'hvn 2K 149
Portland Vs. BN3: Hove 6F 130
Port Rd. BN22: Eastb 3D 154
Portsdown Way BN20: Will 2M 153
Portside BN2: Brig 1A 146
PORTSLADE 4C 130
PORTSLADE-BY-SEA 6E 130
Portslade Sports Cen. 2C 130
Portslade Station (Rail) 5F 130
Portsmouth La. RH16: Hay H 1G 49
Portsmouth Wood RH16: Lind 1G 49
Portsmouth Wood Cl. RH16: Lind 1G 49
Portsmouth Wood Dr.
RH16: Lind 1G 49
Possingworth Cl. TN21: Cross H 9K 55
Possingworth Pk. 1J 75
Possingworth Workshops
TN22: B'boys 3G 75
Postern, The *TN6: Crow 9D 24*
(off Croft Rd.)
Post Horn Cl. RH18: F Row 2A 22
Post Horn La. RH18: F Row 2N 21
Post Office Pas. *TN34: Hast 6A 128*
(off High St.)
Post Office Rd. TN18: Hawk 9N 31
Post Office Sq. TN1: Tun W 1D 16
Potato La. BN8: Ring 1D 116
POTMAN'S HEATH 5K 47
Potmans La. TN33: Cats 1G 124
Potman's La. TN39: Bex S 4F 124
Pottens Mill La. TN21: B Oak 5J 57
Potteries, The BN6: Ditch 7H 69
TN22: Uck .4J 73
Potters Fld. BN8: Ring 9C 94
POTTER'S GREEN 6A 54
Potters La. BN7: Lewes 6J 115
RH15: Burg H 7A 68
TN18: Hawk 5N 31
Pottery Cl. TN31: Brede 6M 83
Pottery La. TN31: Brede 6M 83
Pottingfield Rd. TN31: Rye 2E 86
Potts Marsh Ind. Est. BN24: W'ham . . .8B 142
Pouchlands Dr. BN8: S Chai 9C 70
Pound Cl. BN23: Eastb 6J 155
POUNDFIELD .9F 24
Poundfield Farm TN6: Crow 9F 24
Poundfield Rd. BN26: Selm 8E 118
BN27: Chal, Selm 7E 118
TN18: Sandh 5H 45
POUNDFORD .4L 55
POUNDGATE .4M 35
POUND GREEN 5B 54
POUND HILL .2B 74
Pound La. BN8: Laug 8A 96
BN26: B'wck 6E 138
TN22: B'boys, Buxt, Fram 2B 74
POUNDSBRIDGE 5H 7
Poundsbridge Hill
TN3: F'cmbe, Pens 7H 7
TN11: Pens .7H 7
Poundsbridge La. TN11: Pens 3H 7
POUND, THE 6L 101
Pound, The RH15: Burg H 4A 68
POUSLEY 9F 54
Powder Mill Cl. TN4: South 5F 8
Powder Mill La. TN4: South, Tun W 6D 8
Powdermill La. TN31: B Oak 3L 83
TN33: Batt, Cats 6G 102
Powell Gdns. BN9: N'hvn 3K 149
Powell Rd. BN8: N'wck 1K 71
Powerfield Rd. TN6: Crow 9F 24
Powis Gro. BN1: Brig 7A 132 (6C 162)
Powis Rd. BN1: Brig 7N 131 (6B 162)
Powis Sq. BN1: Brig 7N 131 (5B 162)
Powis Vs. BN1: Brig 7A 132 (6C 162)
POYNINGS .1E 110
Poynings Cl. BN25: Sea 1H 157
Poynings Dr. BN3: Hove 2H 131
Poynings Rd. BN5: Fulk, Poyn 3B 110
BN45: Poyn 1E 110
Poynter Rd. BN3: Hove 5J 131
Pratt's Folly La. TN6: Crow 1C 36
Prescott Gdns. RH15: Burg H 5B 68
PRESTON 4N 131
Preston Cir. BN1: Brig 3E 162
Preston Drove BN1: Brig 3N 131
Preston Grange BN1: Brig 4N 131
Preston Gro. TN22: Fram 2N 73
Preston Manor (Mus.) 4N 131
Preston Mans. BN1: Brig 1D 162
Preston Pk. Av.
BN1: Brig 3A 132 (1D 162)
Preston Park Station (Rail) 3M 131
Preston Rd. BN1: Brig 3N 131 (1B 162)
TN39: Bex S 7J 125
Preston St. BN1: Brig 8N 131 (8B 162)
Preston Village M. *BN1: Brig 4N 131*
(off Middle Rd.)
Prestonville Ct. BN1: Brig 3B 162
Prestonville Rd.
BN1: Brig 6A 132 (3C 162)
Prestonville Ter. BN1: Brig 3C 162
Prideaux Ct. BN21: Eastb 7C 154 (1J 161)
Prideaux Rd.
BN21: Eastb 7B 154 (1G 161)
Pride Vw. BN24: Sto C 8L 141
PRIMMERS GREEN 5B 28
Primrose Acre BN27: Chal 3F 118
Primrose Cl. BN23: Lang 1E 154
Primrose Hill TN35: Fair 1L 129
TN39: Bex S 8G 124
Primrose La. RH18: F Row 2N 21
Prince Albert St.
BN1: Brig 8B 132 (8E 162)
Prince Albert Ter. TN32: Rob 5J 61
Prince Charles Cl. BN42: S'wck 4B 130
Prince Charles Rd. BN7: Lewes 3L 115
Prince Edward's Rd. BN7: Lewes 5H 115
Prince of Wales Ct. *BN3: Hove 7H 131*
(off Kingsway)
Prince Regent's Cl. BN2: Brig 9F 132
Prince Regents Ct. BN2: Brig 8F 132
Prince Regent Swimming Complex
. . . . .8B 132 (7F 162)
Princes Av. BN3: Hove 7J 131
Princes Cl. BN25: Sea 7D 150
TN22: Uck .1F 72
Princes Ct. BN3: Hove 7J 131
Prince's Cres. BN2: Brig 5C 132 (2G 162)
Princes Cres. BN3: Hove 7J 131
Princes Fld. BN26: B'wck 2F 138
Prince's Pl. BN1: Brig 8B 132 (8E 162)
Prince's Rd. BN2: Brig 5C 132 (1G 162)
Princes Rd. BN23: Eastb 6H 155
Prince's Rd. TN37: St Leo 7K 127
Princess Dr. BN25: Sea 7B 150
PRINCESS ROYAL HOSPITAL 6H 49
Princes Sq. BN3: Hove 7J 131
Prince's St. BN2: Brig 8B 132 (8F 162)
Princes St. TN2: Tun W 1F 16
Princes Ter. BN2: Brig 9F 132
Prince William Pde. BN23: Eastb 6H 155
Principal Cl. TN39: Bex S 1A 144
Prinkle La. BN27: Bodle G 6E 100
Prinsep Rd. BN3: Hove 5J 131
Prior's Way TN8: C'den 7F 4
Priory Av. TN34: Hast 5L 127
Priory Cl. BN24: Pev B 8F 142
TN34: Hast 5L 127
Priory Ct. BN1: Brig 1D 162
BN7: Lewes 6K 115
BN20: Eastb 8H 161
TN40: Bex S 9M 125
Priory Cres. BN7: Lewes 6J 115
Priory Flats BN7: Lewes 6J 115
PRIORY GRANGE, THE 7L 57
Priory Hgts. BN20: Eastb 7L 153
Priory Ho. BN7: Lewes 6K 115
Priory La. BN23: Lang 1H 155
Priory Lane Stadium 1J 155
Priory Mdw. Shop. Cen.
TN34: Hast 6M 127
Priory Orchard BN23: Lang 3H 155
Priory Rd. BN6: Hass 2A 90
BN23: Lang 1H 155
RH15: Burg H 7B 68
RH18: F Row 5G 21
Priory Rdbt. BN23: Lang 1H 155
Priory St. BN7: Lewes 6J 115
TN34: Hast 6L 127
Priory Ter. *BN7: Lewes 6K 115*
(off Mountfield Rd.)
Priory, The BN1: Brig 9M 111
BN3: Hove 8K 131
RH16: Hay H 5G 48
Priory Way RH16: Hay H 6G 48
Promenade BN21: Eastb 1E 160 (6N 161)
BN25: Sea 9B 150
TN38: St Leo 8F 126
TN39: Bex S 3E 144
TN40: Bex S 2M 145
Promenade, The BN10: Peace 7E 148
(Cornwall Av.)
BN10: Peace 6B 148
(Edith Av., not continuous)
BN10: Peace 5A 148
(Lincoln Av. Sth.)
BN10: Peace 6A 148
(Phyllis Av.)
BN24: Pev B 9F 142
Prospect Gdns. BN21: Eastb 8A 154
Prospect Pk. TN4: South 4C 8
Prospect Pl. TN34: Hast 7L 127
Prospect Rd. TN2: Tun W 1E 16
TN4: South .4C 8
TN21: H'fld 2E 76
Prospect Ter. TN21: H'fld 1D 76
Providence Cotts. *TN3: Groom 5G 14*
(off Corseley Rd.)
TN6: Crow .6B 24
Providence Pl. BN1: Brig 6B 132 (3E 162)
(not continuous)
Prowting Mead TN39: Bex S 1D 144
Puddingcake La. TN22: Uck 9H 53
Pulborough Av. BN22: Eastb 3B 154
Pulborough Cl. BN2: Brig 6G 132
Pump Ho., The BN3: Hove 5F 130
Pump La. TN22: Fram 6B 74
PUNNETT'S TOWN 2M 77
Purbeck Cl. BN23: Lang 9M 141
Purbeck Ho. BN2: Brig 8G 162
Putlands Cres. TN39: Bex S 6H 125
Pychers Pl. TN2: Pem 7N 9
PYECOMBE .1L 111

Q

QUABROOK 2B 22
Quadrangle, The BN8: E Hoath 2H 97
Quadrant, The BN6: Hass 3B 90
BN21: Eastb 8B 154
Quakers La. RH16: Hay H 4H 49
Quantock Cl. BN23: Lang 1G 154
TN2: Tun W .8G 9
Quantock Gdns. TN34: Hast 3A 128
Quarry Bank Rd. BN1: Brig 3C 132
Quarry Cl. RH15: Burg H 5E 68
Quarry Cotts. TN5: Wadh 4N 27
Quarry Cres. TN34: Hast 5N 127
Quarry Hill RH16: Hay H 3D 48
TN38: St Leo 7H 127
Quarry Ho. TN38: St Leo 7H 127
Quarry La. BN25: Sea 7F 150
Quarry Ri. RH19: E Grin 1G 10
Quarry Rd. BN9: N'hvn 7J 149
TN1: Tun W .8E 8
TN34: Hast 5M 127
Quarry Rd. Ind. Est. BN9: N'hvn 6J 149
Quarry Vw. *TN6: Crow 2D 36*
(off Harecombe Ri.)
Quebec Cl. BN23: Eastb 5J 155
TN39: Bex S 9H 125
Quebec Rd. TN38: St Leo 3G 126
Quebec St. BN2: Brig 7C 132
Queen Alexandra Av. BN3: Hove 2J 131
Queen Alexandra's Cott. Homes
BN23: Eastb 5G 155
(off Seaside)
Queen Anne's Cl. BN7: Lewes 5J 115
Queen Caroline Cl. BN3: Hove 2J 131
Queen Elizabeth Av. RH15: Burg H 6A 68
Queen Mary Av. BN3: Hove 2J 131
Queens App. TN22: Uck 8J 53
Queen's Av. *TN34: Hast 7M 127*
(off Queen's Rd.)

Queensbury M.—Rochester Rd.

Queensbury M.
BN1: Brig ... 8N 131 (8B 162)
Queens Cliff BN21: Eastb ... 2H 161
Queens Cotts. TN5: Wadh ... 6A 28
Queens Ct. BN23: Eastb ... 5G 155
RH16: Hay H ... 3G 48
TN18: Hawk ... 1A 44
TN39: Bex S ... 2J 145
Queen's Cres. BN23: Eastb ... 5G 155
Queens Cres. RH15: Burg H ... 6B 68
Queensdown School Rd.
BN1: Brig ... 2D 132
BN2: Brig ... 2D 132
Queens Dr. BN6: Hass ... 3A 90
TN22: Mare ... 5E 52
Queen's Gdns.
BN1: Brig ... 7B 132 (6E 162)
BN3: Hove ... 8L 131
BN21: Eastb ... 9E 154 (5N 161)
TN4: Tun W ... 7E 8
Queens M. TN18: Hawk ... 1A 44
Queensmount TN20: F Ashes ... 2M 55
Queen's Pde. BN3: Hove ... 3G 131
Queens Pk. Gdns. BN25: Sea ... 8B 150
Queen's Pk. Ri. BN2: Brig ... 7D 132
Queen's Pk. Rd. BN2: Brig ... 8C 132
Queen's Pk. Ter. BN2: Brig ... 7D 132
Queen's Pl. BN1: Brig ... 6B 132 (4F 162)
BN3: Hove ... 7L 131
Queen Sq. BN1: Brig ... 8A 132 (7D 162)
Queen's Rd. BN1: Brig ... 8A 132 (7D 162)
BN7: Lewes ... 3K 115
BN23: Eastb ... 5G 155
Queens Rd. BN27: Herst ... 1A 122
BN42: S'wck ... 4A 130
RH16: Hay H ... 3F 48
Queen's Rd. RH19: E Grin ... 4E 10
TN4: Tun W ... 8D 8
Queens Rd. TN6: Crow ... 2D 36
Queen's Rd. TN18: Hawk ... 1A 44
TN34: Hast ... 7M 127
Queen's Rd. Quad.
BN1: Brig ... 7A 132 (6D 162)
Queens Sq. TN34: Hast ... 6M 127
Queen St. TN18: Sandh ... 4G 45
Queens Wlk. RH19: E Grin ... 3E 10
Queensway BN2: Brig ... 7E 132
BN25: Sea ... 7F 150
RH19: E Grin ... 3E 10
TN37: St Leo ... 1F 126
TN38: St Leo ... 3D 126
Queen Victoria Av. BN3: Hove ... 2J 131
QUEEN VICTORIA HOSPITAL ... 1F 10
Quickbourne La. TN31: North ... 2B 64
Quinnell Dr. BN27: Hails ... 4E 120
Quintin Cl. BN27: Hails ... 9D 120
Quintins, The BN27: Hails ... 6F 120

R

RACE HILL ... 5G 132
Radcliffe Cl. TN37: St Leo ... 3J 127
Radinden Dr. BN3: Hove ... 4M 131
Radinden Mnr. Rd. BN3: Hove ... 5L 131
Radnor M. TN38: St Leo ... 4E 126
Ragged Dog La. TN21: Wald ... 5M 75
Raglan Ct. BN1: Brig ... 7D 162
BN24: Pev B ... 1M 155
Railway App. BN9: N'hvn ... 5K 149
RH19: E Grin ... 3E 10
Railway Cotts. RH17: Hors K ... 2A 32
TN38: St Leo ... 8F 126
Railway La. BN7: Lewes ... 5K 115
Railway Rd. BN9: N'hvn ... 5K 149
Railway St. BN1: Brig ... 7A 132 (5D 162)
Railway Vw. *TN6: Jar B ... 2G 37*
(off Victoria Rd.)
Rainbow Pde. *TN21: B Oak ... 8H 57*
(off Burwash Rd.)
Rainey Ct. BN21: Eastb ... 9E 154 (4M 161)
Raleigh Cl. BN23: Eastb ... 6H 155
Ramsay Way BN23: Eastb ... 5H 155
RAMSLYE ... 3B 16
Ramslye Rd. TN4: Tun W ... 3A 16
Ranalah Est. BN9: N'hvn ... 4K 149
Randolph Ho. TN39: Bex S ... 9F 124
Randolph La. TN31: Iden ... 6E 66
Ranelagh Ct. BN23: Eastb ... 6H 155
Ranelagh Vs. BN3: Hove ... 5K 131
Rangemore Dr. BN21: Eastb ... 5A 154
Rankine Rd. TN2: Tun W ... 6G 8
Ranmore Cl. TN34: Hast ... 9L 105
Rannoch Rd. TN6: Crow ... 9B 24
Rannoch Rd. W. TN6: Crow ... 9B 24
Ranscombe Hill BN8: Glyn ... 8N 115
Ranscombe La. BN8: Glyn ... 8A 116
Ranworth Cl. BN23: Lang ... 9L 141
Raphael Rd. BN3: Hove ... 6H 131
Rapley Ct. RH16: Hay H ... 5G 48
Rapson's Rd. BN20: Will ... 1K 153
Rastrick Cl. RH15: Burg H ... 7A 68
Rattle Rd. BN24: Sto C, W'ham ... 8L 141
Ratton Dr. BN20: Will ... 5M 153
Ratton Gdns. BN20: Will ... 5M 153
Ratton Rd. BN21: Eastb ... 8B 154
RATTON VILLAGE ... 5M 153
Raven Ct. TN33: Batt ... 3N 103
TN38: St Leo ... 3E 126
Ravens Cl. TN39: Bex S ... 2D 144
Ravens Ct. *BN20: Eastb ... 3C 160*
(off St John's Rd.)
Ravens Cft. BN20: Eastb ... 3C 160
Ravenside Retail & Leisure Pk.
TN40: Bex S ... 9A 126
Ravenswood Av. TN2: Tun W ... 8F 8
Ravenswood Dr. BN2: W'dean ... 7N 133
Ravenswood Rd. RH15: Burg H ... 5C 68
Ravine Cl. TN34: Hast ... 3N 127
Rayford Cl. BN10: Peace ... 5C 148
Rayford Ct. *BN25: Sea ... 1D 156*
(off St John's Rd.)
TN40: Bex S ... 1L 145
(off Buckhurst Rd.)
Raymond Cl. BN25: Sea ... 7F 150
Rayner Cl. TN6: Crow ... 8D 24
Readers La. TN31: Iden ... 5D 66
Reading Rd. BN2: Brig ... 9G 132
Rear, The *TN4: Tun W ... 2D 16*
(off Pantiles, The)
Reba Ct. BN2: Salt ... 4L 147
Rectory Cl. BN3: Hove ... 6F 130
BN8: E Hoath ... 2E 96
BN9: N'hvn ... 6J 149
BN20: Eastb ... 9A 154
TN19: B'wsh ... 3K 59
TN38: St Leo ... 5H 127
Rectory Dr. TN3: Bid ... 2N 7
Rectory Fld. TN7: Hart ... 8K 13
Rectory La. TN31: Buck ... 4D 64
TN31: Play ... 9F 66
TN36: Winch ... 9C 86
Rectory Pk. TN35: Pett ... 6K 107
Rectory Rd. BN9: N'hvn ... 2L 149
Rectory Way TN40: Bex S ... 9L 125
Red Barn M. TN33: Batt ... 3L 103
Redbridge La. TN6: Crow ... 5B 36
Redbrook La. TN22: Buxt ... 4B 54
Red Dyke Cotts. BN24: Sto C ... 7J 141
Redford Cl. BN23: Lang ... 3H 155
Redford Ct. *TN39: Bex S ... 1G 145*
(off Collington La. E.)
Redgarth Ct. RH19: E Grin ... 1B 10
Redgeland Ri. TN38: St Leo ... 4F 126
Redgill La. BN8: N'wck, N Cha ... 9G 51
Redhill Cl. BN1: Brig ... 9L 111
Redhill Dr. BN1: Brig ... 9L 111
Red Lake Ter. TN35: Hast ... 2C 128
Redlands La. TN32: Rob ... 5K 61
Redleaf Cl. TN2: Tun W ... 7G 8
Redman King Ho.
BN20: Eastb ... 1C 160 (7H 161)
Redmayne Dr. TN34: Hast ... 7L 127
Red Oak TN18: Hawk ... 2M 43
Redoubt Fortress (Military Mus. of Sussex)
... 8F 154
Redoubt Rd. BN22: Eastb ... 8F 154 (2N 161)
REDPALE ... 9F 78
Redswood Rd. TN31: B Oak ... 3A 84
Redvers Rd. BN2: Brig ... 4E 132
Redwell Av. TN39: Bex S ... 6J 125
Redwings La. TN2: Pem ... 3N 9
Redwood Dr. RH16: Hay H ... 6E 48
Reed Ct. BN7: Lewes ... 3J 115
Reedham Rd. BN23: Lang ... 9L 141
Reed Pond Walk RH16: Hay H ... 5H 49
Reedswood Rd. TN38: St Leo ... 6E 126
Reef Way BN23: Eastb ... 3K 155
Reeves Hill BN1: Brig ... 9E 112
Reeves Ter. *TN5: Tice ... 1N 41*
(off High St.)
Refectory Rd. BN1: Falm ... 6J 113
Regal Dr. RH19: E Grin ... 4F 10
Regency Cl. TN22: Uck ... 9H 53
Regency Ct. BN1: Brig ... 2M 131
BN20: Eastb ... 3C 160
Regency Gdns. TN38: St Leo ... 6G 126
Regency Hall TN4: Tun W ... 2D 16
Regency M. BN1: Brig ... 8N 131 (7B 162)
BN20: Eastb ... 2D 160 (9K 161)
Regency Rd. BN1: Brig ... 8A 132 (8C 162)
(not continuous)
Regency Sq. BN1: Brig ... 8N 131 (7B 162)
Regency Town House ... 8M 131
Regent Arc. BN1: Brig ... 8E 162
Regent Hill BN1: Brig ... 8A 132 (7C 162)
Regent Pk. TN21: H'fld ... 9D 56
Regent Pl. TN2: Tun W ... 1G 16
TN37: St Leo ... 8F 104
Regent Row BN1: Brig ... 8A 132 (7C 162)
Regents Cl. BN25: Sea ... 7D 150
Regents Pl. BN22: Eastb ... 4A 154
Regent Sq. TN31: Rye ... 2G 86
Regent St. BN1: Brig ... 8B 132 (7E 162)
Regina Ct. TN4: Tun W ... 9C 8
Reginald Rd. TN39: Bex S ... 1J 145
Regnum Cl. BN22: Eastb ... 9H 141
Reigate Rd. BN1: Brig ... 4M 131 (1A 162)
Renascent Ho. BN21: Eastb ... 5M 161
Renfields RH16: Hay H ... 6D 48
Renfrew Ct. *BN22: Eastb ... 6G 154*
(off Allfrey Rd.)
Renown Cl. TN40: Bex S ... 8L 125
Reservoir La. TN31: Sed ... 6H 83
TN33: Sed ... 6H 83
Residence, The BN22: Eastb ... 4N 161
Resting Oak Hill BN8: Cooks ... 4F 92
Reynolds Dr. TN40: Bex S ... 9M 125
Reynolds La. TN4: Tun W ... 6C 8
Reynolds Rd. BN3: Hove ... 6H 131
BN23: Lang ... 3G 155
Reynoldstown La. BN26: Pole ... 7C 140
Ricard M. TN3: Lamb ... 7K 19
Riccards La. TN33: What ... 6A 82
Rices Hill RH19: E Grin ... 3F 10
Richard Allen Ct. BN1: Brig ... 4D 132
Richardson Ct. BN3: Hove ... 6H 131
Richardson Rd. BN3: Hove ... 6H 131
TN4: Tun W ... 7D 8
Richborough Cl. TN34: Hast ... 2K 127
Rich Ind. Est. BN9: N'hvn ... 3L 149
Richington Way BN25: Sea ... 8G 150
Richland Cl. TN35: Hast ... 2D 128
Richmead Gdns. TN20: May ... 8E 38
Richmond Av. TN39: Bex S ... 2G 145
Richmond Cl. TN39: Bex S ... 2H 145
Richmond Ct. BN3: Hove ... 4A 162
BN25: Sea ... 9D 150
(off Richmond Rd.)
Richmond Gdns.
BN2: Brig ... 7C 132 (5G 162)
Richmond Gro. TN39: Bex S ... 3H 145
Richmond Hgts. BN2: Brig ... 7C 132 (6G 162)
Richmond M. *BN25: Sea ... 9D 150*
(off Richmond Rd.)
Richmond Pde.
BN2: Brig ... 7B 132 (6G 162)
Richmond Pl. BN2: Brig ... 7B 132 (5F 162)
BN21: Eastb ... 8C 154 (4H 161)
TN2: Tun W ... 3E 16
Richmond Rd. BN2: Brig ... 5C 132
BN24: Pev B ... 8F 142
BN25: Sea ... 9D 150
TN39: Bex S ... 2H 145
Richmond St. BN2: Brig ... 7C 132
TN35: Hast ... 4B 128
Richmond Ter. BN2: Brig ... 4G 162
BN25: Sea ... 9D 150
Richmond Way RH19: E Grin ... 4F 10
RICKNEY ... 3N 141
Riddens Cl. BN7: Plump G ... 2M 91
Riddens La. BN7: Plump G ... 1M 91
Riddlesdale Av. TN4: Tun W ... 7D 8
Riders Bolt TN39: Bex S ... 9F 124
Ride, The BN1: Brig ... 4A 132 (1D 162)
Ridge Cl. BN41: Ports ... 1C 130
TN22: Nut ... 5B 34
Ridgelands TN3: Bid ... 1N 7
Ridgelands Cl. BN20: Eastb ... 9N 153
Ridgelands La. BN8: N'wck, S Chai ... 7J 71
Ridge Rd. BN1: Falm ... 6K 113
Ridgeside Av. BN1: Brig ... 9N 111
Ridge, The BN20: Eastb ... 3C 160
TN3: Groom ... 6E 14
TN34: Hast ... 1M 127
TN36: Winch ... 2F 108
TN37: St Leo ... 8H 105
Ridge Vw. BN1: Brig ... 9F 112
Ridgeway BN42: S'wck ... 4B 130
RH19: E Grin ... 5E 10
TN2: Pem ... 6N 9
TN18: Hawk ... 2L 43
TN19: Hur G ... 7G 43
Ridgeway Cl. BN42: S'wck ... 4B 130
TN21: H'fld ... 9E 56
Ridgewaye, The TN4: South ... 4E 8
Ridgeway Gdns. BN2: W'dean ... 6M 133
Ridgeway Paddock BN7: King L ... 8E 114
Ridgeway, The BN20: Fris ... 2E 158
BN25: Sea ... 7E 150
BN27: Herst ... 9A 100
RH15: Burg H ... 4C 68
Ridge West, The TN37: St Leo ... 8F 104
RIDGEWOOD ... 4J 73
Ridgewood Av. BN2: Salt ... 1K 147
Ridgewood Cl. TN22: Uck ... 4J 73
Ridgewood Gdns. TN34: Hast ... 1L 127
TN40: Bex S ... 1N 145
Ridgewood Ind. Pk. TN22: Uck ... 4K 73
Ridgewood Ri. *TN22: Uck ... 4J 73*
(off Highview La.)
Ridgway Cl. BN2: W'dean ... 5L 133
Ridgway, The BN2: W'dean ... 5L 133
Ridings, The BN2: Oving ... 9L 133
BN8: N'wck ... 1J 71
BN10: Tels C ... 3B 148
BN25: Sea ... 7E 150
RH15: Burg H ... 7D 68
TN2: Tun W ... 7J 9
TN37: St Leo ... 1J 127
TN39: Bex S ... 7G 124
Rigden Rd. BN3: Hove ... 5L 131
Riley Rd. BN2: Brig ... 5D 132
Rill Wlk. RH19: E Grin ... 3H 11
Ringle Grn. TN18: Sandh ... 5J 45
RINGLES CROSS ... 7H 53
RINGMER ... 1C 116
Ringmer Bus. Cen. BN8: Ring ... 9E 94
Ringmer Cl. BN1: Brig ... 1F 132
Ringmer Dr. BN1: Brig ... 1G 132
Ringmer Rd. BN1: Brig ... 1F 132
BN9: N'hvn ... 6G 149
BN25: Sea ... 1D 156
Ringmer Way BN23: Lang ... 9K 141
Ringwood Cl.
BN22: Eastb ... 7E 154 (1M 161)
Ringwood Ct. BN22: Eastb ... 7F 154
Ringwood Dr. TN39: Bex S ... 7K 125
Ringwood Rd.
BN22: Eastb ... 7E 154 (1M 161)
RIPE ... 5C 118
Ripe La. BN8: Ripe ... 5C 118
Ripley Chase BN21: Eastb ... 9B 154
Ripsley Cl. BN23: Lang ... 2H 155
Risden La. TN18: Hawk ... 3C 44
RISEDEN ... 1L 39
Riseden Rd. TN5: Tide, Wadh ... 9L 27
Rise Pk. Gdns. BN23: Lang ... 2G 155
Rise, The BN41: Ports ... 3B 130
RH16: Hay H ... 4J 49
RH19: E Grin ... 4F 10
TN21: Horam ... 9C 76
Risings, The BN25: Sea ... 8E 150
Rising, The BN23: Lang ... 2G 155
Rissom Ct. BN1: Brig ... 3N 131
Riverbourne Ho.
BN22: Eastb ... 8E 154 (3N 161)
Riverdale BN7: Lewes ... 4J 115
Riverhall Hill TN5: Frant ... 3J 27
River La. BN26: Alfr ... 1M 151
Riverside BN9: N'hvn ... 5K 149
BN42: S'wck ... 7A 130
RH18: F Row ... 9L 11
TN22: B'boys ... 8G 55
Riverside Bus. Cen. BN7: Lewes ... 4K 115
Riverside Ct. *BN9: N'hvn ... 5J 149*
(off North La.)
Riverside Gdns. TN6: Jar B ... 2G 37
Riverside Ho. BN9: N'hvn ... 6K 149
Riverside Ind. Est. BN7: Lewes ... 4K 115
Riverside Nth. BN9: N'hvn ... 5K 149
Riverside Sth. BN9: N'hvn ... 6K 149
River Way TN22: Uck ... 2H 73
Rixons Cl. RH17: Hors K ... 5C 32
Rixons Orchard RH17: Hors K ... 5C 32
Robert Ho. BN21: Eastb ... 2J 161
Robert Lodge BN2: Brig ... 9G 132
ROBERTSBRIDGE ... 5J 61
Robertsbridge Abbey
Remains of ... 5M 61
Robertsbridge Station (Rail) ... 5H 61
Robert's Hill TN36: Winch ... 9C 86
Robertson Pas. *TN34: Hast ... 7M 127*
(off Robertson St.)
Robertson Rd. BN1: Brig ... 3M 131
Robertsons Hill TN34: Hast ... 4A 128
Robertson St. TN34: Hast ... 7L 127
(not continuous)
Robertson Ter. TN34: Hast ... 7M 127
Robert St. BN1: Brig ... 7B 132 (6E 162)
Robert Tressell Cl.
TN34: Hast ... 5L 127
Robert Tressell Workshops
TN34: Hast ... 6M 127
Robian Cl. TN22: Mare ... 5F 52
Robin Cl. BN23: Lang ... 2F 154
RH19: E Grin ... 2F 10
Robin Ct. TN39: Bex S ... 2H 145
Robin Davis Cl. BN2: Brig ... 5F 132
Robin Dene BN2: Brig ... 9F 132
Robin Hill TN39: Bex S ... 1E 144
Robinia Lodge BN1: Brig ... 3N 131
Robinson Ct. BN22: Eastb ... 6F 154
Robinson Rd. BN9: N'hvn ... 4J 149
Robins Post La. BN26: Hails ... 3A 140
(not continuous)
BN27: Hails ... 1B 140
Robins Row BN41: Ports ... 4C 130
Robion Post La. BN26: Wilm ... 4M 139
Roborough Cl.
BN21: Eastb ... 8D 154 (3L 161)
Roborough Ct.
BN21: Eastb ... 8D 154 (3K 161)
ROBOROUGH DAY HOSPITAL
... 8D 154 (3K 161)
Robsack Av. TN38: St Leo ... 4E 126
Rochdale Rd. TN1: Tun W ... 8F 8
Rochester Cl. BN3: Hove ... 7M 131
BN20: Eastb ... 3N 159
Rochester Ct. *BN3: Hove ... 7M 131*
(off Rochester Gdns.)
Rochester Gdns. BN3: Hove ... 7M 131
Rochester Ho. *TN6: Jar B ... 1G 37*
(off Bracken Cl.)
Rochester Rd. TN37: St Leo ... 4H 127

Sackville Trad. Est.—Saltdean

Sackville Trad. Est. BN3: Hove 5J **131**
Saddlers Cl. RH15: Burg H 7E **68**
Saddler's Ct. *TN38: St Leo 8H 127*
(off Mews Rd.)
SADDLESCOMBE **3G 110**
Saddlescombe Farm Cotts.
BN45: Brig 2G **110**
Saddlescombe Rd. BN1: Brig 3G **111**
BN1: Brig 7H **111**
BN45: Newt, Poyn 1F **110**
Sadlers Way BN8: Ring 2B **116**
Sadler Way BN2: Brig 7G **132**
Saffron Gdns. BN26: Alfr 1L **151**
Saffron Ga. BN3: Hove 6L **131**
Saffrons Ct. BN20: Eastb 1B **160** (7G **161**)
Saffrons Ga.
BN20: Eastb 1C **160** (7H **161**)
Saffrons Mead
BN20: Eastb 1C **160** (7H **161**)
Saffrons Pk. BN20: Eastb 2B **160** (8G **161**)
Saffrons Rd.
BN21: Eastb 9B **154** (5G **161**)
Saffrons, The RH15: Burg H 3A **68**
St Agnes Rd. RH19: E Grin 2E **10**
St Aidan's Ct. BN22: Eastb 7F **154**
St Andrews Cl. BN27: Hails 5D **120**
St Andrew's Ct. BN9: N'hvn 5H **149**
St Andrews Ct. TN4: South 4D **8**
St Andrew's Dr. BN25: Sea 6N **149**
St Andrew's La. BN7: Lewes 5K **115**
St Andrew's Pk. Rd. TN4: South 4D **8**
St Andrews Pl. *BN7: Lewes 6K 115*
(off St Andrews La.)
St Andrew's Rd. BN1: Brig 4B **132**
BN41: Ports 6D **130**
St Andrews Rd. RH15: Burg H 4D **68**
St Andrew's Rd. TN40: Bex S 9K **125**
St Andrews Sq. *TN34: Hast 6M 127*
(off Cornwallis St.)
St Andrews Vs. *TN34: Hast 5N 127*
(off Stonefield Rd.)
St Anne's Cl. TN40: Bex S 9L **125**
St Anne's Ct. BN1: Brig 4D **162**
BN2: Brig 9D 132
(off Burlington St.)
St Anne's Cres. BN7: Lewes 6H **115**
St Anne's Gdns. BN6: Hass 4B **90**
St Annes Grn. TN19: B'wsh 3J **59**
St Anne's Ho. BN1: Brig 4D **162**
St Annes Rd. BN20: Will 1M **153**
St Anne's Rd.
BN21: Eastb 8B **154** (2G **161**)
St Annes Well Ho. BN3: Hove 7M **131**
St Ann's Ct. BN3: Hove 6M **131**
St Anns Mans. BN3: Hove 4A **162**
St Ann's Well Gardens 6M **131** (5A **162**)
St Anthonys BN8: Ring 9D **94**
St Anthony's Av. BN23: Eastb 4H **155**
ST ANTHONY'S HILL **5G 154**
St Aubyns BN3: Hove 7J **131**
TN40: Bex S 2L 145
(off Brassey Rd.)
St Aubyn's Cres. BN41: Ports 6D **130**
St Aubyn's Gdns. BN3: Hove 7J **131**
St Aubyn's Mans. *BN3: Hove 8J 131*
(off King's Esplanade)
St Aubyn's Mead BN2: Rott 3H **147**
St Aubyn's Rd.
BN22: Eastb 9E **154** (4N **161**)
BN41: Ports 6E **130**
BN41: Ports 6C **130**
St Aubyn's Sth. BN3: Hove 8J **131**
St Augustines Cl. RH17: Scay H 6N **49**
St Augustine's Cl. TN39: Bex S 2G **145**
St Barnabas Cl. TN1: Tun W 8E **8**
St Boswells Cl. BN27: Hails 6D **120**
St Brelades BN21: Eastb 7M **161**
St Bridget's TN40: Bex S 8L **125**
St Catherines Cl. TN37: St Leo 6K **127**
St Catherines Ct. RH19: E Grin 2D **10**
St Catherine's Ter. BN3: Hove 8J **131**
St Clements Ct. BN21: Eastb 6A **154**
St Crispians BN25: Sea 9C **150**
St Crispians Ct. BN25: Sea 9C **150**
St Cuthman's Cl. BN2: Brig 7F **132**
St David's Av. TN40: Bex S 9K **125**
St Davids Cl. BN22: Eastb 9G **141**
St David's Ct. BN10: Peace 4B **148**
St David's Rd. TN4: Tun W 7E **8**
St Denys BN21: Eastb 8B **154**
St Dominic Cl. TN38: St Leo 6G **126**
St Edmund's Rd. RH16: Hay H 6F **48**
St Edward's Cl. RH19: E Grin 3C **10**
St Elizabeth's BN25: Sea 8E **150**
St Francis Chase TN39: Bex S 9H **125**
St Francis Cl. RH16: Hay H 7G **48**
St George's BN8: N Cha 1D **70**
St Georges BN21: Eastb 8N **153**
St Georges Ct. RH19: E Grin 1C **10**
St George's M. BN1: Brig 7B **132** (6F **162**)
St George's Pk. TN2: Tun W 4C **16**
St George's Pl. BN1: Brig 7B **132** (5F **162**)
St George's Rd. BN2: Brig 9D **132**
BN22: Eastb 8E **154** (3N **161**)
St George's Rd. TN34: Hast 5N **127**
TN40: Bex S 9K **125**
St George's Ter. BN2: Brig 9D **132**
St Georges Vineyard 5L **75**
St Giles Cl. TN36: Winch 9C **86**
St Gregory Cl. BN20: Eastb 3B **160**
St Helena Ct. BN21: Eastb 8B **154**
St Helena La.
BN6: Plump G, Streat 8K **69**
BN7: Plump G 8K **69**
ST HELEN'S **1N 127**
St Helen's Av. TN34: Hast 3L **127**
(not continuous)
St Helen's Ct. TN34: Hast 4L **127**
St Helen's Cres. BN3: Hove 2F **130**
TN34: Hast 4L **127**
St Helen's Down TN34: Hast 3N **127**
(not continuous)
St Helen's Dr. BN3: Hove 2F **130**
St Helen's Pk. Rd. TN34: Hast 3L **127**
(Baird Dr.)
TN34: Hast 4L **127**
(Laton Rd.)
TN34: Hast 1M **127**
(Sandrock Pk.)
St Helen's Rd. BN2: Brig 6E **132**
TN34: Hast 2J **127**
ST HELEN'S WOOD **2M 127**
St Helen's Wood Rd. TN34: Hast 1L **127**
St Heliers Av. BN3: Hove 6G **131**
SAINT HILL **8D 10**
Saint Hill Grn. RH19: E Grin 8D **10**
Saint Hill Manor **8C 10**
Saint Hill Rd. RH19: E Grin 6B **10**
St Ives Ct. BN21: Eastb 8C **154** (2G **161**)
St James BN24: Nor B 5M **143**
St James' Av. TN40: Bex S 7K **125**
St James' Cl. TN40: Bex S 7K **125**
St James Ct. RH19: E Grin 3D **10**
TN1: Tun W 9E **8**
St James Cres. TN40: Bex S 7L **125**
St James' Ho. *BN2: Brig 8C 132*
(off High St.)
St James Ho. RH19: E Grin 3E **10**
St James Pk. TN1: Tun W 8F **8**
St James Rd. BN22: Eastb 8F **154** (3N **161**)
RH19: E Grin 3D **10**
St James' Rd. TN1: Tun W 8F **8**
TN40: Bex S 8K **125**
St James's Av. BN2: Brig 8C **132**
St James's La. TN22: Nut 6B **34**
St James's Pl. BN2: Brig 8B **132** (8F **162**)
St James Sq. TN5: Wadh 7C **28**
St James's Rd. TN34: Hast 5M **127**
St James's St. BN2: Brig 8B **132** (8F **162**)
St James's St. M.
BN2: Brig 8C **132** (8G **162**)
St James St. BN7: Lewes 6J **115**
St James Wlk. BN8: S Chai 7E **70**
ST JOHN'S
TN4 **8D 8**
TN6 **7B 24**
St John's Av. RH15: Burg H 5A **68**
St Johns Bank BN8: S Chai 8D **70**
St Johns Cl. *BN8: S Chai 9D 70*
(off Mill La.)
St John's Cl. RH19: E Grin 2E **10**
TN6: Crow 8C **24**
ST JOHN'S COMMON **4A 68**
St John's Dr. BN24: W'ham 7A **142**
St John's Hill BN7: Lewes 5J **115**
St Johns Ho. BN20: Eastb 9H **161**
St John's M. BN2: Brig 9D **132**
St John's Mt. *BN2: Brig 8C 132*
(off Mt. Pleasant)
St John's Pk. **5A 68**
St John's Pk. TN4: Tun W 5D **8**
St John's Pl. BN2: Brig 8C **132**
BN3: Hove 7L **131**
St John's Rd. BN3: Hove 8L **131**
BN20: Eastb 3B **160** (9H **161**)
BN25: Sea 1D **156**
BN26: Pole 7D **140**
RH15: Burg H 5B **68**
RH16: Hay H 7F **48**
RH19: E Grin 2E **10**
TN4: South, Tun W 5D **8**
TN6: Crow 6A **24**
TN37: St Leo 7J **127**
St Johns Rd. TN40: Bex S 8K **125**
St John's Ter. BN7: Lewes 5J **115**
St John St. BN7: Lewes 5K **115**
St Joseph's Cl. BN3: Hove 5J **131**
St Joseph's Trad. Est. BN3: Hove 5J **131**
St Josephs Way RH16: Hay H 5F **48**
St Keyna Av. BN3: Hove 7F **130**
St Kilda Mans. BN21: Eastb 4H **161**
St Kitts TN39: Bex S 2H **145**
St Kitts Dr. BN23: Eastb 5K **155**
St Laurence Cl. BN10: Tels C 3A **148**
St Lawrence Av. TN4: Bid 2A **8**
St Lawrence M. BN23: Eastb 3K **155**
St Lawrence Pl. BN23: Eastb 3K **155**
St Lawrence Rd. TN39: Bex S 7J **125**
St Lawrence Way BN23: Eastb 3K **155**
ST LEONARDS **7J 127**
St Leonard's Av. BN3: Hove 7E **130**
St Leonard's Cl. BN9: N'hvn 2M **149**
St Leonard's Ct. TN38: St Leo 8G **126**
St Leonards Gardens *7H 127*
(off Maze Hill)
St Leonard's Gdns. BN3: Hove 7F **130**
ST LEONARDS GREEN **5H 127**
St Leonards Pk. RH19: E Grin 3E **10**
St Leonard's Pl. BN20: Eastb 9N **153**
St Leonard's Rd. BN2: Brig 5D **132**
BN3: Hove 7E **130**
BN9: N'hvn 2M **149**
BN21: Eastb 9C **154** (4J **161**)
St Leonards Rd. TN40: Bex S 2K **145**
St Leonards Ter. BN26: Pole 6C **140**
St Leonards Warrior Square Station (Rail)
7J 127
St Louie Cl. BN42: S'wck 5C **130**
St Lucia TN39: Bex S 2H **145**
St Lucia Wlk. BN23: Eastb 4J **155**
St Lukes Ct. *RH15: Burg H 5B 68*
(off Crescent Way)
St Lukes La. BN9: N'hvn 5K **149**
St Luke's Rd. BN2: Brig 7D **132**
TN4: Tun W 7E **8**
St Luke's Swimming Pool **7D 132**
St Luke's Ter. BN2: Brig 7D **132**
St Margaret's BN2: Rott 3H **147**
St Margarets Cres. TN39: Bex S 6C **124**
St Margaret's Pl.
BN1: Brig 8A **132** (8C **162**)
St Margaret's Ri. BN25: Sea 6N **149**
St Margaret's Rd. RH19: E Grin 1F **10**
TN37: St Leo 7K **127**
St Margarets Ter *TN31: Rye 3F 86*
(off Rock Channel)
St Margaret's Ter. TN37: St Leo 7K **127**
St Marks Cl. TN39: Bex S 9E **124**
St Marks Fld. TN22: Had D 4F **54**
St Mark's M. *BN2: Brig 9F 132*
(off St Mark's St.)
St Mark's Rd. TN2: Tun W 4C **16**
St Mark's St. BN2: Brig 9F **132**
St Martins TN33: Batt 2L **103**
St Martin's Ct. *BN2: Brig 5C 132*
(off St Martin's St.)
St Martins Cres. BN9: N'hvn 3K **149**
St Martin's Flats *BN2: Brig 6D 132*
(off Picton St.)
St Martins Ho. *BN8: Ring 9D 94*
(off Lewes Rd.)
St Martin's La. BN7: Lewes 6J **115**
St Martin's Pl. BN2: Brig 6C **132**
St Martins Rd. BN22: Eastb 1A **154**
BN22: Eastb 1A **154**
St Martin's St. BN2: Brig 6C **132**
St Martins Way TN33: Batt 2L **103**
St Mary-In-The-Fields TN20: May 8E **38**
St Mary Magdalene St.
BN2: Brig 5C **132**
St Mary's BN26: Pole 7F **140**
St Mary's Av. BN27: Hails 7F **120**
St Mary's Cl. BN22: Will 2M **153**
BN25: Sea 8D **150**
TN5: Tice 1M **41**
TN31: Brede 6N **83**
St Mary's Cotts. BN20: Eastb 9A **154**
TN39: Bex S 6G **125**
St Marys Ct. BN21: Eastb 9A **154**
St Mary's Ct. *TN37: St Leo 7J 127*
(off Terrace Rd.)
St Marys Flats TN21: Cross H 1J **75**
St Marys Gth. TN22: Buxt 5A **54**
St Mary's La. TN3: Speld 5L **7**
TN5: Tice 1M **41**
TN39: Bex S 7G **124**
St Marys Mead *TN22: Buxt 6N 53*
(off Church Rd.)
St Mary's Pl. BN2: Brig 8C **132**
St Mary's Rd. BN21: Eastb 8A **154**
RH15: Burg H 4A **68**
TN34: Hast 5N **127**
St Mary's Sq. BN2: Brig 9E **132**
St Mary's Ter. TN33: Batt 4N **103**
TN34: Hast 5N **127**
St Mary's Vs. TN33: Batt 4M **103**
St Marys Wlk. *BN27: Hails 7F 120*
(off High St.)
St Mary the Virgin
Battle **3M 103**
St Matthews Ct. *BN2: Brig 8D 132*
(off College Ter.)
St Matthew's Dr. TN38: St Leo 5H **127**
St Matthews Gdns. TN38: St Leo 5H **127**
St Matthews Rd. TN38: St Leo 5H **127**
St Mellion Cl. BN27: Hails 6C **120**
St Michaels Cl. BN24: Sto C 7K **141**
TN6: Crow 2F **36**
ST MICHAEL'S HOSPICE **7H 127**
St Michael's Pl. BN1: Brig 7N **131** (6B **162**)
TN34: Hast 7L 127
(off Prospect Pl.)
St Michael's Rd. BN41: Ports 6D **130**
St Michaels Rd. RH19: E Grin 2E **10**
St Michael's Rd. TN4: Tun W 6E **8**
St Michael's Ter. BN7: Lewes 4K **115**
St Nicholas Cl. BN24: Pev 7D **142**
St Nicholas Ct. *BN1: Brig 7A 132*
(off Buckingham Rd.)
RH16: Lind 2H **49**
St Nicholas La. BN7: Lewes 5K **115**
St Nicholas Lodge BN1: Brig 7D **162**
BN1: Brig 6D **162**
St Nicholas Rd.
BN1: Brig 7A **132** (6C **162**)
BN41: Ports 6D **130**
St Olive's Cl. TN21: Cross H 1N **75**
St Pancras Gdns. BN7: Lewes 6H **115**
St Pancras Grn. BN7: King L 9D **114**
St Pancras Rd. BN7: Lewes 6H **115**
St Patricks Cres. TN40: Bex S 9K **125**
St Patrick's Rd. BN3: Hove 6J **131**
St Paul's Cl. BN22: Eastb 1A **154**
RH16: Hay H 4G **48**
St Pauls Ct. TN4: R'hall 9N **7**
St Pauls Pl. TN37: St Leo 6K **127**
St Pauls Rd. TN37: St Leo 5J **127**
St Paul's St. BN2: Brig 5C **132**
TN4: R'hall 9N **7**
ST PETER & ST JAMES HOSPICE **4M 69**
St Peter's Av. BN10: Tels C 4A **148**
St Peter's Cl. BN3: Hove 3H **131**
BN25: Sea 7D **150**
St Peter's Ct. *TN40: Bex S 9L 125*
(off De La Ware Rd.)
St Peter's Cr. TN40: Bex S 8L **125**
St Peters Mead TN6: Roth 3L **37**
St Peter's M. *TN40: Bex S 9L 125*
(off Church St.)
St Peter's Pl. BN1: Brig 7B **132** (5F **162**)
St Peters Pl. BN7: Lewes 5J **115**
St Peter's Rd. BN25: Sea 7D **150**
BN41: Ports 6D **130**
St Peters Rd. RH15: Burg H 5B **68**
St Peter's Rd. TN37: St Leo 5J **127**
St Peter's Row TN3: F'cmbe 8F **6**
St Peter's St. BN1: Brig 6B **132** (4F **162**)
St Peters St. TN2: Tun W 1F **16**
St Philips Av.
BN22: Eastb 7E **154** (1M **161**)
St Philips Ct. TN2: Tun W 7G **8**
St Philips M. BN3: Hove 6H **131**
St Raphaels TN22: Buxt 5B **54**
St Richard's Ct. BN3: Hove 4F **130**
St Richard's Flat BN41: Ports 6D **130**
St Richard's Ho. *TN38: St Leo 7J 127*
(off Pevensey Rd.)
St Richard's Rd. BN41: Ports 6D **130**
St Richards Rd. TN6: Crow 3E **36**
St Ritas BN20: Eastb 2A **160**
St Saviours *TN22: Uck 2J 73*
(off Framfield Rd.)
St Saviours Ct. BN1: Brig 2F **162**
St Saviour's Rd. TN38: St Leo 8E **126**
SAINT'S HILL **5E 6**
Saints Hill TN11: Pens 4E **6**
St Stephens Ct. TN1: Tun W 8E **8**
St Swithun's Cl. RH19: E Grin 3F **10**
St Swithuns La. BN7: Lewes 6J **115**
St Swithuns Ter. *BN7: Lewes 6J 115*
(off Stewards Inn La.)
St Thomas TN39: Bex S 2H **145**
St Thomas's Rd. TN34: Hast 5N **127**
St Thomas' St. TN36: Winch 9D **86**
St Vincents Flats TN37: St Leo 2H **127**
St Vincents Pl. BN20: Eastb 2B **160**
St Vincents Rd. TN38: St Leo 7F **126**
St Wilfred's Grn. BN27: Hails 6F **120**
St Wilfreds Rd. RH15: Burg H 4C **68**
St Wilfrid's Ct. RH16: Hay H 5F **48**
St Wilfrid's Flat *BN2: Brig 6D 132*
(off Whippingham Rd.)
ST WILFRID'S HOSPICE **8C 154** (3H **161**)
St Wilfrids Pl. BN25: Sea 9G **150**
St Wilfrid's Way RH16: Hay H 5F **48**
Salamons Rd. TN4: R'hall 9N **7**
Salcey Cl. TN38: St Leo 4E **126**
SALEHURST **4L 61**
Salehurst Gdns. TN38: St Leo 4D **126**
Salehurst Rd. BN21: Eastb 9N **153**
Salisbury Cl. BN22: Will 2N **153**
Salisbury Rd. BN3: Hove 7L **131**
BN20: Eastb 3N **159**
BN25: Sea 9D **150**
TN3: Lang G 1K **15**
TN4: Tun W 5F **8**
TN37: St Leo 5J **127**
TN40: Bex S 9J **125**
Salisbury Ter. *TN21: Cross H 9M 55*
(off Firgrove Rd.)
Salisbury Yd. *TN37: St Leo 5J 127*
(off Salisbury Rd.)
Salmans La. TN11: Pens 1E **6**
Saltcote La. TN31: Rye 1G **86**
Saltcote M. TN31: Rye 1G **86**
SALTDEAN **2K 147**

Southwick Sq.—Stone Hill

Southwick Sq. BN42: S'wck . . . 6A 130
Southwick Station (Rail) . . . 6A 130
Southwick St. BN42: S'wck . . . 6A 130
Southwick Tunnel
BN42: S'wck . . . 2A 130
BN43: Shor S . . . 2A 130
Southwood Av. TN4: Tun W . . . 7D 8
Southwood Cl. TN38: St Leo . . . 5G 127
Sth. Woodlands BN1: Brig . . . 9N 111
Southwood Rd. TN4: R'hall . . . 8M 7
Sovereign Cen. BN22: Eastb . . . 6H 155
Sovereign Cl. BN25: Sea . . . 7F 150
TN34: Hast . . . 2N 127
Sovereign Ct. BN2: Brig . . . 1B 146
BN22: Eastb . . . 7F 154
TN40: Bex S . . . 9M 125
SOVEREIGN HARBOUR . . . 3K 155
Sovereign Harbour Marina . . . 4K 155
Sovereign Harbour Retail Pk.
BN23: Eastb . . . 3J 155
Sovereign Ho. BN21: Eastb . . . 6M 161
Sovereign Rdbt. BN22: Eastb . . . 6H 155
Spa Ct. *BN3: Hove* . . . *8K 131*
(off King's Esplanade)
Spa Ind. Pk. TN2: Tun W . . . 5H 9
Spaldings, The TN38: St Leo . . . 5E 126
Spa Lea RH17: Cuck . . . 3A 48
Spanish Ct. RH15: Burg H . . . 4C 68
Sparke Gdns. TN33: Nin . . . 9B 102
SPARROW'S GREEN . . . 6B 28
Sparrows Grn. Rd. TN5: Wadh . . . 6B 28
Sparrows, The BN10: Peace . . . 3D 148
Spatham La. BN6: Ditch . . . 5G 90
Spa Valley Railway . . . 5H 15
Speckled Wood TN35: Hast . . . 3B 128
SPELDHURST . . . 5L 7
Speldhurst Hill TN3: Speld . . . 6L 7
Speldhurst Rd. TN3: Lang G . . . 9J 7
TN4: South . . . 5A 8
Spelmonden Rd. TN12: Hors . . . 1N 19
Spencer Av. BN3: Hove . . . 2F 130
Spencer Ct. BN21: Eastb . . . 7K 161
Spencer Ho. BN21: Eastb . . . 7K 161
Spencer M. *TN1: Tun W* . . . *2D 16*
(off Berkeley Rd.)
Spencer Rd. BN21: Eastb . . . 1D 160 (7K 161)
Spences Ct. BN7: Lewes . . . 4L 115
Spences Fld. BN7: Lewes . . . 3L 115
Spences La. BN7: Lewes . . . 4K 115
Spicers Cl. RH15: Burg H . . . 3A 68
Spindlewood Country Holiday Pk.
TN35: Hast . . . 1B 128
Spindlewood Dr. TN39: Bex S . . . 1D 144
Spinneys, The BN7: Lewes . . . 4L 115
TN21: H'fld . . . 2E 76
Spinney, The BN3: Hove . . . 2L 131
BN6: Hass . . . 2A 90
BN27: Chal . . . 3F 118
RH15: Burg H . . . 3C 68
Spinney, The RH16: Hay H . . . 6G 49
(Eastern Rd.)
RH16: Hay H . . . 1E 48
(Penland Rd.)
TN32: Rob . . . 6G 61
TN33: Batt . . . 4N 103
TN34: Hast . . . 5L 127
TN39: Bex S . . . 2E 144
Spire Cl. BN7: Plump G . . . 9M 69
Spital Rd. BN7: Lewes . . . 5G 115
SPITHURST . . . 9M 71
Spithurst Rd.
BN8: Barc, Barc C, Isf, N'wck . . . 2L 93
SPLAYNE'S GREEN . . . 4N 51
Spode La. TN8: C'den . . . 4E 4
Sponden La. TN18: Sandh . . . 2F 44
Spooners Indoors Bowls Club
RH19: E Grin . . . 6E 10
Sportcentre Rd. BN1: Falm . . . 8H 113
Spotted Cow La. TN22: Buxt . . . 4C 54
Spout Hill TN6: Town R . . . 9A 26
Spratts La. TN33: Cats . . . 2G 124
Spray Hill TN3: Lamb . . . 7K 19
Spray's La. TN33: Sed . . . 3H 105
Springate Rd. BN42: S'wck . . . 5B 130
Spring Cl. BN20: Will . . . 3M 153
Spring Copse RH19: E Grin . . . 1F 10
Springett Almshouses TN18: Hawk . . . 2M 43
Springett Av. BN8: Ring . . . 1C 116
Springett Cotts. BN8: Ring . . . 9C 94
Springfield RH19: E Grin . . . 1D 10
Springfield Av. BN10: Tels C . . . 4N 147
Springfield Cl. BN24: W'ham . . . 7B 142
TN6: Crow . . . 9F 24
Springfield Ind. Est. TN18: Hawk . . . 8N 31
Springfield Pl. *TN3: Groom* . . . *5G 14*
(off Corseley Rd.)
Springfield Rd.
BN1: Brig . . . 5A 132 (2D 162)
BN22: Eastb . . . 8E 154 (2N 161)
TN3: Groom . . . 5G 14
TN4: South . . . 4C 8
TN38: St Leo . . . 5H 127
TN40: Bex S . . . 8K 125
Springfields Arches Ri. TN5: Tice . . . 1N 41
Springfields Farm Ind. Est.
RH17: Burg H . . . 3G 69
Springfield Valley TN38: St Leo . . . 5H 127
Spring Gdns. BN1: Brig . . . 8B 132 (7D 162)
BN7: Lewes . . . 5K 115
BN8: Bedd . . . 9E 116
BN42: S'wck . . . 6A 130
TN4: R'hall . . . 9M 7
Springhead TN2: Tun W . . . 8G 8
Springhead Way TN6: Crow . . . 2C 36
Spring Hill TN3: F'cmbe . . . 7E 6
TN11: Pens . . . 6E 6
TN31: North . . . 2A 64
Spring La. BN6: Clay . . . 7A 90
RH16: Lind . . . 1J 49
TN3: Bid . . . 2N 7
TN19: B'wsh . . . 1D 58
TN20: F Ashes . . . 4L 55
TN39: Bex S . . . 9D 124
Spring Lodge Cl. BN23: Lang . . . 2H 155
Spring Mdw. RH18: F Row . . . 2M 21
Spring Pk. TN21: H'fld . . . 9D 56
Springshaw Ct. TN2: Tun W . . . 7G 8
Springside Wlk. TN38: St Leo . . . 5F 126
Spring Steps *TN36: Winch* . . . *8D 86*
(off Barrack Sq.)
Spring St. BN1: Brig . . . 8N 131 (7B 162)
TN37: St Leo . . . 5J 127
Springwood Rd. TN21: H'fld . . . 9C 56
Spruce Cl. BN22: Eastb . . . 2A 154
Spur Rd. BN26: Pole . . . 8E 140
Spurway Pk. BN26: Pole . . . 8E 140
Spurway, The TN4: Tun W . . . 2A 16
Squab La. BN27: Mag D . . . 1K 121
Square, The BN1: Brig . . . 8N 111
BN24: Pev B . . . 7H 143
BN27: Hails . . . 7D 120
TN6: Roth . . . 2M 37
TN8: C'den . . . 7G 4
Squires Farm Ind. Est.
TN22: Fram . . . 6B 74
Squirrel Cl. TN38: St Leo . . . 3F 126
TN39: Bex S . . . 9F 124
Squirrel Drey BN27: Chal . . . 3F 118
Squirrel La. BN27: Herst . . . 1L 121
Squirrel Wlk. BN27: Chal . . . 3F 118
Squirrel Way TN2: Tun W . . . 8H 9
Sreet, The BN8: W Firle . . . 1G 136
(not continuous)
Stabledene Way TN2: Pem . . . 7N 9
Stable Fld. TN35: W'fld . . . 3L 105
Stable M. TN37: St Leo . . . 1J 127
Stables La. BN21: Eastb . . . 5K 161
Stable Theatre . . . *6A 128*
(off Bourne, The)
Stade, The . . . 7A 128
Stafford Ct. *BN23: Lang* . . . *3H 155*
(off Etchingham Rd.)
BN25: Sea . . . *9D 150*
(off Stafford Rd.)
Stafford Ho. BN21: Eastb . . . 5J 161
Stafford Rd. BN1: Brig . . . 5N 131 (2B 162)
BN25: Sea . . . 9D 150
TN2: Tun W . . . 9H 9
Stafford Way BN6: Hass . . . 4B 90
Stag Rd. TN2: Tun W . . . 5G 9
Stainsby St. TN37: St Leo . . . 7J 127
Stalkers La. BN8: C'gly, E Hoath . . . 1H 97
Stamford *RH16: Hay H* . . . *3E 48*
(off Great Heathmead)
Stamford Bldgs. BN8: W Firle . . . 9K 117
Stamford Ct. TN35: Hast . . . 4C 128
Stamford Lodge *BN1: Brig* . . . *3N 131*
(off Cumberland Rd.)
Stammers Hill BN5: Fulk . . . 3B 110
STANDARD HILL . . . 9A 102
Standard Hill Cl. TN33: Nin . . . 9A 102
STANDEAN . . . 5A 112
Standean Cl. BN1: Brig . . . 8E 112
Standen . . . 8D 10
Standen Cl. RH19: E Grin . . . 1A 10
STANDEN STREET . . . 1L 45
Standen St. TN4: Tun W . . . 8D 8
TN17: Ben, Sandh . . . 1K 45
Stanford Av. BN1: Brig . . . 5A 132 (1D 162)
Stanford Cl. BN3: Hove . . . 4L 131
Stanford Ct. BN1: Brig . . . 2D 162
Stanford Rd. BN1: Brig . . . 5N 131 (1B 162)
Stanhope Cvn. Pk. TN36: Winch . . . 2E 108
Stanhope Ct. BN20: Eastb . . . 9H 161
Stanhope Pl. TN38: St Leo . . . 8J 127
Stanhope Rd. TN1: Tun W . . . 8F 8
Stanier Rd. TN38: St Leo . . . 1F 126
Stanley Av. BN41: Ports . . . 1B 130
Stanley Av. Sth. BN41: Ports . . . 2B 130
Stanley Deason Leisure Cen. . . . 8G 133
Stanley Rd. BN1: Brig . . . 6B 132 (3E 162)
BN10: Peace . . . 3B 148
BN22: Eastb . . . 8E 154 (2N 161)
BN41: Ports . . . 5C 130
TN1: Tun W . . . 8E 8
TN34: Hast . . . 6L 127
Stanley St. BN2: Brig . . . 8C 132
STANMER . . . 6G 112
Stanmer Av. BN2: Salt . . . 1L 147
Stanmer Ct. *BN1: Brig* . . . *3B 132*
(off Stanmer Pk. Rd.)
Stanmer Dr. BN22: Will . . . 3A 154
Stanmer Ho. *BN1: Brig* . . . *3B 132*
(off Stanmer Pk. Rd.)
BN21: Eastb . . . 1C 160 (7J 161)
Stanmer House (Mus.) . . . 7G 112
Stanmer Pk. Rd. BN1: Brig . . . 3B 132
Stanmer St. BN1: Brig . . . 3C 132
Stanmer Vs. BN1: Brig . . . 2C 132
Stansfield Rd. BN7: Lewes . . . 4H 115
Stanstead Cres. BN2: W'dean . . . 7N 133
Stansted Rd.
BN22: Eastb . . . 8D 154 (2L 161)
Stanton Dr. RH15: Burg H . . . 4A 68
Stanton Prior BN20: Eastb . . . 3A 160
STAPLECROSS . . . 8E 62
Staplefield Dr. BN2: Brig . . . 2G 132
Stapley Ct. BN3: Hove . . . 5F 130
Stapley Rd. BN3: Hove . . . 5F 130
Starboard Ct. BN2: Brig . . . 1A 146
Starfield TN6: Crow . . . 1C 36
Star Gallery . . . *5J 115*
(off Fisher St.)
Star La. BN26: Alfr . . . 1M 151
TN20: May . . . 8E 38
TN22: B'boys . . . 2F 74
Star M. *TN20: May* . . . *8E 38*
(off High St.)
Star Rd. BN21: Eastb . . . 9B 154
Starrs Cotts. *TN34: Hast* . . . *6A 128*
(off All Saints' St.)
Starrs Grn. La. TN33: Batt . . . 4N 103
Starrs Mead TN33: Batt . . . 4N 103
Starvecrow La. TN31: Peas . . . 2G 84
Starwell Cl. TN34: Hast . . . 3K 127
Station App. BN1: Falm . . . 8J 113
BN3: Hove . . . 5K 131
BN22: Eastb . . . 3C 154
BN25: Sea . . . 9D 150
RH17: Ard, Hors K . . . 4A 32
TN1: Tun W . . . 1D 16
TN19: Etch . . . 9D 42
TN20: May . . . 8C 38
TN21: H'fld . . . 1D 76
TN31: Rye . . . 3F 86
TN33: Batt . . . 4M 103
TN34: Hast . . . 6L 127
TN37: St Leo . . . 7J 127
Station App. E. BN6: Hass . . . 3A 90
Station Cl. BN7: Plump G . . . 2M 91
TN6: Town R . . . 1N 37
Station Cotts. BN6: Hass . . . 3A 90
Station Hill TN5: Wadh . . . 4M 27
Station Pde. BN21: Eastb . . . 5J 161
Station Rd. BN1: Brig . . . 2M 131
(not continuous)
BN7: Lewes . . . 6K 115
BN7: Plump G . . . 1M 91
Station Rd. BN8: N'wck, N Cha . . . 1E 70
BN9: N'hvn . . . 3M 149
BN25: Sea . . . 8A 150
BN26: B'wck . . . 6E 138
BN26: Pole . . . 6D 140
BN27: Hails . . . 7E 120
BN27: Hell . . . 1D 120
BN41: Ports . . . 7E 130
BN42: S'wck . . . 6A 130
RH15: Burg H . . . 6A 68
(not continuous)
RH17: Hors K . . . 5C 32
RH18: F Row . . . 9M 11
RH19: E Grin . . . 3D 10
RH19: Sharp . . . 5A 20
TN3: Groom . . . 5G 14
TN5: S'gate . . . 7F 40
TN5: Wadh . . . 4L 27
(not continuous)
TN6: Roth . . . 2M 37
TN7: Withy . . . 8N 13
TN8: C'den . . . 6H 5
TN19: Hur G . . . 7G 43
TN20: May . . . 8C 38
TN21: H'fld . . . 1D 76
TN22: Buxt . . . 6L 53
TN22: Isf . . . 7C 72
TN31: North . . . 2A 64
TN32: Rob . . . 6H 61
TN33: C'hrst . . . 1N 125
TN34: Hast . . . *7M 127*
(off Queen's Rd.)
TN34: Hast . . . 6M 127
(Devonshire Rd.)
TN36: Winch . . . 7C 86
TN40: Bex S . . . 1K 145
Station Rd. Ind. Est. BN27: Hails . . . 8F 120
Station Rdbt.
BN21: Eastb . . . 9C 154 (5J 161)
Station St. BN1: Brig . . . 7B 132 (5E 162)
BN7: Lewes . . . 5K 115
BN21: Eastb . . . 9D 154 (5J 161)
Staveley Ct. *BN20: Eastb* . . . *3B 160*
(off Staveley Rd.)
Staveley Mead *BN20: Eastb* . . . *3B 160*
(off Buxton Rd.)
Staveley Rd. BN20: Eastb . . . 3B 160
Steelands Ri. TN5: Tice . . . 1A 42
STEEL CROSS . . . 7F 24
Steep Hill TN31: Brede . . . 6K 83
Steeple Grange BN21: Eastb . . . 8B 154
Steep Rd. TN6: Crow, Roth . . . 4G 36
Steine Gardens . . . 9F 162
Steine Gdns. BN2: Brig . . . 8B 132 (8F 162)
Steine La. BN1: Brig . . . 8E 162
Steine St. BN2: Brig . . . 9B 132 (9F 162)
Stennings, The RH19: E Grin . . . 2C 10
Stephens Cl. BN8: Ring . . . 1C 116
Stephenson Dr. RH19: E Grin . . . 5F 10
Stephens Rd. BN1: Brig . . . 3C 132
Stephen's Rd. TN4: Tun W . . . 7D 8
Stevens Cl. TN39: Bex S . . . 7K 125
Stevens Ct. BN3: Hove . . . 6G 130
STEVEN'S CROUCH . . . 4C 102
Stevenson Cl. BN23: Lang . . . 1H 155
Stevenson Rd. BN2: Brig . . . 8D 132
TN37: St Leo . . . 3H 127
Stewards Inn La. BN7: Lewes . . . 6J 115
Stewart Rd. TN4: Tun W . . . 6F 8
Steyne Cl. BN25: Sea . . . 1E 156
Steyne Ct. BN25: Sea . . . 1D 156
Steyne Rd. BN25: Sea . . . 1D 156
Steyne, The BN25: Sea . . . 1D 156
Steyning Av. BN3: Hove . . . 2H 131
BN10: Peace . . . 6C 148
(not continuous)
Steyning Cl. BN25: Sea . . . 1H 157
Steyning Ct. BN3: Hove . . . 6K 131
Steyning Rd. BN2: Rott . . . 3G 147
BN25: Sea . . . 1H 157
Sth Cliff Av. BN20: Eastb . . . 2C 160 (9J 161)
STICK HILL . . . 2F 4
Stiles, The BN27: Hails . . . 7F 120
Still La. TN4: South . . . 3C 8
Stirling Av. BN25: Sea . . . 8H 151
Stirling Cl. BN25: Sea . . . 9H 151
RH15: Burg H . . . 4D 68
Stirling Ct. BN3: Hove . . . 6L 131
BN23: Lang . . . 3H 155
Stirling Ct. Rd.
RH15: Burg H . . . 4D 68
Stirling Pl. BN3: Hove . . . 6J 131
Stirling Rd. TN38: St Leo . . . 1F 126
Stirling Way RH19: E Grin . . . 1H 11
St-Mary-In-The-Castle Theatre & Arts Cen.
. . . 7N 127
Stock Dale TN35: Fair . . . 2L 129
STOCKLAND GREEN . . . 4N 7
Stockland Grn. Rd.
TN3: South, Tun W . . . 5M 7
Stockland La. TN22: Had D . . . 3F 54
Stocklands Cl. RH17: Cuck . . . 1A 48
Stockleigh Rd. TN38: St Leo . . . 7J 127
Stocks Mdw. TN33: Nin . . . 1C 124
Stockwell Ct. RH15: Burg H . . . 5A 68
RH16: Hay H . . . *6F 48*
(off Gower Rd.)
Stockwell Rd. RH19: E Grin . . . 6E 10
Stoddards La. TN31: Buck . . . 4D 64
Stoke Cl. BN25: Sea . . . 9G 150
Stoke Mnr. Cl. BN25: Sea . . . 8G 150
Stokes Ho. *TN39: Bex S* . . . *1H 145*
(off Sutherland Av.)
Stonebeach Ri. TN38: St Leo . . . 8E 104
Stonebridge La. TN22: B'boys . . . 3D 74
Stonecott Cl. TN6: Crow . . . 2D 36
Stone Ct. La. TN2: Pem . . . 5N 9
Stonecroft Cl. BN3: Hove . . . 1G 130
STONE CROSS
BN24 . . . 8M 141
TN3 . . . 2D 14
TN5 . . . 8C 28
TN6 . . . 4D 36
Stone Cross TN20: May . . . 8C 38
Stone Cross Bus. Cen.
BN8: Laug . . . 9C 96
Stonecross Rd. BN2: Brig . . . 1G 132
Stone Cross Rd. TN5: Wadh . . . 7C 28
TN6: Crow . . . 4D 36
Stone Cross Towermill
BN24: Sto C . . . 8L 141
STONECROUCH . . . 4A 30
Stonedene Cl. RH18: F Row . . . 1A 22
Stonefield Pl. TN34: Hast . . . 6M 127
Stonefield Rd. TN34: Hast . . . 6M 127
Stonefield Way RH15: Burg H . . . 3A 68
STONEGATE . . . 4H 41
Stonegate Cl. BN23: Lang . . . 9K 141
Stonegate Ct. TN5: S'gate . . . 5H 41
Stonegate Rd. TN5: Wadh . . . 1E 40
Stonegate Station (Rail) . . . 7F 40
Stonegate Way TN21: H'fld . . . 9E 56
STONEHAM . . . 2L 115
Stoneham Cl. BN7: Lewes . . . 3J 115
Stoneham Rd. BN3: Hove . . . 6H 131
Stonehaven Ct. *TN40: Bex S* . . . *2L 145*
(off Knole Rd.)
Stone Hill RH19: E Grin . . . 1C 20

Stonehouse Dr.—Teise Cl.

Stonehouse Dr.
TN33: Batt, St Leo 7F 104
TN38: St Leo 4G 126
TN38: St Leo 7F 104
Stonehurst Ct. BN2: Brig 7D 132
Stonehurst La. TN20: F Ashes 9H 37
TN22: Had D, Roth 3G 55
Stoneleigh Av. BN1: Brig 8A 112
Stoneleigh Cl. BN1: Brig 8A 112
RH19: E Grin 3F 10
Stonelink Cl. TN37: St Leo 8F 104
Stonepark Dr. RH18: F Row 1N 21
Stone Pit La. TN18: Sandh 5L 45
STONEQUARRY 1G 10
Stone Quarry Rd.
RH17: Chel C, Chel G 4J 33
Stone Row TN3: F'cmbe 8F 6
Stonery Cl. BN41: Ports 3C 130
(not continuous)
Stonery Rd. BN41: Ports 3C 130
Stonestile La. TN35: Hast, W'fld 4L 105
Stone St. BN1: Brig 8N 131 (7B 162)
TN1: Tun W 9E 8
TN34: Hast 6M 127
Stonewall Pk. Rd. TN3: Lang G 1K 15
Stonewood Cl. BN25: Sea 8H 151
TN4: Tun W 5D 8
Stoneworks Cotts. *TN31: Rye 5K 87*
(off Rye Harbour Rd.)
Stoney Down *BN20: Eastb 3B 160*
(off Milnthorpe Rd.)
Stoney La. BN27: Hails 7F 120
Storrington Cl. BN3: Hove 3G 131
Story of Rye, The *3F 86*
(off Deals, The)
Stour Cl. BN24: Sto C 8J 141
Stour Cft. BN8: N'wck 1K 71
Straight Half Mile TN22: Mare 4G 52
Straight La. TN33: Hooe 4A 124
Straight Mile TN19: Etch 1A 60
Strand TN31: Rye 3F 86
Strand Ct. *TN31: Rye 3F 86*
(off Deals, The)
Strand Hill TN36: Winch 9D 86
Strand Mdw. TN19: B'wsh 2K 59
Strand Quay *TN31: Rye 3F 86*
(off Deals, The)
Strand, The BN2: Brig 1A 146
TN36: Winch 8D 86
Stratford Ho. BN21: Eastb 4M 161
Stratford St. TN1: Tun W 1F 16
Stratheden Ct. BN25: Sea 1D 156
Strathfield Cl. RH16: Hay H 5G 48
Strathmore Ct. *TN40: Bex S 2M 145*
(off De La Warr Pde.)
Strawberry Cl. TN2: Tun W 4B 16
Strawberry Flds. TN31: North 2N 63
Strawberry Hill TN3: Tun W 6A 16
Strawlands BN7: Plump G 1M 91
Stream La. TN18: Hawk 3N 43
TN33: Sed, What 6B 82
TN35: Fair 9M 107
Stream Pk. RH19: E Grin 1A 10
Streampit La. TN18: Sandh 5H 45
Streamside Cl. TN34: Hast 3L 127
Stream, The TN31: North 6B 64
TN33: Cats 9E 102
STREAT 4K 91
Streat Bostall BN6: Streat 8K 91
Streatfield Gdns. TN21: H'fld 9D 56
Streatfield Ho. TN22: Uck 9H 53
Streatfield Rd. TN21: H'fld 9C 56
TN22: Uck 1G 72
Streat La. BN6: Streat 7K 91
Streele La. TN22: Fram 8B 54
Streele Vw. TN22: Uck 9K 53
Street End La. TN20: B Oak, May 8H 39
TN21: B Oak 2H 57
STREETER'S ROUGH 3L 33
Streetlands TN33: Sed 7E 82
Street, The BN5: Fulk 3B 110
BN6: W'ton 7G 91
BN7: King L 9E 114
BN8: Glyn 7E 116
BN8: Ripe 5B 118
BN26: Arl 3J 139
BN26: Lit, Lull 4M 151
BN26: Milt S, Wilm 1A 152
BN26: Selm 3B 138
BN45: Poyn 2E 110
Street, The TN21: Dall 5F 78
TN22: Fram 3N 73
TN33: Sed 7D 82
Stretton Ct. *BN3: Hove 6H 131*
(off Rutland Gdns.)
Stringer Way BN1: Brig 2A 132
(not continuous)
Stringwalk, The BN27: Hails 7F 120
Stroma Gdns. BN27: Hails 4C 120
Strome Ho. TN39: Bex S 7K 125
Strongs Pas *TN34: Hast 6A 128*
(off Tackleway)
Strood Ga. RH17: Wivel G 3K 69
Strood Rd. TN37: St Leo 4J 127
Stroudley Ct. *RH19: E Grin 2F 10*
(off Badger's Way)
Stuart Av. BN21: Eastb 6N 153
Stuart Cl. TN2: Tun W 4C 16
Stuart Way RH19: E Grin 5F 10
Stubb La. TN31: Brede, B Oak 7A 84
Stud Cotts. BN27: Up D 6L 119
Studdens La.
BN27: Cowb, Herst 8M 99
Stud Farm Stables, The
BN26: Pole 7B 140
STUNTS GREEN 8N 99
Sturdee Cl. BN23: Eastb 5J 155
Sturdee Pl. TN34: Hast 7N 127
Sturton Pl. BN27: Hails 7E 120
Sudeley Pl. BN2: Brig 9E 132
Sudeley St. BN2: Brig 9E 132
Sudeley Ter. BN2: Brig 9E 132
Suffolk Ct. BN22: Eastb 8F 154
Suffolk Ho. TN40: Bex S 2L 145
Suffolk Rd. TN39: Bex S 7K 125
Suffolk St. BN3: Hove 5H 131
Sugar La. RH17: Hors K 5C 32
Sugar Loaf, The 4H 79
Sugworth Cl. RH16: Hay H 2E 48
Sullington Cl. BN2: Brig 1G 132
Sumach Cl. BN22: Eastb 2B 154
Summer Cl. BN41: Ports 6C 130
Summer Ct. BN20: Eastb 4A 160
BN27: Hails 6E 120
Summerdale Rd. BN3: Hove 3F 130
Summerdown Cl. BN20: Eastb 9A 154
Summerdown La. BN20: E Dean 2G 158
Summerdown Rd. BN20: Eastb 9N 153
Summerfields Av. BN27: Hails 6E 120
Summerfields Leisure Cen. 6K 127
Summerheath Rd. BN27: Hails 6E 120
SUMMER HILL 2D 140
Summerhill TN5: Tice 1J 41
Summer Hill TN38: St Leo 6G 127
Summerhill Av. TN4: South 4C 8
Summerhill Cl. RH16: Hay H 2G 48
Summerhill Dr. RH16: Lind 2G 49
Summerhill Grange RH16: Lind 2G 49
Summer Hill La. BN27: Hails 2C 140
Summerhill La. RH16: Hay H 2G 49
Summer Hill Rd. TN39: Bex S 8G 124
Summerlands Rd. BN22: Will 2M 153
Summersdeane BN42: S'wck 4B 130
Summervale Rd. TN4: Tun W 3A 16
Sunhill Ct. TN2: Pem 7M 9
Sun La. TN34: Hast 7N 127
Sunningdale Cl. BN25: Sea 1F 156
BN27: Hails 5D 120
TN40: Bex S 1M 145
Sunningdale Dr. TN38: St Leo 7F 126
Sunninghill Av. BN3: Hove 3G 131
Sunninghill Cl. BN3: Hove 3G 131
Sunnybank TN5: Flim 8F 30
TN31: Peas 7N 65
Sunnybank Cl. *TN20: May 8E 38*
(off Fletching St.)
Sunnybrooke Cl. TN22: Uck 1J 73
Sunnycroft Cl. RH17: Scay H 6M 49
Sunnydale Av. BN1: Brig 8B 112
Sunnydale Cl. BN1: Brig 8B 112
Sunnymead BN20: Eastb 3B 160
SUNNYSIDE .5E 10
Sunnyside TN5: Tice 1M 41
Sunnyside Pk. BN25: Sea 8A 150
Sunnyside Rd. TN4: R'hall 9N 7
Sunnywood Ct. RH16: Hay H 6E 48
Sunnywood Dr. RH16: Hay H 6E 48
Sun Patch BN27: Hails 7F 120
Sunset Av. BN27: Chal 3F 118
Sunset Cl. BN10: Tels C 2B 148
BN24: Pev B 7G 143
Sunstar La. BN26: Pole 7B 140
Sun St. BN7: Lewes 5J 115
Sunte Av. RH16: Lind 2G 49
Sunte Cl. RH16: Hay H 2F 48
Sunview Av. BN10: Peace 6D 148
(not continuous)
Surrendean Ct. *BN1: Brig 2A 132*
(off Varndean Gdns.)
Surrenden Cl. BN1: Brig 1A 132
Surrenden Cres. BN1: Brig 2N 131
Surrenden Holt BN1: Brig 2A 132
Surrenden Lodge BN1: Brig 3A 132
Surrenden Pk. BN1: Brig 1B 132
Surrenden Rd. BN1: Brig 2A 132
Surrey Cl. BN25: Sea 8B 150
TN2: Tun W 4C 16
Surrey Ho. BN2: Brig 9E 132
Surrey Rd. BN25: Sea 8B 150
Surrey St. BN1: Brig 7A 132 (5D 162)
Susans Cl. BN8: E Hoath 2E 96
Susan's Rd. BN21: Eastb 9D 154 (4L 161)
Sussex Av. BN27: Hails 6E 120
SUSSEX BEACON (HOSPICE), THE . . .4F 132
Sussex Border Path TN18: Hawk 1L 43
Sussex Cl. BN27: Hails 6E 120
TN2: Tun W 3F 16
TN39: Bex S 9G 124
Sussex County Cricket Ground 6L 131
Sussex Ct. BN3: Hove 7L 131
BN22: Eastb 7E 154
RH16: Hay H 6F 48
TN40: Bex S 1L 145
SUSSEX EYE HOSPITAL 9E 132
Sussex Gdns. BN20: E Dean 2G 158
Sussex Hgts. BN1: Brig 8B 162
Sussex Ho. BN10: Tels C 5N 147
BN21: Eastb 6L 161
RH15: Burg H 6B 68
RH16: Hay H 3F 48
(off Perrymount Rd.)
Sussex Ho. Bus. Pk. BN3: Hove 5H 131
Sussex Mans. BN21: Eastb 6K 161
Sussex M. BN2: Brig 9F 132
TN2: Tun W 2D 16
SUSSEX NUFFIELD HOSPITAL 5K 133
Sussex Pl. BN2: Brig 7C 132 (6F 162)
BN27: Herst 9A 100
Sussex Rd. BN3: Hove 8K 131
RH16: Hay H 6F 48
TN38: St Leo 8G 127
Sussex Sq. BN2: Brig 9F 132
RH16: Hay H 5F 48
Sussex St. BN2: Brig 7C 132
Sussex Ter. BN2: Brig 7C 132
Sussex Toy & Model Mus.
. . . . .7B 132 (5E 162)
Sussex University Sports Cen. 8H 113
Sussex Way BN10: Tels C 5N 147
RH15: Burg H 3A 68
Sussex Yacht Club 7B 130
Sutherland Av. TN39: Bex S 2H 145
Sutherland Cl. TN39: Bex S 1H 145
Sutherland Rd. BN2: Brig 8D 132
TN1: Tun W 1E 16
TN39: Bex S 1H 145
Sution Wall BN7: Ifrd 2J 135
SUTTON 8G 150
Sutton Av. BN10: Peace 5B 148
BN25: Sea 1F 156
Sutton Av. Nth. BN10: Peace 4B 148
Sutton Cl. BN2: W'dean 4M 133
Sutton Cotts. BN7: Ifrd 2H 135
Sutton Cft. La. BN25: Sea 9D 150
Sutton Drove BN25: Sea 8E 150
Sutton Ho. *BN20: Eastb 2B 160*
(off Meads Rd.)
Sutton Pk. Rd. BN25: Sea 9D 150
Sutton Pl. BN25: Sea 8G 150
TN40: Bex S 1M 145
Sutton Rd. BN21: Eastb 9D 154 (5K 161)
BN25: Sea 9D 150
Suttons Ind. Pk. TN36: Winch 9E 86
Suttons, The TN31: Camb 7D 88
TN38: St Leo 4F 126
SWAILE'S GREEN 1C 82
Swaine's Pas. *TN34: Hast 6A 128*
(off All Saints' St.)
Swaines Way TN21: H'fld 2D 76
Swainham La. TN38: St Leo 3A 126
Swainsthorpe Cl. RH16: Hay H 6G 48
Swale Cl. BN24: Sto C 8K 141
Swallow Bank TN38: St Leo 4F 126
Swallow Cl. BN23: Lang 2E 154
Swallow Ct. *BN2: Brig 6G 132*
(off Albourne Cl.)
TN22: Uck 3J 73
Swallow Dr. TN2: Tun W 7J 9
TN33: Batt 3N 103
Swallows, The BN10: Tels C 3B 148
Swan Av. TN34: Hast 6N 127
Swan Barn Bus. Cen. BN27: Hails 8G 120
Swan Barn Cvn. Site BN27: Down 9G 120
Swanborough Dr. BN2: Brig 6G 132
Swanborough Drove BN7: King L 2F 134
Swanborough Hollow
BN7: Ifrd, King L 9G 114
Swanborough Pl. BN2: Brig 6G 132
Swan Cl. BN8: S Chai 9E 70
Swan Ct. BN8: S Chai 9E 70
Swanley Cl. BN23: Lang 2G 154
Swann Cl. RH15: Burg H 5E 68
Swannee Cl. BN10: Peace 3D 148
Swan Rd. BN27: Hails 8F 120
Swansbrook La.
TN21: Gun H, Horam 6A 98
Swans Ghyll RH18: F Row 9L 11
Swan St. TN30: Witter 7N 47
Swan Ter. TN34: Hast 6N 127
Swattenden La. TN17: Cran 1N 31
Swaylands Av. TN6: Crow 3D 36
Sweda Ct. BN2: Brig 9E 132
Sweeps Hill Cl. TN2: Pem 6N 9
SWEETHAWS 4A 36
Sweethaws La. TN6: Crow 4A 36
Sweetings La. TN3: Cous W 2F 28
TN5: Cous W 2F 28
Sweetlands BN6: Hass 2C 90
Swife La. TN20: May 2A 58
TN21: B Oak 7L 57
Swift Cl. TN6: Crow 1B 36
TN22: Uck 3J 73
SWIFTSDEN .4G 43
Swinburne Av. BN22: Will 1M 153
SWINGATE CROSS 1E 120
Swing Bri. BN9: N'hvn 4K 149
Swynford Dr. TN38: St Leo 1F 126
Sybron Way TN6: Jar B 2H 37
Sycamore Cl. BN2: W'dean 5M 133
BN22: Eastb 1A 154
BN25: Sea 9H 151
BN41: Ports 2E 130
(not continuous)
TN21: H'fld 2E 76
TN38: St Leo 5G 127
TN39: Bex S 1D 144
Sycamore Cotts. TN2: Pem 7M 9
Sycamore Ct. *BN2: Brig 5E 132*
(off Fitzherbert Dr.)
TN22: Uck 9J 53
Sycamore Dr. BN27: Hails 9E 120
RH19: E Grin 3G 11
Sycamores, The BN10: Peace 3C 148
BN21: Eastb 8C 154 (2H 161)
Sydenham Ct. TN40: Bex S 2L 145
Sydney Cl. TN38: St Leo 3H 127
Sydney Rd. BN22: Eastb 9E 154 (4M 161)
RH16: Hay H 3F 48
Sydney St. BN1: Brig 7B 132 (6E 162)
Sydney Tidy Ho. *BN2: Brig 7D 132*
(off Queen's Pk. Rd.)
Sylvan Cl. RH16: Hay H 5J 49
Sylvester Way BN3: Hove 2E 130
Symbister Rd. BN41: Ports 6E 130
Syresham Gdns. RH16: Hay H 5F 48

T

Tackleway TN34: Hast 6A 128
Taddington Ho. *BN22: Eastb 8F 154*
(off Taddington Rd.)
Taddington Rd. BN22: Eastb 8F 154
Tainter's Brook TN22: Uck 9K 53
Talbot Cres. BN1: Brig 8E 112
Talbot Pk. TN2: Tun W 8G 8
Talbot Rd. TN18: Hawk 2N 43
Talbot Ter. BN7: Lewes 5J 115
Talland Pde. BN25: Sea 1D 156
Tall Ash Dr. TN37: St Leo 2J 127
Tall Oaks RH16: Hay H 4J 49
Tall Timbers BN27: Chal 2F 118
Tall Trees RH19: E Grin 4F 10
Tamarack Cl. BN22: Eastb 2A 154
Tamar Cl. BN24: Sto C 8K 141
Tamarisk Steps *TN34: Hast 6A 128*
(off Rock-A-Nore Rd.)
Tamplin Ter. BN2: Brig 7C 132 (5G 162)
Tamworth Rd. BN3: Hove 6H 131
Tanbridge Rd. BN23: Lang 2J 155
Tandridge Rd. BN3: Hove 7G 130
Tangier La. TN3: Tun W 6D 16
Tanglewood Coppice TN39: Bex S 2F 144
Tangmere Cl. TN39: Bex S 2F 144
Tangmere Pl. BN1: Brig 8B 112
Tangmere Rd. BN1: Brig 8B 112
Tanhouse La. TN31: Peas 7L 65
Tanneries, The BN27: Mag D 2J 121
Tanners Brook BN7: Lewes 6K 115
Tanners Fld. RH17: Wivel 3H 69
Tanners Way TN6: Crow 1E 36
Tanyard TN18: Sandh 5H 45
Tanyard Av. RH19: E Grin 4G 10
Tanyard Cotts. TN22: Buxt 7A 54
Tanyard La. RH17: Dane 6J 33
TN4: South .4C 8
TN22: Dane, Fur G 7J 33
TN36: Winch 8C 86
Tapsells La. TN5: Wadh 6M 27
Tarland Ho. TN2: Tun W 1G 16
Tarner Rd. BN2: Brig 7C 132
Tarring Cl. BN9: N'hvn 2K 149
TARRING NEVILLE 9C 136
Tas Combe Way BN20: Will 2M 153
Tasmania Way BN23: Eastb 2K 155
Tate Cres. RH15: Burg H 3A 68
Tates TN18: Hawk 1A 44
Taunton Gro. BN2: Brig 4H 133
Taunton Pl. *BN2: Brig 4H 133*
(off Taunton Rd.)
Taunton Rd. BN2: Brig 4G 133
Taunton Way BN2: Brig 4H 133
Tavern Pl. BN1: Brig 8E 162
Tavistock BN21: Eastb 7L 161
Tavistock Down BN1: Brig 3D 132
Taylor Cl. TN38: St Leo 2F 126
Taylor St. TN4: South 5C 8
Tea Gdn. La. TN3: R'hall, Tun W 2N 15
Teal Ct. BN27: Hails 7H 121
TN38: St Leo 3E 126
Teasley Mead TN3: B'ham 9A 6
Tedder Rd. TN4: Tun W 6E 8
Tedder Ter. TN35: Hast 1C 128
Teg Cl. BN41: Ports 3D 130
Teise Cl. TN2: Tun W 2F 16

Tweedsmuir Cl.—Wadhurst Bus. Pk.

Tweedsmuir Cl. BN23: Lang 1F **154**
TWELVE OAKS 3M **79**
Twineham Cl. BN2: Brig 6G **132**
Twineham Rd. BN21: Eastb 5A **154**
Twitten Cl. BN42: S'wck 6A **130**
Twitten, The BN2: Rott 3H **147**
BN6: Ditch 4E **90**
*BN24: Pev B 8F **142***
(off Richmond Rd.)
BN42: S'wck 6A **130**
RH15: Burg H 4C **68**
TN5: Tice .1M **41**
(off St Mary's La.)
TN6: Crow 1C **36**
(not continuous)
TN39: Bex S 9E **124**
TWYFORD 8F **20**
Twyford Cres. TN37: St Leo 2J **127**
Twyford Rd. BN1: Brig 8F **112**
Twyfords TN6: Crow 1B **36**
Twyhurst Ct. RH19: E Grin 1D **10**
Twysden Cotts. TN18: Sandh 6G **44**
Tye Cl. BN2: Salt 4L **147**
Tyedean Rd. BN10: Tels C 4N **147**
Tye Hill La. BN26: Arl 2J **139**
Tye Hill Rd. BN26: Arl 1K **139**
TYES CROSS 6C **20**
Tye, The BN26: Alfr 2M **151**
Tye Vw. BN10: Tels C 3A **148**
Tyhurst Pl. TN22: Uck 2H **73**
Tyler's Grn. RH17: Cuck 4B **48**
Tylers La. TN22: Nut 9D **34**
Tyndale Av. TN39: Bex S 2D **144**
Tyrone Ct. BN23: Lang 3G **154**
Tyson Pl. *BN2: Brig 8C **132***
(off Grosvenor St.)

U

UCKFIELD .1H 73
Uckfield Cl. BN2: Brig 7G **132**
UCKFIELD COMMUNITY HOSPITAL 2J 73
Uckfield Gymnastics Club 5F 52
Uckfield La. TN8: Hever 1H **5**
Uckfield Rd. BN8: Ring 8A **94**
TN6: H Hur 4L **35**
TN22: H Hur 4L **35**
Uckfield Station (Rail) 2H 73
Uckham La. TN33: Batt 1M **103**
UDIAM 4C 62
Udiam La. TN32: Ewh G 5D **62**
UDIMORE 6H 85
Udimore Rd.
TN31: B Oak, Rye, Udim 4A **84**
UGC Cinema
Brighton 1A 146
Eastbourne 3J 155
Undercliff TN38: St Leo 8H **127**
Undercliff Ter. *TN38: St Leo 8J **127***
(off Undercliff)
Undercliff Wlk.
BN2: Brig, Oving, Rott 1C **146**
Underdown Rd. BN42: S'wck 5A **130**
Underhill TN22: Mare 4G **52**
Underhill La. BN6: Clay 7A **90**
BN6: Ditch, W'ton 7E **90**
Under Rd. BN27: Mag D 3K **121**
Underwater World 7A 128
Union Cl. BN27: Hails 3E **120**
Union Point TN22: Uck 3J **73**
Union Rd. BN2: Brig 6C **132** (3G **162**)
Union Sq. TN4: Tun W 2C **16**
Union St. BN1: Brig 8E **162**
TN5: Flim .8C **30**
TN38: St Leo 7J **127**
Univeristy of Brighton (Leaf Hospital)
. . . . .3H 161
University of Brighton
Circus St. Annexe 8B 132 (7F 162)
Grand Pde. 8B 132 (7F 162)
Mithras House 4D 132
***Phoenix Halls of Residence** 6C 132*
(off Southover St.)
University of Brighton Annexe 8F 162
University of Brighton
(Falmer Campus) 9J 113
University of Brighton
(Hillbrow Site) *2B 160*
(off Gaudick Rd.)
University of Brighton
(Moulsecoomb Campus) 3D 132
University of Brighton
(Welkin Site) *2B 160*
(off Carlisle Rd.)
University of Sussex 7J 113
Updown Hill RH16: Hay H 7D **48**
Upland Rd. BN20: Eastb 9M **153**
Uplands *TN21: B Oak 8H **57***
(off Burwash Rd.)
TN22: Uck 8H **53**
Uplands Cl. TN22: Uck 8H **53**
TN39: Bex S 8G **125**
Uplands Dr. TN22: Uck 8J **53**
Uplands Pk. TN21: B Oak 8H **57**
Uplands Rd. BN1: Brig 3D **132**
Uplands, The TN38: St Leo 7H **127**
Up. Abbey Rd. BN2: Brig 9E **132**
Upper Av. BN21: Eastb 8D **154** (3K **161**)
Upper Av. Rdbt. BN21: Eastb 3K **161**
Upper Avenue Rdbt. *BN23: Lang 9L **141***
(off Wroxham Rd.)
Up. Bannings Rd. BN2: Salt 1M **147**
Up. Bedford St. BN2: Brig 9D **132**
Up. Belgrave Rd. BN25: Sea 8D **150**
UPPER BEVENDEAN 4K 133
Up. Bevendean Av. BN2: Brig 4F **132**
Up. Broomgrove Rd. TN34: Hast 3A **128**
Up. Carlisle Rd. BN20: Eastb 3N **159**
Up. Chalvington Pl. BN2: Brig 8F **132**
Up. Church Rd. TN37: St Leo 2H **127**
Up. Chyngton Gdns. BN25: Sea 8G **150**
Up. Clarence Rd. TN37: St Leo 4J **127**
Upper Cl. RH18: F Row 1M **21**
Upper Cotts. BN2: Oving 9L **133**
Up. Cumberland Wlk. TN2: Tun W 3D **16**
(not continuous)
UPPER DICKER 6L 119
Upper Dr., The BN3: Hove . . .5L **131** (1A **162**)
Up. Duke's Dr. BN20: Eastb 4N **159**
Up. Dunstan Rd. TN4: Tun W 7E **8**
Up. Gardner St.
BN1: Brig 7B **132** (6E **162**)
Up. Glen Rd. TN37: St Leo 1G **127**
Up. Gloucester Rd.
BN1: Brig 7A **132** (5D **162**)
Up. Greenwood La. TN21: Punn T 2L **77**
Up. Grosvenor Rd. TN1: Tun W 9D **8**
TN4: Tun W .7F **8**
Up. Hamilton Rd.
BN1: Brig 5N **131** (2B **162**)
UPPER HARTFIELD 1G 22
Up. Hollingdean Rd. BN1: Brig 4C **132**
UPPER HORSEBRIDGE 3D 120
Up. Horsebridge Rd. BN27: Hails 3B **120**
Up. King's Dr. BN20: Will 3M **153**
Up. Lake TN33: Batt 3L **103**
Up. Lewes Rd. BN2: Brig . . .6C **132** (3G **162**)
Up. Market St. BN3: Hove 8M **131**
Up. Maze Hill TN38: St Leo 6H **127**
Upper Nellington TN3: Lang G 9M **7**
Up. North St. BN1: Brig 7N **131** (6B **162**)
Up. Park Pl. BN2: Brig 8C **132**
Up. Park Rd. TN37: St Leo 5J **127**
UPPER PARROCK 1D 22
Up. Platts TN5: Tice 1A **42**
Upper Profit TN3: Lang G 1L **15**
Up. Ratton Dr. BN20: Will 4M **153**
Up. Rock Gdns. BN2: Brig 8C **132**
Up. Roedale Cotts. BN1: Brig 1B **132**
Up. St James's St. BN2: Brig 9C **132**
Up. St John's Rd. RH15: Burg H 4B **68**
Up. Sea Rd. TN40: Bex S 1L **145**
Up. Sherwood Rd. BN25: Sea 8E **150**
Up. South Rd. TN37: St Leo 5J **127**
Upper Sq. RH18: F Row 9M **11**
Upper Stables RH16: Hay H 6D **48**
Up. Station Rd. TN21: H'fld 2E **76**
Up. Stephens TN3: Lang G 1L **15**
Up. Stoneham BN8: Lewes 2M **115**
Upper St. BN20: E Dean 3F **158**
TN4: R'hall .9A **8**
(not continuous)
Up. Sudeley St. BN2: Brig 9E **132**
UPPERTON 8B 154 (2H 161)
Upperton Gdns.
BN21: Eastb 9C **154** (4H **161**)
(not continuous)
Upperton La.
BN21: Eastb 9C **154** (4H **161**)
Upperton Rd.
BN21: Eastb 8B **154** (4G **161**)
Up. Valley Rd. BN9: N'hvn 6H **149**
UPPER WELLINGHAM 7A 94
Up. Wellington Rd. BN2: Brig 6D **132**
Up. Winfield Av. BN1: Brig 8A **112**
Up. Wish Hill BN20: Will 4M **153**
Upton Av. BN42: S'wck 4A **130**
Upton Quarry TN3: Lang G 1K **15**
Upwick Rd. BN20: Eastb 9N **153**
Upwyke Ho. BN21: Eastb 8N **153**
Utopia Leisure Cen. 1J 73

V

Vale Av. BN1: Brig 7N **111**
TN1: Tun W 1D **16**
TN4: South .4C **8**
Valebridge Cl. RH15: Burg H 2D **68**
Valebridge Dr. RH15: Burg H 3D **68**
Valebridge Rd. RH15: Burg H 3D **68**
Vale Cl. BN25: Sea 8F **150**
Vale Ct. BN41: Ports 6D **130**
RH16: Hay H 7F **48**
TN4: South .3D **8**
Vale Gdns. BN41: Ports 6D **130**
Valence Rd. BN7: Lewes 5H **115**
Valentine Ct. BN3: Hove 6L **131**
BN21: Eastb 6K **161**
Valerie Cl. BN41: Ports 3D **130**
Vale Rd. BN2: Salt 1L **147**
BN25: Sea 8E **150**
BN41: Ports 6D **130**
RH16: Hay H 7E **48**
TN1: Tun W 1D **16**
TN4: South .3C **8**
TN18: Hawk 8N **31**
TN20: May .8E **38**
TN33: Batt .2J **103**
TN37: St Leo 4J **127**
Vale, The BN2: Oving 8M **133**
Vale Vw. Rd. TN21: H'fld 2E **76**
Vallance Ct. *BN3: Hove 7J **131***
(off Hove St.)
Vallance Gdns. BN3: Hove 7J **131**
Vallance Rd. BN3: Hove 7J **131**
Vallensdean Cotts. BN41: Ports 3E **130**
Valley Cl. BN1: Brig 1L **131**
BN9: N'hvn 4H **149**
Valley Dene BN9: N'hvn 5H **149**
Valley Dr. BN1: Brig 1K **131**
BN25: Sea 7F **150**
Valley Ri. BN25: Sea 8E **150**
Valley Rd. BN7: Lewes 6G **115**
BN9: N'hvn 5G **149**
(not continuous)
BN10: Peace 2C **148**
BN41: Ports 2B **130**
TN4: R'hall .9N **7**
TN6: Crow 1D **36**
Valley Side Rd. TN35: Hast 3B **128**
Valley Vw. TN4: South 3D **8**
TN22: Fur G 1G **51**
Valley Vw. Cl. TN6: Crow 1D **36**
Val Prinseps Rd. BN24: Pev B 9E **142**
Valverde Ho. BN3: Hove 6L **131**
Vanburgh Ct. BN3: Hove 6K **131**
Vancouver Rd. BN23: Eastb 2L **155**
Vantage Point BN1: Brig 3E **162**
Vantage Wlk. *TN38: St Leo 4H **127***
(off Sedlescombe Gdns.)
Varndean Cl. BN1: Brig 2N **131**
Varndean Dr. BN1: Brig 2N **131**
Varndean Gdns. BN1: Brig 2N **131**
Varndean Holt BN1: Brig 2A **132**
Varndean Rd. BN1: Brig 2N **131**
Vauxhall La. TN4: South, Tonb 2C **8**
(not continuous)
TN11: Tonb .1E **8**
Vega Cl. BN27: Hails 7G **121**
Ventnor Cl. BN23: Lang 9L **141**
Ventnor Vs. BN3: Hove 7K **131**
Venture Cl. TN40: Bex S 1N **145**
Verbania Way RH19: E Grin 3H **11**
Verdant Cl. TN34: Hast 6K **127**
Vere Rd. BN1: Brig 5B **132** (2F **162**)
Veric BN3: Hove 6L **131**
Vermont Rd. TN4: R'hall 9N **7**
Vermont Way TN38: St Leo 9F **104**
Vernon Av. BN2: W'dean 4K **133**
BN10: Peace 6D **148**
(not continuous)
Vernon Cl. BN23: Eastb 5H **155**
Vernon Ct. BN1: Brig 5B **162**
Vernon Gdns. BN1: Brig 5B **162**
Vernon Lodge BN21: Eastb 7K **161**
Vernon Rd. TN1: Tun W 7F **8**
TN22: Uck .2J **73**
Vernons Rd. BN8: N'wck 1J **71**
Vernon Ter. BN1: Brig 7N **131** (5B **162**)
Veronica Way BN2: Brig 9C **132**
Verralls Wlk. BN7: Lewes 6J **115**
Verulam Pl. TN37: St Leo 7L **127**
Viaduct Rd. BN1: Brig 6B **132** (3E **162**)
Vian Av. BN23: Eastb 5J **155**
Vicarage Cl. BN8: Ring 1B **116**
BN9: N'hvn 2L **149**
BN25: Sea 9E **150**
Vicarage Dr. BN20: Eastb 9A **154**
Vicarage Field BN27: Hails 6F **120**
Vicarage Flats *TN34: Hast 5N **127***
(off St George's Rd.)
Vicarage La. BN2: Rott 3G **147**
BN20: Eastb 9A **154**
BN27: Hails 6F **120**
BN27: Hell .9D **98**
RH17: Scay H 6N **49**
TN19: B'wsh C 6C **58**
TN35: W'fld 4K **105**
Vicarage Rd. BN20: Eastb 9A **154**
BN27: Hails 7F **120**
TN4: South .3C **8**
TN19: B'wsh C 6C **58**
TN34: Hast 5N **127**
Vicarage Ter. BN2: Rott 3G **147**
Vicarage Wlk. RH19: E Grin 3F **10**
Vicarage Way BN8: Ring 1C **116**
TN19: Hur G 7H **43**
Viceroy Lodge BN3: Hove 7J **131**
Victor Cl. BN25: Sea 7C **150**
Victoria Av. BN10: Peace 6C **148**
(not continuous)
TN35: Hast 2B **128**
Victoria Cl. BN26: Pole 6C **140**
RH15: Burg H 6A **68**
Victoria Cotts. *BN3: Hove 8K **131***
(off Sussex Rd.)
TN6: Roth .4N **37**
Victoria Ct. BN3: Hove 7K **131**
BN21: Eastb 1D **160** (7L **161**)
BN41: Ports 5E **130**
TN2: Tun W .9G **9**
TN38: St Leo 8H **127**
Victoria Dr. BN20: Eastb 6M **153**
Victoria Gardens 7F 162
Victoria Gdns. BN20: Eastb 8M **153**
RH15: Burg H 6A **68**
Victoria Gro. BN3: Hove 7L **131**
TN4: Tun W 1C **16**
VICTORIA HOSPITAL (LEWES) 5G 115
Victoria Mans. BN21: Eastb 6M **161**
Victoria M. *BN2: Rott 3G **147***
(off West St.)
Victoria Pk. 5F 48
Victoria Pk. Gdns. *BN41: Ports 5E **130***
(off Old Shoreham Rd.)
Victoria Pl. BN1: Brig 7N **131** (6B **162**)
Victoria Rd. BN1: Brig 7N **131** (6B **162**)
BN20: Eastb 7M **153**
BN26: Pole 6C **140**
BN27: Bore S 1D **122**
BN27: Hails 7F **120**
BN41: Ports 5D **130**
BN42: S'wck 6A **130**
RH15: Burg H 6A **68**
RH16: Hay H 6G **49**
TN1: Tun W .9E **8**
TN4: South .4B **8**
TN6: Jar B .2G **37**
TN20: May .7D **38**
TN37: St Leo 7K **127**
TN39: Bex S 1J **145**
Victoria Rd. Trad. Est.
BN41: Ports 5E **130**
Victoria St. BN1: Brig 7N **131** (6B **162**)
Victoria Ter. BN3: Hove 8K **131**
RH19: E Grin 1E **10**
Victoria Way RH15: Burg H 6A **68**
RH19: E Grin 5F **10**
TN36: Winch 2E **108**
Victory M. BN2: Brig 1B **146**
View Bank TN35: Hast 4C **128**
View Rd. BN10: Peace 4C **148**
Views Path RH16: Hay H 5J **49**
Views Wood Path TN22: Uck 8J **53**
Viking Cl. BN25: Sea 6A **150**
Viking Way BN23: Eastb 4H **155**
Village Barn, The BN1: Brig 7N **111**
Village Cl. BN41: Ports 3D **130**
TN39: Bex S 1D **144**
Village Grn. BN9: Pidd 1H **149**
Village M. TN39: Bex S 1D **144**
Village Sq. BN2: Brig 1A **146**
Village, The BN20: Eastb 3A **160**
BN26: Alc .5B **138**
BN26: B'wck 6D **138**
Village Way BN1: Falm 8J **113**
Villa Rd. TN37: St Leo 7K **127**
Villiers Cl. BN2: W'dean 5M **133**
Villiers Ct. BN1: Brig 5E **162**
Vincent Cl. BN23: Eastb 5J **155**
Vincent's Ct. BN2: Brig 1B **146**
Vine Cotts. TN6: Jar B 3G **37**
Vinehall Cl. TN34: Hast 1N **127**
Vinehall Rd. TN32: Mount 2L **81**
VINEHALL STREET 2M 81
Vine Pl. BN1: Brig 7A **132** (6C **162**)
Vineries, The
BN3: Hove 7N **131** (4A **162**)
BN23: Lang 2G **155**
RH15: Burg H 5E **68**
VINE'S CROSS 8F 76
Vines Cross Rd. BN2: Brig 6G **133**
TN21: Horam 8C **76**
Vine Sq. BN22: Eastb 6G **154**
Vine St. BN1: Brig 7B **132** (6F **162**)
Vineyard La. TN5: Tice 9K **29**
Vintry, The BN21: Eastb 5N **153**
TN22: Nut .6B **34**
Virgin's Cft. TN33: Batt 1L **103**
Virgin's La. TN33: Batt 1L **103**
Vogue Gyratory BN2: Brig 5D **132**
Volks Electric Railway 9C 132 (9G 162)
Vulcan Ho. Farm Bus. Units
TN22: Five D 6K **53**

W

Wade Cl. BN23: Eastb 5J **155**
WADHURST .7C 28
Wadhurst Bus. Pk. TN5: Wadh 4L **27**

West Common—Winchester Ho.

West Common RH16: Hay H, Lind 3G 48
West Common Dr. RH16: Lind 2H 49
Westcourt Dr. TN39: Bex S 2G 144
WESTDEAN .8N 151
Westdean Av. BN9: N'hvn 7G 149
W. Dean Ri. BN25: Sea 8F 150
WESTDENE .1L 131
Westdene Cl. TN37: St Leo 9J 105
Westdene Dr. BN1: Brig 9L 111
Westdown Ho. BN21: Eastb 6L 161
Westdown La. TN19: B'wsh C 6C 58
Westdown Pk. TN19: B'wsh C 6C 58
Westdown Rd. BN25: Sea 8C 150
West Down Rd. TN39: Bex S 9H 125
West Dr. BN2: Brig 8C 132
West End BN27: Herst 9A 100
Westergate Rd. BN2: Brig 1F 132
Westerham Rd. BN23: Lang 3G 155
Westerings, The *TN21: H'fld 2D 76*
(off Hailsham Rd.)
Westerleigh Cl. TN38: St Leo 6G 126
Westerman Complex BN3: Hove 5H 131
Western Av. BN26: Pole 7E 140
TN18: Hawk 9N 31
TN33: Batt 3L 103
(off High St.)
Western Concourse BN2: Brig 2A 146
Western Ct. BN9: N'hvn 6J 149
Western Esplanade BN41: Ports 7F 130
Western Pde.
BN20: Eastb 4C 160 (9K 161)
BN21: Eastb 4C 160 (9K 161)
Western Rd. BN3: Hove 7L 131 (7A 162)
BN7: Lewes 5H 115
BN8: N'wck 1H 71
BN9: N'hvn 6H 149
BN22: Eastb 8E 154 (2M 161)
BN24: Pev B 9F 142
BN27: Hails 6D 120
(not continuous)
RH15: Burg H 5A 68
RH16: Hay H 6G 48
TN1: Tun W .8F 8
TN4: South .4C 8
TN5: Wadh 5B 28
TN6: Jar B 3G 36
TN18: Hawk 9N 31
TN37: St Leo 7J 127
TN40: Bex S 2K 145
Western St. BN1: Brig 8M 131 (8A 162)
Western Ter.
BN1: Brig 8N 131 (7A 162)
WESTFIELD .4L 105
Westfield Av. BN2: Salt 1L 147
Westfield Av. Nth. BN2: Salt 1L 147
Westfield Av. Sth. BN2: Salt 1L 147
Westfield Cl. BN1: Brig 1B 132
BN26: Pole 6D 140
TN20: F Ashes 3M 55
Westfield Ct. BN26: Pole 6D 140
Westfield Cres. BN1: Brig 9B 112
Westfield La. TN35: W'fld 7K 105
TN37: St Leo, W'fld 7J 105
Westfield Ri. BN2: Salt 1L 147
Westfield Rd. BN21: Eastb 6A 154
Westfield Ter. TN17: Cran 2N 31
WEST FIRLE 2H 137
West Ga. BN7: Plump G 1M 91
Westgate St. BN7: Lewes 5J 115
WESTHAM .7B 142
Westham BN2: Brig 8G 132
Westham Cl. TN39: Bex S 2F 144
Westham Dr. BN24: Pev B 7H 143
WEST HILL 5A 128
West Hill RH19: E Grin 4D 10
Westhill Dr. RH15: Burg H 5A 68
W. Hill Pl. BN1: Brig 7A 132 (5C 162)
W. Hill Rd. BN1: Brig 7A 132 (5C 162)
TN38: St Leo 8F 126
W. Hill St. BN1: Brig 7A 132 (5C 162)
W. Hoathly Rd. RH19: E Grin 7D 10
(not continuous)
West Ho. BN21: Eastb 1D 160 (7K 161)
West Jetty BN2: Brig 2A 146
Westland Ct. *BN41: Ports 6C 130*
(off West Rd.)
Westlands Rd. RH16: Hay H 4J 49
West La. RH19: E Grin 4D 10
West Leigh RH19: E Grin 5E 10
Westlords BN21: Will 4N 153
West Mallion *RH16: Hay H 6G 49*
(off Collwell Cl.)
WEST MARINA 8F 126
WESTMESTON 7G 90
Westmeston Av. BN2: Salt 2J 147
Westmeston Bostall
BN6: W'ton 8G 91
Westminster Cl. BN22: Eastb 9G 140
Westminster Cres. TN34: Hast 2N 127
Westmoreland Cl. TN38: St Leo 3G 126
Westmoreland Ct. *TN22: Uck 3H 73*
(off High St.)
Westmorland Ct. BN3: Hove 4B 162
BN20: Eastb 5M 153
Westmount BN2: Brig 7D 132
West Parade TN39: Bex S 3H 145
West Pk. Av. TN4: South 4C 8
West Pier
Brighton 9N 131 (9B 162)
West Point BN8: N'wck 1J 71
West Quay BN2: Brig 2A 146
BN9: N'hvn 6K 149
Westren Gdns. TN6: Jar B 2H 37
West Rd. BN41: Ports 6C 130
TN17: Kiln .1A 30
West St Leonards Station (Rail) 7F 126
West St. BN1: Brig 8A 132 (8D 162)
BN2: Rott 3G 147
BN6: Ditch 4D 90
BN7: Lewes 5K 115
BN21: Eastb 1C 160 (6J 161)
BN25: Sea 1D 156
BN26: Alfr 9D 138
BN41: Ports 6E 130
RH15: Burg H 4A 68
RH19: E Grin 4E 10
TN20: May .8D 38
TN31: Rye .3G 86
TN34: Hast 7N 127
West St. La. TN21: Horam, May G 6B 76
West St. M. BN21: Eastb 6J 161
West Ter. BN21: Eastb 1C 160 (5J 161)
BN27: Herst 9A 100
West Undercliff TN31: Rye 3E 86
West View BN3: Hove 6L 131
West Vw. BN25: Sea 1D 156
RH16: Lind .3J 49
TN22: Uck .8J 53
TN34: Hast 4A 128
West Vw. Ct. BN25: Sea 1D 156
W. View Gdns. RH19: E Grin 4E 10
W. View Ter. BN9: N'hvn 2K 149
Westville Rd. TN39: Bex S 1H 145
West Way BN3: Hove 3F 130
Westway TN2: Pem 6N 9
Westway Cl. BN41: Ports 1A 130
Westway Gdns. BN41: Ports 1A 130
Westwood Rd. TN4: R'hall 8M 7
Wexford Ct. *BN23: Lang 3G 155*
(off Biddenden Cl.)
Wharf Rd. BN21: Eastb 9C 154 (5J 161)
BN41: Ports 7F 130
WHATLINGTON 7A 82
Whatlington Rd. TN33: Batt, What 1L 103
Whatlington Way TN38: St Leo 4D 126
Wheatfield Ct. TN37: St Leo 1J 127
Wheatfield Way BN2: Brig 2G 132
Wheatlands Cl. BN10: Tels C 2B 148
Wheatsheaf Gdns. BN7: Lewes 4L 115
Wheatsheaf La. RH17: Cuck 3B 48
Wheeler Ct. RH16: Hay H 7G 48
Wheelers La. TN22: Had D 4H 55
Wheel Farm Bus. Pk. TN35: W'fld 3K 105
Wheel La. TN35: W'fld 2J 105
Wheelwright Cl. BN22: Eastb 9G 141
Wheelwright La. RH15: Burg H 7E 68
Whichelo Pl. BN2: Brig 7D 132
Whiffens Cl. BN27: Hails 8D 120
Whincroft Pk. TN6: Crow 2B 36
Whineham Way TN40: Bex S 1N 145
Whippingham Rd. BN2: Brig 5D 132
Whippingham St. BN2: Brig 5D 132
Whipping Post La. BN2: Rott 3G 147
Whistler Ct. BN1: Brig 4A 132
Whitbread Cl. BN23: Lang 9L 141
White Bear Pas. TN1: Tun W 2D 16
Whitebread La. TN31: Buck, North 9C 46
White Chimneys *TN6: Crow 1E 36*
(off Crowborough Hill)
White Ct. BN26: Alfr 2L 151
Whitecross St. BN1: Brig 7B 132 (5E 162)
WHITE DYKE 8H 121
White Dyke Rd. BN27: Hails 8H 121
Whitefield Rd. TN4: Tun W 7D 8
Whitefriars Rd. TN34: Hast 5N 127
White Gables
BN21: Eastb 2C 160 (8J 161)
Whitegate Cl. TN4: Tun W 5D 8
Whitegates Cl. BN8: S Chai 9E 70
Whitegates La. TN5: Wadh 2M 27
Whitegates Pk. TN35: W'fld 5K 105
Whitehall Pde. *RH19: E Grin 3E 10*
(off London Rd.)
WHITEHAWK 7G 132
Whitehawk Cl. BN2: Brig 8F 132
Whitehawk Cres. BN2: Brig 8F 132
Whitehawk Hill Rd. BN2: Brig 8E 132
Whitehawk Rd. BN2: Brig 7F 132
Whitehawk Way BN2: Brig 7G 132
WHITEHILL 3D 36
White Hill BN7: Lewes 5J 115
Whitehill Cl. BN20: Eastb 7M 153
TN6: Crow .1D 36
Whitehill Ct. *TN39: Bex S 9F 124*
(off White Hill Av.)
White Hill Dr. TN39: Bex S 1F 144
Whitehill Rd. TN6: Crow 1D 36
White Horse, The 6K 151
Whitehouse Av. TN39: Bex S 7J 125
Whitehouse La. TN21: Wald 5L 75
Whiteing La. BN26: Arl 3K 139
Whitelands RH16: Hay H 6G 48
White Lodge BN3: Hove 5L 131
TN1: Tun W .9F 8
Whitelot Cl. BN42: S'wck 3A 130
Whitelot Way BN42: S'wck 3A 130
WHITEMANS GREEN 1A 48
WHITE POST 6B 6
White Rock TN34: Hast 7L 127
White Rock Gardens 7K 127
White Rock Gdns. TN34: Hast 7L 127
Whiterock Pl. BN42: S'wck 6A 130
White Rock Theatre *7L 127*
(off White Rock)
White's La. TN18: Hawk 1C 44
WHITESMITH .7F 96
White St. BN2: Brig 8C 132
Whitethorn Dr. BN1: Brig 1K 131
White Way BN7: Rod 6H 135
Whiteway Cl. BN25: Sea 6D 150
Whiteway La. BN2: Rott 2H 147
(not continuous)
Whitfield La. BN8: H'sey 9H 93
Whitley Rd. BN22: Eastb 8D 154 (2L 161)
Whittinghame Gdns. BN1: Brig 2A 132
Whittingtons Way TN34: Hast 2A 128
Whittle Dr. BN23: Eastb 3D 154
Whittlewood Cl. TN38: St Leo 4E 126
Whitworth Ho. TN40: Bex S 1K 145
Whitworth Rd. TN37: St Leo 8H 105
Whybourne Crest TN2: Tun W 3F 16
WHYDOWN .6C 124
Whydown Cotts. TN39: Bex S 7D 124
Whydown Hill TN33: Sed 1E 104
Whydown Rd. TN39: Bex S 6B 124
TN39: Bex S 7D 124
Wickets, The RH15: Burg H 3A 68
Wick Hall BN3: Hove 7M 131 (5A 162)
Wickham Av. TN39: Bex S 2J 145
Wickham Cl. RH16: Hay H 2F 48
Wickham Gdns. TN4: R'hall 8A 8
Wickham La. BN8: Cooks 5E 92
Wickham Rock La.
TN36: Ick, ...2A 108
(not continuous)
Wickham Way RH16: Hay H 2F 48
Wickhurst Cl. BN41: Ports 3B 130
Wickhurst Ri. BN41: Ports 2B 130
Wickhurst Rd. BN41: Ports 3B 130
Wicklands Av. BN2: Salt 3K 147
Wicklow Ct. *BN23: Lang 3G 155*
(off Biddenden Cl.)
WICKSTREET 8J 119
Wick St. BN8: W Firle 9H 117
Widbury TN3: Lang G 1K 15
Widdicombe Way BN2: Brig 3F 132
Wigmore Cl. BN1: Brig 4C 132
Wilbury Av. BN3: Hove 5K 131
Wilbury Cres. BN3: Hove 6L 131
Wilbury Gdns. BN3: Hove 5L 131
Wilbury Grange BN3: Hove 7L 131
Wilbury Gro. BN3: Hove 7L 131
Wilbury Lodge BN3: Hove 6L 131
Wilbury Mans. *BN3: Hove 5M 131*
(off Wilbury Vs.)
Wilbury Rd. BN3: Hove 7L 131
Wilbury Vs. BN3: Hove 6L 131
Wilby Av. BN42: S'wck 4A 130
Wilderness Gdns. TN31: North 2A 64
Wilderness La. TN8: Hever, M'bch 2J 5
TN22: Had D 8F 54
Wilderness Pk. TN6: Crow 9C 24
Wilderness, The RH16: Lind 1J 49
Wilderness Wood 5G 55
Wilderwick Rd. RH19: E Grin 1H 11
Wild Pk. Cl. BN2: Brig 2F 132
Wildwood BN23: Lang 9M 141
Wilfrid Rd. BN3: Hove 5F 130
Wilkinson Cl. BN2: Rott 1G 146
Wilkinson Way BN25: Sea 8D 150
Wilkins Way TN40: Bex S 8N 125
Willard Cl. BN22: Eastb 6D 154
WILLARD'S HILL 4D 60
Willets Fld. BN8: C'gly 7J 97
Willetts La. TN3: B'ham 9A 6
William Allen La. RH16: Hay H 4J 49
William Rd. TN38: St Leo 7E 126
Williams Ct. BN23: Lang 3H 155
William St. BN2: Brig 8B 132 (7F 162)
BN41: Ports 6D 130
TN4: Tun W .8D 8
William Sutton Ho. BN1: Brig 7E 162
William Ter. TN33: Batt 4M 103
Willicombe Pk. TN2: Tun W 9G 9
WILLINGDON 3M 153
Willingdon Av. TN38: St Leo 1G 126
TN39: Bex S 1H 145
Willingdon Cl. BN20: Will 3M 153
TN38: St Leo 1G 126
Willingdon Ct. BN20: Will 1L 153
Willingdon Drove
BN23: Eastb, Lang 3D 154
Willingdon La. BN26: Jev 5G 153
Willingdon Pk. Dr. BN22: Will 2N 153
Willingdon Rd. BN2: Brig 4F 132
BN20: Eastb, Will 3N 153
(not continuous)
BN21: Eastb 5N 153
Willingdon Rdbt. BN20: Will 4N 153
Willingdon Way BN22: Will 2M 153
TN38: St Leo 1G 127
Willingford La.
TN19: B'lng, B'wsh C 6E 58
TN32: B'lng 6E 58
Willoughby Cres. BN22: Eastb 6F 154
Willow Av. BN27: Hails 5E 120
Willow Bank TN32: Rob 5J 61
Willowbed Wlk. TN34: Hast 1L 127
Willowbrook Way BN6: Hass 4B 90
Willow Cl. BN2: W'dean 5M 133
RH19: E Grin 1D 10
TN19: Etch .1C 60
TN21: H'fld 9E 56
TN22: Uck 9J 53
(off Larnach Cl.)
Willow Ct. BN3: Hove 6M 131
BN26: Pole 7D 140
(off Walnut Wlk.)
Willowdowne Cl. BN26: Pole 8D 140
Willow Dr. BN25: Sea 9H 151
BN26: Pole 8D 140
TN39: Bex S 9D 124
Willow End TN34: Hast 2M 127
Willow Est., The BN9: N'hvn 4L 149
Willowfield Rd.
BN22: Eastb 9E 154 (4N 161)
Willowfield Sq.
BN22: Eastb 9E 154 (4N 161)
Willow Glen TN37: St Leo 1G 127
Willow La. TN36: Winch 1F 108
Willow Mead RH19: E Grin 4F 10
TN6: Crow .2C 36
Willow M. TN32: Rob 6J 61
Willow Pk. RH16: Hay H 5J 49
Willows Ri. TN22: Fram 3N 73
Willows, The *BN2: Brig 5C 132*
(off Prince's Cres.)
BN8: Barc C 2L 93
BN25: Sea 9D 150
BN27: Hails 3D 120
RH15: Burg H 3C 68
TN37: St Leo 9G 105
Willow Stream Cl. TN35: T Oaks 4D 106
Willow Tree Rd. TN2: Tun W 3B 16
Willow Wlk. BN9: N'hvn 4J 149
BN22: Eastb 2A 154
TN2: Tun W .5H 9
Wilman Rd. TN4: Tun W 6D 8
WILMINGTON 8J 139
Wilmington Cl. BN1: Brig 9B 112
BN6: Hass .3A 90
Wilmington Gdns.
BN21: Eastb 2D 160 (8K 161)
Wilmington Pde. *BN1: Brig 9A 112*
(off Wilmington Way)
Wilmington Priory 8J 139
Wilmington Rd. BN9: N'hvn 6H 149
BN25: Sea 8C 150
TN34: Hast 3N 127
Wilmington Sq.
BN21: Eastb 2D 160 (8K 161)
Wilmington Way BN1: Brig 9A 112
RH16: Hay H 4H 49
Windmill La. TN36: Ick 2L 107
Wilson Av. BN2: Brig 9G 132
Wilson Gro. TN22: Uck 1F 72
Wilton *RH16: Hay H 3E 48*
(off Great Heathmead)
Wilton Av. BN22: Eastb 1C 154
Wilton Ct. *TN40: Bex S 2K 145*
(off Wilton Rd.)
Wilton Ct. Flats *TN40: Bex S 2K 145*
(off Wilton Rd.)
Wilton Rd. TN40: Bex S 2K 145
Wiltshire Ct. BN23: Lang 3H 155
Wiltshire Ho. *BN2: Brig 8C 132*
(off Lavender St.)
Wiltshire Way TN2: Tun W 6G 9
Winceby Cl. TN39: Bex S 3F 144
Winchcombe Rd. BN22:
Eastb 8D 154 (3L 161)
WINCHELSEA .9C 86
WINCHELSEA BEACH 2F 108
Winchelsea Beach Cvn. Pk.
TN36: Winch 3E 108
Winchelsea Cl. BN25: Sea 7G 151
Winchelsea La. TN31: Rye, Udim 6L 85
TN35: Hast 1C 128
Winchelsea Rd. BN22: Eastb 6G 154
TN31: Rye .3F 86
TN35: Gues T 9E 106
TN35: Hast 2C 128
Winchelsea Sands Holiday Village
TN36: Winch 2E 108
Winchelsea Station (Rail) 7B 86
Winchester Ho. BN22: Eastb 1B 154

Winchester Rd.—Zion Gdns.

Winchester Rd. TN18: Hawk 9N 31
Winchester St. BN1: Brig 5B 132 (2E 162)
Winchester Way BN22: Will 2M 153
Wincombe Rd. BN1: Brig 4M 131
Windemere Ct. BN2: Brig 7D 132
Windermere Ct. BN21: Eastb 6L 161
Windermere Cres. BN22: Eastb 7F 154
Windermere Rd. RH16: Hay H 5G 49
Winding St. TN34: Hast 6A 128
Windlesham Av.
BN1: Brig 7N 131 (5B 162)
Windlesham Cl. BN41: Ports 4C 130
TN6: Crow .1D 36
Windlesham Ct. BN1: Brig 4B 162
Windlesham Gdns.
BN1: Brig 7N 131 (5B 162)
Windlesham Ho. BN1: Brig 5A 162
Windlesham Mans. BN3: Hove 4B 162
Windlesham Rd.
BN1: Brig 7N 131 (5A 162)
Windmill Av. BN6: Hass 4A 90
Windmill Cl. BN3: Hove 3H 131
BN21: Eastb 6A 154
TN21: H'fld .9E 56
Windmill Ct. *TN2: Tun W* *1F 16*
(off North St.)
Windmill Dr. BN1: Brig 8L 111
RH15: Burg H 4B 68
TN39: Bex S 8H 125
Windmill Grn. BN24: Sto C 8L 141
WINDMILL HILL 1D 122
Windmill Hill Place Golf & Tennis Academy
. . . . .2F 122
Windmill La. BN20: Fris 2E 158
RH19: E Grin 5J 11
(Lewes Rd.)
RH19: E Grin 1D 10
(Lowdell's La.)
TN5: Cous W 3E 28
TN5: Wadh .7N 27
Windmill Pde. BN42: S'wck 4A 130
Windmill Pk. TN36: Winch 1F 108
Windmill Pl. BN26: Pole 8D 140
TN36: Winch 1F 108
Windmill Rd. BN26: Pole 8D 140
BN42: S'wck 4A 130
TN38: St Leo 4H 127
Windmill St. BN2: Brig 7C 132
TN2: Tun W 1F 16
Windmill Ter. BN2: Brig 7C 132
Windmill Vw. BN1: Brig 8B 112
Windover Cres. BN7: Lewes 4G 114
Windover Way BN22: Will 1M 153
Windsor Bldgs.
BN1: Brig 8A 132 (7D 162)
Windsor Cl. BN3: Hove 2J 131
BN23: Lang 1F 154
BN25: Sea 6A 150
RH16: Hay H 7F 48
Windsor Ct. BN1: Brig 7D 162
BN1: Brig 1M 131
BN22: Eastb 9E 154 (4N 161)
BN26: Pole 6D 140
TN6: Jar B 2G 37
Windsor Lodge BN1: Brig 7D 162
BN2: Brig *8C 132*
(off High St.)
BN3: Hove 7K 131
Windsor Pl. RH19: E Grin 4G 10
TN6: Jar B 2G 37
Windsor Rd. BN27: Hails 8E 120
TN6: Jar B 2G 36
TN37: St Leo 3H 127
TN39: Bex S 1J 145
Windsor St. BN1: Brig 8A 132 (7D 162)
Windsor Way BN26: Pole 6D 140
TN36: Winch 3E 108
Windward Quay BN23: Eastb 4J 155
Windy Fld. TN5: Tice 9L 29
Winfield Av. BN1: Brig 8A 112
Winfield Cl. BN1: Brig 9A 112
BN41: Ports 1C 130
Wingate Cl. TN38: St Leo 5G 127
Wingle Tye Rd. RH15: Burg H 8B 68
Winkfield Ct. RH16: Hay H 4E 48
Winkhurst Way RH15: Burg H 7E 68
Winkney Rd. BN22: Eastb 1C 154
Winnals Park RH16: Hay H 4E 48
Winscote La. TN6: Crow 1B 36
Winser Rd. TN17: Rolv L 1F 46
Winston Cres. BN23: Eastb 5G 155
Winston Dr. TN39: Bex S 1F 144
Winston Scott Av. TN3: Lang G 9J 7
Winterbourne Cl. BN7: Lewes 6G 115
TN34: Hast 6K 127
Winterbourne Hollow BN7: Lewes 6H 115
Winterbourne La. BN7: Lewes 6G 114
(not continuous)
Winterbourne M. BN7: Lewes 6H 115
Winter Garden Theatre 2D 160 (8K 161)
WINTON 9D 138
Winton Av. BN2: Salt 2K 147
Winton St. BN26: Alfr 9D 138
Wisden Av. RH15: Burg H 3A 68
Wiseacre TN3: Lamb 9J 19
Wish Ct. BN3: Hove 5G 130
Wish Hill BN20: Will 3M 153
Wishing Tree Cl. TN38: St Leo 4F 126
Wishing Tree La. TN38: St Leo 5F 126
Wishing Tree Rd. TN38: St Leo 4F 126
Wishing Tree Rd. Nth.
TN38: St Leo 2G 126
Wish Rd. BN3: Hove 7G 130
BN21: Eastb 1D 160 (6K 161)
Wish St. TN31: Rye 3F 86
Wish Tower Puppet Mus., The
. . . . .2D 160 (9L 161)
Wish Ward TN31: Rye 3F 86
Wiston Rd. BN2: Brig 6G 132
Wiston Way BN2: Brig 6G 132
WITHDEAN 1M 131
Withdean Av. BN1: Brig 3M 131
Withdean Cl. BN1: Brig 2M 131
Withdean Ct. BN1: Brig 2N 131
Withdean Ct. Av. BN1: Brig 2M 131
Withdean Cres. BN1: Brig 2N 131
Withdean Hall BN1: Brig 2N 131
Withdean Ri. BN1: Brig 2M 131
Withdean Rd. BN1: Brig 2M 131
Withdean Sports Complex 1M 131
Withdean Stadium 2M 131
WITHERENDEN HILL 9D 40
Witherenden Rd. TN20: May 9H 39
TN21: May 9A 40
WITHYHAM .8M 13
Withyham Av. BN2: Salt 3K 147
Withyham Cl. BN22: Eastb 3C 154
Withyham Rd.
TN3: Groom, Withy 5D 14
TN39: Bex S 3D 144
Wittersham La. TN31: Iden 4F 66
Wittersham Ri. TN38: St Leo 4E 126
Wittersham Rd. TN30: Iden 1E 66
TN30: Witter 5L 47
TN31: Iden .1E 66
TN31: Peas .4L 65
Wittersham Road Station 4J 47
WIVELSFIELD 3J 69
WIVELSFIELD GREEN 4K 69
Wivelsfield Rd. BN2: Salt 1K 147
RH16: Hay H 7F 48
Wivelsfield Station (Rail) 4D 68
Wnhams Wood TN6: Crow 7B 24
Woburn Cl. BN27: Hails 5D 120
Woburn Pl. BN1: Brig 9G 112
Woburn Way BN22: Eastb 1A 154
Wolfe Cl. TN6: Crow 2E 36
Wolseley Rd. BN1: Brig 8E 112
BN41: Ports 5C 130
TN4: Tun W .6F 8
Wolstonbury Ct. RH15: Burg H 6C 68
Wolstonbury Rd.
BN3: Hove 6N 131 (3A 162)
Wolstonbury Way RH15: Burg H 6C 68
Wolverstone Dr. BN1: Brig 3D 132
Woodbine La. BN8: N'wck 1J 71
Woodbourne Av. BN1: Brig 1A 132
Woodbrook Rd. TN34: Hast 4M 127
Woodbury Av. RH19: E Grin 4H 11
Woodbury Cl. RH19: E Grin 4G 11
(not continuous)
TN4: Tun W .8D 8
Woodbury Pk. Gdns. TN4: Tun W 8E 8
Woodbury Pk. Rd. TN4: Tun W 8D 8
Woodbury Rd. TN18: Hawk 9N 31
Woodcombe TN34: Hast 2M 127
Woodcote Rd. RH18: F Row 1L 21
(not continuous)
Woodcrest Rd. RH15: Burg H 7A 68
Woodcroft RH15: Burg H 3A 68
Woodcroft Dr. BN21: Will 5N 153
Woodcutters RH17: Scay H 6N 49
Woodeland Way TN21: H'fld 2E 76
Woodgate Mdw. BN7: Plump G 9M 69
Woodgate Rd.
BN22: Eastb 7E 154 (1N 161)
Woodhall Cl. RH17: Cuck 2A 48
Woodhams Cl. TN33: Batt 2L 103
Woodhill Pk. TN2: Pem 7M 9
Woodhouse Cl. BN3: Hove 6G 131
Woodhouse Rd. BN3: Hove 6G 130
WOODINGDEAN 5L 133
Woodingdean Bus. Pk.
BN2: W'dean 4L 133
Woodland Av. BN3: Hove 3K 131
BN22: Will 4N 153
RH15: Burg H 4D 68
Woodland Cl. BN3: Hove 3K 131
RH15: Burg H 4D 68
TN4: Tun W .6F 8
Woodland Ct. BN3: Hove 1K 131
RH15: Burg H *5C 68*
(off Mill Rd.)
Woodland Cres. RH15: Burg H 4D 68
Woodland Dr. BN3: Hove 3K 131
Woodland M. TN21: H'fld 2E 76
Woodland Pde. BN3: Hove 2K 131
Woodland Ri. TN40: Bex S 1M 145
Woodland Rd. TN4: Tun W 6F 8
Woodlands BN3: Hove 3L 131
Woodlands Cl. BN10: Peace 3B 148
BN27: Hails 4F 120
RH15: Burg H 7C 68
TN21: H'fld .3E 76
TN22: Uck .9J 53
TN31: Peas 7A 66
Woodlands Ct. TN4: South 3D 8
Woodlands Pk. TN35: W'fld 6K 105
Woodlands Rd. RH16: Hay H 5G 48
RH19: E Grin 1G 10
Woodlands, The BN1: Brig 9N 111
TN2: Tun W .9F 8
TN34: Hast 1L 127
Woodlands Way TN34: Hast 9L 105
Woodland Vale Cotts. *BN26: Pole* *8C 140*
(off Wannock Rd.)
Woodland Va. Rd. TN37: St Leo 6J 127
Woodland Vw. Touring Pk.
TN21: Horam 1D 98
Woodland Wlk. BN2: Oving 9L 133
Woodland Way BN1: Brig 1A 132
TN4: Bid 1A 8
TN6: Crow .2D 36
TN33: C'hrst 2N 125
TN35: Fair 2K 129
Wood La. BN27: Bore S, Wart 4E 122
Woodleigh Rd. RH15: Burg H 4D 68
Woodpecker Dr. BN27: Hails 6D 120
Woodpecker La. BN27: Chal 3F 118
Woodpecker Rd. BN23: Lang 2E 154
Woodpecker Way BN27: Chal 3F 118
TN22: Uck .3J 73
Wood Ride RH16: Hay H 6E 48
Woodridge Cl. RH16: Hay H 6H 49
Woodruff Av. BN3: Hove 3K 131
WOOD'S CORNER 5H 79
Woodsgate Av. TN40: Bex S 8K 125
Woodsgate Pk. TN39: Bex S 8H 125
Woodsgate Way TN2: Pem 7L 9
WOOD'S GREEN 3B 28
Wood's Grn. Cotts. TN5: Wadh 4B 28
Woods Hill Cl. RH19: A'hstw 6K 11
Woods Hill La. RH19: A'hstw 6K 11
Woods Ho. *BN3: Hove* *5J 131*
(off Sackville Rd.)
Woodside TN6: Crow 9C 24
Woodside Av. BN1: Brig 3M 131
Woodside Lodge BN1: Brig 3M 131
Woodside Rd. TN4: R'hall 9A 8
Woodside Way BN27: Hails 1D 140
Woodsland Cl. BN6: Hass 3A 90
Woodsland Rd. BN6: Hass 3A 90
Wood's Pas. *TN34: Hast* *6A 128*
(off All Saints' St.)
Woodspring Cl. TN37: St Leo 1H 127
Woodstock RH19: E Grin 2C 10
Woodstock Rd. TN39: Bex S 8D 124
Wood St. RH19: E Grin 3D 10
TN1: Tun W .9E 8
Woodvale Crematorium BN2: Brig 5E 132
Woodview Cl. BN1: Brig 8E 112
Woodville Rd. TN39: Bex S 2J 145
Woodward Cl. BN23: Eastb 5H 155
Woolley Cl. TN4: South 4C 8
Woolley Rd. TN4: South 4C 8
Worcester Ct. BN1: Brig 5B 162
Worcester Vs. BN3: Hove 6E 130
Wordsworth Dr. BN23: Lang 2H 155
Wordsworth Ri. RH19: E Grin 3C 10
Wordsworth St. BN3: Hove 6J 131
Workhouse La. TN35: W'fld 3L 105
TN36: Ick .2L 107
WORLD'S END 4E 68
Worsham Ct. *TN39: Bex S* *1D 144*
(off Mansell Cl.)
Worsham La. TN40: Bex S 7N 125
Worsted La. RH19: E Grin 4H 11
Wray Cl. RH19: A'hstw 6K 11
Wren Cl. TN21: H'fld 1D 76
Wren Ct. TN33: Batt 3N 103
Wrens Warren TN7: Hart 6H 23
Wrestwood Av. BN22: Will 3N 153
Wrestwood Cl. TN40: Bex S 8L 125
Wrestwood Rd. TN40: Bex S 8K 125
Wrotham Cl. BN23: Lang 3G 154
TN34: Hast 1L 127
Wroxham Rd. BN23: Lang 9L 141
Wyatts La. RH17: Hors K 5D 32
Wyberlye Rd. RH15: Burg H 4B 68
Wybourne Ri. TN2: Tun W 3E 16
WYCH CROSS 7L 21
Wychperry Rd. RH16: Hay H 4E 48
Wychurst Gdns. TN40: Bex S 8L 125
Wyck Ct. *BN41: Ports* *6C 130*
(off St Aubyn's Rd.)
Wykeham Rd. TN34: Hast 5L 127
Wykeham Ter. BN1: Brig 8A 132 (7D 162)
Wykeham Way RH15: Burg H 6D 68
Wyndham St. BN2: Brig 9C 132
Wynnes M. BN3: Hove 6J 131
Wynnstay RH15: Burg H 6C 68
Wythwood RH16: Hay H 8F 48
Wyvern Way RH15: Burg H 5D 68

Y

Yardley St. BN1: Brig 5B 132 (2F 162)
Yarrow Rd. BN7: Lewes 4H 115
Yates Cl. TN31: Camb 6D 88
Yeomans BN8: Ring 8F 94
Yew Ct. RH19: E Grin 2D 10
Yew La. RH19: E Grin 1B 10
Yew Tree Cl. BN8: Ring 8E 94
TN21: H'fld 2D 76
TN34: Hast .9L 105
Yew Tree Cotts. TN31: Buck 4G 65
Yew Tree Ct. *BN21: Eastb* *6L 161*
(off Trinity Trees)
Yew Tree Ct. RH17: Cuck 3A 48
Yewtree La. TN6: Town R 1A 38
Yew Tree Rd. TN4: South 5D 8
Yieldings Cl. BN21: Eastb 7A 154
York Av. BN3: Hove 7N 131 (6A 162)
RH19: E Grin 4F 10
York Bldgs. *TN34: Hast* *7M 127*
(off Wellington Pl.)
York Ct. BN3: Hove 4A 162
York Gdns. *TN34: Hast* *7M 127*
(off Queen's Rd.)
York Gro. BN1: Brig 6A 132 (3C 162)
York Hill BN1: Brig 6B 132 (3E 162)
York Ho. *BN41: Ports* *5C 130*
(off Crown Rd.)
Yorklands BN3: Hove 1K 131
York Mans. BN3: Hove 5A 162
York Pl. BN1: Brig 7B 132 (5F 162)
BN3: Hove 5A 162
York Rd. BN1: Brig 7N 131 (6A 162)
BN3: Hove 7N 131 (6A 162)
BN10: Peace 6E 148
BN21: Eastb 1C 160 (6J 161)
TN1: Tun W 5F 74
TN37: St Leo 4J 127
TN40: Bex S 9A 126
Yorkshire Ct. BN20: Eastb 5M 153
York Vs. BN1: Brig 6A 132 (3C 162)
Youl Grange BN20: Eastb 2A 160
Youngsmere Cl. BN1: Brig 8C 112
Ypres Tower
Rye Castle Mus. 3G 86
Yvonne Robertson Ho.
TN40: Bex S 9L 125

Z

Zion Gdns. BN1: Brig 8A 132 (7D 162)

HOSPITALS and HOSPICES
covered by this atlas.

N.B. Where Hospitals and Hospices are not named on the map, the reference
given is for the road in which they are situated.

ALDRINGTON HOUSE DAY HOSPITAL 7H **131**
35 New Church Road
HOVE
East Sussex
BN3 4AG
Tel: 01273 778383

AMBERSTONE HOSPITAL 2H **121**
Carters Corner
HAILSHAM
East Sussex
BN27 4HU
Tel: 01323 844676

BEXHILL HOSPITAL 8K **125**
Holliers Hill
BEXHILL-ON-SEA
East Sussex
TN40 2DZ
Tel: 01424 755255

BRIGHTON GENERAL HOSPITAL 6E **132**
Elm Grove
BRIGHTON
BN2 3EW
Tel: 01273 696955

BURRSWOOD 4E **14**
Groombridge
TUNBRIDGE WELLS
Kent
TN3 9PU
Tel: 01892 863637

CONQUEST HOSPITAL 9K **105**
The Ridge
ST LEONARDS-ON-SEA
East Sussex
TN37 7RD
Tel: 01424 755255

CROWBOROUGH WAR MEMORIAL HOSPITAL 1C **36**
Southview Road
CROWBOROUGH
East Sussex
TN6 1HB
Tel: 01892 652284

EASTBOURNE DISTRICT GENERAL HOSPITAL 6B **154**
Kings Drive
EASTBOURNE
East Sussex
BN21 2UD
Tel: 01323 417400

ESPERANCE BMI HOSPITAL, THE 1D **160** (6L **161**)
Hartington Place
EASTBOURNE
East Sussex
BN21 3BG
Tel: 01323 411188

EVERSFIELD CENTRE 8G **126**
West Hill Road
ST LEONARDS-ON-SEA
East Sussex
TN38 0NG
Tel: 01424 710110

HASTINGS BUPA HOSPITAL 9K **105**
The Ridge
ST LEONARDS-ON-SEA
East Sussex
TN37 7RE
Tel: 01424 757400

HAWKHURST COTTAGE HOSPITAL 9L **31**
High Street
Hawkhurst
CRANBROOK
Kent
TN18 4PU
Tel: 01580 753345

HAYWARDS HEATH NUFFIELD HOSPITAL 3E **48**
Burrell Road
HAYWARDS HEATH
West Sussex
RH16 1UD
Tel: 01444 456999

HELLINGLY HOSPITAL 1G **121**
The Drive
Hellingly
HAILSHAM
East Sussex
BN27 4EP
Tel: 01323 440022

HOMOEOPATHIC HOSPITAL 1D **16**
Church Road
TUNBRIDGE WELLS
Kent
TN1 1JU
Tel: 01892 542977

HORDER CENTRE FOR ARTHRITIS, THE 7A **24**
St. Johns Road
CROWBOROUGH
East Sussex
TN6 1XP
Tel: 01892 665577

HOSPICE IN THE WEALD 4N **9**
Maidstone Road
Pembury
TUNBRIDGE WELLS
Kent
TN2 4TA
Tel: 01892 820500

HOVE NUFFIELD HOSPITAL 6H **131**
55 New Church Road
HOVE
East Sussex
BN3 4BG
Tel: 01273 779471

HOVE POLYCLINIC 4H **131**
Nevill Avenue
HOVE
East Sussex
BN3 7HY
Tel: 01273 696011

KENT & SUSSEX HOSPITAL 9D **8**
Mount Ephraim
TUNBRIDGE WELLS
Kent
TN4 8AT
Tel: 01892 526111

MARTLETS HOSPICE, THE 4H **131**
Wayfield Avenue
HOVE
East Sussex
BN3 7LW
Tel: 01273 273400

MILL VIEW HOSPITAL 4G **131**
Nevill Avenue
HOVE
East Sussex
BN3 7HZ
Tel: 01273 696011

NEVILL HOSPITAL 4G **131**
Laburnum Avenue
HOVE
East Sussex
BN3 7JW
Tel: 01273 821680

NEWHAVEN DOWNS HOUSE 5J **149**
Church Hill
NEWHAVEN
East Sussex
BN9 9HH
Tel: 01273 513441

PEMBURY HOSPITAL 6K **9**
Tonbridge Road
Pembury
TUNBRIDGE WELLS
Kent
TN2 4QJ
Tel: 01892 823535

PRINCESS ROYAL HOSPITAL 6H **49**
Lewes Road
HAYWARDS HEATH
West Sussex
RH16 4EX
Tel: 01444 441881

PRIORY GRANGE, THE 7L **57**
Tottingworth Park
Broad Oak
HEATHFIELD
East Sussex
TN21 8UN
Tel: 01435 864545

QUEEN VICTORIA HOSPITAL 1F **10**
Holtye Road
EAST GRINSTEAD
West Sussex
RH19 3DZ
Tel: 01342 410210

ROBOROUGH DAY HOSPITAL 8D **154** (3K **161**)
Carew Road
EASTBOURNE
East Sussex
BN21 2AX
Tel: 01323 638972

ROYAL ALEXANDRA CHILDREN'S HOSPITAL 7A **132** (5C **162**)
Dyke Road
BRIGHTON
BN1 3JN
Tel: 01273 328145

ROYAL SUSSEX COUNTY HOSPITAL 9E **132**
Eastern Road
BRIGHTON
BN2 5BE
Tel: 01273 696955

ST MICHAEL'S HOSPICE 7H **127**
25 Upper Maze Hill
ST LEONARDS-ON-SEA
East Sussex
TN38 0LG
Tel: 01424 445177

ST PETER & ST JAMES HOSPICE 4M **69**
North Common Road
North Chailey
LEWES
East Sussex
BN8 4ED
Tel: 01444 471598

ST WILFRID'S HOSPICE 3H **161**
2 Mill Gap Road
EASTBOURNE
East Sussex
BN21 2JH
Tel: 01323 644500

SUSSEX BEACON (HOSPICE), THE 4F **132**
Bevendean Road
BRIGHTON
BN2 4DE
Tel: 01273 694222

SUSSEX EYE HOSPITAL 9E **132**
Eastern Road
BRIGHTON
BN2 5BF
Tel: 01273 606126

SUSSEX NUFFIELD HOSPITAL 5K **133**
Warren Road
BRIGHTON
BN2 6DX
Tel: 01273 624488

TICEHURST HOUSE PRIORY HOSPITAL, THE 9L **29**
Ticehurst
WADHURST
East Sussex
TN5 7HU
Tel: 01580 200391

TUNBRIDGE WELLS BUPA HOSPITAL 1F **14**
Fordcombe Road
Fordcombe
TUNBRIDGE WELLS
Kent
TN3 0RD
Tel: 01892 740047

TUNBRIDGE WELLS NUFFIELD HOSPITAL, THE 1F **16**
Kingswood Road
TUNBRIDGE WELLS
Kent
TN2 4UL
Tel: 01892 531111

UCKFIELD COMMUNITY HOSPITAL 2J **73**
Framfield Road
UCKFIELD
East Sussex
TN22 5AW
Tel: 01825 769999

VICTORIA HOSPITAL (LEWES) 5G **115**
Nevill Road
LEWES
East Sussex
BN7 1PE
Tel: 01273 474153

The representation on the maps of a road, track or footpath is no evidence of the existence of a right of way.

The Grid on this map is the National Grid taken from Ordnance Survey mapping with the permission of the Controller of Her Majesty's Stationery Office.

Copyright of Geographers' A-Z Map Co. Ltd.

No reproduction by any method whatsoever of any part of this publication is permitted without the prior consent of the copyright owners.